Lifestyle Workshops

Lifestyle
Workshops

Martha Imrie Carey, MS
University of Illinois

Human Kinetics Books
Champaign, Illinois

Library of Congress Cataloging-in-Publication Data

Carey, Martha I., 1957-
   Lifestyle workshops / Martha I. Carey.
     p.   cm.
   ISBN 0-87322-930-4
   1. College students--health and hygiene--United States. 2. Health
education--United Sates. 3. Health promotion--United States.
4. College students--United States--Life skills guides--Study and
teaching.   I. Title.
LB3497.3.C37 1989
378'.197'1--dc19   88-9142
                                                                  CIP

Developmental Editor: Lisa Busjahn
Production Director: Ernie Noa
Copyeditors: Dianne Frances, Claire M. Mount, Molly Bentsen
Proofreader: Laurie McGee
Managing Editor: Holly Gilly
Typesetter: Sandra Meier
Text Design: Keith Blomberg
Cover Design: Jack Davis
Text Layout: Denise Mueller
Printed By: Versa Press

ISBN: 0-87322-930-4

Printed in the United States of America

10 9 8 7 6 5 4 3 2 1

Human Kinetics Books
A Division of Human Kinetics Publishers, Inc.
Box 5076, Champaign, IL 61820
1-800-DIAL-HKP
1-800-334-3665 (in Illinois)

To Clare, Anne, Bruce, Laura, and Melinda, my first health education team.

Contents

Preface

The Lifestyle Workshop Program, developed in 1985 at the University of Illinois at Urbana-Champaign, is a model for training undergraduates as health promotion paraprofessionals. The title *paraprofessional* describes the college student who becomes trained to present health promotion workshops. The program information and workshops in *Lifestyle Workshops* are addressed to professional health educators who want to develop or revise their own health promotion programs. The workshops have all been tried and tested at the University of Illinois, and they provide the framework for implementing a successful program.

Lifestyle Workshops centers on the concept of health promotion. Its emphasis is prevention, based on the fact that many lifelong health behaviors are adopted and reinforced during young adult years. Some of those behaviors may have long-term effects on degenerative diseases suffered later in life; the leading causes of death are lifestyle related. Health promotion is aimed at prevention of disease through behavioral and attitudinal change. The World Health Organization (1986) has stated that "health promotion involves the population as the whole in the context of their everyday life, rather than focusing on people at risk for specific diseases" (p. 245).

As the health needs of university students develop and change each year, the challenge to the campus health-education community increases. We have witnessed health concerns, including AIDS, anorexia nervosa, aerobic fitness, stress management, contraception, and drug abuse. This increased interest in health and fitness brings increased responsibility for health educators to disseminate up-to-date information efficiently to both groups and individuals.

At large universities this responsibility is often too demanding for one educator or even a small team of educators. Students respond to trends in health topics with demands for practical information. The scope of the task makes it difficult for professional health educators alone to approach the growing number of interested young adults. Over the years, in many different forums, university health educators have branched out to reach the groups requesting or needing health information.

The Lifestyle Workshop Program educates groups of students in structured training programs and entrusts them to deliver health information to their peers. The effect is that many more students can be reached by educational efforts. At the University of Illinois, students interested in becoming paraprofessionals train in a credited two-semester class that provides them with the opportunity to use their health-education skills as they learn them.

The advantages of a paraprofessional program are numerous. A survey of 237 coordinators of paraprofessional programs in student affairs divisions of colleges and universities (Ender & Winston, 1984) found that 51% believed "that students could be more effective than professionals in assisting [other] students with their normal developmental concerns" (p. 7). Other factors ranked highly as reasons for using paraprofessional programs were the impact of the experience on the paraprofessionals themselves (67%), the ability of departments to offer more services (62%) at consequently lower costs (50%), and the inclusion of the paraprofessional program in the student's overall educational program (22%).

Lifestyle Workshops is divided into two parts. Part I addresses the issues of designing, implementing, and evaluating a paraprofessional health promotion program. Chapter 1 provides a program overview. Chapter 2 discusses administrative requirements, including budgeting, marketing, structuring personnel, and advertising. That chapter should answer health educators' questions about the two major concerns in implementing a paraprofessional program: budget and administrative support. Chapter 3 lists the roles and responsibilities of the trainer and the paraprofessional and provides tools with which to evaluate their expertise. Chapter 4 outlines fundamental presentation skills, which should be incorporated into the paraprofessional training sessions. Chapter 5 provides a brief introduction to explain the workshop section. Part I concludes with a reference list for the first five chapters.

Part II details the 16 workshops in the five general areas of nutrition, fitness, sexuality, stress management, and drug and alcohol education. Each workshop contains an outline, handouts, suggestions for visual aids, a list of frequently asked questions, and references on which the workshop is based. The trainers instruct the paraprofessionals to use this material in workshops for various interested student organizations and groups. The content and format of the workshops may need to be modified, depending on the requirements of the program audience or setting. The workshops are designed to be flexible; health educators are invited to make changes where appropriate.

Encouraging young adults to become interested in their health is a rewarding challenge. By training paraprofessionals, health educators can reach many more students with vital, up-to-date health information. From their peers, students can learn a sense of control over their health-related decisions. It is my hope that health educators in various settings will garner many new ideas from *Lifestyle Workshops* about delivering health information effectively to their audiences.

Acknowledgments

This book is a result of the collaboration of many people. I'd like to thank the contributing authors for each of the Lifestyle Workshop health promotion areas, who were graduate or undergraduate students when this book was begun. Their insight into student lifestyles has been invaluable.

Fitness: Bruce Elmore, PhD

Stress Management: Anne Brinkmann

Nutrition: Clare Sente

Drugs and Alcohol: Melinda Paul, MA; Laura Tubbs; Joanne Smogor, MS; Victoria Merkel, Michelle Adler

Sexuality: Donna Richter; Beth Chamberlain; Lela Jones Olszweski, MS

Many of the handouts in the Lifestyle Workshops were written by the staff of the Health Education Department at the University of Illinois's McKinley Health Center at Urbana-Champaign. These fine people provided their expertise, ideas, and support: Mary Ellen O'Shaughnessey, Sara Kelley, Joanne Smogor, Michele Easterling, Melanie Tyner-Wilson, Judy Simon, Joyce Phares, Paula Swinford, and Phyllis Butler, who typed many ''final'' drafts.

I'd like to express my appreciation and thanks to Sue Wilmoth, who first saw the value of this book, and to Lisa Busjahn at Human Kinetics.

To all of these people, my thanks. A part of you is in this book.

Martha Imrie Carey

Implementing the Lifestyle Workshops Program

Part I of *Lifestyle Workshops* addresses much of the background work that must be tackled before and during implementation of a paraprofessional health promotion program. A secure foundation of goals, policies, evaluation, and philosophy must be laid and referred to repeatedly as the program evolves. This is especially pertinent to preparing paraprofessionals, because the coordinator or supervisor is ultimately responsible for the actions of the trainees. If decisions are not firm or well thought out, the paraprofessionals may develop an attitude of "anything goes," which is certainly not the case. A paraprofessional program must be highly structured, and the key to that structure is planning.

The goal of the first four chapters is to offer practical, hands-on applications for your paraprofessional health promotion program. Many theoretical books are available on peer/paraprofessional education, health promotion, and workshop design, and those theories have been applied in the development of the Lifestyle Workshop Program. However, because the focus of this manual is application, those theories are not detailed here. The appendices provide examples for the suggestions offered in the chapters with the understanding that you may need to modify them for your particular situation.

Although you will learn a multitude of lessons each year of your program, you will save a great deal of time and expense by making a commitment to planning. If you are developing a new program, plan to spend at least half of an academic year or up to four months to plan the program before you start it. Your efforts to analyze the different components of your program will pay off with fewer loopholes and better communication among staff and paraprofessionals.

Chapter 1 is especially helpful for those starting a program from scratch or expanding an existing paraprofessional program. The chapter deals with some of the administrative work that should be completed before the details of program delivery are decided. Getting your program's goals and objectives down on paper is an unenviable task, but one that will give your program direction and meaning. Shaping your staff and their time allocations will determine the size and scope of your program. Selecting the workshop topics for your target audience is a final undertaking that deserves time and research. The topics you choose can make or break your operation; obviously, if the topics are not applicable to your audience, they won't attend.

Chapter 2 addresses many of the details of implementing a successful paraprofessional program. More examples are provided; they can serve as a starting point for a program or as modifications to one. The information is most useful to the program administrator or coordinator and involves decision making necessary before program implementation.

Chapter 3 delineates the roles of the paraprofessional trainers and the paraprofessionals themselves. (In this manual the program coordinator and the paraprofessional trainer are treated as having distinct roles, although in most cases both roles are filled by one individual.) The necessary paperwork may seem excessive, but when paraprofessionals are responsible for carrying out your program, it is better to err on the side of inclusion of materials. The spirit of the detailed procedures listed in this chapter is to encourage

1

as much communication as possible between trainer and paraprofessional. You may require more or fewer procedures depending on your paraprofessionals and your training program.

Chapter 4 describes workshop presentation skills needed by the paraprofessionals. The chapter can be used as an outline for the trainer and a learning guide for the paraprofessional.

The overriding purpose of Part I is to outline the variety of planning details that you should address before and during the implementation of your paraprofessional health promotion program. The time and effort you spend planning specific details will improve communication among your staff and will increase the success of your health promotion program.

CHAPTER 1

The Paraprofessional Health Promotion Program

The Lifestyle Workshops are a service for university students provided by the Health Education Department. The Workshops cover the general areas of nutrition, fitness, drugs and alcohol, sexuality, and stress management. Students initiate these presentations by coordinating programs for their organizations or residence halls, calling the student health center, and requesting a specific Lifestyle Workshop.

Program Goals and Objectives

The goal of the Lifestyle Workshop Program is to encourage students to take control over lifestyle behaviors, motivate them to assume an active role in the maintenance and improvement of their own health condition and needs, and affect the university environment in ways that promote and reinforce low-risk health behaviors.

The mission is twofold: (a) to provide workshops, based on the interests and needs of university students, that encourage examination of present and future lifestyle needs; and (b) to train paraprofessionals to present interesting and timely health workshops. The primary concern is that students receive accurate, up-to-date information in an unbiased manner.

The specific objectives of the Lifestyle Workshop Program are divided into program objectives and behavior and attitude objectives. Health educators use these objectives as guidelines and as a means to evaluate the overall success of the program in terms of the student population. The four program objectives follow:

1. The Lifestyle Workshop Program delivers paraprofessional health promotion workshops in the areas of nutrition, sexuality, fitness, stress management, and drug and alcohol education to students requesting workshops for university residence halls, Greek houses, and other student groups.
2. The Lifestyle Workshop Program promotes participation and discussion based on the premise that people learn more from activities than from lectures.
3. The Lifestyle Workshop Program presents new health information that increases the participant's knowledge in that specific area.
4. Individual Lifestyle Workshop objectives are subject to periodic evaluations.

The Lifestyle Workshops also attempt to promote health-related behaviors that lead students to reinforce or reevaluate their lifestyle choices. The behavior and attitude objectives are more difficult to evaluate because a cause-and-effect relationship cannot be identified between the health promotion workshop and behavioral change. However, the workshop may affect the participants' *perception* of their desire or ability to change. Therefore, health educators ask students to fill out surveys before and after the workshop to identify individual intent to change. These surveys appear with a more detailed explanation in chapter 2. Questions focus on the participants' *likelihood* of changing behaviors or attitudes based on information presented in the workshops.

Administrative Structure

The Lifestyle Workshop Program is based on a three-tiered paraprofessional structure (see Figure 1.1): the program coordinator, the trainers—

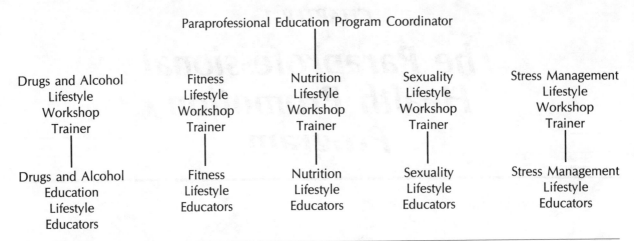

Figure 1.1 The Lifestyle Workshop three-tiered paraprofessional program.

graduate students who teach and train the paraprofessionals, and the paraprofessionals—undergraduate students who lead the Lifestyle Workshops. Graduate students at the University of Illinois also participate at the paraprofessional level with several modifications to the program that take their advanced training and special needs into account. The paraprofessionals are referred to as Lifestyle Educators, a title broad enough to encompass the five lifestyle areas and the program mission, which is to encourage students to examine present and future lifestyle needs.

The Lifestyle Workshop Program is unique in its combination of trainers and professional support. Each trainer works not only with the paraprofessional program coordinator but also with a full-time professional health educator on staff at the student health center. Trainers meet regularly with their professional counterparts to discuss issues, facts, and ideas concerning their Lifestyle Workshops. This arrangement provides for quality assurance by introducing accurate, up-to-date information and dividing the paraprofessional tasks among several responsible experts. Hiring trainers may not be feasible for some institutions. In this case, the program coordinator will be training the paraprofessionals. Any reference to trainers in this book is a generic term for the person or staff who are training the paraprofessionals.

Selecting Workshop Topics

Starting a new program involves a number of tasks and a good deal of research prior to implementation. After the administrative structure of the pro-

gram is approved, one of the most important tasks is determining the health promotion topics the paraprofessionals will deliver. Although it may sound relatively straightforward, the selection of topics actually involves a combination of research, surveys, and intuition.

At the University of Illinois, we determined many of the topics that developed into the 16 Lifestyle Workshops by noting the frequency of requests made by students to the health center. Professional health educators had found themselves spending many evenings each week repeating fundamental health information and, frankly, getting tired in the process. Hiring a full-time paraprofessional program coordinator and developing a structured training course for students offered both a reprieve for the health educators and a challenge for the paraprofessionals. Professional health educators were then free to develop and deliver selective and advanced programs to the student population, whereas trained student paraprofessionals delivered regular workshops on the most frequently requested health topics.

These topics were contraception, alcohol awareness, weight control, and stress management. We began by designing workshops on these topics and gradually included more workshops within the five general health areas of fitness, nutrition, drugs and alcohol, sexuality, and stress management.

In addition to student requests, the health educator can use a variety of methods for determining health interests and needs at both the local and the national level. To design appropriate health promotion workshops for the college population, the health educator can use the following sources: national health data, college health concerns studies, needs assessments, interest surveys, and in-depth health interviews.

National Health Data

The literature on U.S. morbidity and mortality rates for different age groups offers some insight into necessary topics, including health behaviors that are lifestyle related and that can be altered through preventive action. For example, health status trends provided by the Department of Health and Human Services exist for age groups as well as for the entire population.

The U.S. Department of Health and Human Services (1987) listed these three leading causes of death among young adults (age 15-24):

- Accidents and adverse effects (48%) (motor vehicle accidents account for 74% of those),
- Homicide (12%), and
- Suicide (12%).

Adults (age 24-65) are most likely to die from (a) diseases of the heart, (b) cancer, (c) accidents and adverse effects, and (d) stroke. Two questions arise concerning these causes of death: Over which causes do people have the most control? And, can they benefit from health education/promotion programs? Wearing seat belts and avoiding driving while under the influence of alcohol will help reduce motor vehicle accidents. Homicide involves a different set of social issues not usually associated with health promotion activities. Suicide prevention deals primarily with individual emotional issues, although some stress management strategies, such as refuting irrational beliefs, may be appropriate.

The lifestyle habits and practices that young adults develop affect their future chances for premature death or disability. Consequently, this is an opportune time to present workshops that encourage young adults to develop a healthy lifestyle pattern. Reducing health risk factors related to heart disease, cancer, accidents, and stroke is one of the long-range goals of a health promotion program. Prevention activities "within the practical grasp of most Americans are simple measures to enhance the prospects of good health . . . [These] include:

- elimination of cigarette smoking;
- reduction of alcohol misuse;
- moderate dietary changes to reduce intake of excess calories, fat, salt, and sugar;
- moderate exercise;
- periodic screening . . . for high blood pressure and certain cancers;
- adherence to speed laws and use of seat belts" (U.S. Department of Health and Human Services, 1979, p. 10).

We found when we offered smoking cessation programs, few students attended. Therefore, we have not put our efforts into a regular paraprofessional workshop on smoking cessation, but periodically our health center offers such programs. Alcohol misuse, dietary change, and exercise are primary issues for young adults, who are often on their own for the first time and will be making many of these decisions on a regular basis. We have thus built 9 of our 16 workshops on these topics.

During many of the workshops, particularly fitness and nutrition, students are encouraged to participate in the health center's preventive medicine clinic, which offers a variety of screenings including blood pressure, cholesterol, triglycerides, and blood glucose (for diabetes). In 1985, wearing seat belts became a state law in Illinois. Adherence to speed laws and use of seat belts is a good example of health promotion that lends itself to information campaigns rather than to workshops.

College Health Concerns Studies

A study conducted at Indiana University indicated that the health concerns of college students have been stable over the past 12 years (Engs & Hanson, 1985). The study compared the results of the same "Health Concerns" survey given in 1970, 1976, and 1982 and found little change in attitudes and specific health concerns. For instance, 6 items ranked in the top 10 during the 1970 and 1982 surveys: birth control, use of contraceptives, "What I'll be like in 10 or 15 years," auto accidents, nuclear war, and air pollution. Sexually transmitted diseases, drug and alcohol dependence, and smoking stayed relatively the same in ranking. Students indicated that cancer and auto accidents were among their top four health concerns.

Needs Assessments and Interest Surveys

Conducting a needs assessment and/or interest survey of the target population is key to the success of the health promotion program. The age, perspective, and values of the program coordinator may be entirely different from the intended audience. Therefore, it is vital to gather as much information from the population as possible before the planning begins. Needs assessments and interest surveys are two common methods used in this process.

The health educator is responsible for devising a timetable for conducting systematic needs assessments or interest surveys (e.g., annually or biannually). These assessments do not have to be expensive—simple 1- or 2-page surveys distributed at the health center for a couple of days will suffice—but money should be budgeted for this phase. The value of the information is so important to the rest of the program that to conduct a haphazard assessment would most likely jeopardize the program's success.

Needs assessments come in a variety of forms that can be purchased, such as computerized needs assessments, or self-designed for a specific group or population. Using a multimethod approach, the health educator can gather information from a variety of sources, providing a more refined picture of the target population. As different sources point to similar health needs and interests, the topics for workshops will become apparent.

Computerized health risk assessments are an efficient means of collecting data from many individuals. Many computer or paper-and-pencil health risk assessments are on the market today (see Appendix 1.A). For various costs, these health risk assessments can be self-scored, computer-scored, or sent to a company to be batch-processed, or the individual can interact with a microcomputer to find out his or her health needs and receive suggestions for lifestyle improvements.

University health centers are often the students' one health care institution. Another way to determine students' health needs (i.e., conduct a needs assessment) is to look at the common reasons for visits to the student health center. Statistics can usually be obtained from the medical services administrator at the health center. Health educators can use this information to develop medical self-care paraprofessional programs that may result in a decrease in visits.

Interest surveys are a popular method of collecting data on a specific group. It is essential to have information about a population's health needs, but people are not always interested in what they need. It is often more effective to query students about *health interests* and then integrate *health needs* into programs based on those interests. For example, if the results of a survey show stress management as a popular topic, the workshop could be designed to include a discussion on negative coping methods used to combat stress such as abuse of alcohol, drugs, and over-the-counter stimulants or sleeping aids. In this format, students are more likely to relate reasons for the use and abuse of chemicals. In contrast, a workshop

on chemical abuse could be seen by students as too threatening or irrelevant.

Each college or university will want to find out whether there are unique student health interests on its campus. At the University of Illinois, we have conducted a number of surveys to determine current interests. Three surveys are described here, each providing clues for designing successful health promotion programs.

The first survey draws on information from one of the captive audiences on campus, the students living in residence halls. The University of Illinois Housing Division conducts a computerized interest survey each fall semester of all students living in the residence halls. The students are asked to respond to the statement, "I am interested in attending the following programs," which is followed by an extensive list of different interest areas. Many of the choices are health-related, but there are also topics relating to careers, hobbies, social awareness, and housing programs. We found this survey useful in tracking students' interests and observing trends over the years.

Results from this survey have shown surprisingly consistent trends in the top 10 health interest topics. Cardiopulmonary resuscitation (CPR) training, stress reduction, time management, male and female relationships, and first aid are consistently in the top five rankings, followed by dieting in the dining halls, test anxiety, rape awareness, and dating skills. Based on these results, we have addressed some of these topics in our Lifestyle Workshops; CPR and first aid are handled by a separate paraprofessional program.

A comparison of this information to the national health concerns studies reveals a different ranking of interests. This is due in part to the fact that different surveys were used and different topics were queried. For example, birth control, a major interest in the health concerns study (Engs & Hanson, 1985) was not placed on the University of Illinois housing survey until 1986. In developing an interest survey like this, the health educator should circulate ideas among colleagues and other professionals to get as many different topic suggestions as possible.

The second survey is conducted each semester by the Health Advocates, a University of Illinois student health organization. A health interest survey (Table 1.1) is given to each of the members of a residential group (e.g., residence hall floors and Greek houses). Large or small numbers of students are polled, depending on the size of the organization each semester. For example, in the

Table 1.1 Student Health Interest Survey

I am interested in attending the following programs:

Sexual health

☐ AIDS
☐ Prevention of sexually transmitted diseases
☐ Contraceptive choices
☐ Sexual decision-making
☐ Acquaintance rape prevention
☐ Premenstrual syndrome
☐ Abortion
☐ Incest
☐ Other _____

Stress

☐ Stress management
☐ Massage
☐ Progressive relaxation
☐ Time management
☐ Text anxiety
☐ Roommate or living group stress
☐ Other _____

Alcohol and drugs

☐ Helping friends who drink
☐ Problem drinking
☐ Alcohol awareness programs
☐ Women and alcohol
☐ Over-the-counter drugs
☐ Drugs (list) _____
_____
_____
_____

☐ Other _____

Nutrition

☐ Weight control
☐ Eating disorders
☐ Eating in the dining halls and fast food
☐ Cholesterol
☐ Vegetarian cooking
☐ Other _____

Fitness

☐ Fat assessment (skin calipers)
☐ Weight training
☐ Starting a fitness program
☐ Sports injuries
☐ Steroids
☐ Stretching
☐ Back care
☐ Other _____

Miscellaneous

☐ Tour or presentation of student health center
☐ Personal defense
☐ Jobs in the health care field
☐ Death and dying
☐ Aging
☐ Diabetes
☐ Consumer health buying
☐ First aid certification
☐ CPR certification
☐ Smoking cessation
☐ Depression
☐ Suicide prevention

Best Times to Attend

☐ Monday	☐ Tuesday	☐ Wednesday	☐ Thursday
☐ 6:00 p.m.	☐ 6:00 p.m.	☐ 6:00 p.m.	☐ 6:00 p.m.
☐ 7:00 p.m.	☐ 7:00 p.m.	☐ 7:00 p.m.	☐ 7:00 p.m.
☐ 8:00 p.m.	☐ 8:00 p.m.	☐ 8:00 p.m.	☐ 8:00 p.m.

fall, 1985, the Health Advocates polled 1,303 students (907 women and 396 men) using a survey that included the topics of the Lifestyle Workshops that were being developed at that time. This provided advanced information for gauging student interest in the workshops being designed. The students were most interested in attending the following 10 workshops:

- Massage* (38)
- Weight control* (9)
- Weight training* (14)
- Starting a fitness program (9)
- Time management* (5)
- Cardiopulmonary resuscitation*
- Contraceptives* (42)
- Fat assessment* (16)
- Stress management*
- Progressive relaxation* (18)

---

*Topics being developed into Lifestyle Workshops at the time of the survey. Numbers in parentheses represent the number of Lifestyle Workshops delivered during the 1985-86 academic year.

The third survey emphasizes the importance of collecting information from a variety of people. At the University of Illinois, the student health center clinicians were asked to identify those health topics they thought would be beneficial for students. Similarly, 834 students were asked to identify the health topics of most interest to them. The survey included items related to health center visits (e.g., meaning of lab test results, sinus/allergy, and headaches), in addition to popular health promotion topics. The results of the survey are listed in Table 1.2.

The providers and the students chose different topics within the top 10 interests. Although 5 of the top 10 student interests were also ranked in the clinicians' top 10, this survey illustrates the importance of gaining different perspectives when addressing the issue of student health care. The information the clinicians offer is important because they deal with students' health needs on a daily basis. Obviously, not all the topics lend themselves well to separate workshops, but some of the topics can be integrated into other workshops. For instance, urinary tract and vaginal infections can be addressed in sexuality workshops about contraceptives, sexually transmitted diseases, or women's health.

In-Depth Health Interviews

In-depth health interviews involve one-to-one questioning of health needs, interests, and opinions. Interviews are an effective means for gathering information from small groups such as the members of a fraternity or sorority or students from the floor of a residence hall or a small apartment building (e.g., married student housing). The following interview questions were used during an interest assessment conducted at the University of Oregon (Carey, 1984).

- Generally, how healthy are you?
- Have you ever taken any health education courses or classes?
- Are you concerned about any aspect of your health?
- What do you think about America's current interest in health and fitness?
- Would you be interested in health workshops/classes here where you live?
- What workshops would you most likely attend? (Offer topic examples such as these:

Nutrition/weight control/body image

Aerobic conditioning/starting an exercise program

Stress management/relaxation techniques

Emotional wellness/interpersonal communication

Sexuality issues, such as AIDS/sexually transmitted diseases/birth control/infertility

Alcohol/cocaine/marijuana)

- What are your specific interests? (For example, if the student is interested in nutrition find out the specific nutrition topics—vitamins, athletes' nutritional needs, cholesterol, dieting, eating disorders, vegetarian cooking, etc.)

Table 1.2 Perceptions of Health Interest: Clinicians and Students

Health care providers	Percent	Students	Percent
Sexually transmitted disease	80.6	Stress/anxiety	45.4
Urinary tract infections	77.6	Birth control	44.7
Stress/anxiety	75.0	Physical fitness	43.6
Vaginal infections	72.2	Cardiopulmonary resuscitation	43.2
Birth control	69.4	Depression	33.6
Self-breast exam	66.7	Nutrition	30.2
Cardiopulmonary resuscitation	66.7	Self-breast exam	26.3
Jogging injuries	66.7	Low back pain	23.1
Alcohol abuse	66.7	Sexual concerns	22.8
Depression	63.9	Meaning of lab tests	21.3
Drug abuse	63.9		
Drug medication	63.9		

- How much time could you afford to spend on a topic? 1-hour workshop? 2-hour workshop? 3-week course on consecutive evenings?
- When would be a convenient time for you?
- Sociodemographic information:

Age:

Place of residence:

Grade:

Major:

Employer:

Married:

Children:

Although they are more time-consuming, health interviews offer a different perspective from the forced-choice style of a paper-and-pencil survey. Participants can speak freely, so the interviewer can see the individual's reaction as well as gather data. Through in-depth questioning, the interviewer can obtain more details and try out ideas with the student about his or her health interests and concerns.

Note. Much of the material in this chapter comes from "Peer Health Advisor Program to Reduce the Health Risks of University Students" by M. Carey, 1984, *Public Health Reports, 99*(6), 614-620. Copyright 1984 by *Public Health Reports*.

These types of surveys and collection methods are just a few techniques available for developing workshop topics and content. The ultimate evaluation is analyzing workshop surveys, workshop requests, and attendance figures. Health educators are constantly revising, restarting, or continuing health promotion workshops based on feedback from participants and reviews of yearly figures and trends.

Summary

This chapter has shown that careful planning and organization can work to save time and enhance the paraprofessional experience, as well as to provide a basis, through interest surveys and needs assessments, for a current and useful workshop program that will serve the target population. By keeping objectives in mind, the health educator can assess the strengths and weaknesses of the program and work with the paraprofessional team for continued success and improvement. Chapter 2 looks at the responsibilities of the program coordinator and many of the behind-the-scenes operations that lead to a successful and efficient program.

APPENDIX 1.A

Health Risk Assessments

HRA Ordering Information

The Health Risk Assessments (HRAs) listed below were compiled from "Healthfinder," a service of the Office of Disease Prevention and Health Promotion, Public Health Service, U.S. Department of Health and Human Services, as well as information from HRA's providers. The HRAs have not been evaluated by the government or by the author but are provided for your information in case you are considering a HRA for your health promotion program.

Symbol key:

CI = Computer interactive with a microcomputer. The individual sits at a computer terminal to input and receive the information.

CB = Computer batch processing. The forms are either sent to a computer facility for processing, or can be processed by a microcomputer.

PP = Paper-and-pencil forms and self-scored.

Computer Interactive Health Risk Assessments

Following each brief description is a listing of the microcomputer(s) on which the HRA is designed to run, the cost of the program, and ordering information.

Medical Age (CI). Thirty lifestyle practices are considered either to add or subtract months and years from actual age. Summary includes a comparison of chronological to medical age and a listing of

practices that add months/years to one's age. IBM-PC and compatibles.
Order: The University of Vermont
Student Health Center
284 East Avenue
Burlington, VT 05401
(802) 656-3350

Lifestyle Survey (CI). An adaptation of a lifestyle survey from the Berkeley Holistic Health Center. The program computes a personal profile using 216 questions about relaxation, exercise, eating habits, mental-emotional state, social values, environment, and sexual health. IBM-PC and compatibles.
Order: The University of Vermont
Student Health Center
284 East Avenue
Burlington, VT 05401
(802) 656-3350

Circle of Wellness (CI). A short and quick assessment of wellness using 16 questions about nutrition, exercise, relaxation, and personal ecology. As the questions are answered, the computer fills in segments of a circle representing high level wellness. If most of the circle is filled at the end, the user is treated to a tune and congratulations. If some areas are lacking, the user is advised to seek help in these areas. IBM-PC and compatibles.
Order: The University of Vermont
Student Health Center
284 East Avenue
Burlington, VT 05401
(802) 656-3350

Health Awareness Games (CI). This is a set of five microcomputer programs that draw on statistics about lifestyle and health as they relate to life expectancy. The five programs are: Coronary Risk, Why Do You Smoke?, Exercise and Weight, Life Expectancy, and Lifestyle. The set is appropriate for students in junior high school through college, as well as for home use. Teaching guide included. Apple, Commodore, TRS-80, Model III and 4 IBM-PC.
Order: HRM Software
175 Tompinks Avenue
Pleasantville, NY 10570
(914) 769-6900

Health Maintenance, Volume II (CI). MECC, known for its educational software, has developed this health education tool for high school students. The first program on the diskette is an interactive HRA; the second concerns ideal weight. About 20 questions address diet, exercise, smoking, and other health habits. The profile displays mortality risks by age group. Apple II.
Order: MECC Distribution Center
3490 Lexington Avenue North
St. Paul, MN 55112
(612) 481-3527

Health Risk Appraisal (CI). This interactive HRA asks 35 questions concerning lifestyle and physiological indicators. The user's risks for 10 leading causes of death are displayed; a one-page summary printout is also provided. Apple II+ or IIe.
Order: University of Minnesota Media
Distribution
Box 734 Mayo Building
420 Delaware Street, SE
Minneapolis, MN 55455
(612) 376-8340

Healthstyle (CI). Based on "HealthStyle: A Self Test," a self-scoring questionnaire, this program is designed for individual users. The scores, rather than being displayed on the screen, are printed out in bar graphs with values ranging from unhealthful to healthful. The individual's and the group's scores are compared to those of the general population. An explanation sheet interprets the scores and gives advice on reducing risks. TRS-80, Model III.
Order: Wellsource
15431 Southeast 82nd Drive, Suite F
Clackamas, OR 97015
(503) 656-7446

Hospitalization Risk Assessment Program (CI). This HRA is designed to assess hospitalization risks but concerns only those risks that an individual can modify. A short (5 to 10 minutes) or a long (15 to 20 mintues) version can be chosen. Questions cover alcohol consumption, driving habits, weight, blood pressure, cholesterol levels, depression, and smoking. The user can ask why certain information is requested and receive explanations. The on-line profile gives an overall risk score adjusted for age and sex, the contribution of each risk factor to the score, and suggestions for modifying risks. IBM-PC.
Order: Tulane University Medical Center
School of Public Health and Tropical
Medicine
Department of Health Systems
Management
1430 Tulane Avenue
New Orleans, LA 70112
(504) 588-5428

Lifescore M (CI). This program is based on "Lifescore for Your Health," a self-scoring questionnaire. In addition to habits and lifestyle, the questions cover environmental factors, utilization of health care, and family medical history. Scores are interpreted in items of general health and life expectancy. IBM-PC.
Order: Center for Corporate Health Promotion
11490 Commerce Park Drive, Suite 140
Reston, VA 22091
(703) 620-5666

Personal Health Inventory (CI). The 96 items in this appraisal cover health habits and lifestyle, medical care, and women's health. Results are shown in a 5-minute, color graphic analysis of the participant's risks of dying from the 10 most frequent causes of death. Appraisal age, achievable age, and ways to reduce risks are also given. Apple II, IBM-PC.
Order: American Corporate Health Program
85 Old Eagle School Road
Strafford, PA 10987
(215) 293-9367

Wellness Inventory (CI). Adapted from the self-scoring questionnaire of the same name, this interactive program emphasizes stress, personal relationships, and social attitudes. It is not based on statistical data. The 120 items assess the user's lifestyle in 12 areas of personal energy expenditure, such as "eating," "feeling," and "transcending."

The resulting report shows the balance or lack of balance in the 12 areas, prints an individualized list of priorities for personal growth, and cites references for further reading. IBM-PC, Apple, TRS-80, C/PM.
Order: Wellness Associates
Box 5433
Mill Valley, CA 94942
(415) 383-3806

Health Risk Assessments Available as Computer Interactive and Computer Batch Processed

Sphere (CI & CB). Available in English and French versions based on Canadian statistics and in a second English version based on U.S. statistics. The 25 items cover medical and lifestyle characteristics. Graphic displays as well as narratives explain each user's risks and appraisal and achievable ages. IBM-PC, Apple II.
Order: Division of Health Systems
Office of the Coordinator of Health Sciences
University of British Columbia
#400-2194 Health Sciences Hall
Vancouver, BC V6T IZ6
Canada
(604) 228-2258

Compute-A-Life I and II (CI & CB). Part I is an interactive HRA and Part II is batch processing of the same version. Using color graphics, the profile provides information on risk factors, appraisal and achievable ages, life expectancy, and ways to reduce risks. IBM-PC.
Order: National Wellness Institute
University of Wisconsin-Stevens Point
South Hall
Stevens Point, WI 54481
(715) 346-2611

Health Age (CI & CB). The report computes a health age in contrast to chronological age. It also gives achievable age and suggests ways to reduce risks. Ten items collect information on seven health habits in this program, which can be run either interactive or batch processing. Apple II+, IBM-PC, TRS-80, Model III.
Order: Wellsource
15431 Southeast 82nd Drive, Suite F
Clackamas, OR 97015
(503) 656-7446

MICRO-HRA (CI & CB). This is the instrument developed at Fort Leavenworth, KS from which the Center for Disease Control derived its HRA for microcomputers. Three reports are possible: the standard CDC profile, a graphics program that combines bar graphs with narrative, and a whole-life projection. A program called "Why Do You Smoke?" is included on the disk. IBM-PC.
Order: Planetree Medical Systems
870 East 9400 South, #104
Sandy, UT 84070
(801) 572-1419

Personal Health Appraisal (CI & CB). The personal version is interactive while the professional version can be used in either interactive or batch-processing mode and can store and update profiles. The 84 items cover medical history and occupational health information as well as lifestyle. An additional 20 questions concern women's health. In the interactive mode, feedback is given throughout the interaction and the user's life expectancy is calculated at the end. The professional version also allows for an 8-page, explanatory printout, on which an organization's logo may be imprinted. IBM-PC.
Order: Medmicro
The Center for Medical Microcomputing
P.O. Box 9615
Madison, WI 53715
(608) 798-3002

Computer Batch Processed Health Risk Assessments

Take Charge of Your Health (CB). A computer-scored health profile designed to motivate individuals to strive for optimal health. The questionnaire addresses three aspects of health: health history, current health status, and lifestyle. Provides employers with aggregate data on employees' health risks, covers all aspects of an individual's health-related behavior, identifies health risk factors for eight major diseases, includes a full section on dietary risk and adequacy, and utilizes the concept of achieving optimal health rather than statistics. Batch processing mailed to:
Order: American Health Promotion, Inc.
7115 Crail Drive
Bethesda, MD 20817
(202) 822-3213

CHART: Comparative Health Age Relationship Testing (CB). The 16 questions collect information on physiological and laboratory measurements, history of serious diseases, and number of cigarettes smoked per day. In brochure format with a print-out attached, the profile explains risks and how they are computed, compares the individual's measurements to "normal" values, and gives appraisal and achievable ages. Batch processing mailed to:

Order: Medichart Corporation
(212) 982-9635

Computes (CB). Developed for corporations, this HRA calculates costs and savings related to employee health in addition to individual risks. Approximately 200 items collect data on habits, stress, and medical history. A section on women's health is included. The individual profile, 13 pages long, combines narrative and tabular data, explaining each client's deviation from "average" for 39 risk indicators, risk of hospitalization, and mortality risks. Three types of corporate profiles are available, all including information on health-related costs. Also marketed by HealthLine at St. Louis University and by Health Enhancement Systems in Princeton, NJ. Batch processing mailed to:

Order: Overman Associates
P.O. Box 171
Bonne Terre, MO 63628
ATTN: Ralph T. Overman
(314) 562-7020

General Well-Being Questionnaire (CB). This instrument emphasizes current levels of fitness rather than future disease. The report provides numerical scores for various indicators of physical and emotional well-being, based on a comprehensive set of factors "that can be supported scientifically as contributing to health." Batch processing mailed to:

Order: HealthLine
St. Louis University Medical Center
1325 South Grand Blvd.
St. Louis, MO 63014
ATTN: Robert Wheeler
(314) 771-7601

Health and Lifestyle Questionnaire (CB). This is another HRA that emphasizes current quality of life over long-term risks. The 38 questions collect data on health habits, psychological and job attitudes, and social relationships. The resulting two-page profile, in the form of a personal letter, does not report statistics but assigns scores ranging from "excellent" to "immediate attention" and dis-

cusses the individual's risks. Batch processing mailed to:

Order: Health Enhancement Systems
9 Mercer Street
Princeton, NJ 98540
(609) 924-7799

Health Hazard Appraisal (CB). This appraisal is the statistically updated version of the original HRA developed at Methodist Hospital by Drs. Jack Hall and Lewis Robbins. The approximately 80 questions cover medical history, family history, lifestyle, stress, and women's health. Computer analysis provides a four-page report that is a combination of narrative, bar graph, and tabulated data showing risks, appraisal age, and ways to reduce appraisal age. Batch processing mailed to:

Order: Prospective Medicine Center
Suite 219
3901 North Meridian
Indianapolis, IN 46208
(317) 923-3600

Health Hazard Appraisal Questionnaire (CB). Personal and family medical history are substantial parts of this questionnaire, but it also includes sections on alcohol, smoking, and driving. A special section for women is included. The computer analysis gives appraisal and achievable ages, recommends ways to reduce risks, and compares the client's risk factors with those of others of the same age, sex, and race. Batch processing mailed to:

Order: University of California
Department of Epidemiology and
International Health
1699 HSW
San Francisco, CA 94143
(415) 666-1158

Healthline (CB). Forty-four questions gather data on medical history and lifestyle, women's health, stress, and psychological and social factors. The 15-page report displays bar graphs on specific risks for the client's age and race and on stressors such as "frustrations" and "satisfactions." Brief narrative explanations and recommendations for reducing risks accompany the graphs. Batch processing mailed to:

Order: Health Logics
P.O. Box 3430
San Leandro, CA 94578
(415) 573-7222

Health Risk Appraisal (CB). This HRA covers a flexible range of behaviors. The basic form includes 36 items covering health habits and medical status. A wider-ranging "Lifestyle Analysis Questionnaire" is available. The standard nine-page report tabulates risks for five leading causes of death, gives appraisal and achievable ages, and recommends ways to reduce risks. A deluxe version includes extensive background information on risk factors. Batch processing mailed to:
Order: University of Michigan
       Fitness Research Center
       401 Washtenaw Avenue
       Ann Arbor, MI 48109
       (313) 763-2462

Health Risk Appraisal Questionnaire (CB). This HRA is based on the Methodist Hospital instrument. The 39 questions cover personal and family medical history, health habits, and women's health. The 10-page report, a combination of narrative and tabular data, explains the client's risk factors for the 12 leading causes of death as percentages by which the client deviates from the average; appraisal and achievable ages are also given as are behavioral changes that could reduce risks. Batch processing mailed to:
Order: St. Louis County Health Dept.
       504 East Second Street
       Duluth, MN 55805
       (218) 727-8661

Health Risk Assessment Questionnaire (CB). Topics covered in this 58-question HRA are lifestyle, health habits, and personal and family medical history. The resulting five-page printout, in tabular form with some narrative, describes risks that the client can and cannot control, and gives the most likely causes of death over the next 10 years for the client's demographic group. It also gives appraisal and achievable ages and suggests ways to reduce risks. Batch processing mailed to:
Order: Wisconsin Center for Health Risk Research
       University of Wisconsin Center
         for Health Sciences
       600 Highland Avenue, Room H4/414
       Madison, WI 53792
       (608) 263-1771

Health Risk Profile (CB). Although it was designed as part of Control Data's Staywell Program, this HRA is available separately. About 100 questions emphasize medical and family history; health habits and lifestyle, particularly stress factors, are

also covered. The profile emphasizes behavior change rather than risk of death. The left-hand pages of the 17-page report give general information on particular risk indicators; the right-hand pages provide data on the client's own risk factors for these indicators. This HRA is also available through distributors who are hospitals and other health providers. Batch processing mailed to:
Order: Control Data Corporation
       Benefit Services Division
       P.O. Box O-HQCO2P
       8100 34th Avenue South
       Minneapolis, MN 55440
       (800) 853-7777; (612) 853-6807

Health Risk Questionnaire (CB). This program is flexible, allowing volume users to consider modifications. The 39 questions ask about lifestyle, medical history, and some physical and laboratory measurements. The report is a combination of narrative and tabulated data, discussing risk factors for 15 major diseases. "General Well-Being Questionnaire" to measure stress is optional. Batch processing mailed to:
Order: Health Enhancement Systems
       9 Mercer Street
       Princeton, NJ 08540
       (609) 924-7799

Health Status Profile (CB). Volume users may modify this instrument also. The 23-page questionnaire collects information on current symptoms, medication used, and medical history, and probes nutrition, stress, and exercise habits in detail. Each questionnaire allows the client to write out questions that will be reviewed by a physician and answered individually by letter. The individual feedback averages 10 pages, gives appraisal age and achievable age, and discusses individual findings in detail. It also provides suggested readings for each section. Batch processing mailed to:
Order: Health Enhancement Systems
       9 Mercer Street
       Princeton, NJ 08540
       (609) 924-7799

Innerview Health Assessment (CB). This HRA (formerly "Health 80's Questionnaire") is available in several versions that differ in the amount of information they request. The two-, four-, and eight-page versions all collect detailed medical information, including diagnosed conditions, and ask questions on personal habits and behaviors. The longest version includes a section called "Quality of Life," which explores the client's emotional and social outlook. Computer analysis produces a printout, also available in several versions, on which risks are described and compared to the risks of others of the same age and sex. Appraisal and achievable age are given with suggestions for reducing risks. Batch processing mailed to:

Order: National Computer Systems
1100 Prairie Lake Drive
Eden Prairie, MN 55344
(612) 893-8370
(612) 893-8171

LIFE (CB). Included in the 13-page questionnaire are sections on personal and family medical histories, habits and lifestyle, attitudes to health, and physical measurements. Diet, exercise, and other health habits are explored in detail. The printout lists 20 major risk indicators (mostly physical measurements), the client's values for these, and the recommended values. It also lists the 20 leading causes of death for the client's age and sex, making recommendations to reduce risks where appropriate. A nutrition profile, a stress profile, and appraisal and achievable ages are included. IBM-PC software or batch processed.

Order: Wellsource
15431 Southeast 82nd Dr., Suite F
Clackamas, OR 97015
(503) 656-7446

Lifestyle Assessment Questionnaire (CB). Information on resources is an unusual feature of this HRA. The 270 questions cover habits, behavior, medical history, and women's health. A section entitled "Topics for Personal Growth" asks the client to select topics on which to receive more information. The printout suggests specific movies, books, and resources on topics selected by the client's level of wellness to the average of all others who have taken the test, and displays risk factors and ways to reduce them. Batch processing mailed to:

Order: National Wellness Institute
University of Wisconsin-Stevens Point
South Hall
Stevens Point, WI 54481
(715) 346-2172

Personal Health Profile (CB). A full-color, book-style report, this HRA consists of 221 items that collect demographic data and information on general well-being, stress, health status, and habits. A section on women's health is included.

Forty-eight pages give detailed background information on specific risk factors combined with a narrative report on the individual client's appraisal and achievable ages, mortality risks, and recommended actions. Full-color charts and photographs are included. Batch processing mailed to:

Order: General Health
3299 K Street NW
Washington, DC 20007
(800) 424-2775
(202) 965-4881

Personal Risk Profile (CB). Over half of the 109 questions collect data on personal and family medical history, the remainder on behavior, habits, socioeconomic status, and women's health. Computer analysis yields a two-page report that contains brief descriptions of each individual's risks and background information on risk estimation. Batch processing mailed to:

Order: General Health
3299 K Street NW
Washington, DC 20007
(800) 424-2775
(202) 965-4881

PULSE (CB). The PULSE questionnaire includes 143 questions on personal and family medical history, lifestyle, and women's health. The 20-page narrative report describes personal health status, compares the individual's mortality risks with those of others in the same demographic group, and evaluates nutrition, exercise, weight, stress, dental status, and health knowledge. Appraisal and achievable ages and ways to reduce risks are also given. Batch processing mailed to:

Order: International Health Awareness Center
148 East Michigan Avenue
Kalamazoo, MI 49007
(800) 531-4076
(616) 343-0770

Regional Health Resource Center Health Hazard Appraisal (CB). In addition to assessing individual risks, this HRA estimates the impact of workplace wellness programs. Covering lifestyle, medical history, frequency of medical screening, optional laboratory data, and women's health, this HRA consists of 39 questions plus a "General Well-Being Questionnaire" to measure stress. The five-page report, a combination of narrative and tabular data, includes 10-year mortality estimates for the 12 leading causes of death and estimated hospital days per year. Advice on reducing risks is provided. A group profile includes the estimated reduction in workforce mortality and hospitalization achievable through specific wellness programs. Batch processing mailed to:

Order: Regional Health Resource Center
Medical Information Laboratory
1408 West University Avenue
Urbana, IL 61801
(217) 367-0076

Well Aware Health Risk Appraisal (CB). The emphasis of this HRA, developed under a five-year Kellogg Foundation research grant, is on quality of life and current risks. The questionnaire gathers information on health habits and lifestyle, health knowledge, stress, and women's health. The 16-page report includes mortality predictions but stresses practical measures to improve health. Sections are titled Eating/Diet, Motor Vehicle Safety, Alcohol Use, Smoking, Medication/Drug Use, Stress Index, Sociability Index, and Life Contentment Index, and the HRA includes results of physical and laboratory measurements. Background information on risk indicators appears on the left-hand pages; the client's risk level (low, medium, high) and prescriptions for change are on the facing four-color, computer-printed pages. Batch processing mailed to:

Order: Well Aware About Health
P.O. Box 43338
Tucson, AZ 85733
ATTN: Sabrina Dunton
(602) 297-2819
(602) 297-2960

Health Rap (CB). This HRA uses the 37 questions of the CDC instrument plus another 46 questions on wellness. Both a standard risk profile and a wellness index are provided. The three- to four-page printout uses a narrative format. This instrument is also distributed by Random House in conjunction with its college textbook series *Life and Health*. Apple Macintosh software or Batch processed.

Order: Health Enhancement and Promotion
Company
P.O. Box 546
Ames, IA 50010
(515) 233-3552

Healthchec (CB). This batch processing program can be used with an optical scanner and can be modified to include an organization's own program title. The questions and profile are based on

the Center for Disease Control's HRA. IBM-PC software.

Order: Partnership for Good Health
Martin Luther Hospital Medical Center
1830 West Rommeya Drive
P.O. Box 3304
Anaheim, CA 92803
Attn: Kevin Olsen
(714) 535-2783

I'm a Health Nut (CB). This HRA, designed for adolescents, consists of 55 to 60 questions on family and personal health data, lifestyles, feelings, and locus of control. Each participant receives a printout describing appraisal age and suggesting ways to improve it. The profile also shows how each student's lifestyle will affect his or her risks at age 40. Feedback on health attitude is provided. Apple II software, IBM-PC software.

Order: St. Paul Division of Public Health
Health Education Section
555 Cedar Street
St. Paul, MN 55101
(612) 292-7712

Regional Health Resource Center Health Hazard Appraisal (CB). Like the large-computer version of the same name, this HRA estimates the impact of workplace wellness programs. The 39 questions cover lifestyle, medical history, and frequency of medical screening; "General Well-Being Questionnaire" can be included to measure stress. The narrative report is combined with tabular material to provide 10-year mortality estimates for 12 leading causes of death, estimated hospital days per year, and advice on reducing risks. Group reports can be generated. IBM-PC.

Order: Regional Health Resources Center
Medical Information Library
1408 W. University Avenue
Urbana, IL 61901
(217) 367-0076

Wellness Check (CB). Data for this HRA, which is designed for batch processing, can be entered either at the keyboard or by an optical scan system. Forty-seven questions collect information on health habits, family medical history, occupational exposure to hazardous substances, and women's health. The microcomputer produces a printout that identifies both healthful habits and those that pose a risk to health. Ways to reduce risks are suggested, and a booklet with more extensive information is provided. Adolescent and Spanish-

language versions are also available. Apple II or IIe, TRS-80, Model II, 12 or 16, IBM-PC or PCXT.
Order: Chief of Health Promotion
Rhode Island Department of Health
75 Davis Street
Providence, RI 02908
(401) 227-6957

Paper-and-Pencil Health Risk Assessments

Determine Your Medical Age (PP). This brief, fold-out questionnaire has four sections: lifestyle, physical health, family, and women's health. It is designed for healthy adults over 25 and allows them to calculate their medical age in contrast to actual age. Adapted from *How To Be Your Own Doctor Sometimes* by Keith W. Sehnert with Howard Eisenberg.
Order: The Health Education Center
Blue Cross/Blue Shield
of Greater New York
3 Park Avenue at 34th St.
New York, NY 10016
(212) 481-2323

Go to Health (PP). The 35-item questionnaire in this pamphlet is adapted from the Canadian "Your Lifestyle Profile" and covers health status, nutrition, exercise, smoking, substance abuse, and safety. Most of the pamphlet is a discussion of major health risks and ways to reduce them. It concludes with a contract on which the user can record lifestyle changes that he or she wishes to undertake.
Order: Blue Cross/Blue Shield of Michigan
Editorial Services (1909)
600 East Lafayette
Detroit, MI 48226
(313) 225-8430

Health Graph (PP). In addition to the basic wellness categories, this 53-item quiz includes sections on heredity, health fads, sexuality, and health resources. Brief summaries of risks follow each section; there is no totaling of scores.
Order: University of Rhode Island Health Services
Health Education Department
4th Floor, Roosevelt
Kingston, RI 02881
(401) 792-5954

Healthstyle: A Self Test (PP). This pamphlet, published by the U.S. Public Health Service, includes an introductory section explaining how personal habits influence one's health and a concluding section that gives specific suggestions for reducing risks. Areas covered in the 24 questions are nutrition, alcohol and drug use, smoking, fitness, stress, and safety. Each section is scored on a scale of 1 to 10 and the scores for each section are explained in general terms with ideas for improvement. Printing negatives for this brochure may be borrowed, and a two-page version, suitable for reproduction in newsletters, is also available.
Order: National Health Information
Clearinghouse
P.O. Box 1133
Washington, DC 20013-1133
(800) 336-4797
(703) 522-2590

Is Your Body Older Than You Are? (PP). This colorful fold-out brochure consists of the same Blue Cross questionnaire used in "Determine Your Medical Age" (adapted from *How To Be Your Own Doctor Sometimes* by Keith W. Sehnert with Howard Eisenberg, Grosset and Dunlap, New York).
Order: Blue Cross of Oregon
Corporate Communications
100 Southwest Market St.
Portland, OR 97201
(503) 225-5221

Lifescore for Your Health (PP). Designed for employee health programs, this questionnaire comes with an attached carbon copy. Each employee keeps a self-scored copy, while the carbons are batch processed to yield a group profile. Questions cover lifestyle, environmental factors, family medical history, and utilization of health care. Scores are given for general health and life expectancy. See also "Lifescore M" under Computer-Interactive HRAs. (Adapted from *Lifeplan for Your Health* by Donald M. Vickery.)
Order: Center for Corporate Health Promotion
11490 Commerce Park Dr., Suite 140
Reston, VA 11091
(703) 620-5666

Start Taking Charge (PP). This HRA notebook is one in a series of "Start Taking Charge" materials on fitness and lifestyle. Twenty questions address exercise, diet, safety, stress, and substance abuse.
Order: Aetna Life and Casualty
P.O. Box 1106
Hartford, CT 06143
ATTN: Start Taking Charge

Wellness Index/Wellness Inventory (PP). Both the index with 120 questions and the inventory with 330 questions assess wellness in 12 areas of personal energy expenditure, emphasizing stress factors, personal relationships, and social attitudes. Scores are entered on a "Wellness Index Wheel" to demonstrate graphically the balance or lack of balance among the 12 areas. Follow-up is provided in *Wellness Workbook* by R. Ryan and J.W. Travis (Ten Speed Press, 1981, $9.95). A microcomputer-based version of the inventory is available.

Order: Wellness Associates
Box 5433
Mill Valley, CA 94942
(415) 383-3806

Your Health Profile (PP). This questionnaire comes in teen, adult, and senior citizen versions with 20 to 35 questions focusing on the health habits and lifestyle most relevant to each age group. The senior citizen version, in large type, does not include scores; it is intended to be used in conjunc-

tion with personal counseling.

Order: Health Education Center
200 Ross Street
Pittsburgh, PA 15219
(412) 392-3160

Your Lifestyle Profile (PP). Adapted from the Canadian quiz of the same name, this questionnaire is one component of the Kansas PLUS employee health program. The questions are identical to those in "Go To Health," previously cited. It is available as a separate one-page handout or as part of a workbook that provides information on each risk indicator and concludes with a personal contract to be filled out by the client.

Order: Kansas Dept. of Health and Environment
Forbes Field
Topeka, KS 66620
ATTN: Health Promotion PLUS
Administrator
(913) 862-9360

CHAPTER 2

Implementing a Paraprofessional Program

An effective and efficient paraprofessional program requires a clear delineation of duties and responsibilities among the professionals and paraprofessionals involved. The responsibilities of the program coordinator include maintaining a balance between serving the trainers, paraprofessionals, and students, and keeping administration happy and aware of the program's assets. Ongoing coordination and communication between the program coordinator and the trainers is the key to success. This chapter deals with many of the activities the program coordinator engages in to implement a successful health promotion program. Budgetary considerations and management support will play an enormous role in deciding whether the activities listed here will fit into a given program.

The Program Coordinator's Initial Tasks

The program coordinator is responsible for the development and design of the health promotion workshops, the paraprofessional training program, and the execution of the two. This covers a wide variety of duties and challenges ranging from advertising and marketing to developing the specific group activities within a workshop.

Gathering Program Support

The coordinator's initial tasks may be selling or justifying paraprofessional education and eliciting as many different bases of support as possible.

Those who would benefit from this program in the college or university environment include

- the students who train in the program;
- the academic departments that offer practical experiences for their students who train in the program;
- the student groups who request and participate in the workshops;
- resident advisor and directors in residence halls who are often required to coordinate programs for their residents;
- health educators and others who would ordinarily present workshops and eventually burn out from giving beginning-level programs;
- the student health center, or student affairs division sponsoring the program, which can expand its offerings of different types of workshops, increase the number of workshops available, and, ultimately, increase the number of students who will have the opportunity to participate in a workshop; and
- the workshop participants, whose knowledge is increased and whose attitudes and behaviors are affected in a positive direction.

The stronger the program's base of support, the more likely it is that upper administration will approve and fund it. The health educator should elicit the help of those who would benefit from the program by encouraging them to include the ideas for the program in meetings and conversations with administrators. This enables others to rally for the cause in a variety of settings. If there are blockades to getting approval, the health educator may consider forming a committee of representatives from the list of those who would benefit from the program to study the project and document the benefits for all concerned. This may lead to acquiring funds from some of those resources and operating as a jointly funded program. The campus network system should be used to the program's advantage in gaining support and funding. Forming a group of enthusiastic proponents of paraprofessional health promotion may lead to creative ideas for funding.

Once the program has been approved and funded, there are many managerial responsibilities to consider, such as budget writing and cost analysis, marketing, advertising, maintaining quality assurance, conducting needs assessments and interest surveys, designing and piloting workshops, recruiting paraprofessionals, evaluating, and writing reports.

Preparing the Budget

At the University of Illinois, the money for the student health center is budgeted from student fees. Consequently, all the programs are for students only, not faculty or staff, and all programs are free of charge. Each year, the students have a strong voice in the health center's budget, so it's important to develop the program to reflect their interests and to justify an increase in the programming budget, not only for administrators, but also for the students who pay for the services and programs.

The Lifestyle Workshop Program itself is not expensive for the health educator to operate. Trainers' salaries are the largest expenditure, as high as 75% to 80% of the total budget, but this buys the necessary brainpower, creativity, imagination, and intelligence for a successful program. The Lifestyle Workshop Program hires graduate students as trainers, who receive a tuition waiver and monthly stipend or salary. It is considerably less expensive than using a full-time professional health educator, and it is an invaluable experience for the graduate students.

The program coordinator's salary is another large budget expense and varies according to the time spent on the program. For some coordinators, their paraprofessional program may be small and represents 30% of their job. At the end of the year the percentage of time the coordinator puts into the paraprofessional program is calculated into the yearly cost analysis. An example of computing a yearly cost analysis is described in Appendix 2.A.

Budget situations vary from year to year, but forethought is the most important aspect of planning. The first year is, of course, the most difficult for the health educator, who doesn't know what to expect or may not have a clear picture of what to take into account. Beyond salaries, which will not change during the fiscal year, an easy method of accounting is to break down the rest of the operating costs into account categories. The following are some suggested account categories as well as an example of an accounting method to track expenditures.

Duplicating Services. This is often the largest account after salaries. Approximately 10% to 15% of the budget should be designated for duplicating handouts and pamphlets, including the purchase of colored paper. It's best to contact as many available services as possible and find out if the cost goes down as the number of reproductions goes up. The costs for duplication in using a paper-and-pencil health risk assessment, sending out surveys, or mailing letters in bulk to advertise the program would be incorporated here.

Expendable Supplies. These are items that usually have to be bought only once or replaced only as they become worn out or used up. This is the second largest account after salaries, using about 8% to 10% of the budget. These supplies include poster boards, art supplies, prizes, playing pieces for games, portfolios for carrying workshop supplies to presentations, books, and training supplies.

Equipment. These choices will depend on both program needs and its budget. The list may include a videocassette recorder and camera to film trainees and create a library of the workshops, 16 mm film projectors and films for use in training classes and workshops, overhead projector, slide projector, light stand to produce slide shows, tape recorders for paraprofessionals to tape their first workshops and for stress management relaxation tapes, typewriter, computer hardware and software, and copier. If other institutional programs can share a piece of equipment, there will be further justification for its purchase.

It may also be possible for several programs to purchase equipment jointly. Depending on the situation and how much equipment is needed, this account will vary considerably from year to year. For the first year, the program will require a great deal of new equipment if it is being developed from scratch, and for the following year the program may not need much. Each year an allocation of approximately 2% to 5% of the budget should be requested. The health educator should find out if it's possible to share equipment with others in the institution before making major purchases. Some equipment is more difficult to share, however, such as film projectors if the program uses a number of different films for workshops.

Mailing Services. These need to be accounted for in plans to mail out surveys, evaluation forms, and marketing letters. Costs include postage, and self-addressed, return business reply envelopes. About 0.5% to 1% of the budget should be allotted for mailing services. The health educator should check with the postal service for bulk-mailing options.

Professional Services. These include paying honorariums to guest speakers for training classes and using the services of others on or off campus for the program. For example, we ask a professional from the university's instructional media services division to videotape the paraprofessionals, after which we give individual feedback for improving presentation skills. The people who do the actual taping are paid from this account. Other examples of professional services are library computer literature searches, graphic design work for posters, and survey and statistical assistance for evaluations. This account is approximately 0.5% to 2% of the yearly budget.

Continuing Education. This is a fund for travel, lodging and food for conferences, seminars, and further training for the program coordinator and the trainers. In our situation, this fund comes from administration and is not a program cost. If it is a budget item, approximately 5% to 8% should be allocated for continuing education.

It is vitally important to keep an accurate account of program costs. It is easier to estimate the budget request for the following year if the expenses are broken into accounts each year. When the new budget comes in, the requested money should be kept separate in the different accounts, and the expenditures should be subtracted from each account during the year. This allows the program coordinator to know always how much has been spent and how much remains in the budget.

In addition, in the following year this method provides a better estimate of the amount of money to request. For example, let's say a program coordinator requested $8,000 for the health promotion program, $700 of which was estimated to be used for duplicating services. At the start of the new fiscal year, devise an accounting sheet, similar to a checkbook register, for each account category. According to the example of duplicating services, the coordinator would subtract from $700 each duplicating expenditure during the fiscal year (Table 2.1).

At the end of the year, money may remain in some accounts and have been overspent in others. Ultimately the budget must balance. This process helps those involved in making the following year's budget request to come up with a more accurate estimate.

Designing the Marketing Plan

The program coordinator is responsible for seeing that all the careful planning described in this chapter and in chapter 1 pays off in terms of results. This includes developing a marketing plan so that students will be aware of the health education benefits that are available to them.

Social marketing has been defined as ''the design, implementation, and control of programs seeking to increase the acceptability of a social idea, cause, or practice in a target group(s)'' (Kotler,

Table 2.1 Account Category—Duplicating Services

Date	Quantity	Description	Balance
8-14-87	—	—	700.00
8-15-87	500	''Communicating Your Concerns'' handout	− 10.80
			689.20
8-30-87	200	''Lifestyle Workshop'' posters	−6.75
			682.45

1976, p. 495). Health educators and administrators are becoming interested in the concept of marketing because of the changes in the health care industry in this country. Marketing concerns often address big-picture issues such as determining who can deliver the best quality health care. The health industry is highly competitive, and if a target market decides another health care institution can provide better service, the competition is going to go out of business. Thus today's health care institutions need to establish themselves solidly in the marketplace. Although of relatively small size, even the paraprofessional health promotion program can institute a marketing plan to better deliver the program to the students so they will want more.

The health educator initiates a marketing plan by looking at the attitudes of the health center workers, the health education department, the program coordinator, the trainers, and, most important, the paraprofessionals who deliver the service. Is everyone giving the same message about the program? Is there a unifying theme connecting the program with the institution? What ideas do other people in the institution have that will eventually enhance the program?

Market research and plans are carried out when problems arise or opportunities present themselves in the form of student opinion. Those who are interested in developing a marketing plan, conducting market research, or finding out more about what marketing means should take classes, seminars, or read books such as *Marketing Health Care Communications* by R. MacStravic (1986) to become better educated. Through these resources, one can learn about price, promotion, and product, and the how-tos of implementing a systematic plan in which everyone can be involved. The following are the fundamentals of a marketing effort.

1. Clarify the marketing objectives. What are you trying to achieve in your marketing plan?
2. Determine the specific products to market. What do you want to sell to your market?
3. Define the target market population. To whom do you want to sell your product or service?
4. Choose the best promotion methods to carry out your plan. What tools should you use to take your product to the market population?

Carrying out these steps can be an exciting and innovative challenge. An example from the University of Illinois program will describe this process in more detail. We had some concerns about four Lifestyle Workshops geared to women; the workshops were not getting as many requests as we'd hoped. We thought the problem may have been one of two things, the workshops themselves, or the fact that the target market population was unaware of the workshops. The evaluations from these workshops did not indicate major problems with the content, activities, or presenters. So, to find out if potential requesters were unaware of the workshops, we implemented a marketing plan using the four steps described above.

1. Objective: To increase awareness of the Lifestyle Workshops directed toward women.
2. Products: The following Lifestyle Workshops: "Women and Alcohol," "There's More to Eating Than Food," "Winning at Weight Control," and "Acquaintance Rape Prevention for Women."
3. Target market population: The female resident advisors in the University residence halls and sorority program coordinators. These are two large workshop-requester groups.
4. Promotion method: Direct mailing of letters to the target market population describing the workshops designed primarily for women.

We continued to analyze the workshop evaluations and watched workshop requests for 15 weeks. Requests increased for three of the four workshops. Based on the information we collected from our marketing plan, we decided to merge the information in "Women and Alcohol" into one of the other drugs and alcohol Lifestyle Workshops, "A Winner's Alcohol Facts Game." By monitoring responses to marketing efforts, the program coordinator is better able to serve specific groups within the market population.

Preparing Program Advertising

Advertising is another important tool for any community program, and it is especially necessary at a college or university because of the constant turnover in the student population. The Lifestyle Workshop Program requires two kinds of advertising strategy: advertising to the people who request the workshops, and advertising to those who will attend the workshop once a presentation date has been set.

Advertising to Workshop Requesters. This entails finding the groups of people most likely to coordinate health or special interest programs. In our case the larger groups are resident directors and resident assistants of residence halls, sorority and fraternity officers, presidents of student organizations, and the student group, Health Advocates, mentioned in chapter 1.

After identifying these groups, the health educator should set up visits to the groups that meet regularly. At these meetings, staff members can explain the purpose of the program and give out descriptions of the workshops along with instructions on how to arrange for a specific workshop. If individual visits are not feasible, the program coordinator should send mailings to the potential workshop requesters. It is also useful to maintain contact with the people who request workshops by sending mailings to them in the future.

Advertising a Requested Workshop. Once a requester books a Lifestyle Workshop, it is that person's responsibility to advertise the workshop. We offer suggestions for placing posters to help the requester coordinate a successful workshop. After a workshop is requested, the Lifestyle Educator who will be presenting the workshop confirms by making a follow-up phone call and sending a confirmation packet to the requester.

The confirmation packet consists of materials designed to advertise and to improve attendance at the workshop: a confirmation letter and a suggested advertising poster that can be reproduced (see pages 26, 27). The packet also includes one set of the handouts used in the requested workshop that the requester can display to attract attention and publicize the upcoming workshop.

The effectiveness of the advertising should be evaluated periodically. It is useful to ask requesters how they found out about the workshop when the request is made. The program coordinator should develop a checklist of all the possible ways a requester could hear about the workshops. Keeping track of this information for a given time period indicates which method is making the most impact.

Designing a logo for the program distinguishes it from other departments and programs and can be used on advertisements, handouts, and posters. The University of Illinois's Lifestyle Workshop logo expresses movement with a staircase design and the slight slant of the word "Lifestyle." The logo should take into account the program's mission, the target population, and the sponsoring institution.

Facilitating Quality Assurance

Many educational programs highly support quality assurance in concept but have not put together a formalized plan. The goal of a quality assurance program is to identify a problem, which, if changed, would improve the quality of care (or education) provided by a department, program, or service. Quality assurance has traditionally dealt with medical and clinical care issues. But education departments, and their individual programs in health care institutions, need to move into quality assurance programs along with their clinical counterparts. Most education departments receive funding from the same sources as the clinical departments and should be held to the same criteria of quality care.

It is not enough to have a good concept of quality assurance. Ongoing and realistic plans must be developed for meeting those ideals. The quality assurance program designed for the Lifestyle Workshop Program is adopted from the Boynton Health Service at the University of Minnesota and is based on a plan developed at the St. Louis Park Medical Center in Minneapolis, Minnesota (Batalden & O'Connor, 1980). The process includes these steps:

1. Data is collected from a variety of sources concerning the services provided by the Lifestyle Workshop Program. Sources include past workshop participants, health educators and other health center personnel, and students who request workshops for their groups.
2. A telephone survey is designed to interview past workshop participants' opinions and reactions to the workshop and the paraprofessional presenter. The health center's quality assurance director randomly chooses and calls 30 workshop participants for the survey. If your institution does not employ a quality assurance director, request another administrator to fulfill these tasks.
3. The quality assurance director meets with the Lifestyle Workshop Program staff to review the data and identify problems and concerns regarding the program.
4. Each staff member selects a specific problem or concern he or she would like to see resolved. After all problems have been identified, each member selects and ranks the three highest priority problems from the list. The scores are tallied, and the problem

Lifestyle Workshops

WILL BE PRESENTED

AT _____ *PM*

ON _____

IN _____

CONTACT _____
FOR MORE INFORMATION

Letter of Confirmation

Dear _____

   This letter is to confirm that the Lifestyle Workshop _____
will be presented to your group on _____ at _____ p.m.
If you have any questions or concerns, the Lifestyle Educator(s) for your workshop is/are:

(name) _____ (phone) _____

(name) _____ (phone) _____

   We have discovered that the most successful workshops have been promoted within the group by group members. Following is a list of ideas to help you promote the workshop:

1. Have key people (officers, RAs, etc.) "talk up" the program, encouraging people to come.
2. Put up posters in halls, bathrooms, bulletin boards, etc., advertising the workshop.
3. Place catchy leaflets in members' mailboxes and in your lobby.
4. List the workshops on your calendar of events.

Two other tips for a successful workshop:

1. Refreshments are a pleasant accompaniment to a workshop; however, please don't let them interfere with the workshop.
2. Conduct the workshop in a room that is quiet and out-of-the-way, so participants won't be distracted.

PLEASE NOTE: If something unusual comes up, or if there seems to be no one planning to attend, *please* call your Lifestyle Educator to cancel the workshop, or call and leave a message at _____ .
Cancellation will be regarded as a courtesy, not as a failure! Thank you.

receiving the most points is selected as the focus of the program's quality assurance efforts for the year. If more than one problem stands out as an urgent priority, the team may be able to tackle both at the same time, depending on the time and energy required for each.

5. Remedy coordinators from the staff are selected to work with the quality assurance director in resolving the problem. The staff sets a level of desired performance and a target date for problem resolution.

6. The problem-resolution phase consists of conducting a pretest study to determine the extent of the problem, identifying and implementing a remedy to reduce or eliminate the problem, and conducting a posttest study to determine whether the remedy has resulted in the desired level of performance. If the desired level of performance has not been met, the remedy is reevaluated and modified until an acceptable level of performance is reached. When the desired level of performance is achieved, the problem is considered resolved, and no activity on that issue occurs until a reevaluation is done 1 or 2 years later.

7. The staff then reassembles and begins working on the next prioritized issue. Periodically, on an annual or a biannual basis, past quality assurance matters are reevaluated to make sure that the same problems have not reappeared.

A common quality assurance issue in health promotion programs is the production of handouts and pamphlets distributed in workshops. Handouts are often a major component of a workshop; they provide participants with reference information after the workshop and thus facilitate the educational process. Studying the value and justifying the expense of the workshop handouts was a quality assurance issue tackled by our department. During the quality assurance telephone survey (Step 2) (see Appendix 2.B), a group of questions were written specifically to query interviewees' reactions to the workshop handouts.

We needed to find out the following: Are the handouts worth the cost? (Remember, we're spending student money.) Are the handouts helpful? Are the handouts written at an appropriate level for college students? Do they just get thrown away after the workshop? Objective data collection and thoughtful review by a program's staff will result in a successful quality assurance process. In turn, the process can also include seeking the population's feedback for improved service.

Designing and Piloting Workshops

Once there is justification for the workshops, based on needs assessments or other criteria, the creative work begins. Unfortunately, not everyone has the time to develop, design, and test the kinds of creative and informative workshops they'd like to offer in their programs. That's why this book was written! For 3 years we've been designing, implementing, and evaluating the 16 workshops that form the core of this book.

The workshops have evolved because of participants' suggestions and comments on workshop evaluations. The content of each workshop addresses many of the health needs and interests of today's college student. As explained in the budget section, the workshops are not expensive to produce and maintain. They may need modification to a particular audience or program, but it is not necessary to reinvent the wheel. Some of the Lifestyle Workshops adapt or use, with permission, activities and handouts from other programs rather than starting from scratch.

It is imperative to pilot any workshop even if the program is based on predesigned workshops. A professional health educator or the program coordinator must pilot the workshop before a paraprofessional is sent out to present it. By first piloting the workshop, especially to a practice audience, the coordinator will be able to work out some of the bugs and get feedback on the workshop, the presentation, visual aids, and handouts. A very helpful piloting method is to conduct a pre- and posttest on the audience to evaluate changes in knowledge or potential changes in behavior or attitude.

Recruiting Paraprofessionals

Before each new training session starts, the coordinator needs to determine how many new paraprofessionals are needed. This number will not be evident in the beginning until the workshops are fully advertised and evaluated for number of requests and participants. The coordinator can get the program off the ground by starting with at least two paraprofessionals per workshop. After one or two semesters of the program, the program coordinator will be able to determine a more accurate number of recruits based on requests for workshops. The recruitment quota should be padded with a few extra students in case anyone drops out of the program. If this were to happen and there were just enough recruits to begin with, the program will be limited by not being able to offer as many workshops as are demanded because of a shortage of paraprofessionals.

Recruitment of paraprofessionals for the Lifestyle Workshop Program can be accomplished through a number of mechanisms. During all-campus registration, the program can be advertised in the campus newspaper. The program coordinator or staff members can make brief presentations in classes, describing the program and benefits. Another effective method is to contact undergraduate academic advisors of different disciplines to direct students who are in need of practical experiences to take the course, which prepares them in public speaking.

Screening or interviewing prospective paraprofessionals is a technique used by many programs and may be necessary if more students than your program can accommodate are interested in participating. Alternatively, the coordinator may want only students who have taken certain prerequisite classes so they come into the program with a base of knowledge about the health area—this reduces the amount of training time needed. The philosophy of the University of Illinois program has been to allow any students the opportunity to train in the Lifestyle Workshop Program. The program is offered as a university class with credits, so it should be open to anyone who wants to take it. We could ask for prerequisite classes, such as basic nutrition, for those wanting to train in the nutrition Lifestyle Workshops, but so far we haven't chosen to do so. If we screened out those students who initially appeared clumsy, softspoken, or nervous, they would not get the opportunity to practice and develop a much needed communication skill. It has been our experience that any above-average student can master the material in the workshop, but it takes time and practice to be able to teach that same material to others, especially peers.

Each prospective Lifestyle Workshop paraprofessional completes an application form (see pages 30, 31) about his or her background and interests. From this initial information, the trainer gains some idea of the student's experiences in public speaking and extracurricular involvement, and this helps to break the ice as the trainer and paraprofessional begin their yearlong relationship.

Program Evaluation

All health educators and program coordinators recognize and must be committed to the importance of evaluating the success of their programs. The current emphasis on health and fitness requires health educators to show that this emphasis is a necessary one. If we expect the profession of health education and health promotion to continue to grow, we must be able to answer the difficult question: Does health education work? The public is also looking to us for proof that the education they seek will have the desired effects. Evaluation, with its many facets, is a challenge, but it is one challenge that cannot be ignored.

Demonstrating Accountability

Evaluation is used for many different purposes, and it is important that a programmer decide before implementation of a program what kind of evaluation will be conducted. There may be information or data that must be collected before the program begins in order to carry out a successful evaluation. For example, if the purpose of the workshop is to increase participants' knowledge, a pretest must be administered before the workshop begins. Green and Lewis (1986) describe three levels of evaluation if the purpose is accountability.

Level 1: Formative Evaluation. This involves measurements obtained and judgments made before or during the implementation of materials, methods, activities, or programs to improve the quality of performance or delivery (Green & Lewis, 1986). An example of formative evaluation is a post-workshop evaluation survey (see pages 32, 33) that asks about the workshop process. Examine question 9 in this survey for examples of how to elicit a range of feedback.

The paraprofessional tallies all the evaluations onto one sheet and reviews the results with his or her trainer, discussing ways to improve the presentation and the workshop.

Level 2: Impact Evaluation. This is the immediate observable effects of a program, leading to intermediate and intended outcomes (Green & Lewis, 1986). Examples of impact evaluation are measuring the workshop objectives aimed at knowledge, attitudes, and behavior or conducting a cost-effective analysis of your program. According to Green, ''. . . impact evaluation . . . is the most

Paraprofessional Application

Name: _____ Phone: _____

Local Address: _____

_____

Best time to reach is: _____

☐ Fresh.   ☐ Soph.   ☐ Jr.   ☐ Sr.   ☐ Grad.   (Fall of _____)

College: _____ Major: _____

1. What specialty are you interested in applying for (1st, 2nd choice):

   _____ Alcohol and Drugs   _____ Sexuality   _____ Stress Management

   _____ Nutrition   _____ Fitness

2. Why do you want to be a health promotion paraprofessional? _____

   _____

   _____

   _____

3. What experience have you had in teaching or small group leadership? _____

   _____

   _____

   _____

   _____

4. What do you feel you can contribute as a paraprofessional? _____

   _____

   _____

   _____

5. How would you describe your experiences or knowledge about alcohol and drugs/sexuality/stress/
   nutrition/fitness? (Answer based on specialty areas chosen): _____

   _____

   _____

   _____

6. What courses have you taken in small group leadership, group work, or health education? (Or any
   other courses you feel are relevant): _____

   _____

   _____

   _____

7. List your leadership/service experiences:

Position(s)	How long	Responsibilities
_____	_____	_____
_____	_____	_____
_____	_____	_____
_____	_____	_____
_____	_____	_____

8. Please list your extracurricular activities: _____
_____
_____
_____

9. Have you had experience in:

☐ Public speaking   ☐ Media development (posters, ads, etc.)

☐ Teaching   ☐ Group leadership

☐ Program development (workshops, seminars, projects, etc.)

10. How did you hear about the Lifestyle Workshop Program?

☐ Poster   ☐ Health advocates

☐ Campus newspaper   ☐ Resident advisor

☐ Staff/faculty   ☐ Other (specify) _____

11. Is there anything else you would like to include on this application? _____
_____
_____
_____
_____
_____

Workshop Evaluation Survey

In order for us to adequately meet the needs of the student population, we need to know what you are thinking. Please take a few minutes to fill out this questionnaire. It will be of great help to us. Thank you.

1. Name of workshop _____

Circle answers that apply.

2. How did you find out about this workshop?
   a. Poster
   b. Friend
   c. Announcement at meeting
   d. Health advocate/lifestyle educator
   e. Newspaper ad
   f. Other

3. Was your attendance . . .
   a. Mandatory
   b. Voluntary

4. How likely is it your behavior will change due to the information presented?
   a. Unlikely
   b. Somewhat unlikely
   c. Somewhat likely
   d. Likely

5. How likely is it your attitude will change due to the information presented?
   a. Unlikely
   b. Somewhat unlikely
   c. Somewhat likely
   d. Likely

6. If you answered ''unlikely'' to question 4 and/or 5, please explain why in the space below.

7. I have learned something new from this workshop.
   a. Yes
   b. No

8. Due to this workshop, I have increased my knowledge in this specific area.
   a. Yes
   b. No

9. We would also like to evaluate the style and process of the workshop. On a scale of 1 to 5, please respond to each of the following items:

a. Comfort of setting   poor   1   2   3   4   5   excellent

b. Knowledge of presenter(s)   1   2   3   4   5

c. Clarity of material   1   2   3   4   5

d. Sensitivity of presenter(s)   1   2   3   4   5

e. Organization of presentation   1   2   3   4   5

f. Meaningful activities   1   2   3   4   5

g. Involvement of participants   1   2   3   4   5

h. Style of presenter(s)   1   2   3   4   5

i. Applicability to your lifestyle   1   2   3   4   5

10. In the space below, please list ways we could improve this workshop.

Thank you for your cooperation. The following questions are optional, but would help us in planning future programs. Circle answer:

1. Place of residence
   a. Residence hall
   b. Sorority
   c. Fraternity
   d. Private university housing
   e. Off-campus housing

2. Year in school
   a. Freshman
   b. Sophomore
   c. Junior
   d. Senior
   e. Graduate level

3. Sex
   a. Male
   b. Female

likely evaluation to result in improved programs" (Green, 1986, p. 237), whereas formative evaluation is concerned with the quality of professional performance.

The University of Illinois health promotion program uses an impact evaluation to determine whether there has been an increase in the knowledge of the participants after a workshop. A survey is given to participants at the start of the workshop, and that same survey is mailed to them 4 weeks afterward. The 4-week interval allows for changes or improvements in the participants' behavior to have been initiated. In addition, the survey reveals how much information has been retained. The impact survey for the workshop "Positively Stressed!" (pages 35, 36) is an excellent example of how to assess retention of information.

Level 3: Outcome Evaluation. Outcome is the ultimate goal or product of a program or treatment, generally measured in the health field in terms of morbidity or mortality statistics in a population, or vital measures, symptoms, signs, or physiological indicators in individuals. The outcome evaluation is a long-term undertaking. Ultimately, medical outcomes and public health criteria or standards must be related to social definitions of health problems and the quality of life (Green & Lewis, 1986). The outcome evaluation looks for signs that correlate the health promotion intervention to an actual decrease in illness, disability, or death, or to an increase in quality of life. For example, is a worker more productive because he or she is involved in a regular exercise program? Or, does a decrease in saturated fats in turn decrease heart disease? Questions like these are being answered through long-term, controlled studies at many health institutions and agencies.

These three levels of evaluation represent the spectrum of health programming efforts, from immediate workshop activities to ultimate health outcomes and social benefits. For example, suppose an agency is going to implement a health promotion program to reduce heart disease. Conducting a telephone survey to find out how many people saw a newspaper advertisement for a cholesterol-reducing class is an example of formative evaluation. Pre- and posttesting the class participants' cholesterol levels is an example of impact evaluation. Long-term studies of the participants' illnesses and eventual causes of death is an example of outcome evaluation.

Determining Evaluation Criteria

The program coordinator must have a clear view of the place evaluation holds in the program design. The objectives—program, behavioral, educational, attitudinal, and/or performance—must be well written and include measurements to determine the effects and success of the program. Therefore, once the objectives and criteria are determined and the program is implemented, the evaluation criteria phases are already in place. For example, a common objective for a health promotion workshop is to increase the knowledge of the participants: "At the end of the workshop 80% of the workshop participants will be able to differentiate correctly between dietary cholesterol and serum cholesterol."

The objective is for the participants to be able to differentiate between the two types of cholesterol, and the criteria for success is set at 80% of the participants being able to do so. This objective can be evaluated by conducting a pre- and post-workshop quiz, asking for the differentiation. If 80% or more of the participants who did not know the answer before the workshop can correctly answer it after the workshop, the objective has been met. If less than 80% answer correctly, it is an indication that either the presenter is not clearly defining the terms or that aspect of the workshop needs improvement.

The most difficult task in the evaluation process is setting the criteria. Is there a difference between choosing 30% or 50% of the program participants to quit smoking? What if only 5 of the 30 dieters lose weight? Is that successful? Practitioners must set criteria by which success will be measured before the program begins and be willing to learn how to redefine their expectations or make necessary changes in the workshops as they are evaluated. Each workshop will have different goals and objectives along with a targeted audience, and these factors together should determine the criteria measurement. The frequency and duration of health promotion workshops will affect the criteria. A series of weekly workshops will have higher expectations than a one-time, one-hour workshop.

Writing the Annual Report

Finally, the program coordinator is responsible for writing a variety of reports, one of the most

"Positively Stressed!" Impact Evaluation

Where applicable, circle the number of your response.

1. *Stress is bad.*

    Strongly agree 1

    Agree 2

    Disagree..............................3

    Strongly disagree 4

2. *An individual's perception of an event determines whether it is stressful or not.*

    Strongly agree 1

    Agree 2

    Disagree..............................3

    Strongly disagree 4

3. *Prioritize, in order, the three greatest stressors affecting your life today.*

    1 _____

    2 _____

    3 _____

4. *At the present time, would you say that you are experiencing*

    A lot of stress 1

    A moderate amount of stress 2

    Relatively little stress 3

    Almost no stress at all................4

5. *In the past six months how much effect has stress had on your health?*

    A lot 1

    Some 2

    Hardly any 3

    None at all 4

6. *List your health problems that you think may be associated with stress.*

    1 _____

    2 _____

    3 _____

7. *Do you think you have any control over these health problems?*

    Yes 1

    No..................................2

8. *Are you willing to learn some methods of relaxation?*

    Yes 1

    No..................................2

9. *Do you now use any relaxation techniques?*

    Yes 1

    No (skip to question 11) 2

10. *Which relaxation techniques work best for you?*

    1 _____

    2 _____

    3 _____

11. *Coping with stress is a way of reducing its effects on us.*

    Strongly agree 1

    Agree 2

    Disagree..............................3

    Strongly disagree 4

12. *On a scale of 1 to 10, where 10 is excellent, how would you rate your methods of coping?*

    1   2   3   4   5   6   7   8   9   10

13. *List the coping methods you are currently using.*

    1 _____

    2 _____

    3 _____

14. *What coping method do you use most often?*

    _____

15. *If you are not currently using any coping method, circle the number that best describes why.*

    Do not have the time.................1

    Do not see them as useful 2

    Tried, but they did not work..........3

    Do not know any 4

    Other _____ 5

16. *What year in school are you?*

    Freshman 1

    Sophomore 2

    Junior 3

    Senior.............................4

    Graduate student 5

17. *Please indicate whether you are*

    Male 1

    Female 2

18. *Living arrangement*

    Residence hall 1

    Sorority 2

    Fraternity..........................3

    Certified housing 4

    Apartment off-campus................5

19. *What is your major area of study?*

    _____

Survey author: Geraldine Guttenberg, R.N., a master's degree candidate in community health, Dept. of Health & Safety Studies, University of Illinois at Urbana-Champaign.

significant being the annual report, which presents the achievements and impact of the program, to the institution's administration. Because the purpose of the annual report is to show the progress and success of the program, it should include documentation, evaluation results, significant accomplishments, and future considerations (see Appendix 2.C). The cost analysis should also be included in the annual report for a complete picture of the program.

Summary

The information in this chapter indicates how many opportunities there are for the program coordinator to keep busy! We've looked at the results of a marketing plan, different types of advertising, a quality assurance program, three levels of evaluation, and the span of a fiscal year from requesting the budget to writing the annual report. In the next chapter we'll examine the roles of the paraprofessional trainers and the paraprofessionals themselves and how they influence each other and the program.

APPENDIX 2.A

Cost Analysis

At the end of each fiscal year conduct a cost analysis of program expenses and compare that to the total number of participants who attended your workshops for the year. Although there is no charge for most paraprofessional programs, this method gives a final dollar accountability and cost per participant.

Account for all salary and program expenses in each of the budget account categories and add them together. If the coordinator does not work on the paraprofessional program full-time, compute the appropriate salary percentage. These are program debits:

Lifestyle Workshop Program Cost Analysis for 19__-19__

Salaries and Other Expenses.

Coordinator's salary	$xxxx
Trainers' salaries	xxxx
Expendable supplies	xxx
Duplicating costs	xxx
Professional services	xxx
Mailing	xx
	$xxxx (a)

Approximate Time Invested.

Coordinator	xxx hours
Trainers	xxx hours
Lifestyle Educators	xxx hours
	xxxx hours (b)

Cost per hour to maintain the Lifestyle Workshop Program during 19__-19__	$a \div b$

Statistics of Workshops Presented.

Total Lifestyle Workshops presented	xxx (c)
Cost per Lifestyle Workshop	$c \div a$
Total Lifestyle Workshop participants	xxxx (d)
Cost per participant	$d \div a$

Quality Assurance Telephone Survey

	Yes	No	N/A*	Can't recall
1. Were you given any handouts or pamphlets during the workshop?	☐	☐	☐	☐
2. Do you recall which handouts you received?	☐	☐	☐	☐

If "Yes," recalled: _____

_____

_____

_____

3. Did you read it/them?	☐	☐	☐	☐

4. Which handout(s) were most helpful?

Recall: _____

_____

_____

_____

5. About the handouts—were they understandable? For example, was the terminology clear?	☐	☐	☐	☐

Comments: _____

_____

_____

_____

Was the overall appearance of the handout(s) professional?	☐	☐	☐	☐
Did you have questions after reading the material(s) because it was confusing?	☐	☐	☐	☐

(Cont.)

Quality Assurance Telephone Survey (Continued)

	Yes	No	N/A*	Can't recall
Did the material(s) provoke new questions for you?	☐	☐	☐	☐
If "Yes," did you call the program for more information?	☐	☐	☐	☐

Comments: _____

_____

_____

_____

| 6. Did you keep the handout(s)? | ☐ | ☐ | ☐ | ☐ |

Comments: _____

_____

_____

_____

7. Have you referred to the handout(s) since the workshop?	☐	☐	☐	☐
8. Did you share the handout(s) with another person?	☐	☐	☐	☐
9. Was the material in the handout(s) explained during the workshop?	☐	☐	☐	☐

10. Was the number of handout(s) given
☐ too many   ☐ not enough   ☐ sufficient

Comments: _____

_____

_____

_____

*N/A = Not Applicable

Annual Report

Introduction

Provide a brief description of the program including a history of the program, its purpose, and other unique characteristics.

Goals and Objectives

List the goals and objectives for the health promotion program.

Staff

Identify the staff members, trainers, and paraprofessionals involved in the program.

Significant Activities and Accomplishments

This category will outline the special contributions your program has made. Briefly list the activities and accomplishments so the reader can quickly scan these most significant successes.

Special Problems and Concerns

Be honest here and point out barriers or issues that may have delayed or changed your plans during the year. Here you have the opportunity to explain extenuating circumstances. If possible, offer a solution or alternative so administration will know you are aware of the problem and that you plan to correct it.

Personnel and Budget Issues

If anyone on your staff was replaced or hired, and if raises were awarded, give that information here. Provide a breakdown of the budget for the year divided into the amount allocated for each budget account category and the amount spent, including an end-of-year balance.

Staff Development

List committees, seminars, and conferences you and members of your staff attended, served on, or presented at during the year.

Evaluations

Briefly provide information on any evaluations conducted and analyzed concerning the program.

Statistical Documentation

Break down by health area and then summarize the number of workshops presented, the attendance figures, and location of the workshops for the year. Here is an example for structuring the statistical documentation:

Yearly Documentation
The Lifestyle Workshop Program
June 1, 1987-May 31, 1988

Nutrition Lifestyle Workshops

1. Workshops:
   40 TOTAL
   10 (25%) Winning at Weight Control
   15 (37.5%) There's More to Eating Than Food
   15 (37.5%) Designer Diets
2. Presented at:
   20 (50%) Residence Halls
   20 (50%) Greek letter houses
3. Attendance:
   600 Participants Total
   20 Participants per workshop (overall average)
      400 (80%) Greek letter houses
         275 (69%) Sororities
         125 (31%) Fraternities
      200 (20%) Residence halls

Continue this format for each health area or workshop, then summarize:

Documentation Summary
Lifestyle Workshops
June 1, 1987-May 31, 1988

Total Lifestyle Workshops   202

Total Lifestyle Workshops in residence halls	123 (61%)
Total Lifestyle Workshops in Greek letter houses	69 (34%)
Sororities 31 (44%)	
Fraternities 38 (56%)	
Total participants	3881 (11% of total University population)

Average Attendance Per Workshop   *19*

Total attendance in Greek letter houses	1970 (51%)
Sororities 1050 (53%)	
Fraternities 920 (47%)	
Total attendance in residence halls	1810 (46%)
Total Lifestyle Educators	30
Average workshops per lifestyle educator	6.7

Future Considerations

This is a good place to describe plans you have for the next year. Include upcoming events, evaluations that will be conducted, ideas for new workshops or training procedures, and any local or national presentations about the program you plan to make.

CHAPTER 3

The Role of Trainers and Paraprofessionals

All the work thus far has been in preparation for delivering timely and quality health promotion workshops. The workshops presented in this book, along with the suggestions for implementing them, won't mean much if they aren't presented by knowledgeable, enthusiastic, and qualified paraprofessionals. Unfortunately, potential paraprofessionals don't walk in the door fully prepared to present a workshop. In this chapter we'll look at both the trainer and the paraprofessional and how they interact to bring about a successful health promotion program.

The Trainer's Role in the Program

The program coordinator may train the paraprofessionals or there may be a number of different trainers involved in the process. The training issues involved are relatively the same for either circumstance. The trainer's primary responsibilities are to assist in the development, implementation, and evaluation of the paraprofessional training program. The communication between the program coordinator and the trainers is crucial, just as it is between the trainer and the paraprofessionals. The program coordinator and trainers in the Lifestyle Workshop Program meet individually once a week in addition to a weekly staff meeting. The trainer and paraprofessionals meet a minimum of once a week for 3 hours or twice a week for 1 1/2 hours each. This facilitates the training, flow of information, new policies and procedures, and the exchange of ideas in an ongoing process.

Responsibilities

The trainer's responsibilities include the following:

- Teaching the specific content areas (drug and alcohol education, fitness, nutrition, sexuality, or stress management), as well as the workshop presentation and group-facilitation skills
- Supervising and evaluating paraprofessionals, enabling them to present health promotion workshops
- Updating, revising, and maintaining the workshops
- Assisting in the development of new workshops
- Piloting new or significantly revised workshops
- Contributing to the growth and development of the paraprofessional program

The two primary goals of the trainer are to provide thorough instruction and training in the content of each workshop, and to encourage a variety of successful presentation and group-facilitation skills for the trainees. Achieving these goals means having skills in the following areas:

- Coordinating the smooth flow of training operations
- Writing goals and objectives
- Teaching the content of the workshop and background information needed to answer questions during the workshop presentation
- Teaching workshop presentation skills (e.g., eye contact, gestures, use of notes, ease with the topic, and audience control)

- Teaching group-facilitation skills, such as leading discussions, coordinating group activities, fielding questions, and motivating the group
- Updating the workshops, including content, activities, handouts, and visual aids
- Supervising and evaluating the paraprofessionals on workshop presentations
- Writing examinations

Qualifications

Trainers should have a measure of self-confidence and some experience in teaching or presenting workshops. The trainer is a role model and a coach for the paraprofessionals. Careful selection of a trainer is a crucial element to the entire program. There are a number of qualities and previous experience to look for in a prospective trainer. These are discussed below.

The relationship between the trainer and the paraprofessionals is a close one, and it will span the course of a year. Therefore, it is imperative that the trainer enjoy working with students and be interested in their success as paraprofessionals. In selecting trainers, the program coordinator should ask candidates about their teaching experience. Have they taught before? Are their students' evaluations available? What do they like best about teaching?

The trainers must have a background in the areas they will be teaching—a strong interest is not enough. The ideal trainer is one who is working or studying in the area in which they will be training. In addition, the trainers need an understanding of and appreciation for the field of health promotion. This is something that may be cultivated during their experience as trainers; however, asking what their definition or concept of health promotion is will be an indication of their exposure to it. Trainers must be very organized, training paraprofessionals in different workshops while at the same time evaluating presentations and keeping the booking calendar up to date.

The trainers must be able to give constructive feedback to the paraprofessionals. They are the last line of quality control before the workshop is presented. Consequently, it is the trainer who will decide when the paraprofessional is fully qualified to present the workshop. If the student needs more time to prepare, the trainer must explain to him or her why and then set up time for additional training. The trainer also gives feedback on the paraprofessionals' presentations, evaluating each workshop twice. The trainer cannot hesitate to make recommendations or suggestions for improvements. The paraprofessional wants most of all to present a good workshop, so the trainer must offer constructive feedback and prepare the student for what lies ahead.

In summary, the trainers ideally should enjoy teaching, have a strong background in their content area, understand health promotion, be organized, and have the ability to offer honest, constructive feedback to the training paraprofessionals.

Training Sessions and Competency Exams

Sample training sessions for each Lifestyle Workshop have been developed by experienced trainers in the program. The sessions are located at the beginning of each workshop in this book. The training for each workshop is broken into sessions with suggested methods, activities, and readings. It takes an average of 10 to 15 hours to train a paraprofessional to present a workshop, not including outside required reading.

The training format is fairly consistent for the 16 workshops. The number of sessions will depend on the background of the paraprofessional trainees. The first session is a demonstration of the workshop by the trainer. The next four sessions review the content of the workshop and its various components. During these sessions, as many opportunities as possible are created to allow the paraprofessional trainee to practice segments of the workshop, such as an explanation of a handout or a workshop activity.

The final training sessions are called "Review and Hot Seat" and "Practice Presentation." The former reviews the most frequently asked questions and introduces a game called the "Hot Seat." In this activity, each trainee must be in the "hot seat" and present a few minutes of the workshop. For the next 10 minutes, the other trainees and the trainer ask as many questions as they can think of pertaining to the subject. Each paraprofessional practices fielding questions and responding to questions he or she may not know the answer to. In this way, they become confident in saying, "I don't know, but I can refer you to . . ."

The final training session is a practice presentation, in which each trainee is responsible for a section of the workshop. This avoids having to sit through the same workshop three or four times while all the trainees practice. During this session, the trainer evaluates the paraprofessionals and decides whether each is prepared to deliver the workshop solo. The trainer provides honest and constructive feedback and helps those trainees who have to be held back individually so that they can progress to the next step: the competency exam.

Competency Exams accompany the sample training sessions for each Lifestyle Workshop. The exam questions are based on the information covered or assigned during the training sessions. The specific exam questions are numbered in each training session to provide a guide for emphasis of various topics. Often the information for an exam question is overlapped in several training sessions, and that is indicated by repeating the exam number in each appropriate session. We require the paraprofessionals to pass each exam with a minimum of 90% correct. If that is not achieved, the trainee must research and correctly answer each missed question. They are not required to repeat the entire exam, but the original score is recorded in the grade book.

Evaluation

The trainer receives feedback about the training program from the coordinator and the paraprofessionals. The Trainer Evaluation form, completed by the coordinator, is useful for the professional growth of the trainer (see pages 50-53). At the same time, it's important for the paraprofessionals to voice their opinions about the training program and the trainer.

At the end of each of the two semesters, the paraprofessionals complete an Instructor and Course Evaluation form (see pages 54-56). The evaluations are completed anonymously while the trainer is out of the room, collected in a manila envelope, and sent to the program coordinator.

The coordinator reviews the evaluations and returns them to the trainer with appropriate comments and encouragement. The paraprofessionals are encouraged to offer suggestions throughout their year in the program. The remarks on the evaluation should not come as a surprise to the trainer if open communication has been the norm.

The Paraprofessional's Role in the Program

The Lifestyle Workshop paraprofessionals are university students, both undergraduate and graduate, who want practical experience in lead-

ing workshops and specialized training in one of the lifestyle areas. Paraprofessionals come from different academic disciplines, including business administration, community health, library science, and dietetics. Their remuneration is three academic credits for each semester they are in the program. We prefer this method to student wages or volunteering because students are already heavily tied into the grading process and place a great deal of importance on good grades.

At the University of Illinois, the paraprofessionals register for a class called "Health Promotion Practicum," offered by the Health and Safety Studies Department in the College of Applied Life Sciences. The student chooses one of the five lifestyle areas in which to train and specialize. He or she then becomes a Lifestyle Educator in that chosen field. Often students are strongly interested in one of the lifestyle areas over the other four. In that case we always try to allow the student to train in that area, believing they will do a better job if they are already interested in that topic. A two-semester commitment (a total of 1 academic year or 9 months) is required of each paraprofessional.

Standards on Use of Student Paraprofessionals

A common concern for all paraprofessional programs is quality assurance. Programs that have not developed standard policies and procedures are in danger of hiring paraprofessionals who are not carrying out the philosophy of the program. This issue of quality assurance applies both to the treatment of student paraprofessionals and to the actions and behaviors of the paraprofessional trainers. For programs in the university setting, the "Proposed Standards on Use of Student Paraprofessionals in Student Affairs" has been drafted (Ender & Winston, 1984) addressing 10 areas associated with paraprofessional programs: purpose and goals, human resources, programs/services/ activities, facilities, financial and other resources, relationships with faculty and other groups and agencies, planning, evaluation, ethics, and legal issues. The proposed standards have been reprinted in Appendix 3.A. The standards are general in nature but provide an excellent format for writing standards for a specific program. Taking the time to write thoughtful, clear standards and distributing them to associates of the program is a strong step toward quality assurance and ultimately a successful program.

Trainer Evaluation

	Exceeds expectations	Meets expectations	Needs improvement	Doesn't apply
Training staff issues:				
1. Cooperates in staff decisions, policy making, and overall program functioning. Comments:	☐	☐	☐	☐
2. Responds to requests by other staff for information within a reasonable amount of time. Comments:	☐	☐	☐	☐
3. Informs health center and health education department staff of workshops and services available in their specific area. Comments:	☐	☐	☐	☐
4. Accessible and available to para-professionals and staff on a flexible basis. Comments:	☐	☐	☐	☐
5. Shares information willingly; seeks out research and program information to contribute to individual staff. Comments:	☐	☐	☐	☐
6. Demonstrates foresight in planning so as not to disrupt the program with projects. Comments:	☐	☐	☐	☐

	Exceeds expectations	Meets expectations	Needs improvement	Doesn't apply
Workshop management issues:				
7. Displays knowledge of campus and community resources and referrals, in terms of both people and programs.	☐	☐	☐	☐
Comments:				
8. Produces high quality work representing a thorough knowledge of specialty area.	☐	☐	☐	☐
Comments:				
9. Includes appropriate staff in the development of new workshops, handouts, and educational material.	☐	☐	☐	☐
Comments:				
10. Demonstrates ability to assess needs of the student population and incorporate those needs into the workshops.	☐	☐	☐	☐
Comments:				
11. Manages the smooth flow of training program operations so that workshops are always available and paraprofessionals are trained.	☐	☐	☐	☐
Comments:				

	Exceeds expectations	Meets expectations	Needs improvement	Doesn't apply
Paraprofessional issues:				
12. Effectively communicates paraprofessionals' needs and recommendations.	☐	☐	☐	☐
Comments:				
13. Demonstrates a sincere interest in the growth and development of paraprofessionals.	☐	☐	☐	☐
Comments:				
14. Regularly evaluates paraprofessionals' workshop presentations and offers constructive feedback for improvement.	☐	☐	☐	☐
Comments:				
15. Presents himself/herself as a good role model for paraprofessionals.	☐	☐	☐	☐
Comments:				
Professional development issues:				
16. Receives criticism in a professional, nondefensive manner, using it to review job performance and negotiate appropriate actions.	☐	☐	☐	☐
Comments:				

	Exceeds expectations	Meets expectations	Needs improvement	Doesn't apply
17. Displays a positive attitude regarding job responsibilities. Comments:	☐	☐	☐	☐
18. Treats colleagues in a respectful, cooperative manner. Comments:	☐	☐	☐	☐
19. Communicates effectively in both verbal and written exchanges. Comments:	☐	☐	☐	☐
20. Uses time efficiently; accomplishes required work on or ahead of schedule. Comments:	☐	☐	☐	☐
21. Demonstrates the ability to deal with conflict in a constructive and appropriate manner. Comments:	☐	☐	☐	☐

Instructor and
Course Evaluation

Directions: Use pencil only. Circle the appropriate number in responding to the objective questions. Use the last page of this form for your personal comments on teacher effectiveness and other aspects of the course. Your instructor will not see your completed evaluation until final grades are in for your course.

1. Rate the course content. — excellent 5 4 3 2 1 very poor

2. Rate the instructor. — excellent 5 4 3 2 1 very poor

3. Rate the course in general. — excellent 5 4 3 2 1 very poor

4. Did instructor present topics in logical sequence? — yes, almost always 5 4 3 2 1 no, almost never

5. Should more/less time be provided to review and synthesize course material? — much more time 5 4 3 2 1 much less time

6. Did the instructor give assignments that were useful for learning subject matter? — almost always 5 4 3 2 1 almost never

7. Did the instructor provide practice for students to master course material? — almost always 5 4 3 2 1 almost never

8. Were the grading procedures for the course fair/unfair? — very fair 5 4 3 2 1 very unfair

9. Were grading standards too high/low? — too high 5 4 3 2 1 too low

10. How appropriate was the amount of work required for the credit earned? — very appropriate 5 4 3 2 1 very inappropriate

11. Was course too demanding/easy? — overly demanding 5 4 3 2 1 too easy

12. Was pace too fast/slow? — too fast 5 4 3 2 1 too slow

13. Have you become more competent in this area due to this course? — to a great extent 5 4 3 2 1 not at all

14. Would you recommend this course to other students? — highly 5 4 3 2 1 not at all

15. Did the course give you skills and techniques directly applicable to your career? — yes 5 4 3 2 1 no

16. Did your interest in this course increase or decrease as the semester progressed? — greatly increased 5 4 3 2 1 greatly decreased

17. Did you develop some leadership skills because of course? — to a great extent 5 4 3 2 1 not at all

18. Was the instructor's knowledge of subject excellent/poor? — excellent 5 4 3 2 1 poor

19. Was the instructor enthusiastic about teaching? — very enthusiastic 5 4 3 2 1 very unenthusiastic

20. Did the instructor make good use of examples and illustrations?   yes, very often 5 4 3 2 1 no, seldom

21. Did the instructor raise challenging questions in class?   yes, often 5 4 3 2 1 no, seldom

22. Did the instructor encourage you to express your opinion or experience?   almost always 5 4 3 2 1 almost never

23. Was the instructor sensitive to student needs?   almost always 5 4 3 2 1 almost never

24. Were the instructor's criticisms and comments about your work helpful?   very helpful 5 4 3 2 1 not helpful at all

25. Did the instructor have confidence in you as a student?   a great deal 5 4 3 2 1 very little

26. Was a good balance of student participation and instructor contribution achieved?   always 5 4 3 2 1 never

Please write comments below:

A. What are the major strengths and weaknesses of the instructor?

B. What aspects of this course were most beneficial to you?

C. What do you suggest to improve this course?

D. Comment on the grading procedures and exams.

E. Instructor option question

F. Instructor option question

Note. From *The Instructor and Course Evaluation System,* Office of Instructional Resources, Measurement and Research Division, University of Illinois at Urbana-Champaign. Adapted by permission.

Paraprofessional Development

The following is a scenario of a paraprofessional's first year in the program. Bonnie has registered to be a Fitness Lifestyle Educator. During her first semester or 15 weeks, Bonnie will train for two workshops. Her fitness trainer starts Bonnie with the "Fat Assessment and Weight Management" workshop. The training takes approximately 6 weeks because the sessions meet 3 hours a week with additional outside readings. When the training is finished and the trainer feels she is ready, Bonnie is videotaped and given feedback on her skill level (Presenter Evaluation). Then Bonnie takes the competency exam for "Fat Assessment and Weight Management." If Bonnie achieves a 90% or above, her name is then put in the Workshop Calendar, and she will start presenting the workshop when reservations are made for her nights. Bonnie is evaluated twice during the semester on her presentation of "Fat Assessment and Weight Management."

The fitness trainer then begins training Bonnie for the "Getting In Shape" workshop, which takes about 4 to 5 weeks to train for, followed by another competency exam. Bonnie is now beginning the second semester and is prepared to present both "Fat Assessment and Weight Management" and "Getting In Shape." Bonnie starts training for "Body Building," the last of the Fitness Lifestyle Workshops. By midterm Bonnie's name is in the calendar for all three Fitness Lifestyle Workshops.

The requirement of a 1-year commitment has worked well for our program for two reasons. First, the amount of time it takes to train for a workshop allows a paraprofessional to learn only two of the three or four workshops available in each lifestyle area. And second, while a new crew of paraprofessionals is being trained, the veterans can be delivering workshops learned in their first semester. It is also to the benefit of the paraprofessional to be in the program for 1 year so she or he has ample opportunity to practice and improve skills and knowledge.

Each paraprofessional is videotaped during the training program. A professional from the University's Division of Instructional Development reviews the tape with the paraprofessional, offers suggestions for improving the workshop presentation, and notes the strengths that person is bringing to the workshop. The program coordinator or trainer could also give this feedback (using the Presenter Evaluation form), but it is advantageous for the paraprofessional to hear suggestions from an outside professional. Videotaping the paraprofessionals also gives us a library of the workshops to show trainees and others interested in the program.

The five paraprofessional sections meet and train separately. These training sessions are scheduled at the same time, however, so that the entire group can meet on occasion to train or discuss issues common to all.

Evaluation

The Lifestyle paraprofessionals are evaluated both as trainees and as presenters. The objective of the evaluation process for the Lifestyle Educators is to provide feedback from many different sources using a variety of evaluation tools.

After the Lifestyle Educator passes the Competency Exam she or he delivers a workshop solo. Because educators are already nervous about giving the first presentation, we avoid giving them the added pressure of a formal evaluation at that time. We also realize that students are usually their own worst critics. Therefore, we have the trainer wait until the paraprofessional's second presentation to evaluate him or her. The Presenter Evaluation instrument (see pages 58, 59) uses a 50-point scale, which could be doubled if it's easier to use a score out of 100 points. This same form is then used by the trainer at the end of the semester to evaluate the Lifestyle Educator's last presentation of that workshop. This allows for recording improvement over time.

Two other forms of paraprofessional evaluation have already been mentioned: the participants fill out the Workshop Evaluation Survey, and the paraprofessional is videotaped to review presentation strengths and weaknesses with an outside professional.

Procedures for the Paraprofessional Program

This section describes the operations of the Lifestyle Workshop Program and the responsibilities of the paraprofessionals. It provides examples of how to deal with some of the logistics of the program. First is a chronological description of program procedures, from a workshop request to the

Presenter Evaluation

Presenter _____

Delivery variable	Points 0-1	Skill level: low	Points 2-3	Skill level: medium	Points 4-5	Skill level: high
Voice		Monotone; no inflection or variation. Difficult to understand.		Pleasant variations of pitch, volume, and speed. Clear articulation.		Speech and voice are varied, uplifting. Clear changes in tone, pitch, and rate.
Eyes		Appears bored. Little or no eye contact. Dull expression.		Appears interested. Eyes light up, open wide often. Frequent eye contact with audience.		Shows expression with eyes and eyebrows. Almost constant eye contact with the audience.
Gestures		Little or no arm movement. Arms rigid or folded across body. Constantly "talks with hands."		Uses hands and arms to demonstrate or point. Occasional motions using body, head, arms. Steady gestures.		Appropriate demonstrative body movements that enhance presentation.
Body movements		Seldom moves from one spot. May grasp podium. Nervous or repetitive movements.		Moves freely and slowly, so as not to distract from presentation. Steady movements.		Uses fluid body movements, changes pace appropriately, and appears energetic.
Facial expressions		Appears deadpan, expresses no feeling, frowns. Keeps lips closed.		Looks pleased, smiles frequently. Changes expressions when needed.		Appears vibrant, uses variety of expressions. Uses total smile. Demonstrative.
Overall delivery		Lethargic, dull, or sluggish.		Appears energetic and demonstrative, uses some variation.		Appears exuberant. High degree of energy, vitality. Changes in voice, eyes, gestures, and body movements.

Delivery variable	Points 0-1	Skill level: low	Points 2-3	Skill level: medium	Points 4-5	Skill level: high
Knowledge of topic		Appears to be unpracticed and unsure of topic.		Presentation flows smoothly, can answer most questions. Well practiced.		Very well rehearsed and practiced, answers almost all questions, and offers more information when fielding questions.
Use of visual aids and handouts		Does not use visual aids/handouts or rarely refers to them.		Uses visual aids/handouts at correct times during presentation.		Able to clearly tie the presentation and visual aids/handouts together.
Fielding questions		Rarely or never answers questions raised by audience.		Answers many questions. Says "I don't know" when necessary.		Answers most questions. Offers further resources or referrals.
Audience participation/ discussion		Audience appears bored, uninterested, "lectured to."		Audience appears interested and joins in game/discussion.		Audience freely discusses the topic. Seems to "energize" the group.

Evaluator _____ Date _____

final paperwork and evaluation, followed by a further explanation of each step.

1. A student calls to request a Lifestyle Workshop.
2. A reservation is made in the Lifestyle Workshop Calendar.
3. A Lifestyle Educator checks in once a week for reservations for the next week and initials each reservation checked.
4. The Lifestyle Educator calls the requester to confirm the information taken during the reservation.
5. The Lifestyle Educator sends a confirmation letter and poster to the requester.
6. On the day of the workshop, the Lifestyle Educator checks out the necessary materials, handouts, and forms.
7. The Lifestyle Educator presents the Lifestyle Workshop.
8. Workshop participants complete a Lifestyle Workshop Evaluation form.
9. The Lifestyle Educator tallies evaluations and completes a Presentation Documentation form.
10. The trainer reviews the evaluation tally and adds the workshop to the Workshop Tally Sheet.

University of Illinois students requesting a workshop call the health center's resource room to make a reservation. The resource room is an informational center offering patient education material, pamphlets, books, videotapes, and articles. Students seeking health information for themselves or for research papers often use the resource room. This room is also the central station for the Lifestyle Workshop Program.

The reservation is recorded in the Lifestyle Workshop Calendar (see pages 61, 62) along with the appropriate information. The trainer for each lifestyle area is in charge of the calendar pages for his or her specific area. The trainer completes the information for the dates each workshop will be available and which Lifestyle Educators will present the workshops they are trained to present. Each Lifestyle Educator's name must be in the calendar once a week to present workshops.

Reservations must be made a minimum of one working week in advance of the requested date. In this way, the paraprofessionals can check the calendar once a week for the upcoming week and not miss a reservation. Reservations will not be taken more than three weeks in advance because

we have found requesters lose their enthusiasm and do a poorer job of advertising and encouraging attendance.

Because there are so many steps for the paraprofessional to complete for the cycle of each workshop, they keep track of the steps on the Educator's Workshop Checklist (see page 63). This is especially helpful when the educator is regularly presenting three or four different workshops.

The Lifestyle Educator calls the requester to confirm the information that was recorded in the Lifestyle Workshop Calendar. This follow-up call is also a good time to explain the workshop in more detail to be sure the requester understands what will happen. The educator asks about the layout of the room in which the workshop will be held and requests any special equipment or arrangements necessary for the workshop. The educator should encourage different methods for advertising, such as placing posters in the bathrooms and putting reminder slips in mailboxes the day of the workshop. It's also a good idea to recommend serving food or beverages at the conclusion of the workshop.

The Lifestyle Educator follows up the phone call with a confirmation letter and workshop poster. Occasionally, the Lifestyle Educator cannot reach the requester by phone and sends the confirmation letter and workshop poster as the first confirmation. In this case, the Lifestyle Educator includes his or her phone number so the requester can call if necessary.

If requesters need to cancel a workshop, we encourage them, when they make the reservation, to do so as soon as possible by calling the resource room. Sometimes the requester cancels the day of the workshop. The resource room worker who takes the cancellation makes every effort to contact the Lifestyle Educator. If the Lifestyle Educator must cancel a workshop, he or she first tries to enlist another trained educator to present, or calls the requester as soon as possible and reschedules the workshop for the next compatible date.

On the day of the workshop the Lifestyle Educator signs out the needed workshop materials after 1:00 p.m. on the Workshop Materials Sign-Out Sheet (see page 64). The workshop materials must be signed back into the resource room by 1:00 p.m. the following day. The posters, game boards, handouts, and forms are placed in a large portfolio carrier. In addition, the Lifestyle Educator may have to take a film, a projector, or other special equipment for the workshop. It is the Lifestyle

Workshop Calendar

Area (circle): drugs and alcohol, stress, sexuality, fitness, nutrition

Use pencil only.

Month: _____

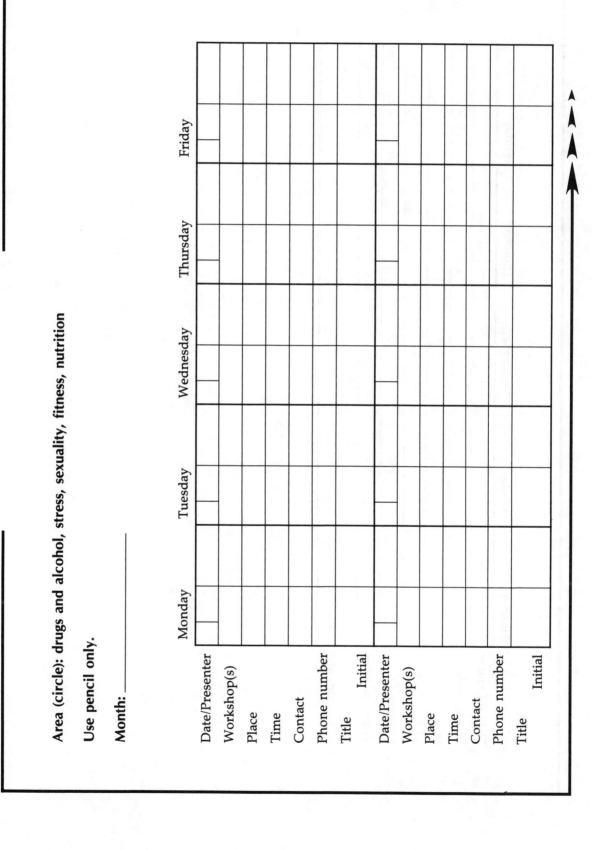

	Monday	Tuesday	Wednesday	Thursday	Friday
Date/Presenter					
Workshop(s)					
Place					
Time					
Contact					
Phone number					
Title Initial					
Date/Presenter					
Workshop(s)					
Place					
Time					
Contact					
Phone number					
Title Initial					

	Monday		Tuesday		Wednesday		Thursday		Friday	
Date/Presenter										
Workshop(s)										
Place										
Time										
Contact										
Phone number										
Title Initial										

Educator's Workshop Checklist

Date	Requester	Location	Phone number	Time	Workshop	Confirmation call	Confirmation packet	Sign-out portfolio	Attendance	Workshop evaluation	Requester evaluation	Presentation documentation

Workshops
Materials Sign-Out Sheet

Name/phone	Lifestyle workshop	Date and time out/ projected return	Date and time in

Educator's responsibility to get the needed materials to the workshop site and return the materials the next day.

The Lifestyle Educator arrives at the workshop site and sets up chairs or rearranges the room for optimal facilitation. The requester may be serving refreshments, which often increases attendance but should be served at the end of the workshop. If stragglers arrive after the workshop has started, the educator should not restart the workshop for each person. If the workshop is a game, latecomers can easily be included. If the workshop is informational, the educator should smile and continue with the presentation. The Lifestyle Educator hands out a Workshop Sign-In Sheet (see page 66) to collect names and addresses of the participants. This information may be necessary for a post-workshop evaluation.

At the end of the workshop, the Lifestyle Educator gives each participant a Workshop Evaluation form to complete. Before the next meeting with his or her trainer, the educator tallies all the evaluation forms and gives the results to the trainer. The trainer reviews the evaluation results with the Lifestyle Educator, offering compliments and suggestions for improvement.

Along with the evaluation tally, the Lifestyle Educator fills out a Presentation Documentation form (see page 67) and turns it in to the trainer.

This information records attendance figures and identifies the requesters and the workshop site.

The trainer transfers this information to the Workshop Tally Sheet (see page 68) in chronological order for all the trainer's Lifestyle Educators. The information is tallied at the end of each semester for the "Lifestyle Workshop Annual Report" documentation figures.

This structure has worked quite well for the University of Illinois paraprofessional health promotion program. The amount of paperwork is justified by the need for quality control and documentation. It doesn't take long for the trainers and the paraprofessionals to learn the system, and it's worth it in the long run.

Summary

We have now completed a description of a model paraprofessional health promotion program. From the choices of workshop topics to the evaluation of the paraprofessional most of the primary elements of a quality program have been explored in these first three chapters. Chapter 4 allows a final element: presentation skills for paraprofessionals. These skills facilitate the presenters in reaching their audience with vital health information.

Workshop Sign-In Sheet

Title of workshop: _____

	Name	Address	Phone #
1.			
2.			
3.			
4.			
5.			
6.			
7.			
8.			
9.			
10.			
11.			
12.			
13.			
14.			
15.			
16.			
17.			
18.			
19.			
20.			
21.			

Presentation Documentation Form

Lifestyle Educator _____

Date of workshop _____

Title _____

Attendance _____

Check the group to which the workshop was presented. Specify the name of the group.

☐ Residence hall _____

☐ Sorority _____

☐ Fraternity _____

☐ Private housing _____

☐ Academic class _____

☐ Student organization _____

☐ Other _____

Check the position of the person who requested the workshop:

☐ Resident advisor

☐ Resident director

☐ Class instructor

☐ Health advocate

☐ Greek house member

☐ Student organization liason

☐ Other _____

Workshop Tally Sheet

Date	Presenter	Title of program	Where presented (be specific) Residence hall floor	Greek house	Other	Attendance

APPENDIX 3.A

Paraprofessional Utilization Standards

by Stephen Ender, Clifford Schuette, and Carmen Nueberger

Purpose and Goals

Paraprofessional student helpers are employed in many student affairs programs. These helpers are assigned to residence halls, counseling centers, learning/tutorial centers, academic advising programs, admissions offices, orientation programs, and student health centers. For purposes of this statement, paraprofessionals are viewed as undergraduate students employed by a division of student affairs for purposes of providing direct services to other students. The goals for utilization of paraprofessionals include:

1. To provide direct services to college students.
2. To maximize the potential positive effects of peers interacting and helping peers.
3. To provide guidance and developmental support programs rather than counseling/ therapeutic interventions. These programs and individual services are designed to provide educational and preventive interventions rather than remedial interventions.
4. To provide a wide range of developmental services at a reduced cost to student affairs staffing budgets.
5. To provide student role models for other students to emulate in regard to self-responsible, self-directed behavior.

Human Resources

The paraprofessional is an individual without extensive training in the helping and education professions but who is specifically selected, trained, and given ongoing supervision in the performance of some designated portion of the tasks usually performed by a professional. While this person can relieve the professional to perform tasks of a more complex nature, it is important to realize the function is an educational rather than remedial one. It is the educational focus of the position that should guide the use of this invaluable human resource.

The professional has a responsibility to insure that the role is carefully defined so that expectations do not exceed capabilities. Correspondingly, the job description must avoid focusing on menial tasks that are not reflective of the educational training experience.

Students serving must model utilization of preventive developmental growth strategies. These helpers are individuals who are actively exploring themselves as human beings, assessing their present levels of developmental growth, and taking advantage of institutional programs, services, and resources.

As staff members, they should represent the population they serve in regard to sex, race, age, and demographic factors. Sharing the environment of those they work with contributes to effectiveness and aids communication. Students receiving help and assistance from paraprofessional student helpers need to have choices about who will assist them. This is made possible through a heterogeneous peer helper staff. The ratio of peer helper to student receiving services should not exceed 1 to 35.

Paraprofessionals must be selected with attention given to the following areas: academic record; recommendations from faculty, staff, and other student helpers; past and present leadership experiences; and a desire and willingness to assist and help other students. Students serving should receive systematic training in helping skills and personal growth strategies. It is strongly recommended that training be given prior to selection.

Training, at the minimum, must cover the following areas if the paraprofessional is to implement student development strategies for himself/herself and others. Extensive initial training and ongoing in-service training is recommended. Areas of training include knowledge of the paraprofessional role; awareness of self and the power of modeling behavior for those students with whom they have contact; community support skills; student (human) development theory; communication skills and the helping interaction; goals setting/behavioral objectives; assessment skills and techniques; cross-cultural relations; study skills techniques; and knowledge of campus and community resources and referral techniques. Other areas of training should be added as determined by the specific services provided to the student consumer and the area of their work assignment.

Programs/Services/Activities

The content of these areas must be determined by the specific student affairs program employing the paraprofessional. The program, service, or activity performed should be developmental and preventive in nature rather than remedial.

Examples of programs/services/activities involving paraprofessionals are orientation, academic advising, academic skills tutoring, admissions, registrar and financial aid programs, international student services, student health centers, and community involvement activities such as Big Buddy, hotline, and companion programs.

Facilities

Paraprofessional activities demand flexibility in the provision of appropriate physical activities. Paraprofessionals do not typically need private offices, but such facilities should be available as the need arises. Three questions should be asked concerning facilities which can be best put in terms of these questions:

1. *What is the paraprofessional expected to do?* Like any human service delivery system, the facilities must be conducive to the particular endeavor.
2. *What circumstances will protect and enhance the well-being of the clientele served by the paraprofessional?* Care must be taken to protect the rights and privileges of the clientele.
3. *What circumstances will protect and enhance the well-being of the paraprofessional?* Care must be taken to protect the paraprofessional from personal risk or injury.

Financial and Other Resources

Student paraprofessionals must be rewarded for their service as would anyone working in a service area. Direct monetary payment, tuition remission, fee waiver, room and board, and academic credit are examples of reward options.

Relationships With Faculty and Other Groups and Agencies

The supervising professional has a responsibility to carefully delineate the paraprofessional's role within the system. If the paraprofessional does not understand his/her relationship to the institution at large, misunderstanding will likely arise.

Work responsibilities and specific duties should be articulated so that both paraprofessionals and professionals have a clear concept of the services they provide. Each paraprofessional should have one professional supervisor with whom he/she maintains a close working relationship. Formal contact between these two individuals should be initiated on a weekly basis, or more often if necessary. The paraprofessional should never be allowed to deliver services without ongoing professional supervision. Paraprofessionals should model for other students the ability to communicate and associate with both faculty and staff at the institution.

Planning

Planning for the use of paraprofessionals should begin early in the academic year for the following year in order to provide for budgetary, staff, and facilities requirements. Long-range planning should be based on evaluative studies of the entire paraprofessional program.

Evaluation

A clear statement of evaluation criteria should be written and distributed to all paraprofessional staff members. They should know how, when, and by what criteria they will be evaluated. Evaluation should be viewed and communicated as a developmental learning opportunity and not as a threat to one's self-esteem. Evaluation should take place at least twice during each academic year. The second of these evaluations should determine whether or not a paraprofessional should be retained on the staff for the following academic year.

Ethics

Ethical considerations must be identified, disseminated to, and discussed with all student paraprofessionals. They should report to their supervisor any concern arising from contact with a student that the paraprofessional feels unqualified to handle. They should not be put in the position of interpreting psychological tests to students. Paraprofessionals should never be employed to offer services in the place of a professional staff member whose qualifications and training are necessary to perform the service, program, or activity.

The paraprofessional must recognize the limitations of his/her knowledge and skills, seek improvement through additional training and supervision, and refer the student to the professional when skills or experience are inadequate. Given this framework, the paraprofessional is expected to act in accordance with the following guidelines:

1. While not a professional, the paraprofessional accepts that he/she is expected to uphold standards of behavior consistent with the profession that he/she is serving.
2. The primary concern of the paraprofessional is the dignity and welfare of the individual.
3. The paraprofessional must become familiar with both campus and community resources available to those being served.
4. The paraprofessional must inform students of the services he/she is able to provide and should avoid acting beyond the realm for which he/she was selected and trained.
5. The paraprofessional needs to recognize his/her limitations and make appropriate referrals when necessary.
6. The paraprofessional is expected to adhere to the confidentiality policy of the sponsoring agency. He/she should always operate within the framework of general institutional policies and procedures.

Legal Issues

Institutions may be held legally responsible for services performed by paraprofessionals. Issues of liability, confidentiality, and nondiscrimination must be carefully covered in training.

Note. Much of the material in this chapter comes from *Students as Paraprofessional Staff* (New Directions for Student Services #27) by S. Ender and R. Winston, 1984, San Francisco: Jossey-Bass. Copyright 1984 by Jossey-Bass.

CHAPTER 4

Workshop Presentation Skills

by Priscilla F. Visek

Communication is the basis for learning; humans communicate verbally and nonverbally by their attitudes and behaviors. An excellent workshop presentation is easily recognized but difficult to define. It piques the participant's interest and holds their attention, and the content engages their minds and emotions. In addition, a presentation involves the participants to increase their interest and their retention of the information. Finally, the design and presentation of the evening workshop must take into account that college and university students have been listening to lectures all day— the paraprofessional must know how to maintain their interest and keep the workshop moving. Training and coaching can improve presentation skills, building on the unique qualities each presenter will bring to the program. The paraprofessionals learn about paying attention to their appearance, coping with excitement and tension, understanding learning-style preferences, making the presentation, using audiovisuals, facilitating groups, improving audience participation, and overcoming potential problems.

Appearance

The paraprofessionals should be aware of how they look when they give a presentation. This includes being neat and clean but not necessarily dressed up. If the presenter looks good, the message to the audience is that the presentation is important and both the information and the presenter should be taken seriously. Presenters should dress according to the audience; student groups tend to dress casually.

Coping With Tension

To be enthusiastic about the presentation, the paraprofessional needs to feel refreshed and energetic. This can be achieved by taking a brisk walk, rehearsing out loud in an exaggerated volume and variety of pitches, and making some grand gestures. Excitement and tension are normal for paraprofessionals, especially before their first presentation. Some level of excitement is helpful (i.e., it motivates one to do a good job), but too much can be harmful. Before the presentation, the student can relieve tension by taking a warm shower or bath, taking a few deep breaths, or laughing out loud. Presenters should avoid drinking caffeinated coffee, tea, or soft drinks, which can heighten the feeling of nervousness.

During the training session, paraprofessionals learn to use their voices to their best advantage. Voices have two important features: the pattern of speech and pitch. When people are nervous, their voices become tense and higher in pitch, their speech becomes more rapid, and they need more air. A high, tense pitch is not pleasant to the ear. To counteract that problem, the paraprofessionals should learn to stand erect with good posture so the lungs have room to expand and take in oxygen.

If presenters are nervous, they sometimes resort to linking phrases with repetitive words (e.g., "ah," "OK," "like," "you know"). This fills in gaps of silence, which are uncomfortable to the nervous presenter who is unsure of what to say next. This bad habit can be suppressed by using periods of silence at the end of an idea. Silence gives the presenter time to think, serves as an effective transition, and gives the audience time to ponder an important point. Pauses always seem longer to the presenter than to the audience.

Men, as a group, tend to have less expressive voices than women; however, their stronger features come across as being confident and powerful. Women tend to have more expressive voices but sometimes are difficult to hear. Paraprofessionals should have the opportunity to rehearse with someone in the back of a room to check their voice volume and clarity.

Accommodating Learning-Style Preferences

Given the same exposure to a piece of knowledge, individuals will acquire it in different ways, at different paces, and with varying degrees of accuracy. Humans learn by hearing, seeing, feeling, touching, smelling, and tasting, and they show variations in learning preferences.

Some people like discussions, whereas others learn better by listening to a lecture; some learn best by working on their own, whereas others look for and follow directions. Some people have low tolerance for distractions, whereas others can study with a radio or television on. Gregorc (1979) states that ''learning style consists of distinctive behaviors which serve as indicators of how a person learns and adapts to his environment. It also gives us a clue as to how a person's mind operates'' (p. 19).

Learning styles emerge from some unknown combination of early environment and inborn inclinations. No one style is best; styles simply differ. Because most people have been in a variety of educational situations over a period of years, they are quite adaptable and capable of learning when presented material in various styles. Each person, however, has a learning-style preference. Selected instructional methods, resources, and programs appear to complement specific elements of an individual's learning style. When these are matched with that learning-style preference, academic achievement increases and general attitudes improve.

If workshop trainers and paraprofessionals appreciate how people learn, they can plan workshops that accommodate various learning-style preferences. To increase interest and the potential for learning in the workshop, the paraprofessional should include a variety of instructional tools, such as mini-lectures, games, simulations, audiotapes, demonstrations, practice sessions, role-playing, group discussions, films, and handouts.

Presenting the Workshop

A great deal of time is spent designing a workshop. It is easy to forget, however, that much of what the audience perceives and retains is what it sees rather than what it hears. Therefore, the presenter must be aware of not only how well the audience hears the content, but also what it sees: posture, gestures, eye contact, body movement, facial expressions, appearance, and enthusiasm. Giving presentations is much like acting on a stage. Acting places importance on how the person looks; in fact, the costume and makeup tell the audience much about the character. Similarly, a fitness paraprofessional who is greatly overweight may cast doubt on his or her credibility as would a stress management paraprofessional who smokes during the presentation.

To get a workshop off to a good start, presenters should organize an introduction. This can include personal information about the presenter, such as her or his name, academic major, hometown, and interest in the paraprofessional program. The presenter should then briefly outline the workshop and the activities in which the participants will be involved that evening. Summarizing two or three main goals of the workshop provides the audience with an idea of what to expect.

Standing or Sitting During the Presentation

It is not a good idea to stand in one spot during an entire presentation; some movement serves to keep the audience alert. However, continual, purposeless movement can interfere with the listeners' concentration. Body movements denote the level of interest in the subject as well as the level of energy. The presenter can wear out the audience as well as put them to sleep!

Sitting down with the audience is useful if participation and exchange of ideas between individuals is desired, but it may make it difficult to remain in control. The presenter should stand or sit at a location above the audience to be in charge, or sit at the same level as the audience to take charge.

Gestures, Eye Contact, and Facial Expressions

Paraprofessionals use gestures to emphasize points and to get attention. Movements need to be purposeful and vigorous. They should vary and be well timed with the content. Inappropriate gestures can distract rather than enhance and complement the presentation. (Keeping elbows next to the body makes gestures ineffective and similar in movement.)

Eye contact is extremely important. The presenter must try to make eye contact with different individuals in the group. The presenter should be able to tell whether the audience is bored or is not understanding the content. Good eye contact maintains the participants' interest by making them feel that the material is being presented to them individually. Facial expression affects the presentation also. There is no reason to be very serious or feel the need to smile during the entire presentation. A pleasant expression that varies as the topic varies keeps the audience alert.

Staying on Schedule

Beginning and ending on time is essential to Lifestyle Workshops. Particularly with university groups, students may drift in and out during the workshop. Despite this kind of distraction, it is still important for the presenter to start the workshop on time and not repeat introductory information for latecomers. Audiences do not like to be held past the stated time, and if they are, the presenter may have to summarize the main points of the presentation while some people are leaving. It is better to stop early than to start a new topic that will take the presentation past the allotted time. So, if the presentation starts late, the paraprofessional should leave out a small section or shorten an activity to end on time.

Using Notecards

Presentation notes can be an outline or incomplete sentences on paper or notecards. Presenters will develop their own methods that work best for them. It's important to bring at least an outline, however, no matter how many times the presenter has given the same workshop. Distractions occur, and presenters can lose their train of thought for no apparent reason. Some presenters learn this lesson from painful experience.

The paraprofessionals should always number the pages or notecards in case they are dropped. Notecards are an acceptable presentation tool, but they should be used inconspicuously. Flipping papers distracts an audience. The presenters should use only one side of the notecard or page, which should not be clipped or stapled together. They should slide each page to one side or to the bottom of the stack rather than flipping it over. They should end a thought or point on the bottom of the page so that they can look at the audience while completing the idea and quietly move to the next page.

The notes should be typed or written legibly to enhance the delivery, incorporating spacing, underlining, indenting, capitalizing, and marking with different colors of ink. Codes will remind the presenter of important points or a thought-provoking question to ask, or indicate where audiovisuals and handouts should be used. The presentation notes will become individualized with experience.

Using Audiovisuals

Audiovisuals add variety to any presentation and emphasize important points; they help people learn by seeing as well as by listening. Examples are handouts and pamphlets; blackboards, overhead transparencies, and posters; and films, slides, and videotapes.

Handouts and Pamphlets

Handouts and pamphlets are especially effective if the presentation deals with complex information. Distribution needs to be planned in advance. There are three choices: before, during, or after the presentation. Each has its advantages, depending on the group. Handouts may be placed so people can pick them up as they walk into the workshop. This is good for very large groups. The disadvantage is that people may be reading them during the presentation. Handouts may be distributed at relevant times during the presentation to help the audience follow concepts. Alternatively, the handouts could be set out at the conclusion of the presentation for people to take with them. This is effective if the purpose of the handout is to summarize or to offer additional resources to complement the presentation.

Blackboards, Overhead Transparencies, and Posters

Whenever presenters use a blackboard, they must remember not to talk into it. They should wait until they have completed writing and then turn to the audience for a discussion. The words should be large, clear, and legible. It's a good idea to ask people sitting in the back whether they can read the blackboard.

Paraprofessionals can place posters on a wall, but using an easel makes them more accessible. Lettering should be large enough for everyone to see. Colors and graphics help to get the point across and may help retention of information.

Films, Slides, and Videotapes

The presenters are responsible for checking to make sure that electrical equipment is in good working order, and they should be trained in using the equipment. They should get in the habit of taking along an extension cord, as suitable outlets are not always available. Films, slides, and videotapes complement information given by the presenter. In addition, the audiovisuals can be followed by a discussion to reinforce what has been seen. A presenter must always preview an audiovisual before showing it to a group.

Facilitating Groups

The presenter should arrive at the site of the presentation early enough to rearrange the physical setting if necessary. This involves knowing the approximate number of people who will be attending to plan an advantageous seating arrangement. The most difficult arrangement for group facilitation is stacked rows of permanent seats. Encourage incoming participants to sit together in the front and close to the presenter. The best is a circular arrangement allowing everyone to have visual contact with each other.

In informal settings, such as university residence halls and Greek houses, most of the participants sit on the floor or on the few available couches and chairs. The furniture should be arranged into an area that accommodates the anticipated group, reserving the best place for the presenter (make sure there's an accessible place for leaving note-

cards). Audiovisuals must be visible from all points of the room, and the presenter should go to the back of the room before the audience arrives to see whether they can be read from all angles. This allows time to make adjustments and avoid interrupting the presentation to move chairs, screens, or people.

Improving Audience Participation

There are two popular techniques paraprofessionals can use to encourage group participation.

Eliciting and Answering Questions

A popular method of presenting information to a group is a short lecture with questions to and from the audience. Questioning increases audience participation but is less likely to occur in large groups. The use of good questions increases learning and motivation. Formulating thought-provoking questions is difficult to do while giving a presentation. Thus quality questions should be written in advance and included in the presentation notes or outline. Once questions are solicited, the presenter has less control over the time and sometimes the direction of the topic. However, getting the audience to participate actively may be more important than maintaining strict control over the time and topic.

Game Format

Another method for increasing audience participation is introducing a game or contest that incorporates the facts and ideas of the presentation. Dividing a group into smaller parts increases the involvement by making it more informal. Competition between teams enhances each person's feeling of being a part of the group. People often learn and remember more by doing than by listening or watching. Consequently, several of the Lifestyle Workshops are in game format; for example, "A Winner's Alcohol Facts Game," a football game in which teams answer questions worth yardage on the football field. Another game, "Winning at Weight Control," is played like the board game "Monopoly," but instead of money, teams play to gain or lose pounds. Inexpensive prizes can add to the fun.

Everyone should understand the rules and the goal of the group activity. Presenters should invite questions from the participants for clarification before beginning the activity. Walking through a short segment of the activity increases the general comprehension.

Overcoming Unexpected Problems

The first rule for all presenters is to respect the audience. During group discussions, the presenter should encourage participants to support their opinions while providing facts to back up statements. A disagreement between the presenter and participant or between two participants should be expressed in a mature and respectful manner. During any disturbance, the presenter should stay calm; the group will usually help deal with unruly, loud, or destructive individuals. The presenter is in charge and can facilitate and end discussions.

Many university meeting rooms and lounges are surrounded by distractions and various disruptions. This will include elevators that open and shut, entrances and hallways that open into the room, and nearby places where students are meeting and talking. In addition, sometimes students from outside the audience will join in. Paraprofessionals and trainers should share such experiences so they can share solutions and learn from problems that they have encountered. Identical circumstances rarely occur, but thinking ahead about these experiences will help paraprofessionals react with more confidence when confronted with a difficult situation. Flexibility comes with experience; when a problem arises, presenters need to be able to change strategies. Humor is especially helpful to dissipate tension so that the presenter can continue with the workshop.

Summary

Students bring their unique personalities to a paraprofessional health promotion program, but few will have sufficient experience in presenting information to groups. Although many of the presentation skills come with experience, learning the basics discussed in this chapter will get paraprofessionals off to a good start.

REFERENCES

Batalden, P., & O'Connor, P. (1980). *Quality assurance in ambulatory care*. Rockville, MD: Aspen Systems Corporation.

Carey, M. (1984). Peer health advisor program to reduce the health risks of university students. *Public Health Reports,* **99**(6), 614-620.

Ender, S., & Winston, R. (1984). *Students as paraprofessional staff* (New Directions for Student Services No. 27). San Francisco: Jossey-Bass.

Engs, R., & Hanson, D. (1985). The drinking patterns and drinking problems of college students: 1983. *Journal of Alcohol and Drug Education,* **31**(1), 65-83.

Green, L., Kreuter, M., Deeds, S., & Partridge, K. (1980). *Health education planning: A diagnostic approach*. Palo Alto, CA: Mayfield.

Green, L., & Lewis, F. (1986). *Measurement and evaluation in health education and health promotion*. Palo Alto, CA: Mayfield.

Gregorac, A. (1979). *Student learning styles: Diagnosing and prescribing programs*. Reston, VA: National Association of Secondary School Principals.

Kotler, P. (1976). *Marketing management*. Englewood Cliffs, NJ: Prentice-Hall.

MacStravic, R. (1986). *Managing health care marketing communications*. Rockville, MD: Aspen Systems Corporation.

U.S. Department of Health and Human Services. (1979). *Healthy people: The surgeon general's report on health promotion and disease prevention* (GPO 1983-0-399-261). Washington, DC: U.S. Government Printing Office.

U.S. Department of Health and Human Services. (1987). *Prevention '86/'87: Federal programs and progress*. Washington, DC: U.S. Government Printing Office.

World Health Organization. (1986). Health promotion—A discussion document on the concept and principles. *Public Health Reviews,* **14**(3-4), 245-250.

SUGGESTED READINGS

American Hospital Association. (1981). *Health education in college health services*. Rockville, MD: American College Health Association.

Brown, W. (1974). Effectiveness of paraprofessionals: The evidence. *Personnel and Guidance Journal, 53*(4), 257-263.

Durlak, J. (1979). Comparative effectiveness of paraprofessional and professional helpers. *Psychological Bulletin, 86*(1), 80-92.

Falck, V., & Kilcoyne, M. (1984). A health promotion program for school personnel. *Journal of School Health, 54*(7), 239-243.

Healthfinder, health risk appraisals. (Available from National Health Information Clearinghouse, P.O. Box 1133, Washington, DC 20013.)

Helm, C. (1972). Health aides: Student involvement in a university health center program. *Journal of the American College Health Association, 20*, 248-251.

Perry, C., Klepp, K., Halper, A., Hawkins, K., & Murray, D. (1986). A process evaluation study of peer leaders in health education. *Journal of School Health, 56*(2), 62-67.

Sciacca, J., & Seehafer, R. (1986). College peer health education: Program rationale, support, and example. *Wellness Perspectives III, 2*, 3-8.

Silverman, M. (1977). *Senior medication education program*. Unpublished manuscript. (Available from the San Francisco Department of Public Health, 101 Grove St., Room 201, San Francisco, CA 94102.)

PART II

Sixteen
Lifestyle Workshops

The 16 Lifestyle Workshops presented in Part II are designed primarily for young adults in a university setting. However, with modification they can be used in secondary schools, community education programs, hospital-based education classes, or workplace health promotion. Health educators should be particularly sensitive in their application of the sexuality workshops, which have been written with the often-liberal and less-inhibited college audience in mind.

Each workshop has two sections: Paraprofessional Preparation Materials and The Workshop Presentation. The paraprofessional preparation materials include training session outlines, a paraprofessional competency exam, and a list of texts and suggested readings. The paraprofessional trainer uses the training session outlines as a guide in teaching prospective paraprofessionals. Major points in the training session are tested by the paraprofessional competency exam; each session lists which questions on the exam correlate to that session. The texts and readings used in each session are listed in the outline and the reference list.

During the last training session for each workshop the prospective paraprofessionals each present a workshop section. The trainer evaluates each presentation and decides whether the student is ready to present a workshop alone. Students repeat their presentations until they are acceptable. Trainers should offer constructive criticism to their students based on evaluation forms (see chapter 3). This presentation-practice session is a time for the paraprofessional students to give each other support. This can be encouraged by trainers who offer positive as well as negative feedback.

The Workshop Presentation includes an outline of the objectives and list of materials used in the workshop (Workshop at a Glance); the basic workshop information as it will be presented by the paraprofessionals (Presenter Information); questions commonly asked of paraprofessionals at the University of Illinois (Most Frequently Asked Questions); handouts and visual aids; and a reference list.

Getting in Shape
Lifestyle Workshop

PARAPROFESSIONAL PREPARATION MATERIALS

Training Sessions

Competency Exam

Texts and Suggested Readings

WORKSHOP AT A GLANCE

Presenter Information

Most Frequently Asked Questions

Handouts and Visual Aids

References

TRAINING SESSIONS

Getting in Shape

Session 1: Workshop Presentation

Time: 60 minutes

Methods: Presentation, demonstration

Description: Trainer presents workshop to Lifestyle Educators

Readings: The workshop

Session 2: Exercise Your Brain

Time: 60 minutes

Methods: Lecture, discussion

Description: Present each question and discuss responses

Activity: Present "Exercise Your Brain" handout, develop each question/answer through discussion.

Readings: The workshop and materials on benefits and myths of exercise

Competency exam question: 1

Session 3: Interest, Goals, and Success

Time: 60 minutes

Methods: Lecture; discussion; film, *For a Change, Breaking Old Habits and Making New Ones* (25 min), which is distributed by Spectrum Films, Inc., 2755 Jefferson Street, Suite 103, Carlsbad, CA 92008, (619) 434-6191

Description: Identify areas of interest; the makings of a successful program; components of goal-setting, motivation, and exercise

Readings: The workshop and materials covering the psychological aspects of human movement

Competency exam questions: 2, 3

Session 4: "Most Frequently Asked Questions" Review and Hot Seat

Time: 60 minutes

Methods: Discussion, lecture, practice

Description: Review workshop components

Activity: Hot Seat: Each Lifestyle Educator is quizzed by other students about the workshop topic for 10 minutes.

Readings: The workshop materials to review the benefits of being active

Competency exam questions: 4, 5, 6

Session 5: Practice Workshop Presentation

Time: 60 minutes

Methods: Presentation

Description: Each Lifestyle Educator presents 20 minutes of the workshop.

Readings: The workshop

COMPETENCY EXAM

1. Instructor will choose three questions from "Exercise Your Brain" and ask students to provide the answer and an appropriate explanation.

2. List two principles that are important in determining activities of interest. Explain each.

3. Explain the proper technique for taking body circumference measurements.

4. Explain why records of progress toward fitness goals should be kept (two reasons and two methods).

5. Explain the relationship between intensity and duration. Give an example.

6. List three benefits of getting in shape.

7. Explain the fallacy of spot reduction.

8. Explain why stretching is important.

9. What are fat-burning exercises? Explain.

10. Identify three possible ways to gain weight.

11. Explain why goals are used for "Getting in Shape."

12. Explain why weight lifting is not the ideal fat-burning exercise.

13. Suggest possible techniques to use in the workshop if an audience participant is one of the following:
    • Recognition Seeker (frequently calls attention to self)
    • Conversationalist (brings up off-the-subject anecdotes and is a noisy distraction)
    • Moralizer (advocates judgmental points of view based on personal convictions)
    • Conservative (convinced that the status quo does not need changing)

TEXTS AND SUGGESTED READINGS

Bucher, C.A., & Prentice, W.E. (1985). *Fitness for college and life*. St. Louis: Times Mirror/Mosby.

Heyward, V.H. (1986). *Designs for fitness: A guide to physical fitness appraisal and exercise prescription*. Minneapolis: Burgess.

Rosato, R.D. (1986). *Fitness and wellness: The physical connection*. New York: West.

Sharkey, B.J. (1984). *Physiology of fitness*. Champaign, IL: Human Kinetics.

WORKSHOP AT A GLANCE

The goal of this workshop is to offer the participants motivational techniques and an opportunity to formulate personal goals in starting or improving their personalized fitness programs. This workshop takes approximately 45 minutes to present. Suggested attendance is 5 to 20 persons.

Objectives

Through the content of this workshop, the following objectives will be met.

- Participants will discuss myths and facts about exercising.
- Participants will determine their body circumference using anthropometric measurements.
- Participants will compute their Target Heart Range.
- Personal fitness goals will be discussed and participants will have the opportunity to write down their own goals and rewards.

Workshop Materials

- Workshop sign-in sheet
- Handouts and visual aids: *Exercise Your Brain, Fitness Goal Card, Computing Your Target Heart Range, Comparable Aerobic Exercise Table,* and *Aerobic Workout Graph*
- Five measuring tapes, preferably nonstretchable
- Stopwatch or watch with a second hand
- Calculator
- 4 × 6 index cards
- Lifestyle Workshop evaluation forms and pencils

Note: Have participants dress in T-shirts and shorts or sweatpants for measuring body circumference.

PRESENTER INFORMATION

Briefly introduce yourself, your background, and any other personal information you choose to share. Describe your health promotion program and the topics available; for example, fitness and nutrition. Stress that the workshops are unique because you bring them to their living areas. Tell them that Lifestyle Workshop paraprofessionals are trained at (your institution or program) to present these workshops. If anyone is interested in the training program, ask him or her to speak to you after the workshop.

This workshop will address the details that should be considered in starting an individualized exercise program. The different components of fitness will be identified and strategies will be offered for sticking with an exercise program once one has been started.

Exercise Your Brain (20 minutes)

Hand out "Exercise Your Brain" and ask participants to complete the true/false questionnaire. Give correct answers and discuss the myths versus the facts that participants question. The questions and answers follow.

1. *The faster you run or jog one mile, the more calories you will use.* (False)

   For all practical purposes, the speed at which one runs will not influence the number of calories expended. A faster pace will involve greater total energy demand, but keeping this pace usually results in running a shorter distance, thus less calories are used. The most important determinant of calories expended is the distance covered. McArdle, Katch, and Katch (1986) state that a good estimate of energy expended by runners may be calculated by the following equation: 1 kilocalorie/kilogram/kilometer. Thus an 80-kg male would burn an average of 80 kcal per kilometer of run, and a 50-kg female would burn approximately 50 kcal per kilometer of run. The male carries more weight, thus performing more work, which is evident in calories expended.

2. *Exercise will change fat to muscle.* (False)

   Fat is an economical way to store energy. Muscle is an active metabolic system. As muscle contracts it uses energy. This energy may come from stored fat (adipose tissue) that is mobilized, put into the blood stream, carried to active muscle, and used to energize further contractility by muscle cells. Fat is deposited in adipose cells, which may grow in size and in number (extreme obesity). The number of fat cells does not change after adolescence, therefore a loss of fat weight from exercise will not reduce the total number of adipose cells. Biochemically, fat does not carry the nitrogen necessary to build protein, and therefore it is impossible to change fat to muscle. However, excess protein in the diet can be deaminated and then synthesized to fat.

3. *A good way to get rid of fat around the stomach area is to do sit-ups.* (False)

   Exercising a group of muscles in a specific area will not selectively diminish those fat deposits. During physical activity, energy is needed to generate body movements. At low to moderate intensity activity a majority of the fuel used is fat. Fat is stored all over the body, both subcutaneously and in internal adipose tissue. When one needs energy, as during exercise, the needs are met by using energy (from fat) from all over the body, not just the areas involved in muscular contraction. Katch and Katch (1986) showed that fat lost from extremely obese females was situated all over the body, but the trunk region lost twice as much fat as the extremities.

4. *Fat people never exercise.* (False)

   Genetics may play a large role in determining the body's morphology, though exercise and caloric intake are also important. Fat people may or may not exercise, but of critical importance is the theory of energy balance. There are three ways that people gain weight in the form of fat:

   a. Caloric intake is increased while energy expenditure is constant;
   b. energy expenditure is decreased while caloric intake is constant; and
   c. increased caloric intake is combined with decreased energy expenditure.

   Thus, fat people may be just as active as everyone else, but their diet contains more calories, and calories not used for activity are thus deposited in adipose tissue.

5. *You need to develop large muscles to develop strength.* (True)

Strength, or the ability to generate force, is directly related to the cross-sectional area of the muscle (size). Thus, larger muscles are generally stronger. There are exceptions, dependent on genetics, muscle fiber types, and motor unit recruitment.

6. *A high-protein diet will give you extra nutrients needed for exercise.* (False)

For muscle tissue to generate force, fuel is needed in the contractile process. The optimal choice of fuel (fat, carbohydrate, or protein) depends on many factors, but two dominate: intensity (high intensity activity requires carbohydrates; low intensity utilizes fat), and availability (which substance is located within the muscle cell or bloodstream). The body uses protein only after carbohydrates are gone, for example, at the finish of a marathon or during severe starvation. Obviously, protein is not the ideal energy source.

Also important in exercise are vitamins and minerals. B-complex vitamins are particularly needed for energy metabolism. B vitamins are found in red meats; but don't overdo it—too much protein stresses the kidney.

7. *When you diet, you should restrict the amount of water you drink.* (False)

Water has no calories, therefore it cannot result in a gain of fat. A glass of water may temporarily cause you to gain nonfat weight, but your body regulates the appropriate amount of fluids it needs and rids itself of the excess.

A can of soda has 150 calories and a glass of milk has 120 calories—a 30-calorie difference. Over the course of a month or a year, the difference adds up. Remember, an excess of 3,500 calories is equal to 1 pound of fat.

8. *You should take in more protein if you are trying to build muscle strength through weight lifting.* (False)

For all practical purposes, the diet of the average American contains more than a sufficient amount of protein. Excess protein, similar to excess carbohydrate, is converted to fat. Most serious weight lifters and bodybuilders increase protein intake in preparation for con-

tests, but this is mostly due to the low caloric value of a gram of protein and the basic belief that more protein is needed in the diet.

Also important for weight lifting is a sufficient intake of carbohydrates. Weight training is very intense activity and carbohydrates are the proper energy source.

9. *The best way to lose weight is to become more active and reduce the number of calories you eat.* (True)

There are a number of reasons for this.

- Negative energy balance (weight loss) is the result of a decreased caloric intake while energy expenditure is constant, increased energy expenditure while caloric intake is constant, and combined increased energy expenditure with decreased caloric intake.
- Weight loss should be from fat, not muscle, and exercise helps prevent muscle tissue from being used for energy.
- Combining increased activity with caloric restriction is like burning the candle at both ends; it is the fastest and safest route to your goal. For example, 300 kcal/day of caloric restriction + 200 kcal/day of exercise = 500 kcal/day (3,500 kcal = 1 pound of fat).
- Proper nutrition is maintained when appropriate nutrients are consumed.

10. *Exercise may affect a woman's menstrual cycle.* (True)

Loss of menses after menarche and before menopause is called amenorrhea. Although commonly found in female athletes who perform long-distance training (running and swimming), it is also found in athletes with very low body fat (gymnasts). Part of the problem may be caused by this less-than-ideal percent of body fat, because female hormones, particularly estrogen, need fat to work properly. Estrogen is important in maintaining metabolism in adult women.

11. *Jogging is the best form of exercise for losing fat weight.* (False)

Jogging is one form of exercise for losing fat. There are countless others, including walking, running, cycling, swimming, and skating. Every person is different, and the type of activity one chooses may not suit someone else. A person starting to exercise should try a variety of activities and find one that he or she likes. Alternate activities to prevent boredom, set goals, and go for them.

Identifying Areas of Interest (5 minutes)

Hand out 4 × 6 cards and ask participants to truthfully answer the following three questions.

- What does it mean to them "to be in shape"? (More than one response is appropriate.)
- Do they consider themselves in shape at the present time? (Yes or No)
- What would they list as possible reasons that they are or are not currently in shape?

Collect the cards. Review and share with the group the most common responses. Ask the group why past exercise and activity programs have failed to keep them active. Next you'll begin to discuss methods to help them get moving so they can get in shape and stay in shape. Choosing the proper activity should be based on two principles.

First, the activity should be specific to the component(s) of fitness one desires or the goals one sets. For example, if the goal of the exercise program is to change body composition (loss of fat weight), one should select an endurance activity. If the goal of the exercise program is to increase strength (power or endurance), one should choose a weight-training program. If the goal is flexibility, one should start a stretching program.

Second, the activity should be one they like. Tell participants not to select an activity they don't enjoy, because they won't stay with this activity very long. If they like time to think and relax, tell them to consider solitary sports such as jogging. If they enjoy socializing, walking with friends or playing team sports like volleyball may be better for them.

A variety of activities and exercises will prevent boredom. After losing interest, it's better to choose a different actvity than to quit altogether. Another possibility is to alternate activities depending on the season and weather, the day of the week, and whether one is exercising with a partner or a group. Examples of aerobic activities are walking, jogging, biking, swimming, skating, and cross-country skiing. Take advantage of activities that are already available. For college students, there probably won't be another time when so many selections are offered. Provide a list of local fitness

and recreational activities and programs available for your participants.

Making a Successful Exercise Program (10 minutes)

Hand out a "Fitness Goal Card" and show the visual aid, "Comparable Aerobic Exercise Table" to each participant. Have participants get a partner, hand out flexible measuring tapes, and take body circumferences. These are the circumference sites that should be measured.

- Upper Arm: The arm hangs limp at the side of the body and the measurement is taken mid-distance from shoulder (acromian process) to elbow (olecronon process).
- Waist: The person stands erect and the measurement is taken at the level of the umbilicus during normal breathing.
- Hip: The person stands erect and the measurement is taken at the greatest girth of the hip area.
- Thigh: The person stands with equal weight on both feet and measurement is taken half way between knee (patella) and hip joint.
- Calf: The person stands with equal weight on both feet and the measurement is taken at the belly (greatest girth) of the calf.

The tape should be pulled snugly, but should not cause an indentation in the surface of the skin. Record measurements on "Fitness Goal Card."

Set Goals and Plan Rewards

Goals should be challenging, but attainable. Allow the activity to be fun, not a task. Remember, high achievers set lower (but achievable) goals, and low achievers set goals that are too high and then make excuses for not achieving them. Everyone is different; therefore, most individual goals will differ. Have them write down their goal and put it where they can see it. Each goal should be measurable, concrete, and realistic. Instruct participants to record their fitness goal on the "Fitness Goal Card."

At intermediate points or after attaining the goal, a reward should be given. It's important that rewards be contingent on some predetermined behavior. For example, after two weeks of regular exercise, a reward could be a new workout T-shirt. Have participants write down one reward they will give themselves if they attain their goal.

Keep Records

Tell participants to keep records to note their progress, and to keep workouts consistent, especially with weight training. Workouts need to be balanced to utilize the progressive overload theory. Have them photograph themselves or use anthropometric measurements (e.g., circumferences, skinfolds)—it would be nice to look back and note the difference.

On the back of the "Goal Card," participants write down the best days and times in their schedules to exercise. Tell them to try to set them at regular times of the day. It is best to start slow and let the activity become part of their daily lifestyle. Suggest that they exercise with a friend or a group of people; the social aspects of partner or group exercise are important. It is important not to exercise while in pain. Tell participants that if they start feeling pain, they should stop—or at least slow down. Remind them that their body is telling them something, and they should listen. The injury must be allowed to heal before they start back, and they should then proceed slowly.

Planning Safe Exercise (10 minutes)

Tell participants to work at the proper intensity, frequency, and duration that their body can handle. Too much too soon means soreness and pain. There are five important factors for a safe exercise program. (You may want to put these points on a poster.)

- Frequency—generally, you should be working out three to five times per week. Spread your workouts out over the course of the week, giving yourself time to rest.
- Duration—15-60 minutes of continuous physical activity. Duration is dependent on the intensity of the activity; in other words, a low intensity activity should be conducted over a long period of time.

- Intensity—60-90% of your maximum heart rate. Maximal heart rate is the fastest the heart will contract related to maximal physical exertion.

  Hand out "Computing Your Target Heart Rate Range" sheets. Explain the steps and have participants calculate their Target Heart Rate range.
- Type of exercise—any activity that is aerobic (meaning it uses oxygen), uses large muscle groups, can be maintained continuously, and is rhythmical in nature. Some examples are running or jogging, walking or hiking, swimming, skating, bicycling, rowing, cross-country skiing, rope-skipping, and endurance games.
- Warm-Up and Cool-Down—studies show the importance of both a warm-up and a proper cool-down. The warm-up should incorporate the muscles the chosen activity will use by starting out very slowly and gradually increasing. Cool down by gradually slowing down. Never stop and stand still after a strenuous workout or blood may pool at your feet, causing dizziness and possible complications. An active cool-down is best.

Conclusion and Evaluation (5 minutes)

Summarize the main points of the workshop:

- Getting in shape will mean something different to each person.
- They should find a physical activity they enjoy and participate in it.
- It is important to provide the proper stimulants and alterations in the activity program to stay involved.

Ask for questions from the participants. Offer resources and referrals for further information. Distribute Lifestyle Workshop evaluation forms and pencils. Allow time for completion and then collect. Briefly list and describe the other Lifestyle Workshops in Fitness.

MOST FREQUENTLY ASKED QUESTIONS

1. *How long and how often do I need to exercise?*

   Ideally, you should exercise four to six times per week, because your conditioning drops off after 72 hours. Exercising just on Saturdays will not help your state of fitness. Attempt to exercise for 20 to 60 minutes to get an aerobic (burn off fat) and a cardiovascular workout.

2. *Is it important to stretch before and after you exercise?*

   Ten minutes of stretching should be included in both the warm-up and cool-down to help prevent injury. Stretching exercises should be specific to the active body segments; for example, running and biking concentrate on lower limb motion, so appropriate stretching exercises would include leg exercises like the hurdler's stretch.

3. *I'm doing 100 sit-ups a day. Why do I still have "love handles"?*

   Spot reduction is a common fitness fallacy. Your body stores fat all over, and when energy is needed, your body retrieves it from all over. Sit-ups tone and develop abdominal muscles, but aerobic activity is needed to burn your body's fat stores.

4. *I seem to reach a comfortable level of fitness and then start to "blow off" exercising for one reason or another. How can I prevent this?*

   Make exercise part of your lifestyle. One reason people join exercise groups is to socialize, but there are many ways to motivate yourself to keep active.

5. *What's the difference between muscular strength and muscular endurance?*

   Muscular strength involves a force exerted by a group of muscles in a single maximum contraction. Muscular endurance involves sustained or repeated contractions.

6. *I've been running for 2 months and I've developed shin splints. I don't want to lose my present conditioning level. What should I do?*

   Shin splints are caused by overpronation of the foot and ankle while running, which results in the muscle being pulled from the bone. To treat the problem, rest, run on softer surfaces, and do lower-leg stretching exercises. Alternately switch to an activity like swimming or biking that will take you off your feet but retain your level of conditioning.

7. *Why does my roommate have a smaller waist but weigh more than I do? We are the same height and wear the same size pants.*

   A pound of fat is 18% larger, in volume, than a pound of muscle. In other words, muscle is more dense; so even though you may weigh the same, if you have a higher percentage of body fat your size will be greater.

8. *What's the best fat-burning exercise?*

   Aerobic activity is the best type of exercise for burning fat. Common aerobic activities include jogging, biking, basketball, swimming, and racquetball. Aerobic activities are those that last longer than 20 minutes, involve large muscle mass, and elevate both heart rate and ventilation rate.

9. ***What's the best way to gain weight?***

For individuals who are naturally thin, gaining weight may be difficult. Increasing body weight may be accomplished by gaining muscle, fat, or both. Muscle tissue will grow (hypertrophy) in size in response to a strenuous weight-training regimen. Once lifting weights stops, the muscles will slowly decrease (atrophy) in size back to the original state. Gaining fat weight is accomplished by eating more calories than you are expending. This is accomplished by eating more, exercising less, or both. Most people do not want to gain fat.

10. ***Why do women have a higher percentage of body fat than men?***

Genetically and evolutionarily women have needed extra fat for reproductive reasons. The female hormone estrogen is dependent on fat stores to work properly.

Exercise Your Brain

Answer these common statements about exercise True or False:

	T	F
1. The faster you run or jog one mile, the more calories you will use.	☐	☐
2. Exercise will change fat to muscle.	☐	☐
3. A good way to get rid of fat around the stomach area is to do sit-ups.	☐	☐
4. Fat people never exercise.	☐	☐
5. You need to develop large muscles to develop strength.	☐	☐
6. A high protein diet will give you extra nutrients needed for exercise.	☐	☐
7. When you diet, you should restrict the amount of water you drink.	☐	☐
8. You should take in more protein if you are trying to build your muscular strength.	☐	☐
9. The best way to lose weight is to be more active and reduce the number of calories that you eat.	☐	☐
10. Exercise may affect a woman's menstrual cycle.	☐	☐
11. Jogging is the best form of exercise for losing fat weight.	☐	☐

Note. Adapted from "Exercise Wise" by L. Lamb, 1980, *The Health Letter*, pp. 1-4.

Fitness Goal Card

Specific fitness goal: _____
_____

Reward: _____
_____

Starting measurements: Starting weight: _____

    Upper arm _____

    Waist   _____   Goal weight: _____

    Hips   _____

    Thighs   _____

    Calf   _____

Computing Your Target Heart Rate Range

1. $220 - \underline{\hspace{2cm}}_{\text{age}} =$ Maximum Heart Rate $\underline{\hspace{2cm}}$

2. Maximum Heart Rate − Resting Heart Rate = Heart Rate Reserve $\underline{\hspace{2cm}}$

3. Heart Rate Reserve × .60 + Resting Heart Rate = Minimum Working Heart Rate $\underline{\hspace{2cm}}$

4. Heart Rate Reserve × .90 + Resting Heart Rate = Maximum Working Heart Rate $\underline{\hspace{2cm}}$

Example:

1. 220 − 20 = 200
2. 200 − 70 = 130
3. 130 × .60 + 70 = 148
4. 130 × .90 + 70 = 187

Target heart rate range is 148–187 beats per min.
Target heart rate is 165 beats per min or 16–17 beats per 6 sec.

Source: American College of Sports Medicine Position Statement on the Recommended Quantity and Quality of Exercise for Developing and Maintaining Fitness in Healthy Adults

Comparable Aerobic Exercise[a]
Table

Activity	Kilocalories[b] (kcal/min)	Oxygen uptake (ml/kg · min⁻¹)	Activity	Kilocalories[b] (kcal/min)	Oxygen uptake (ml/kg · min⁻¹)
Archery	3.7- 5	10.5-14	Horseback riding	3.7-10	10.5-28
Backpacking	6 -13.5	17.5-38.5	Horseshoe pitching	2.5- 3.7	7 -10.5
Badminton	5 -11	14 -31.5	Hunting, walking		
Basketball			Small game	3.7- 8.5	10.5-24.5
Nongame	3.7-11	10.5-31.5	Big game	3.7-17	10.5-49
Game	8.5-15	24.5-42	Mountain climbing	6 -12	17.5-35
Bed exercise (arm movement, supine or sitting)	1.1- 2.5	3.5- 7	Paddleball/racquetball	10 -15	28 -42
			Rope skipping	10 -14	28 -42
Bicycling	3.7-10	10.5-28	Sailing	2.5- 6	7 -17.5
Bowling	2.5- 5	7 -14	Scuba diving	6 -12	17.5-35
Canoeing (also rowing and kayaking)	3.7-10	10.5-28	Shuffleboard	2.5- 3.7	7 -10.5
			Skating (ice or roller)	7 -10	17.5-28
Calisthenics	3.7-10	10.5-28	Skiing (snow)		
Dancing			Downhill	6 -10	17.5-28
Social and square	3.7- 8.5	10.5-24.5	Cross-country	7.5-15	21 -42
Aerobic	7.5-11	21 -31.5	Skiing (water)	6 -85	17.5-24.5
Fencing	7.5-12	21 -35	Snowshoeing	8.5-17	24.5-49
Fishing			Squash	10 -15	28 -42
Bank, boat, or ice	2.5- 5	7 -14	Soccer	6 -15	17.5-42
Stream, wading	6 - 7.5	17.5-21	Softball	3.7- 7.5	10.5-21
Football (touch)	7.5-12	21 -35	Stair-climbing	5 -10	14 -28
Golf			Swimming	5 -10	14 -18
Using power cart	2.5- 3.7	7 -10.5	Table tennis	3.7- 6	10.5-17.5
Walking, carrying bag, or pulling cart	5 - 8.5	14 -24.5	Tennis	5 -11	14 -31.5
			Volleyball	3.7- 7.5	10.5-21
Handball	10 -15	28 -42	Weight training circuit	10	28
Hiking (cross-country)	3.7- 8.5	10.5-24.5			

Note. From *Exercise in Health and Disease* (pp. 258-259) by M.L. Pollock, J. Wilmore, and S.M. Fox, 1985, Philadelphia: W.B. Saunders. Copyright 1985 by W.B. Saunders. Reprinted by permission.

[a]Energy cost values based on an individual of 154 lb of body weight (70 kg).

[b]Kilocalorie: A unit of measure based upon heat production. One kcal equals approximately 200 ml of oxygen consumed.

Aerobic Workout Graph

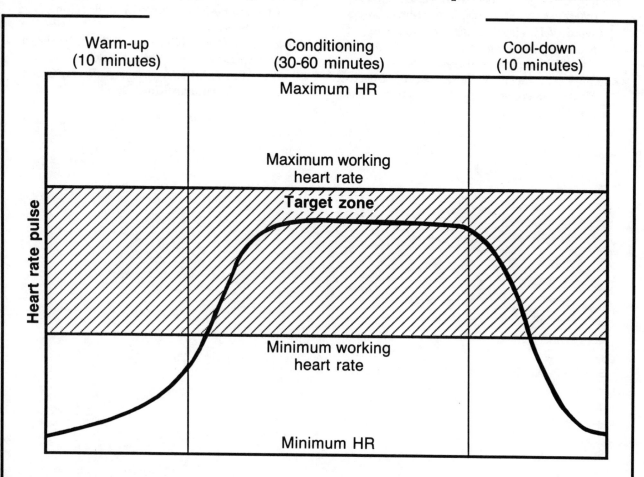

REFERENCES

Bucher, C.A., & Prentice, W.E. (1985). *Fitness for college and life*. St. Louis: Times Mirror/Mosby.

Heyward, V.H. (1986). *Designs for fitness: A guide to physical fitness appraisal and exercise prescription*. Minneapolis: Burgess.

Katch, V., & Katch, F. (1986, April). Success! Those incredible shrinking women. *Shape*, pp. 60-63.

McKardle, W.D., Katch, F.I., & Katch, V.L. (1986). *Exercise Physiology* (2nd ed.). Philadelphia: Lea & Febiger.

Rosato, R.D. (1986). *Fitness and wellness: The physical connection*. New York: West.

Sharkey, B.J. (1984). *Physiology of fitness*. Champaign, IL: Human Kinetics.

Body Building
Lifestyle Workshop

PARAPROFESSIONAL PREPARATION MATERIALS

Training Sessions

Competency Exam

Texts and Suggested Readings

WORKSHOP AT A GLANCE

Presenter Information

Most Frequently Asked Questions

Handouts and Visual Aids*

References

Weight Training and Nutrition was written by Melanie Tyner Wilson, MS, and Sara Kelley, MS, RD.

TRAINING SESSIONS

Body Building

Session 1: Workshop Presentation

Time: 60 minutes

Methods: Presentation, demonstration

Description: Trainer presents workshop to Lifestyle Educators in weight-training room.

Readings: The workshop

Competency exam questions: 1, 2

Next class meets in weight room (dress in sports clothing).

Session 2: Free Weights

Time: 60 minutes

Methods: Demonstration, participation

Description: Warm-up—importance discussed and exercise selection reviewed. Set up free-weight equipment and identify different stations and exercises. Lifestyle Educator performs each exercise (light resistance) and identifies muscles involved. Teach proper spotting techniques for each exercise.

Activity: Introduce the importance of warming up, followed by warm-up activities. Students learn to use free weights properly and to identify muscles used in each exercise by performing the major bodybuilding exercises listed in the manual.

Readings: The workshop material covering free-weight routines

Competency exam questions: 3, 4, 5

Next session meets in weight room.

Session 3: Free Weights

Time: 60 minutes

Methods: Demonstration, practice with free weights and calisthenics

Description: Warm-up; strength and endurance training: resistance, repetitions, sets, rest; calisthenics: push-ups, abdominal exercises.

Activity: Demonstrate and allow participation with warm-up, strength and endurance training, and calisthenics.

Readings: The workshop material covering free-weight routines and calisthenics.

Competency exam questions: 6, 7, 8, 9

Next session meets in weight room.

Session 4: Weight Machines

Time: 60 minutes

Methods: Explanation, practice

Description: Warm-up and review different stations/exercises. Lifestyle Educator performs each exercise and identifies muscles involved. Discuss similarities and differences between machines/free weights with respect to each exercise.

Activity: In this session the Lifestyle Educator learns to use bodybuilding machines (Nautilus, Omni, Universal) and will then discuss differences between machines and free weights.

Readings: Material covering the use of Nautilus, Omni, and Universal machines as a method for body-building.

Competency exam question: 3

Session 5: Designing a Workout, "Most Frequently Asked Questions" Review, and Hot Seat

Time: 60 minutes

Methods: Discussion, practice

Description: Introduce the structuring of a beginning bodybuilding routine, then present tips used by body-builders.

Activity: Hot Seat: Each Lifestyle Educator is quizzed by the other students about the workshop topic for 10 minutes.

Readings: The workshop, beginning and advanced bodybuilding materials

Session 6: Practice Workshop Presentation

Time: 60 minutes

Method: Presentation

Description: Each Lifestyle Educator presents 20 minutes of the workshop.

Readings: The workshop

COMPETENCY EXAM

1. List and briefly explain three purposes for weight training.

2. Support through evidence why females should not be concerned with becoming muscle-bound.

3. List two advantages of using free weights and two advantages of using machines.

4. List three factors that are important for proper warm-up. Explain each.

5. Choose four muscle groups and describe weight-training exercises (both free weight *and* machine) that concentrate on these muscles; identify proper spotting techniques for each free-weight exercise.

6. Explain the process you will use to get the participants actively involved in performing each exercise.

7. Explain the importance of using a spotter.

8. Explain why a workout is designed to begin with exercises that use the large muscle groups.

9. Explain the difference between strength training and endurance training. Include repetitions, resistance, sets, and rest as they pertain to each training program.

10. Explain three exercise tips for weight lifters.

11. Explain the overload principle. Use an example.

12. List and explain in sequence the series of abdominal exercises discussed in the program.

13. Suggest possible techniques to use in your workshop if an audience participant is one of the following:
    - Recognition Seeker (frequently calls attention to self)
    - Conversationalist (brings up off-the-subject anecdotes and is a noisy distraction)
    - Moralizer (advocates judgmental points of view based on personal convictions)
    - Conservative (convinced that the status quo does not need changing)

TEXTS AND SUGGESTED READINGS

Bucher, C.A., & Prentice, W.E. (1985). *Fitness for college and life*. St. Louis: Times Mirror/Mosby.

Heyward, V.H. (1986). *Designs for fitness: A guide to physical fitness appraisal and exercise prescription*. Minneapolis: Burgess.

Rosato, F.D. (1986). *Fitness and wellness: The physical connection*. New York: West.

Sharkey, B.J. (1984). *Physiology of fitness*. Champaign, IL: Human Kinetics.

WORKSHOP AT A GLANCE

The goal of this workshop is to present participants with the concepts, instruction, and safety guidelines for bodybuilding, and to offer an opportunity of supervised experience with weight-lifting equipment. This workshop takes approximately 60 minutes to present. Suggested attendance is 5 to 15 persons.

Objectives

Within the content of this workshop, the following objectives will be met.

- Participants will be able to perform one circuit of a beginning weight-lifting set.
- Various types of resistance equipment will be discussed, with consideration given to their benefits and shortcomings.
- Participants will be able to perform basic weight-training exercises.
- Calisthenic-style resistance training will be modeled as an alternative to equipment-oriented bodybuilding.

Workshop Materials

- Workshop sign-in sheet
- Handout and visual aids: *Weight Training and Nutrition*, and resistance equipment (possible sources of equipment and space are campus recreation facilities, residence hall weight room, and fraternity or sorority weight room).
- Lifestyle Workshop evaluation forms and pencils

Note. Encourage the workshop requester to have participants dress for activity, preferably wearing a T-shirt, shorts, or sweatpants.

PRESENTER INFORMATION

Briefly introduce yourself, your background, and any other personal information you choose to share. Describe your health promotion program and the topics available; for example, fitness and nutrition. Stress that the workshops are unique because you bring them to their living areas. Tell them that Lifestyle Workshop paraprofessionals are trained at (your institution or program) to present these workshops. If anyone is interested in the training program, ask him or her to speak to you after the workshop.

This workshop will address the prerequisites that should be considered before beginning a bodybuilding program. The workshop will provide information on choosing exercises and will offer a beginning program that may be used with or without weights or weight lifting.

Weight-Training Goals (3 minutes)

Not everyone chooses to use weights just to build strength. The reasons for choosing weight lifting are as diverse as the people who lift weights. These are popular weight-lifting goals:

- Working with weights to enhance shape and definition through muscular development. Weight training is not the ideal activity to burn fat and lose weight because weight training does not require the physical intensity necessary to use body fat as the primary energy source. Therefore, it should not be used as a weight loss exercise program. Both males and females can weight-train to improve body shape, but may not want to develop the same areas. Males may be more concerned with upper torso and arms while females may be concerned with hips, thighs, and legs.
- Working with weights for strength development. The most obvious reason for lifting weights is to improve strength. To do so, the program must be designed to add more pounds to your load as you proceed. Strength development, for the purpose of enhancing performance, should be activity-specific. For example, this means that if you want to jump higher you must design your program to strengthen the muscles used in jumping.

- Weight lifting for rehabilitation. Rehabilitation of an injured joint or muscle should include low-intensity activities that mirror the movement and function of that location. An injury will influence which exercises can be performed and how intense the workout should be. Certain exercises are not advisable for specific injured areas. For example, if you have a "bad" knee you should stay away from the leg press and the squat machine. It is also important to start and progress slowly.

It is essential to note that it is a myth that women should not use weights. It is not harmful for women, and there is no evidence that exercising during menstruation is harmful, or that bodybuilding is not feminine. In fact, in skill execution, women possess greater manual dexterity than men. Bodybuilding with weights will

- improve strength,
- develop endurance and muscle tone,
- firm sagging areas,
- improve appearance,
- improve posture, and
- improve physical efficiency.

Females don't have to be concerned with becoming "muscle-bound" because the *male* hormone testosterone produces muscle size and the higher percentage of body fat found in females masks muscular development.

Types of Resistance Equipment (7 minutes)

Choosing which equipment works best will vary from person to person. Remember that results from weight training only occur after a consistent commitment of time and effort. All resistance equipment works upon the overload principle, which requires working a muscle against a resistance (weight load) that is greater than normally encountered. It doesn't really matter which type of workout equipment is chosen—doing either push-ups or bench pressing will influence changes in strength and muscle size. Strength development in military personnel is based on this theory.

Workouts should not be performed daily, but rather every other day. During your workout you are tearing down muscle tissue. A day of rest enables your body to build muscle tissue. Only work specific muscles on alternate days. It is also important to eat well. Here are some advantages of two types of equipment, free weights and machines.

Free Weights

Most clubs and gyms have free-weight equipment. Many people also own their own free-weight equipment. Barbells, dumbbells, benches, and squat racks are the apparatus. The benefits of free weights include flexibility and accessibility. Free weights enable one to perform a greater variety of exercises, and not limit exercises to the prescribed motion of the machines. The amount of resistance used with free weights may be modified in smaller increments than those of machines, lessening the chances of injury that could result from lifting too much weight. Most people who are serious about weight training, such as football players and professional bodybuilders, use free weights.

Machine Weights

The most popular resistance machines today are Nautilus, Omni, and Universal. Resistance machines are effective, but are usually available only at fitness centers or through campus recreation departments. The advantages of using machines are that an exercise circuit is set up for you, providing a good variety of activities, and machines allow for quick change of exercise load, simply by moving the key.

Warm-Up: Worth the Time
(3 minutes)

A warm-up period of 5 to 10 minutes will prepare the body for the strenuous task of weight lifting and reduce the chance of injury. Your warm-up must be activity-specific. Concentrate warm-up activities on muscles and joints that will be used during the workout. For example, to warm up for the military press (shoulder), do arm circles; for toe rises (calf), try the wall stretch with straight legs.

A warm-up should include stretching exercises that get muscles and joints ready for activity as well as improve flexibility. Some good stretches are the anterior thigh stretch, the heel-cord stretch, and the lotus stretch. The warm-up should be intense enough to increase your heart rate and ventilation rate above resting conditions.

Designing a Workout Routine
(8 minutes)

Work large muscles first, then move toward the extremities. If the small muscle groups of the extremities were used first, it would be difficult to hold the heavy weight (fatigue) needed to properly exercise (stress) the large muscle groups. Here is the process for the upper torso, including the muscle exercised and the type of exercise to perform.

1. Chest (pectoralis major)—bench press
2. Trapezius (shoulder-neck)—military press
3. Deltoids (shoulder)—military press
4. Biceps—curls
5. Triceps—forearm extensions
6. Forearms—wrist curls

The same concept applies to the lower body. Remember all muscular areas need to be developed and/or maintained. Don't become disproportioned. Exercise all major areas and muscle groups to get a complete and balanced workout. Your exercise routine should be individualized according to your needs. These will differ from person to person. Be sure to write down your exercise routine because your workouts will be more consistent, and you can chart your progress.

Exercises for Bodybuilders
(10 minutes)

Free weights allow for a greater variety of exercises and allow the lifter to isolate specific muscles. However, some exercises can only be performed on machines. For example, a pulley system is used for pull-downs because the latissimus dorsi muscle contracts (standing position) in the same direction as gravity.

When performing the exercises, keep these guidelines in mind:

- Focus on stance, grip, and form. Take time to prepare yourself before lifting to prevent injury.
- Go through the full range of motion; exercise the total muscle.
- Breathe through the power phase. Air movement is necessary during the power phase of the lift to lessen the pressure on the thoracic cavity; simply talking or counting the repetition number out loud will accomplish this.
- With free weights, have someone spot for you. Have the spotter in a good, ready stance to assist you and to prevent weight from falling.

To involve participants in learning exercises common to most bodybuilding routines, use the following protocol:

1. Review all exercises.
2. Identify the exercise.
3. Perform the exercise (light resistance).
4. Identify the muscles involved.
5. Instruct on proper spotting techniques.

Each weight-lifting activity listed here is followed by the area of the body that will be affected. (This would make an excellent poster.)

- Bench press—chest, shoulders, arms
- Military press—shoulders (deltoids, trapezius), arms
- Rowing—upper back, shoulders
- Squats—thighs, quadriceps, buttocks
- Pull-downs—latissmus dorsi (lats)
- Forearm extensions—triceps
- Calf rise—calves
- Leg extension—quadriceps
- Curls—biceps
- Bent leg sit-ups—abdominal muscles
- Hyperextensions—back muscles

Set up a training circuit and have participants perform each exercise using light resistance. Supervise by providing assistance and correcting faults.

Duration, Intensity, and Frequency (4 minutes)

Remind participants that just as reasons for weight lifting vary widely from person to person, so do training techniques; however, the following tips can be used as general guidelines. For strength or muscle size, set the weight at maximal resistance for five to eight repetitions. You should feel fatigued after the eighth repetition. Perform three to five sets with a minimum of 2 minutes' rest between each set. For endurance, set at maximal resistance for 10 to 15 repetitions. Perform three sets with a minimum of 2 minutes' rest between sets.

How do you determine intensity? For strength—calculate 80% of the value of one repetition at maximal effort. To determine maximal effort, try each weight until you find one that you can only lift once, then take 80% of that weight. For endurance—calculate 40-50% of the value of one repetition at maximal effort. (Determine maximal effort the same as above.) Be sure to warm up properly. While determining maximal effort with free weights, use a spotter. Maximal strength must be determined for each exercise. Proper frequency is best (three to four times per week, preferably every other day), alternating the muscle groups exercised.

Tips for Bodybuilding (3 minutes)

Here are a few tips you can share with the workshop participants. Urge them to set goals. Time guidelines for setting goals follow.

- Long-term goals—3 to 6 months
- Short-term goals—10 days to 2 weeks
- Once you stop weight training, your muscles will naturally atrophy (get smaller and weaker) according to the current level of use. The atrophying process generally takes as long as the developmental process.

Train with a friend so that you can motivate each other. Train consistently, sticking to a scheduled workout routine. Spot for each other and keep workouts short. Don't waste time—during your rest periods, spot for your partner.

Don't forget that variety can be the spice of working out. Here are a few ways to vary your routine:

- Take a week off and come back strong and rested.
- Use different equipment; for example, switch from free weights to machines.
- Once in a while, try an endurance workout instead of a normal strength workout.

- Include a variety of exercises in your program to prevent burnout.
- Listen to music while you work out.

Calisthenic-Style Resistance Training (10 minutes)

This type of training does not use weights or equipment. You may wish to demonstrate both the push-ups and the abdominal workout yourself or choose a volunteer to demonstrate. This is a list of various types of push-ups:

- Military-style push-ups—hands shoulder-width apart, palms on the floor.
- Make fists with knuckles on floor (strengthens wrists).
- Military-style but place palms one hand-width laterally from body.
- Repeat previous exercise, but spread palms one additional hand-width laterally.
- Place palms under chest with thumbs and index fingers touching (fingers forming a triangle).
- First balance on toes, then on knees (changes your resistance and builds endurance).
- Chair push-ups—allows greater extension (greater stretch of chest muscles). Both hands and feet are located on the seat of a chair, which are arranged to allow normal push-up (T position) action. Three chairs are used.

This is a list of various types of abdominal exercises:

- Regular military-style sit-up—Knees bent, hands behind your head; go through the complete range of motion (head up to knees, then all the way back to the floor).
- Curl-up—Start in sit-up position but raise only your head and shoulders (shoulder blades) off the floor, curling halfway up. Knees should be bent, soles of feet flat on the floor. This is

a better exercise than regular sit-ups for people with back problems.

- Knee lifts—Start in sit-up position, with soles of feet on the floor and knees bent; allowing feet to leave the floor, raise knees toward chin so thighs touch chest (as if tucking body into a ball). Lower legs until soles again touch the floor.
- Downers—Like a regular sit-up, but go only halfway back down toward floor, stop, and raise body back up, bringing head to knees.
- V-sits—Raise legs and shoulder simultaneously to form a V-shape with the body.
- Hyperextensions—Usually performed sitting on a bench that allows you to fall back slowly so that shoulders are closer to floor than hips (hyperextended position), with feet locked under a fixture. Extend past 0° to stretch abdominals fully, coming up to 30° past horizontal only.
- Leg lifts—Hanging from a bar (overhand grip), raise straight legs until toes touch fingers. This advanced activity requires considerable abdominal strength.

Conclusion and Evaluation (5 minutes)

Summarize the main points of the workshop:

- Bodybuilding programs should be personalized.
- Choose specific exercises and isolate specific areas of the body.
- Bodybuilding can be accomplished without weight training equipment.

Ask for questions from the participants. Offer resources and referrals for further information. Distribute Lifestyle Workshop evaluation forms and pencils. Allow time for completion and then collect. Briefly list and describe the other Lifestyle Workshops in Fitness.

MOST FREQUENTLY ASKED QUESTIONS

1. *What is a good starting weight for weight lifting exercises?*

When starting out, go slowly using moderate weight. Doing too much too soon will make your body sore 24 to 48 hours later. Beginning weight should be relatively light to moderate (less than 50% of maximal strength). Stay at this weight for the first three or four workouts, to allow your body to adjust to this new physical stress.

2. *How long should you wait to exercise after an injury?*

This will depend on the severity of the injury, but it is best to consult a physician or athletic trainer. The major risk concerning an injury is working out too soon or with too much intensity. Rehabilitation should involve range of motion with very little resistance.

3. *How long does it take before a noticeable difference in strength and size occurs?*

The overload principle applies to this question. Placing a greater stress than normal on the body causes the body to respond by slowly adapting to that stress. It takes a minimum of 14 to 28 days to notice a difference in size. Strength changes may occur sooner, which may be due to increased neural recruitment. There will be considerable difference between individuals because of genetic traits and muscle fiber composition.

4. *Do steroids really work?*

Current literature on this issue is inconclusive. Although many people (football players, bodybuilders) use steroids, the side effects may be hazardous to good health. Steroids may benefit experienced weight lifters, but are not appropriate for beginners, who still have room for improvement.

5. *Is strength related to muscle size?*

Yes. Strength, which is the ability to generate force, is directly related to the cross-sectional area of the muscle (size). Thus, larger muscles are generally stronger. There are exceptions, dependent on genetics, muscle fiber types, and motor unit recruitment.

6. *Can I lose weight (fat weight) by lifting weights?*

Fat is stored energy. One pound of fat is equivalent to 3,500 kcal. This is roughly worth 35 miles of jogging. Weight lifting is an intense exercise of short duration that burns carbohydrates as the major source of fuel. Thus, weight lifting is not a desirable method of losing fat stores (fat weight).

7. *Why do I get sore two days after weight lifting? What can I do to prevent this?*

Soreness after lifting weights is due to the breakdown of muscle and connective tissue. Doing too much too soon may be one reason for soreness and may be the result of doing new exercises or using too much stress in existing exercises. To prevent muscle soreness, perform less strenuous workouts.

8. *How often should I lift weights?*

Do not lift weights more often than every other day for each muscle group. Sometimes weight lifters work upper body muscles one day and exercise lower body muscles the next day.

9. *How often should I increase my training weight?*

The amount of resistance can usually be increased after three to five sets of 3 to 15 repetitions can be performed successfully. The ability to lift more weight will come in alternating phases of increase and maintenance, which may vary in length. A staircase illustration would make an excellent visual aid.

Weight Training and Nutrition

I already run; why should I start weight training?

Weight training causes an increase in strength. Strength is defined as the muscle's ability to exert force against a resistance. Although it is an important component in an athlete's training program, it is also important to people involved in the activities of daily life, such as sitting, walking, lifting, or being involved in recreational activities and sports. Strong muscles aid in making the body more efficient and less prone to injuries. Following a program of progressive resistance is the most effective means of increasing strength.

What happens when a person begins a weight training program?

A basic principle of any physical fitness program is to *safely* overload the body in order for improvement to occur. By giving specific muscle groups a greater load than they are accustomed to, adaptations will take place, causing adjustment in the form of increased strength. Weight training causes specific muscle fiber types (fast twitch) to increase in size, which results in the increased cross-sectional area of individual muscle cells—this is called hypertrophy (a decrease in the size of a muscle cell is called atrophy).

Nervous System: Other factors also improve, such as increased transmission of neuromuscular impulses to the working muscle groups, increased number of muscle fibers recruited at the same time, and longer tonic activity, which enhances muscle tone.

Biochemical Factors: Weight training also produces some biochemical changes within the muscle cells. Creatine phosphate (CP) and adenosine triphosphate (ATP) are energy-rich compounds stored in the muscle cells. When these compounds are broken down, a large amount of energy required for muscular contraction is released. These compounds have been noted to increase in response to a weight training program.

What kinds of changes occur in body composition?

Weight training is considered an anaerobic activity—meaning that it is high intensity work, short duration, works specific muscle groups, and relies mainly on carbohydrates to fuel the activity. Weight training uses 5-12 calories per minute, depending upon your weight, body composition, and fitness level. It has been shown to increase lean body mass (muscle mass), with little or no change in body weight. Fat weight or percent fat has been shown to decrease in response to a weight training program. However, it is important to note that greatest changes in body fat come from programs that combine aerobic activity and dietary modification. Aerobic metabolism requires oxygen, uses large muscle groups, is lower intensity but longer in duration, and relies mainly on carbohydrates and fat. The longer the activity continues, the greater the dependence on fat for the activity.

What is the most important food or drink to consume after a strenuous workout?

After a strenuous workout, it is most important to replace the fluid that has been lost through sweating. Cool water is best as it is more quickly absorbed than warm water and is also more cooling. Juices would be the second choice. The less sugar in a juice, the quicker it can be absorbed. Dilute sugared juice drinks with five parts water to increase their absorption rate.

Weight lost from strenuous exercise is water weight—replace each pound of weight lost with 1 pint of fluid. Dehydration is a common response to a strenuous workout and can affect or impair performance. Rehydration requires 1-2 days to be completed and can be determined by the color of the urine. Adequate hydration causes the urine to be clear-colored and plentiful, as opposed to dark-colored and infrequent.

Although beer is a popular choice for postexercise consumption, it will cause further dehydration by inhibiting the release of the hormone which holds water in the body. Water is by far the best choice after exercise.

I'm starting a weight training program. Do I need to include extra protein in my diet?

Although some extra protein is needed to build muscle tissue, it is doubtful that you need to eat more protein; the typical American diet already supplies more than an ample amount. Meat, fish, poultry, eggs, dairy products, legumes, breads, cereals, and vegetables all contribute protein in varying amounts. To determine a desirable daily protein intake, multiply your weight in pounds by 0.4 to 0.45 grams. For example, a 150-pound weight trainer needs approximately 60 to 68 grams of protein per day. This could be obtained by eating 3 ounces of meat, fish, or poultry (21 grams), 1 cup baked beans (13 grams), 2 cups of milk (9 grams each), and four slices of whole wheat bread (2-3 grams per slice).

Development of muscle mass is dependent on proper exercise and conditioning, not on high protein diets. Any amount of protein eaten over the body's actual needs will be converted to an energy source or stored as body fat. In addition, large intakes of protein can put unnecessary stress on the kidneys and lead to dehydration.

Should I take a vitamin/mineral supplement?

Supplementation is usually not necessary if your diet contains a variety of foods: dairy products, meat, fish, poultry, legumes, fruits, vegetables, breads, and cereals. By taking your nutrients in pill form, it is possible to overdose. Excessive intake of some nutrients can interfere with absorption/metabolism of other nutrients and may sometimes produce serious toxic effects. If you are determined to take a supplement, read the product label carefully before you buy! Choose one that contains a variety of vitamins and minerals in amounts no greater than 100% of your RDA (Recommended Dietary Allowance).

For more information, consult the following publications:

Clark, N. (1981). *The athlete's kitchen: A nutrition guide and cookbook.* Boston: C.B.I.

Flesson, J.L. (1985). *Weight training for life.* Inglewood, CO: Morton.

Fox, E.L. (1984). *Sports physiology.* Philadelphia: Saunders.

Haskell, W., Scala, J., & Whittam, J. (Eds). (1982). *Nutrition and athletic performance.* Palo Alto, CA: Bull.

McArdle, W.D., Katch, F.I., & Katch, V.L. (1981). *Exercise physiology: Energy, nutrition and human performance.* Philadelphia: Lea & Febiger.

Natow, A., & Heslin, J. (1981). *Megadoses: Vitamins as drugs.* New York: Pocket Books.

REFERENCES

Bucher, C.A., & Prentice, W.E. (1985). *Fitness for college and life*. St. Louis: Times Mirror/Mosby.

Heyward, V.H. (1986). *Designs for fitness: A guide to physical fitness appraisal and exercise prescription*. Minneapolis: Burgess.

Rosato, F.D. (1986). *Fitness and wellness: The physical connection*. New York: West.

Sharkey, B.J. (1984). *Physiology of fitness*. Champaign, IL: Human Kinetics.

Fat Assessment and Weight Management Lifestyle Workshop

PARAPROFESSIONAL PREPARATION MATERIALS

Training Sessions

Competency Exam

Texts and Suggested Readings

WORKSHOP AT A GLANCE

Presenter Information

Most Frequently Asked Questions

Handouts and Visual Aids*

References

---

*The *Body Composition Form* was written by Bruce Elmore, MS. The *Fast Food Calorie Counter* was compiled by Judy Simon, RD; Sara Kelley, MS, RD; and Michele Easterling, MPH, RD.

TRAINING SESSIONS

Fat Assessment and Weight Management

Session 1: Workshop Presentation

Time: 60 minutes

Methods: Presentation, demonstration

Description: Trainer presents workshop to Lifestyle Educators.

Activity: Trainer presents workshop to Lifestyle Educators.

Readings: The workshop

For next session participants should wear T-shirts and shorts.

Session 2: Skinfold Measurements and Calculating Percent Fat

Time: 60 minutes

Methods: Demonstration, discussion, participation

Description: Skinfold techniques

Activity: Skinfold technique is explained and demonstrated by coordinator. Students will then practice on each other, assisted by trainer. Introduce and use Body Composition Form and Calculation Tables. Normative values for percent fat will be discussed.

Readings: The workshop material addressing the assessment of body composition using skinfold data.

Competency exam questions: 1, 2, 3, 4, 5, 6, 7, 8, 9, 10, 11, 12

Session 3: Skinfold Technique, Basal Metabolic Rate (BMR)

Time: 60 minutes

Methods: Practice, lecture, discussion

Description: Skinfold measurement is reviewed. Basal Metabolic Rate is presented and calculated; and particularly relevant influential variables discussed.

Activity: Review skinfold technique. Students will practice the proper technique on each other. Each student will calculate their BMR using the BMR handout.

Readings: The workshop, material for the review of basal metabolism

Competency exam questions: 13, 14

Session 4: Diet and Exercise

Time: 60 minutes

Methods: Lecture, discussion

Description: Discuss the roles diet and exercise have, both combined and separate, in weight management. Review how fat cells develop.

Activity: Each Lifestyle Educator brings in one fat diet plan with a critique.

Readings: Nutrition and weight loss material that emphasize the diet-exercise connection

Competency exam questions: 15, 16, 17, 18, 19 20

Session 5: "Most Frequently Asked Questions" Review and Hot Seat

Time: 60 minutes

Methods: Discussion, practice

Description: Review components of workshop.

Activity: Hot Seat: Each Lifestyle Educator is quizzed by the other students on the workshop topic for 10 minutes.

Session 6: Practice Workshop Presentation

Time: 60 minutes

Method: Presentation (videotape presentation)

Description: Each Lifestyle Educator presents 20 minutes of the workshop.

Readings: The workshop

COMPETENCY EXAM

The following questions require short essay responses.

1. Explain the theory for using skinfolds to assess body fatness.

2. Explain the proper technique for measuring skinfolds.

The following are True/False questions. Check the appropriate blanks.

True   **False**

_____   _____   3. The skinfold caliper directly measures body fatness.

_____   _____   4. The skinfold equations are similar for both males and females but differ according to age.

_____   _____   5. Obesity is a health problem that is genetic in origin and nothing but exercise will correct it.

_____   _____   6. Subcutaneous fat is proportional to total body fat.

_____   _____   7. Fatter people have larger skinfold values.

_____   _____   8. Using skinfolds gives a participant his or her true percent body fat.

_____   _____   9. Measurements should be taken more than once to reduce error and to get a more accurate value.

_____   _____   10. Not eating a meal or drinking fluids at least 4 hours before measuring skinfolds will alter one's percent fat.

_____   _____   11. An athlete should strive to attain a level of minimal percent fat for optimal performance.

_____   _____   12. The normative values given in the program are specifically designed for college-age participants and are not valid in other samples.

The following questions require brief responses.

13. Define Basal Metabolic Rate (BMR):

14. To calculate BMR, four factors are involved. Identify each factor and briefly explain how each one influences BMR.

15. Explain the fallacy of spot reduction and include an example.

16. Provide three reasons why exercise is necessary for good health.

17. Plan your exercise prescription for losing fat weight, including the following factors: frequency, intensity, time, type of activity.

18. Diagram the three energy balance equations and label each.

19. Negative balance (weight loss) is the result of three possibilities. Explain the possibilities.

20. How long will it take you to lose 10 pounds of fat by restricting your diet (_____ kcal/day) and exercising (_____ kcal/day)? Choose the energy values and determine the time commitment involved.

21. Suggest possible techniques to use in the workshop if participant is one of the following:
    • Recognition Seeker (frequently calls attention to self)
    • Conversationalist (brings up off-the-subject anecdotes and is a noisy distraction)
    • Moralizer (advocates judgmental points of view based on personal convictions)
    • Conservative (convinced that the status quo does not need changing)

TEXTS AND SUGGESTED READINGS

Allsen, P.E., Harrison, J.M., & Vance, B. (1984). *Fitness for life: An individualized approach*. Dubuque, IA: Brown.

Bucher, C.A., & Prentice, W.E. (1985). *Fitness for college and life*. St. Louis: Times Mirror/Mosby.

Falls, H.B., Baylor, A.M., & Dishman, R. (1980). *Essentials of fitness*. Philadelphia: Saunders College.

Katch, F., & McArdle, W. (1977). *Nutrition, weight control and exercise*. Boston: Houghton-Mifflin.

Katch, V., & Katch, F. (1986, April). Success! Those incredible shrinking women. *Shape*, pp. 60-63.

Oscai, L. (1973). Role of exercise in weight control. *Exercise and Sport Science Reviews*, **1**, 103-123.

Sharkey, B.J. (1984). *Physiology of fitness*. Champaign, IL: Human Kinetics.

WORKSHOP AT A GLANCE

The goal of this workshop is to assess and evaluate an individual's percent fat, with a follow-up discussion concentrating on factors that influence weight management, primarily diet and exercise. This workshop takes approximately 60 minutes to present. Suggested attendance is 5 to 20 persons.

Objectives

Within the content of the workshop, the following objectives will be met.

- Each participant's body composition (percent body fat, ideal body weight, and fat-free body weight) will be estimated using the skinfold caliper technique.
- Using the "Calculating Basal Metabolic Rate" handout, participants will calculate an estimate of their Basal Metabolic Rate.
- The benefits of exercise, both alone and combined with caloric restriction for the purpose of weight management, will be discussed.

Workshop Materials

- Workshop sign-in sheet
- Handouts and visual aids: *Body Composition Form, Percent Body Fat Norms Table, Calculating Basal Metabolic Rate, Fast Food Calorie Counter,* and *Comparable Aerobic Exercise Table*
- Skinfold caliper
- Body Fat Calculation Tables (Appendix A)
- Calculator
- Lifestyle Workshop evaluation forms and pencils

Note. Request that participants wear T-shirts and shorts or sweatpants.

PRESENTER INFORMATION

Briefly introduce yourself, your background, and any other personal information you choose to share. Describe your health promotion program and the topics available; for example, fitness and nutrition. Stress that the workshops are unique because you bring them to their living areas. Tell them that Lifestyle Workshop paraprofessionals are trained by (your institution or program) to present the workshops. If anyone is interested in the training program, ask him or her to speak with you after the workshop.

This workshop will offer an estimation of percent fat for all willing participants, with further calculations to determine ideal body weight. We will discuss factors that affect weight management, such as basal metabolic rate, diet, exercise, and the benefits of combining exercise and caloric restriction.

Fat Assessment and Evaluation (25 minutes)

Explain that percent body fat is the amount of fat in the body, expressed as a percentage of the total body weight. The amount of fat is assessed by using skinfold calipers at selected sites of the body and then putting these values into a predetermined equation to get an estimate of percent body fat. It is the best procedure next to underwater weighing or hydrostatic weighing. There is a layer of fat located underneath the skin (subcutaneous fat) that is proportional to total body fat. The thickness of skinfolds reflect the percentage of body fat.

Skinfold Measurement

Perform the skinfold measurements at the equation-specific sites (see Fat Assessment Procedure, Appendix A), taking three measurements per site. Two body fat equations will be utilized (regardless of gender), the Durnin & Womersley (D & W) equation, and the Pollack, Schmidt, and Jackson (P, S, & J) equation. An average of the two equations is used to determine percent body fat. Select one person to record the skinfold values on the Body Composition Form (see handouts and visual aids section).

Have each participant average the three trial measurement figures for each site and total them.

Collect Body Composition Forms and calculate percent fat estimates using Body Fat Calculation Tables (Appendix A). Be sure to use the proper table with each average mean. The average percent fat of the two equations, D & W and P, S, & J, is the percent body fat estimate recorded on the form. Return forms and assure confidentiality. Review norms of percent fat for selected samples (see handouts and visual aids).

Factors Influencing Percent Body Fat

The genes one receives from parents play a large role in determining one's physical makeup. Genetics does influence body composition, although the dynamics of the relationship are not clearly understood. To illustrate this, ask one small-framed and one large-framed individual if his or her physique is similar to one or both parents. Point out that when both parents are obese, the child has an 80% risk of obesity (Sharkey, 1984). The next step is to show that even though genetics plays a part in obesity, it is not the whole story. Active people, especially those involved in aerobic activities, generally have a lower percent fat. For example, athletes are usually leaner because regimented exercise programs force these individuals to be more active. Another aspect is an individual's diet. Calories and food choices do count.

Home environment will influence one's activity pattern and affect the caloric and nutrient value of the food one consumes. For example, college students living in university housing are quite restricted in the choices of food available, though some flexibility in the menu may be provided. Have participants calculate and write down the rest of the body composition data on the Body Composition Form (use calculators). Participants now have a hard copy of personalized information. Presenter should assist persons having difficulty performing the calculations. Using the information in Table 1, inform participants about where they fall in the percent body fat norms.

Table 1 Percent Body Fat Norms

Sample group	Men (20-24 yrs)	Women (20-24 yrs)
Ideal	15%	25%
Athlete	5-15%	12-22%
Essential	5%	12%
Obesity	> 25%	> 35%
Optimal range (health)	10-25%	18-33%

Weight Management (25 minutes)

Now that estimated percent body fat has been determined and participants have an idea of where they fall in the norms, determine how many calories one needs to function according to height and weight. Basal Metabolic Rate or BMR reflects the minimum amount of energy required to sustain the body's vital functions at rest. BMR is the number of calories expended solely in response to resting metabolic activity of the body. Because able-bodied people are not completely sedentary during the day, one's total daily energy expenditure is greater than one's BMR. Any physical activity one undertakes affects this difference, whether it is getting up to change channels on the television or performing a structured exercise workout. Hand out "Calculating Basal Metabolic Rate" and take the group through these steps:

1. Estimate body surface area (item 1) using participant's height and weight. Use a straight-edge as needed to perform the calculation.
2. Determine BMR factor (item 2) based on age and sex.
3. Multiply estimated body surface area by BMR factor to get BMR: (item 1) × (item 2) = BMR. This value is the number of calories the body uses for 1 hour under resting conditions.
4. Multiply your hourly BMR by 24 to estimate basal metabolic needs for one day: (item 3) × 24 = basal metabolic needs for one day.

Ask volunteers to state their BMRs. From the group, choose one large and one small participant (or male and female) to point out how age, gender, and size (height and weight) influence BMR.

Age and BMR

With increasing age, an individual's BMR naturally decreases. This doesn't mean much now, but if you keep eating the same number of calories with no change in activity level, you will gain weight (fat weight) as the result of a slower metabolism. To counteract this natural aging phenomenon, either be more active, take in fewer calories, or combine both approaches.

Gender and BMR

Males have greater BMRs than females, which is basically the result of greater size and larger percentage of lean body mass. A muscular individual will have a higher BMR than a person of the same body weight but more fat, because muscle tissue is metabolically more active than fat tissue.

Size and BMR

Large persons will have greater resting energy expenditures than small persons. Tall persons have greater BMRs than do short persons (if weight is constant). People who weigh more have greater BMRs.

Physical activity has a pronounced effect on total daily energy expenditure. One's BMR is relatively stable, and day-to-day fluctuations in total caloric expenditure are directly related to the amount of activity one undertakes. The preferred activity for weight loss is aerobic exercise, which has the following characteristics:

- It uses large muscle groups (e.g., hamstrings and quadriceps).
- It is rhythmic in nature (e.g., running, cycling, swimming).
- It is sustained for more than 20 minutes.
- It increases both heart rate and ventilation rate and may cause the person to work up a sweat.

Dieting for Weight Management

You may want to present this material in the following manner: Diets rarely work—diets usually don't last and only a small percentage of all dieters keep the weight off. Ask the participants, "How many have attempted weight loss by dieting?" Have the participants answer by raising their hands. Next ask, "How long did you diet? One day? Two days? Four days? One week? Two weeks? One month?" (Show by raising hands.) Finally, ask, "How many lost weight and kept the weight off?" (Show by raising hands.) Generally, diets don't work because people return to their previous eating habits.

Dieting is one method of controlling the energy balance of the body; it simply reduces the number of calories going in. Energy is then liberated from within body stores, both from carbohydrates and fat, when needed. Hand out the "Fast Food Calorie Counter." Have the participants recall their last meal at one of the eateries listed on the handout, then have each participant calculate an estimate of calories consumed in that meal.

Exercising for Weight Management

People tend to believe they can lose weight in certain places, such as the stomach or thighs. Unfortunately, spot reduction is a fallacy. Fat is stored energy, deposited both subcutaneously and internally (surrounding the major organs). Muscles need energy to contract. First energy is supplied by carbohydrates, and as the activity continues, a greater percentage of energy is derived from fat stored all over the body.

Note. Trained distance runners have very little fat, especially around the midsection (stomach and thighs). This is not from doing sit-ups, but because runners engage in intense training, burning a lot of calories. Even though the leg muscles are the active muscles, energy is obtained from fat stored in all parts of the body.

Present the poster "Where Fat Comes Off" (see handouts and visual aids) depicting areas of fat loss in obese women. The women were measured only after losing 5 pounds of body weight. The amount of fat lost in the trunk region was twice that lost in the extremities, which indicates that there is no way to speed up fat loss at a given body site. Exercise helps to prevent the loss of lean tissue and to mobilize fats; in other words, weight loss should be from fat weight, not muscle or water weight. Examine the Comparable Aerobic Exercise Table (see handouts and visual aids). People will burn a different number of calories depending on their weight and height. This chart shows the same person performing different exercises and burning the same amount of calories.

These activities burn the same amount of calories but require 12, 15, or 20 minutes. In other words, slower activities require more time to burn the same amount of calories as faster activities.

Another benefit of exercising is that it adds up—300 calories kcal/day from exercise, 4 days per week results in 1,200 kcal/week in energy expended, and 3,500 kcal is equal to 1 pound of fat. And, of course, if you're not motivated by other reasons, exercise is healthy! You will maintain and improve your fitness and health level. You will feel better physically and mentally, because you are doing something good for yourself! And best of all for those of us with very busy lives, exercise aids in stress reduction. This is an exercise program outline that will benefit your cardiovascular system as well as your weight management program.

- Frequency: 3 to 5 days per week
- Intensity: Greater than 50% of Predicted Maximal Heart Rate (PMHR). PMHR = 220 – age.
- Time: Longer than 20 minutes at PMHR for each episode
- Type of activity: Aerobic (with oxygen), using large muscle groups rhythmically.

Note. The equation for PMHR determines heartbeat accuracy (± 10) without requiring that the subject be taken to exhaustion. (The only way to get a true maximal heart rate is through a maximal exercise test.)

These are a few suggestions for making exercise more pleasant.

- Start slowly.
- Set challenging but attainable goals.
- Change type of activity periodically to prevent boredom.
- Exercise with a friend or in a group.
- Choose an exercise that you like . . . one that fits into your lifestyle.

This example of calories restricted and expended can be shown and explained to the group.

1. If you make a 300 kcal/day restriction + 200 kcal/day expenditure through exercise for 500 kcal/day total reduction, then a
2. 500 kcal/day × 7 days/wk = 3,500 kcal/wk reduction, and
3. 3,500 kcal = 1 pound of fat lost over 1 week

The best approach for weight management is to combine moderate caloric restriction with moderate physical activity. By sticking to a moderate plan, proper nutrition is maintained and exercising is achievable.

Conclusion and Evaluation (5 minutes)

Summarize the main points of the workshop.

- Your percent fat has been measured by a trained technician using skinfold caliper.

- Your basal metabolic rate is related to your size (weight and height), age, and gender.
- The best and safest means for fat weight loss is moderate caloric restriction combined with increased activity.

Ask for questions from the participants. Offer resources and referrals for further information. Distribute Lifestyle Workshop evaluation forms and pencils. Allow time for completion and then collect. Briefly list and describe the other Lifestyle Workshops in Fitness.

APPENDIX A

Fat Assessment

The information provided in Appendix A details proper skinfold techniques and the specific measurement sites used in each skinfold equation. The equation-specific tables needed for determining the percent body fat are also included.

The Skinfold Measuring Method

The proper method for measuring skinfolds is as follows:

1. Firmly grasp the skinfold between the thumb and forefinger and lift up. The subject should not experience pain.
2. Place the contact surfaces of the caliper 1 cm (1/2 inch) above or below the fingers (depth equal to thickness of fold).
3. Slowly release the grip on the calipers, enabling tongs to exert their full (natural) tension on the skinfold.
4. Read skinfold to nearest 0.5 mm after needle stops (1 to 2 seconds after releasing grip on caliper). The skinfold measurement is registered on the dial of the caliper.

Note that the caliper is not to be placed at the base of the skinfold. The correct distance for measurement is approximately midway between the crest and the base of the skinfold.

If repeated measurements vary by more than 1-2 mm, a third measurement should be taken.

Skinfold thickness should be measured separately for each individual without comment or display. Each participant has the right to share or withhold the results of the test. In all cases, interpretation of results should be given individually.

Note that on occasion, one can grasp a fold and include muscle as well as fat. By having the participant contract the muscle, one can feel the muscle pull away. In that case, a new skinfold measurement should be taken.

Skinfold Sites

Body composition is an important component in sports performance, physical fitness, and health. Determining lean body mass or fat weight in the laboratory setting is usually accomplished through hydrostatic weighing. Since it is not always practical or feasible to use this technique, skinfold calipers and equations were developed to serve as a field method for estimating percent body fat.

Research in the area of body composition indicates that averaging the Durnin and Womersley equations with the Pollack, Schmidt, and Jackson equations most closely matches the results of underwater weighing. Therefore the Fat Assessment and Weight Management Lifestyle Workshop uses the mean of the equations as the estimate of percent fat for the workshop participant.

The Durnin and Womersley Sites

The skinfold sites for Durnin and Womersley (1974) for both males and females are these:

- Triceps—locate a point halfway between the bony part of the shoulder and the tip of the elbow. Measure the skinfold with the arm relaxed and hanging in extension.
- Biceps—locate a point halfway between the armpit and the elbow joint. Measure the skinfold with the arm relaxed and hanging in extension.

- Iliac crest—measure the skinfold over the iliac crest (hip) at the midaxillary line (middle of armpit). Measure fold vertically.
- Subscapula—skinfold is taken at the tip of the scapula (shoulder blade) on a diagonal.

The Pollack, Schmidt, and Jackson Sites

The skinfold sites for the Pollack, Schmidt, and Jackson (1980) equation for *females* are triceps, suprailium, and thigh:

- Triceps—measure the fold vertically on the posterior midline of upper arm, halfway between shoulder and elbow with elbow extended and relaxed.
- Suprailium—measure the fold diagonally above crest of the ilium at the spot where an imaginary line would come down from the anterior axillary line.
- Thigh—measure the fold vertically on the anterior aspect of the thigh, midway between hip and knee joint.

The skinfold sites for the Pollack, Schmidt, and Jackson equation for *males* are chest, abdomen, and thigh:

- Chest—measure the fold diagonally, one-half the distance between axillary line and the nipple.
- Abdomen—take a vertical fold at a lateral distance of approximately 2 cm from the umbilicus.
- Thigh—measure the fold vertically on the anterior aspect of the thigh, midway between the hip and knee joints.

Proper use of the following table is critical in estimation of percent fat. Each table is author-specific, since a different group of skinfold sites are used. Also, Pollack, Schmidt, and Jackson have separate tables according to gender. To use the tables correctly, identify the appropriate table for author and gender, find the skinfold sum (in millimeters), and cross-reference that with participant's age to find percent body fat.

Body Fat Calculation Tables (Durnin and Womersley)

Skinfolds (mm)	Males (age in years)				Females (age in years)			
	17-29	30-39	40-49	50+	16-29	30-39	40-49	50+
15	4.8	—	—	—	10.5	—	—	—
20	8.1	12.2	12.2	12.6	14.1	17.0	19.8	21.4
25	10.5	14.2	15.0	15.6	16.8	19.4	22.2	24.0
30	12.9	16.2	17.7	18.6	19.5	21.8	24.5	26.6
35	14.7	17.7	19.6	20.8	21.5	23.7	26.4	28.5
40	16.4	19.2	21.4	22.9	23.4	25.5	28.2	30.3
45	17.7	20.4	23.0	24.7	25.0	26.9	29.6	31.9
50	19.0	21.5	24.6	26.5	26.5	28.2	31.0	33.4
55	20.1	22.5	25.9	27.9	27.8	29.4	32.1	34.6
60	21.2	23.5	27.1	29.2	29.1	30.6	33.2	35.7
65	22.2	24.3	28.2	30.4	30.2	31.6	34.1	36.7
70	23.1	25.1	29.3	31.6	31.2	32.5	35.0	37.7
75	24.0	25.9	30.3	32.7	32.2	33.4	35.9	38.7
80	24.8	26.6	31.2	33.8	33.1	34.3	36.7	39.6
85	25.5	27.2	32.1	34.8	34.0	35.1	37.5	40.4
90	26.2	27.8	33.0	35.8	34.8	35.8	38.3	41.2
95	26.9	28.4	33.7	36.6	35.6	36.5	39.0	41.9
100	27.6	29.0	34.4	37.4	36.4	37.2	39.7	42.6
105	28.2	29.6	35.1	38.2	37.1	37.9	40.4	43.3
110	28.8	30.1	35.8	39.0	37.8	38.6	41.0	43.9
115	29.4	30.6	36.4	39.7	38.4	39.1	41.5	44.5
120	30.0	31.1	37.0	40.4	39.0	39.6	42.0	45.1
125	30.5	31.5	37.6	41.1	39.6	40.1	42.5	45.7
130	31.0	31.9	38.2	41.8	40.2	40.6	43.0	46.2
135	31.5	32.3	38.7	42.4	40.8	41.1	43.5	46.7
140	32.0	32.7	39.2	43.0	41.3	41.6	44.0	47.2
145	32.5	33.1	39.7	43.6	41.8	42.1	44.5	47.7
150	32.9	33.5	40.2	44.1	42.3	42.6	45.0	48.2
155	33.3	33.9	40.7	44.6	42.8	43.1	45.4	48.7
160	33.7	34.3	41.2	45.1	43.3	43.6	45.8	49.2
165	34.1	34.6	41.6	45.6	43.7	44.0	46.2	49.6
170	34.5	34.8	42.0	46.1	44.1	44.4	46.6	50.0
175	34.9	—	—	—	—	44.8	47.0	50.4
180	35.3	—	—	—	—	45.2	47.4	50.8
185	35.6	—	—	—	—	45.6	47.8	51.2
190	35.9	—	—	—	—	45.9	48.2	51.6
195	—	—	—	—	—	46.2	48.5	52.0
200	—	—	—	—	—	46.5	48.8	52.4
205	—	—	—	—	—	—	49.1	52.7
210	—	—	—	—	—	—	49.4	53.0

Note. From ''Body fat assessed from total body density and its estimation from skinfold thickness: Measurements on 481 men and women aged 16-74 years'' by J. Durnin and J. Womersley, 1974, *British Journal of Nutrition, 32,* 95. Copyright 1974 by Cambridge University Press. Reprinted by permission of Cambridge University Press.

Percent Fat Estimates for Women, Sum of Triceps, Suprailium, and Thigh Skinfolds* (Pollack, Schmidt, and Jackson)

Sum of Skinfolds (mm)	Age to the last year								
	Under 22	23 to 27	28 to 32	33 to 37	38 to 42	43 to 47	48 to 52	53 to 57	Over 58
23-25	9.7	9.9	10.2	10.4	10.7	10.9	11.2	11.4	11.7
26-28	11.0	11.2	11.5	11.7	12.0	12.3	12.5	12.7	13.0
29-31	12.3	12.5	12.8	13.0	13.3	13.5	13.8	14.0	14.3
32-34	13.6	13.8	14.0	14.3	14.5	14.8	15.0	15.3	15.5
35-37	14.8	15.0	15.3	15.5	15.8	16.0	16.3	16.5	16.8
38-40	16.0	16.3	16.5	16.7	17.0	17.2	17.5	17.7	18.0
41-43	17.2	17.4	17.7	17.9	18.2	18.4	18.7	18.9	19.2
44-46	18.3	18.6	18.8	19.1	19.3	19.6	19.8	20.1	20.3
47-49	19.5	19.7	20.0	20.2	20.5	20.7	21.0	21.2	21.5
50-52	20.6	20.8	21.1	21.3	21.6	21.8	22.1	22.3	22.6
53-55	21.7	21.9	22.1	22.4	22.6	22.9	23.1	23.4	23.6
56-58	22.7	23.0	23.2	23.4	23.7	23.9	24.2	24.4	24.7
59-61	23.7	24.0	24.2	24.5	24.7	25.0	25.2	25.5	25.7
62-64	24.7	25.0	25.2	25.5	25.7	26.0	26.7	26.4	26.7
65-67	25.7	25.9	26.2	26.4	26.7	26.9	27.2	27.4	27.7
68-70	26.6	26.9	27.1	27.4	27.6	27.9	28.1	28.4	28.6
71-73	27.5	27.8	28.0	28.3	28.5	28.8	29.0	29.3	29.5
74-76	28.4	28.7	28.9	29.2	29.4	29.7	29.9	30.2	30.4
77-79	29.3	29.5	29.8	30.0	30.3	30.5	30.8	31.0	31.3
80-82	30.1	30.4	30.6	30.9	31.1	31.4	31.6	31.9	32.1
83-85	30.9	31.2	31.4	31.7	31.9	32.2	32.4	32.7	32.9
86-88	31.7	32.0	32.2	32.5	32.7	32.9	33.2	33.4	33.7
89-91	32.5	32.7	33.0	33.2	33.5	33.7	33.9	34.2	34.4
92-94	33.2	33.4	33.7	33.9	34.2	34.4	34.7	34.9	35.2
95-97	33.9	34.1	34.4	34.6	34.9	35.1	35.4	35.6	35.9
98-100	34.6	34.8	35.1	35.3	35.5	35.8	36.0	36.3	35.5
101-103	35.3	35.4	35.7	35.9	36.2	36.4	36.7	36.9	37.2
104-106	35.8	36.1	36.3	36.6	36.8	37.1	37.3	37.5	37.8
107-109	36.4	36.7	36.9	37.1	37.4	37.6	37.9	38.1	38.4
110-112	37.0	37.2	37.5	37.7	38.0	38.2	38.5	38.7	38.9
113-115	37.5	37.8	38.0	38.2	38.5	38.7	39.0	39.2	39.5
116-118	38.0	38.3	38.5	38.8	39.0	39.3	39.5	39.7	40.0
119-121	38.5	38.7	39.0	39.2	39.5	39.7	40.0	40.2	40.5
122-124	39.0	39.2	39.4	39.7	39.9	40.2	40.4	40.7	40.9
125-127	39.4	39.6	39.9	40.1	40.4	40.6	40.9	41.1	41.4
128-130	39.8	40.0	40.3	40.5	40.8	41.0	41.3	41.5	41.8

Note. From "Measurement of cardiorespiratory fitness and body composition in the clinical setting" by M. Pollack, D. Schmidt, and A. Jackson, 1980, *Comprehensive Therapy*, 6(9), 12-27. Copyright 1980 by Laux Co. Reprinted by permission of the Laux Company, Inc.

*Percent fat calculated by the formula of Siri. Percent fat = $[(4.95/BD) - 4.5] \times 100$, where BD = body density.

Percent Fat Estimates for Men, Sum of Chest, Abdominal, and Thigh Skinfolds*
(Pollack, Schmidt, and Jackson)

Sum of Skinfolds (mm)	Age to the last year								
	Under 22	23 to 27	28 to 32	33 to 37	38 to 42	43 to 47	48 to 52	53 to 57	Over 58
8-10	1.3	1.8	2.3	2.9	3.4	3.9	4.5	5.0	5.5
11-13	2.2	2.8	3.3	3.9	4.4	4.9	5.5	6.0	6.5
14-16	3.2	3.8	4.3	4.8	5.4	5.9	6.4	7.0	7.5
17-19	4.2	4.7	5.3	5.8	6.3	6.9	7.4	8.0	8.5
20-22	5.1	5.7	6.2	6.8	7.3	7.9	8.4	8.9	9.5
23-25	6.1	6.6	7.2	7.7	8.3	8.8	9.1	9.9	10.5
26-28	7.0	7.6	8.1	8.7	9.2	9.8	10.3	10.9	11.4
29-31	8.0	8.5	9.1	9.6	10.2	10.7	11.3	11.8	12.4
32-34	8.9	9.4	10.0	10.5	11.1	11.6	12.2	12.8	13.3
35-37	9.8	10.4	10.9	11.5	12.0	12.6	13.1	13.7	14.3
38-40	10.7	11.3	11.8	12.4	12.9	13.5	14.1	14.6	15.2
41-43	11.6	12.2	12.7	13.3	13.8	14.4	15.0	15.5	16.1
44-46	12.5	13.1	13.6	14.2	14.7	15.3	15.9	16.4	17.0
47-49	13.4	13.9	14.5	15.1	15.6	16.2	16.8	17.3	17.9
50-52	14.3	14.8	15.4	15.9	16.5	17.1	17.6	18.2	18.8
53-55	15.1	15.7	16.2	16.8	17.4	17.9	18.5	19.1	19.7
56-58	16.0	16.5	17.1	17.7	18.2	18.8	19.4	20.0	20.5
59-61	16.9	17.4	17.9	18.5	19.1	19.7	20.2	20.8	21.4
62-64	17.6	18.2	18.8	19.4	19.9	20.5	21.1	21.7	22.2
65-67	18.5	19.0	19.6	20.2	20.8	21.3	21.9	22.5	23.1
68-70	19.3	19.9	20.4	21.0	21.6	22.2	22.7	23.3	23.9
71-73	20.1	20.7	21.2	21.8	22.4	23.0	23.6	24.1	24.7
74-76	20.9	21.5	22.0	22.6	23.2	23.8	24.4	25.0	25.5
77-79	21.7	22.2	22.8	23.4	24.0	24.6	25.2	25.8	26.3
80-82	22.4	23.0	23.6	24.2	24.8	25.4	25.9	26.5	27.1
83-85	23.2	23.8	24.4	25.0	25.5	26.1	26.7	27.3	27.9
86-88	24.0	24.5	25.1	25.7	26.3	26.9	27.5	28.1	28.7
89-91	24.7	25.3	25.9	26.5	27.1	27.6	28.2	28.8	29.4
92-94	25.4	26.0	26.6	27.2	27.8	28.4	29.0	29.6	30.2
95-97	26.1	26.7	27.3	27.9	28.5	29.1	29.7	30.3	30.9
98-100	26.9	27.4	28.0	28.6	29.2	29.8	30.4	31.0	31.6
101-103	27.5	28.1	28.7	29.3	29.9	30.5	31.1	31.7	32.3
104-106	28.2	28.8	29.4	30.0	30.6	31.2	31.8	32.4	33.0
107-109	28.9	29.5	30.1	30.7	31.3	31.9	32.5	33.1	33.7
110-112	29.6	30.2	30.8	31.4	32.0	32.6	33.2	33.8	34.4
113-115	30.2	30.8	31.4	32.0	32.6	33.2	33.8	34.5	35.1
116-118	30.9	31.5	32.1	32.7	33.3	33.9	34.5	35.1	35.7
119-121	31.5	32.1	32.7	33.3	33.9	34.5	35.1	35.7	36.4
122-124	32.1	32.7	33.3	33.9	34.5	35.1	35.8	36.4	37.0
125-127	32.7	33.3	33.9	34.5	35.1	35.8	36.4	37.0	37.6

Note. From ''Measurement of cardiorespiratory fitness and body composition in the clinical setting'' by M. Pollack, D. Schmidt, and A. Jackson, 1980, *Comprehensive Therapy,* **6**(9), 12-27. Copyright 1980 by Laux Co. Reprinted by permission of the Laux Company, Inc.

*Percent fat calculated by the formula by Siri. Percent fat = $[(4.95/BD) - 4.5] \times 100$, where BD = body density.

MOST FREQUENTLY ASKED QUESTIONS

1. *What's so bad about skipping the exercise and just dieting?*

   By only dieting to lose weight, your body will use fat and muscle tissue as fuel. Severe caloric restriction will cause the body to adjust to the decreased caloric intake and slow your basal metabolic rate considerably. Exercise prevents the loss of lean tissue while simultaneously contributing to energy expenditure.

2. *How reliable is assessing body fatness using skinfold calipers?*

   The skinfold procedure is reliable within 3-5% of the estimated number obtained. This difference includes variations in measurer's technique, measurement error of instrument, and the possible variance of sites on an individual's body. The most reliable method of fat assessment, at this time, is hydrostatic or underwater weighing. Adequate training and proper techniques will reduce most technical errors associated with the skinfold procedure.

3. *Does BMR mean I should eat that many calories?*

   No, basal metabolic rate (BMR) is the minimum number of calories required to sustain resting metabolism. The number of calories you require above your BMR is determined by your activity level. The more active one is, the greater the amount of energy one expends, thus the more calories one may eat without gaining weight.

4. *Is just walking to class enough exercise?*

   Being a student requires a large amount of sedentary time, either in lecture or studying. Thus, walking would not be enough exercise. Aim for aerobic exercise—exercise that gets the heart pumping faster (130-150 beats/minute)—three to five times per week for at least 20 to 30 minutes each time.

5. *I've tried diet after diet and nothing works. What can I do to lose weight?*

   Try not to emphasize the idea that you're on a diet. That implies painful self-sacrifice. Slightly reduce the number of calories you eat, increase your activity level, and be patient. Remember, for long-term, permanent weight loss, aim to lose 1 to 2 pounds per week. Moderate caloric restriction combined with a moderate increase in activity is the healthiest and safest route to losing weight. It may take a while, but you'll be more likely to keep it off.

6. *Can I exercise too much?*

   Running more than 25 miles a week dramatically increases one's risk of injury. For nonracers, it's best not to run more than 3 miles five days a week. The cardiovascular benefits of running 3 miles five days a week are the same as running 80 miles a week. It's a good idea to take at least one day off each week to allow time for tissue to repair itself. Alternate strenuous workouts with easier ones.

7. *Since I've started an exercise/weight-training program, I have not lost weight. I've actually gone up a pound or two. Why is this?*

   If you are involved in an exercise program that includes weight training, you may have gained weight because you're increasing your muscle mass while losing fat. Per-unit volume, muscle weighs more than fat. As a gauge to monitor your progress in an exercise program, use a flexible tape measure to assess changes in body circumferences, and perhaps have your body fat measured. Don't rely solely on the scale. Your clothes should fit looser if you are losing fat weight.

8. *What can I do to lose the fat on my thighs and hips?*

Spot reducing is a much-publicized fallacy. You can reduce fat stores by adhering to a caloric restricted diet and an exercise program. As you lose weight, fat will be burned from *all* parts of your body, including your thighs. Weight training will tone the muscles in your thighs, but it will not burn fat specifically from these areas.

9. *Do diet pills work?*

Yes, you'll lose pounds—but you may sacrifice nutrition, especially vitamins and minerals. Diet pills are often diuretics, which cause you to lose water weight that is replaced when you go off the pills.

10. *How can a larger, "fatter" person have the same fat percentage as a thinner person?*

Body fat is basically located in two areas: surrounding the vital organs and subcutaneously (beneath the top layer of skin). Subcutaneous fat may be deposited in different areas, usually around the hips and thighs in women, and around the stomach area in men. Skinfold equations rely on standardized measurement sites; if a person does not have fat deposits at these particular sites, a lower percent fat may be calculated even if the person looks "fatter."

11. *Won't some people genetically tend to be overweight or have "fat" parts of their bodies? Is there any way to change that?*

Although genetics plays a part, family environment is often a critical factor that is overlooked. If you come from an inactive family that eats high calorie foods, the whole family might be overweight, but that isn't solely genetic.

12. *What's wrong with going on a crash diet for a few days?*

The biggest problem with this type of diet is that it simply doesn't work. The number of calories allowed is usually so low that the dieter is miserable and consequently finds it difficult to stay on the diet. A large part of the weight lost on a crash diet is stored glycogen (carbohydrates) and water. This weight is replaced rapidly when normal eating patterns are resumed.

13. *Do carbohydrates have more calories than protein?*

No, equal amounts of carbohydrates and protein have the same energy or caloric value. Fats have at least twice the amount of calories per unit weight of carbohydrates or protein. Eating an extra piece of meat (protein) instead of a potato (carbohydrate) won't help you lose weight, but reducing the total number of calories consumed will.

14. *How does the preparation of foods affect their caloric value?*

Ordinary preparation (cooking, freezing, cutting, blending) does not appreciably change the number of calories in a food. To dispel a myth, toasted bread does not have fewer calories than untoasted bread. Frying foods does increase the number of calories to the extent that fat is added. Broiling is the preferred method.

15. *Do some foods or food combinations have special chemical properties that help with weight loss?*

No, this is another attempt to fool people into thinking that a magical reducing diet has arrived. The grapefruit-and-egg diet was supposed to have a special chemical combination that "burned" your fat off. Unless you decrease your caloric intake, you won't lose weight. More important, some of these fad diets may actually be dangerous.

16. *What is "cellulite" and how do I get rid of it?*

Some maintain that cellulite is a particular type of fatty deposit that is lumpy and bumpy and causes the overlying skin to have a puckered appearance similar to an orange peel. However, all creditable nutritionists and medical authorities believe there is no such thing as cellulite, and the lumpy bulges are ordinary fat that will respond to a diet and exercise program that affects energy expenditure.

17. *What's the difference between being obese and being overweight?*

A person is considered overweight when he or she does not meet accepted standards as determined by age, height, and weight, but these standards can be poor indicators. Health insurance companies use height-weight tables in health appraisal, because heavier weight usually indicates excessive fat weight. However, these tables do not account for very muscular individuals, such as football players. Obesity refers to the percentage of fat in the body. In college-age males, 25% body fat or more is considered obese, while in college-age females, obesity is defined as over 35% body fat.

18. *Why shouldn't I attempt to lose weight by exercising with a plastic sweat suit or figure-wrapping device?*

Wearing a vinyl sweat suit during intense physical activity adversely affects the body's heat-regulating mechanism. This may be quite dangerous, as the body is not able to regulate body core-temperature, and individuals may actually undergo heat stress or heat stroke. Excessive sweating is a false loss of weight, because it represents a loss of bodily fluids, not fat. Figure-wrapping does not cause a loss of body fat, but may result in the apparent loss of inches due to bodily fluids shifting from the pressure of the wraps. In time, the fluids will stabilize and the measurements will return to their original diameters.

Body Composition Form

_____   _____

Name _____ Age _____ Date _____

1. Current weight _____
2. Skinfolds

Females	Males	Males & Females
Triceps _____	Chest _____	Biceps _____
Suprailium[a] _____	Abdomen _____	Triceps _____
Thigh _____	Thigh _____	Subscapula _____
		Iliac crest[b] _____
Total _____	Total _____	Total _____

3. Percent fat _____
4. Current fat weight (item 1 × item 3) _____
5. Current lean body weight (item 1 − item 4) _____
6. Desired percent body fat
   Males (average for college age 15%) _____

   Females (average for college age 25%) _____
7. Estimated target weight [item 5 ÷ (1.0 − item 6)] _____
8. Estimated pounds of fat to lose (item 1 − item 7) _____

Note. Columns 1 and 2 from ''Measurement of Cardiorespiratory Fitness and Body Composition in the Clinical Setting'' by M. Pollack, D. Schmidt, and A. Jackson, 1980, _Comprehensive Therapy,_ **6**(9), pp. 12-25. Column 3 from ''Body Fat Assessed From Total Body Density and Its Estimation From Skinfold Thickness: Measurements on 481 Men and Women Aged 16-74 Years'' by J. Durnin and J. Womersley, 1974, _British Journal of Nutrition,_ **32**, p. 95.

[a]Measure diagonal fold.

[b]Measure vertical fold.

Where Fat Comes Off

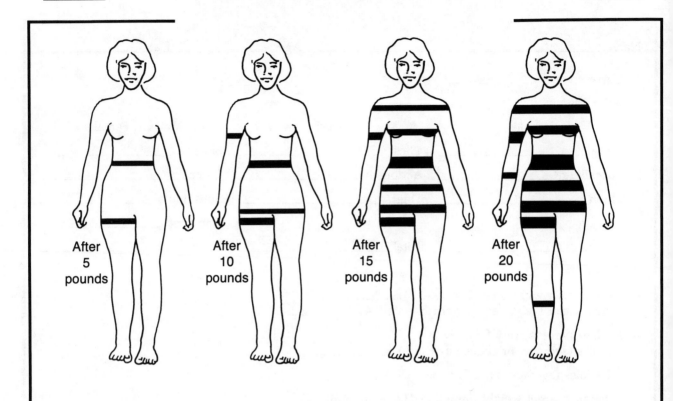

After 5 pounds

After 10 pounds

After 15 pounds

After 20 pounds

Calculating
Basal Metabolic Rate

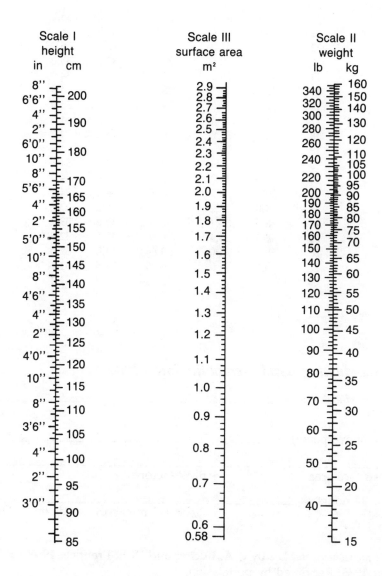

Scale I
height
in   cm

Scale III
surface area
m²

Scale II
weight
lb   kg

Basal Metabolic Rate According to Age and Sex

Age	BMR (kcal/m²/hr)		Age	BMR (kcal/m²/hr)	
	Men	Women		Men	Women
10	47.7	44.9	28	37.8	35.0
11	46.5	43.5	29	37.7	35.0
12	45.3	42.0	30	37.6	35.0
13	44.5	40.5	31	37.4	35.0
14	43.8	39.2	32	37.2	34.9
15	42.9	38.3	33	37.1	34.9
16	42.0	37.2	34	37.0	34.9
17	41.5	36.4	35	36.9	34.8
18	40.8	35.8	36	36.8	34.7
19	40.5	35.4	37	36.7	34.6
20	39.9	35.3	38	36.7	34.5
21	39.5	35.2	39	36.6	34.4
22	39.2	35.2	40-44	36.4	34.1
23	39.0	35.2	45-49	36.2	33.8
24	38.7	35.1	50-54	35.8	33.1
25	38.4	35.1	55-59	35.1	32.8
26	38.2	35.0	60-64	34.5	32.0
27	38.0	35.0	65-79	33.5	31.6
			70-74	32.7	31.1
			75+	31.8	

Worksheet for Calculating Basal Metabolic Rate (BMR)

1. Estimated body surface area = _____
   (see left panel)

2. BMR factor (see above panel) = _____

3. _____ × _____ = _____
   Est. body surface area   BMR factor   BMR

4. _____ × 24 hours = _____
   BMR   Basal metabolic needs for 1 day

Note. From *Fitness for College and Life* by C.A. Bucher and W.E. Prentice, 1985, St. Louis: Times Mirror/Mosby. Copyright 1985. Reprinted by permission.

Fast Food Calorie Counter

BASKIN-ROBBINS

Food item (regular 4-oz. scoop)	Calories	Fat (gm)	% Calories from fat
Vanilla	235	13.1	50
Chocolate	264	12.6	43
Strawberry	226	9.6	38
French Vanilla	290	18.9	59
Pralines 'n' Cream	283	13.1	42
Rocky Road	291	11.2	35
Chocolate Mousse Royale	293	13.6	42
Orange Sherbet	158	2.4	14
Dacquiri Ice	136	0.0	0
Raspberry Sherbet	134	0.0	0
Wild Strawberry (low-fat frozen dairy dessert)	90	1.6	16
Sugar Cone	57	1.0	16
Cake Cone	19	0.3	14

ARBY'S

Food item	Calories	Fat (gm)	% Calories from fat
Jr. Roast Beef	218	8.0	33
Regular Roast Beef	353	15.0	38
Super Roast Beef	501	22.0	40
King Roast Beef	467	19.0	37
Beef 'n' Cheddar	490	21.0	39
Bacon 'n' Cheddar Deluxe	561	34.0	55
Ham 'n' Cheese	353	13.0	33
Chicken Breast Sandwich	592	27.0	41
Turkey Deluxe	375	17.0	41
Potato Cakes	201	14.0	63

BURGER KING

Food item	Calories	Fat (gm)	% Calories from fat
Whopper	628	36.0	52
Whopper w/ Cheese	711	42.0	53
Double Beef Whopper	850	52.0	55
Double Beef Whopper w/ Cheese	950	60.0	57
Whopper Junior	322	17.0	48
Whopper Junior w/ Cheese	364	20.0	49
Hamburger	275	12.0	39
Cheeseburger	317	15.0	43
Bacon Double Cheeseburger	510	31.0	55
Whaler Fish Sandwich	488	27.0	50
Whaler Fish Sandwich w/ Cheese	530	30.0	51
Ham & Cheese Specialty Sandwich	471	23.0	44
Chicken Specialty Sandwich	688	40.0	52
Plain Salad	28	0.0	0
French Fries	227	13.0	52
Onion Rings	274	16.0	53
Apple Pie	305	12.0	35

DOMINO'S PIZZA

Food item (2 slices of an 8-slice pizza)	Calories	Fat (gm)	% Calories from fat
Plain Cheese	218	5.9	24
Pepperoni	265	10.2	35
Sausage	246	8.4	31
Double Cheese	284	10.8	34

LONG JOHN SILVER'S

Food item	Calories	Fat (gm)	% Calories from fat
Fish & Fries (3 fish, fries, 2 hushpuppies)	998	55.0	50
Tender Chicken Plank Dinner (4 chicken planks, fries, slaw)	1037	59.0	51
Shrimp, Fish & Chicken Dinner (2 battered shrimp, 1 fish, 1 chicken plank, fries, slaw, 2 hushpuppies	1022	60.0	53
Seafood Platter (1 fish, 2 shrimp, clams, fries, slaw, 2 hushpuppies)	1133	68.0	54
Clam Dinner (clams, fries, slaw)	955	58.0	55
Cajun Shrimp Platter (Cajun shrimp, fries, slaw)	859	52.0	54
Pasta & Seafood Salad (7 oz pasta & seafood, 4 oz lettuce, 2 tomato wedges, 2 crackers	474	33.0	63
Seafood Salad (4.5 oz seafood, 4 oz lettuce, 2 tomato wedges, 2 crackers)	317	25.0	71
Ocean Chef Salad (4 oz lettuce, 1.75 oz shrimp, 2 oz seafood blend, .5 oz carrots, tomato wedge, .75 oz cheese, 2 crackers)	193	7.0	33
Breaded Clams (1 order)	526	31.0	53
Breaded Fish Sandwich	406	15.0	33
Clam Chowder	128	5.0	35
Cole Slaw	182	15.0	74
Fries	247	12.0	44
Hushpuppies	145	7.0	43

DAIRY QUEEN

Food item	Calories	Fat (gm)	% Calories from fat
Cone			
Small	140	4.0	26
Regular	240	7.0	26
Large	340	10.0	26
Chocolate Dip Cone			
Small	190	9.0	43
Regular	340	16.0	42
Large	510	24.0	42
Milkshake (chocolate)			
Small	490	13.0	24
Regular	710	19.0	24
Large	990	26.0	24
Float	410	7.0	15
Banana Split	540	11.0	18
Mr. Misty Freeze (regular)	250	0.0	0
Dilly Bar	210	13.0	56
D.Q. Sandwich	140	4.0	26
Mr. Misty Kiss	70	0.0	0
Heath Blizzard	800	24.0	27
Peanut Buster Parfait	740	34.0	41

WENDY'S

Food item	Calories	Fat (gm)	% Calories from fat
Single Hamburger	350	18.0	46
Double Hamburger	560	34.0	55
Triple Hamburger	900	56.0	56
Single Hamburger w/ Cheese	420	24.0	51
Double Hamburger w/ Cheese	630	40.0	57
Triple Hamburger w/ Cheese	1040	68.0	59
Chicken Sandwich	320	10.0	28
Chili	260	8.0	28
French Fries (regular)	280	14.0	45
Taco Salad	390	18.0	42
Frosty	400	14.0	32
Hot Stuffed Potatoes			
Plain	250	2.0	7
Sour Cream & Chives	460	24.0	47
Cheese	590	34.0	52
Chili & Cheese	510	20.0	35
Bacon & Cheese	570	30.0	47
Broccoli & Cheese	500	25.0	45
Pick-Up Side Salad	110	6.0	49

HARDEE'S

Food item	Calories	Fat (gm)	% Calories from fat
Hamburger	276	15.3	50
Cheeseburger	309	12.8	37
Big Deluxe	503	28.9	52
Bacon Cheeseburger	556	32.8	53
Roast Beef Sandwich	312	12.4	36
Big Roast Beef Sandwich	440	21.5	44
Turkey Club	426	22.3	47
Fisherman's Filet	469	20.1	39
Chicken Filet	510	26.2	46
Hot Dog	346	22.0	57
French Fries (regular)	239	12.9	49
French Fries (large)	406	22.0	49
Apple Turnover	282	13.8	44
Big Cookie	278	15.3	50
Biscuit	257	12.4	43
Egg Biscuit	334	18.7	50
Sausage Biscuit	426	28.3	60
Sausage & Egg Biscuit	503	34.6	62
Bacon & Egg Biscuit	405	25.7	57
Cinnamon 'n' Raisin Biscuit	276	16.2	53
Hashrounds	200	13.0	59

McDONALD'S

Food item	Calories	Fat (gm)	% Calories from fat
Egg McMuffin	340	15.8	42
Hot Cakes w/ Butter & Syrup	500	10.3	19
Scrambled Eggs	180	13.0	65
Pork Sausage	210	18.6	80
English Muffin w/ Butter	186	5.3	26
Hash Brown Potatoes	144	8.9	56
Big Mac	570	35.0	55
Hamburger	263	11.3	39
Cheeseburger	318	16.0	45
Quarter Pounder	427	23.5	50
Quarter Pounder w/ Cheese	525	31.6	54
Filet-O-Fish	435	25.7	53
McD.L.T.	680	44.0	58
Chicken McNuggets (6)	323	20.2	56
French Fries (regular)	220	11.5	47
Apple Pie	253	14.0	50
Vanilla Shake	352	8.4	21
Chocolate Shake	383	9.0	21
Strawberry Sundae	320	8.7	24
Hot Fudge Sundae	357	10.8	27
Hot Caramel Sundae	361	10.0	25
McDonaldland Cookies	308	10.8	32
Chocolaty Chip Cookies	342	16.3	43
Chef Salad	226	13.0	52
Shrimp Salad	99	2.6	24
Garden Salad	91	5.5	54
Chicken Oriental Salad	146	3.9	24
Side Salad	48	2.6	49
Croutons	52	2.2	38
Chow Mein Noodles	45	2.2	44

KENTUCKY FRIED CHICKEN

Food item	Calories	Fat (gm)	% Calories from fat
Original Recipe			
Wing	181	12.3	61
Side Breast	276	17.3	56
Center Breast	257	13.7	48
Drumstick	147	8.8	54
Thigh	278	19.2	62
Extra Crispy			
Wing	218	15.6	64
Side Breast	354	23.7	60
Center Breast	353	20.9	53
Drumstick	173	10.9	57
Thigh	371	26.3	64
Mashed Potatoes	59	0.6	9
Gravy	59	3.7	56
Cole Slaw	103	5.7	50
Biscuit	269	13.6	46
Kentucky Fries	268	12.8	43
Corn-on-the-Cob	176	3.1	16

TACO BELL

Food item	Calories	Fat (gm)	% Calories from fat
Bean Burrito	360	10.9	27
Beef Burrito	402	17.3	39
Beefy Tostada	322	19.6	55
Tostada	243	10.9	40
Bell Beefer	312	13.1	38
Burrito Supreme	422	18.8	40
Combination Burrito	381	14.1	33
Enchirito	382	20.1	47
Pintos 'n' Cheese	194	9.5	44
Taco	184	10.9	53
Fajita Steak Taco	235	10.9	42
w/ Sour Cream	281	15.4	49
w/ Guacamole	269	13.2	44
Nachos	356	19.2	49
Nachos Bell Grande	719	40.7	51

SALAD DRESSINGS

1 oz = 2 tbsp.	Calories	Fat (gm)	% Calories from fat
Bleu Cheese	130	13.5	93
Italian	133	13.7	93
Ranch	139	14.6	95
French	123	10.4	76
Thousand Island	131	11.7	80
Low-Calorie Italian	32	2.8	79
Low-Calorie Thousand Island	69	5.6	73

CARBONATED BEVERAGES

12 oz	Calories	Fat (gm)	% Calories from fat
Cola types	150	0.0	0
Cream Soda	155	0.0	0
Fruit Flavor Soda	166	0.0	0
Gingerale	126	0.0	0
Root Beer	163	0.0	0
Beer	151	0.0	0

Note. Data from *Bowes & Church's Food Values of Portions Commonly Used* (14th ed.), 1985, J.B. Lippincott Co.; and individual restaurant chains.

Comparable Aerobic Exercise[a]
Table

Activity	Kilocalories[b] (kcal/min)	Oxygen uptake (ml/kg · min⁻¹)	Activity	Kilocalories[b] (kcal/min)	Oxygen uptake (ml/kg · min⁻¹)
Archery	3.7- 5	10.5-14	Horseback riding	3.7-10	10.5-28
Backpacking	6 -13.5	17.5-38.5	Horseshoe pitching	2.5- 3.7	7 -10.5
Badminton	5 -11	14 -31.5	Hunting, walking		
Basketball			Small game	3.7- 8.5	10.5-24.5
Nongame	3.7-11	10.5-31.5	Big game	3.7-17	10.5-49
Game	8.5-15	24.5-42	Mountain climbing	6 -12	17.5-35
Bed exercise (arm movement, supine or sitting)	1.1- 2.5	3.5- 7	Paddleball/racquetball	10 -15	28 -42
			Rope skipping	10 -14	28 -42
Bicycling	3.7-10	10.5-28	Sailing	2.5- 6	7 -17.5
Bowling	2.5- 5	7 -14	Scuba diving	6 -12	17.5-35
Canoeing (also rowing and kayaking)	3.7-10	10.5-28	Shuffleboard	2.5- 3.7	7 -10.5
			Skating (ice or roller)	7 -10	17.5-28
Calisthenics	3.7-10	10.5-28	Skiing (snow)		
Dancing			Downhill	6 -10	17.5-28
Social and square	3.7- 8.5	10.5-24.5	Cross-country	7.5-15	21 -42
Aerobic	7.5-11	21 -31.5	Skiing (water)	6 -85	17.5-24.5
Fencing	7.5-12	21 -35	Snowshoeing	8.5-17	24.5-49
Fishing			Squash	10 -15	28 -42
Bank, boat, or ice	2.5- 5	7 -14	Soccer	6 -15	17.5-42
Stream, wading	6 - 7.5	17.5-21	Softball	3.7- 7.5	10.5-21
Football (touch)	7.5-12	21 -35	Stair-climbing	5 -10	14 -28
Golf			Swimming	5 -10	14 -18
Using power cart	2.5- 3.7	7 -10.5	Table tennis	3.7- 6	10.5-17.5
Walking, carrying bag, or pulling cart	5 - 8.5	14 -24.5	Tennis	5 -11	14 -31.5
			Volleyball	3.7- 7.5	10.5-21
Handball	10 -15	28 -42	Weight training circuit	10	28
Hiking (cross-country)	3.7- 8.5	10.5-24.5			

Note. From *Exercise in Health and Disease* (pp. 258-259) by M.L. Pollock, J. Wilmore, and S.M. Fox, 1985, Philadelphia: W.B. Saunders. Copyright 1985 by W.B. Saunders. Reprinted by permission.

[a]Energy cost values based on an individual of 154 lb of body weight (70 kg).

[b]Kilocalorie: A unit of measure based upon heat production. One kcal equals approximately 200 ml of oxygen consumed.

REFERENCES

Allsen, P.E., Harrison, J.M., & Vance, B. (1984). *Fitness for life: An individualized approach.* Dubuque, IA: Brown.

American Alliance for Health, Physical Education, Recreation and Dance. (1984). *Health-related physical fitness* (Technical manual). Reston, VA: Author.

Brooks, G.A., & Fahey, T.D. (1984). *Exercise physiology.* New York: Wiley.

Bucher, C.A., & Prentice, W.E. (1985). *Fitness for college and life.* St. Louis: Times Mirror/Mosby.

Durnin, J., & Womersley, J. (1974). Body fat assessed from total body density and its estimation from skinfold thickness: Measurements on 481 men and women aged from 16 to 72 years. *British Journal of Nutrition, 32,* 95.

Falls, H.B., Baylor, A.M., & Dishman, R. (1980). *Essentials of fitness.* Philadelphia: Saunders College.

Katch, F., & McArdle, W. (1977). *Nutrition, weight control and exercise.* Boston: Houghton-Mifflin.

Katch, V., & Katch, F. (1986, April). Success! Those incredible shrinking women. *Shape,* pp. 60-63.

Oscai, L. (1973). Role of exercise in weight control. *Exercise and Sport Science Reviews, 1,* 103-123.

Pollock, M.L., Schmidt, D.H., & Jackson, A.S. (1980). Measurement of cardio-respiratory fitness and body composition in the clinical setting. *Comprehensive Therapy, 6*(9), 12-25.

Sharkey, B.J. (1984). *Physiology of fitness.* Champaign, IL: Human Kinetics.

"Positively Stressed!"
Lifestyle Workshop

PARAPROFESSIONAL PREPARATION MATERIALS

Training Sessions
Competency Exam
Texts and Suggested Readings

WORKSHOP AT A GLANCE

Presenter Information
Most Frequently Asked Questions
Handouts and Visual Aids
References

TRAINING SESSIONS

"Positively Stressed!"

Session 1: Workshop Presentation

Time: 60 minutes

Methods: Presentation, demonstration

Description: Trainer presents workshop to Lifestyle Educators.

Readings: The workshop

Session 2: General Adaptation Syndrome

Time: 60 minutes

Methods: Lecture, discussion

Description: Information presented on General Adaptation Syndrome (GAS) and sources and symptoms of stress. Definition and discussion of stress, the psychophysiology of stress, and the relationship between stress and illness.

Activity: Complete "Stress Inventory" and "Symptoms Checklist." Discuss similarities and differences among participants.

Readings: Introductory material on stress. Psychophysiology and GAS stages.

Competency exam questions: 1, 2, 3, 4, 5, 6, 7, 26

Session 3: The Mind: Friend or Foe?

Time: 60 minutes

Methods: Lecture, discussion

Description: Discuss relationship between mind, body, and health. Discuss positive and negative self-talk.

Activity: Demonstrate mind-body relationship using Chevreul's Pendulum. Discuss refuting irrational ideas. Complete and score a beliefs inventory. Practice guided imagery relaxation technique.

Readings: The workshop and materials on modifying stressful behaviors, the mind-body relationship, and self-talk

Competency exam questions: 8, 9, 10, 11, 24, 25, 28

Session 4: Relaxation Techniques

Time: 60 minutes

Methods: Discussion, lecture

Description: Use the "Symptom Effectiveness Chart" to introduce relaxation techniques.

Activity: Massage demonstration and participant practice; progressive relaxation practice

Readings: The workshop and materials covering techniques for managing stress, such as meditation, autogenic training, progressive relaxation, and sensory awareness

Competency exam questions: 12, 13, 14, 15, 16, 17, 18, 19, 27, 29

Session 5: Nutrition, Exercise, and Stress

Time: 60 minutes

Methods: Lecture, discussion

Description: Explain or ask a guest lecturer to speak to the class about the relationship between nutrition and exercise to stress.

Readings: Materials covering diet, exercise, and stress

Competency exam questions: 20, 21, 22, 23, 26

Session 6: "Most Frequently Asked Questions" Review and Hot Seat

Time: 60 minutes

Methods: Discussion, lecture, practice

Description: Review workshop components.

Activity: Hot Seat: Each Lifestyle Educator is quizzed by other students about the workshop topic for 10 minutes.

Readings: The workshop

Session 7: "Positively Stressed!" Lifestyle Workshop

Time: 60 minutes

Method: Presentation

Description: Each Lifestyle Educator presents 20 minutes of the workshop.

Readings: The workshop

COMPETENCY EXAM

The following questions require brief responses.

1. Give an example of a stressor.

2. Explain Selye's definition of stress.

3. Briefly describe the three stages of the General Adaptation Syndrome.

4. Briefly define eustress and distress and give an example of each.

5. The fight-or-flight response is also known as "stress reactivity." Describe five physiological characteristics of this reaction.

6. According to your texts and lecture, mental stress has caused or aggravated symptoms in what percentage of all hospital inpatients in the U.S.?

7. Imagine yourself presenting a stress management program and describing common symptoms of stress. Identify five physical and five emotional symptoms of stress.

8. Explain what self-talk is. Give an example of irrational self-talk.

9. Define "Rational Emotional Therapy" and explain why irrational ideas should be refuted.

10. Why is self-concept an important part of the mind/body relationship?

11. Give an example of a positive affirmation statement.

12. One stress management technique is massage. Briefly explain how being massaged helps a person to relax.

13. The massage instruction handout gives 10 general tips regarding massage. List five of them.

14. How would you respond to a participant asking, "How can I learn more about massage?"

15. Identify four guidelines for practicing progressive relaxation.

16. Based on your readings, describe four advantages of using the progressive relaxation technique to elicit the relaxation response.

17. During your presentation, a student complains, "I tried progressive relaxation once and hated it!" What would your response be?

18. What is meditation?

19. What is autogenic training?

20. Regarding stress-producing foods, what are two of the most harmful substances consumed in excess by most Americans?

21. Explain why they are "stress-producing."

22. Stress can deplete the body of certain vitamins and minerals—the very ones it needs most to combat stress. Identify two of these vitamins and minerals.

23. Exercise is one means of dealing with the stress response. Describe two benefits of exercise for psychological health.

The following are True/False questions. Check the appropriate blanks.

True   False

_____ _____ 24. Thinking about an unpleasant event is never as stressful as actually experiencing the event.

_____ _____ 25. Thinking of one's self as useless and powerless can increase one's stress level.

_____ _____ 26. Stress may decrease the body's ability to defend itself against disease.

_____ _____ 27. Overload occurs when people are able to meet the demands placed on them.

_____ _____ 28. The stress produced by a situation depends more on the situation itself than on how the person perceives it.

_____ _____ 29. To be effective, relaxation exercises must always be used at the same time and place.

30. Suggest possible techniques to use in your workshop if an audience participant is one of the following:
    • Recognition Seeker (frequently calls attention to self)
    • Conversationalist (brings up off-the-subject anecdotes and is a noisy distraction)
    • Moralizer (advocates judgmental points of view based on personal conviction)
    • Conservative (convinced that the status quo does not need changing)

TEXTS AND SUGGESTED READINGS

Ardell, D.B. (1982). *14 days to a wellness lifestyle.* Mill Valley, CA: Whatever.

Curtis, J.D., & Detert, R.A. (1981). *How to relax: A holistic approach to stress management.* Palo Alto: CA: Mayfield.

Davis, M., Eshelman, E.R., McKay, M. (1982). *The relaxation and stress reduction workbook.* Oakland, CA: New Harbinger.

Girdano, D.A., & Everly, G.S. (1986). *Controlling stress and tension: A holistic approach.* Englewood Cliffs, NJ: Prentice-Hall.

Goldberger, L., & Breznitz, C. (Eds.) (1982). *Handbook of stress: Theoretical and clinical aspects.* New York: Macmillan.

Greenburg, J.S. (1987). *Comprehensive stress management.* Dubuque, IA: Brown.

Mason, L.J. (1985). *Guide to stress management.* Berkeley: Celestial Arts.

Pelletier, K.R. (1977). *Mind as healer, mind as slayer: A holistic approach to preventing stress disorders.* New York: Delacorte.

Selye, H. (1978). *The stress of life.* New York: McGraw-Hill.

Van Dolson, L. (1984). *Taming tension through total health.* Washington, DC: Reviewer & Herald.

WORKSHOP AT A GLANCE

The goal of this workshop is to educate participants about stress and to promote stress management as a positive lifestyle behavior. This workshop takes approximately 45 to 60 minutes to present. Suggested attendance is 5 to 30 persons.

Objectives

Within the content of this workshop, the following objectives will be met.

- Participants will be able to identify many of their personal stressors and coping techniques.
- Participants will practice two stress management techniques: visualization and guided imagery.
- Using the "Stress Exhaustion Symptoms" handout and the "Symptom Effectiveness Chart," participants will identify potential stress management techniques.

Workshop Materials Needed

- Workshop sign-in sheet
- Handouts and visual aids: *Your Coping Methods: Are They Working?*, *Symptom Effectiveness Chart*, *Stress Exhaustion Symptoms*, and *The Staircase Effect*
- Blackboard or portable flip-chart pad
- Blank sheets of paper for participants to write on
- Lifestyle Workshop evaluation forms and pencils

PRESENTER INFORMATION

Briefly introduce yourself, your background, and any other personal information you choose to share. Describe your health promotion program and the topics available, for example, nutrition and fitness. Stress that the workshops are unique because you bring them to their living areas. Lifestyle Workshop paraprofessionals are trained at (your institution or program) to present these workshops. If anyone is interested in the training program, ask him or her to speak with you after the workshop.

In this workshop participants will generate a personal list of stressors and identify typical coping strategies. Participants will be introduced to potential skills for dealing with stressors, learn how to recognize individual stress symptoms, and learn techniques for coping with these stress symptoms.

Visualization Exercise (10 minutes)

Explain to participants that the workshop will begin with a stress management exercise to help them clear their minds and make it easier to participate in and benefit from the workshop. Begin by asking the participants to find a position comfortable for them, sitting or lying down. They may want to loosen any tight clothing and uncross their legs and ankles. Ask them to close their eyes and take a deep breath. Once the participants are settled comfortably, gently guide them through the following meditation.

Allow yourself to take a few minutes to focus on the thoughts, worries, and concerns that come into your mind.

Identify these distractions . . . there may be many things on your mind right now . . . homework that needs to be done when you leave here . . . a conversation you had with someone earlier . . . what you are going to do tomorrow . . . your plans for the weekend. . . .

Take a minute to concentrate on what your concerns are—develop a mental list . . . these concerns occupy your thoughts and use your energy, leaving less for you and for this experience.

You probably can't do much about these concerns during the next 45 minutes, except worry . . . and that will interfere with all you can be learning here . . . so put those worries aside for a while.

Imagine yourself seated at a desk . . . in front of you is a pad of blank white paper . . . and a black pen . . . imagine yourself picking up the pen . . . and writing a word on one of the sheets of paper that represents one of your worries . . . picture yourself doing this . . . write one worry on each sheet of paper . . . using as many or as few sheets of paper as you need to clear your mind. . . .

Now imagine yourself placing a sheet of paper into the desk drawer . . . one by one, place each concern inside the desk drawer . . . as you do this, tell yourself, "There is nothing I can do about this right now . . . so I'm putting it in a safe place—for now, while I'm here. I can come back later, and it will be right here when I want it."

Allow yourself to place all your concerns in this safe place. . . .

When you've placed all of your concerns in the desk drawer . . . lock the drawer and put the key in your pocket. . . . At the end of this workshop, you can take the key and unlock the drawer if you choose. . . .

When you're ready, I'd like you to slowly open your eyes."

Personal Stressors and Coping Techniques (15 minutes)

Explain to participants that we will examine personal stressors and ways in which we cope with them. Hand out blank sheets of paper and ask participants to list all of their current stressors—all of the big and little things that nag, worry, upset, or drain them in life right now. Give a variety of examples, such as an annoying roommate, financial difficulties, a hangover, an uncomfortable chair, frustrating classes, and so forth.

Have participants pair up and share their lists. After about 2 minutes, ask each pair to choose one stressor they have in common and one that is unique to each partner. Suggest that it would be interesting to hear what are sources of stress for others. Invite each pair to share their chosen common and unique stressors with the group.

Define eustress and distress, incorporating stressors given by the participants as examples. Explain that the distinction between eustress and distress is determined by the individual's *perception* of a particular stressful experience, not by the stressor. Give examples (such as a job interview) that may be eustress for some people and distress for others. Reemphasize that in most cases it is the *perception* of a person or situation that determines whether or not it will be a source of stress.

Reactions to Frustration

Read "What Your Reaction to a Stuck Window Shade Reveals About Your Personality" (Appendix A). Now ask participants to change their focus of attention from the problems to the solutions. Ask participants to take out their list of stressors and make a second list, this time writing down their favorite coping techniques. Ask the question, "What things do you do to relax when you're feeling really stressed?" Allow them time to write a short list. Offer examples such as smoking, talking to a friend, exercising, drinking, getting organized; and encourage participants to list several copers that they use frequently.

Coping Methods

Hand out "Your Coping Methods: Are They Working?" Instruct participants to look over the list of suggested coping methods and note the copers they put on their original list. List any other copers from their list on the handout under the heading "Other methods you use." Instruct participants to check how often they use each method and how effective that method is for reducing stress. Next describe the following three combinations for participants to analyze. It will help to have an enlarged visual aid of this handout with the examples described below filled in on the chart.

- Look for a combination of a check under the "Frequency" heading in the *Often* column and a check under the "Effectiveness" heading in the *Very* column. This combination indicates a coping method that is successful because you are using it frequently and it is effective in relieving your stress. For example, if you checked "Get it off your chest, blow off steam" under *Often* and *Very*, this is an effective method for you. But if the method is unhealthy, such as "drink more alcohol, use drugs," you must realize that although the method may appear to work, it is actually creating more problems.
- Look for a combination of a check in the *Often* column and a check in the *Not* column. This

combination indicates a coping method you are using that is not effective. Think about why you use this method and be aware of its ineffectiveness the next time you start to use it. For example, if you checked "Take it out on others, blame someone else" in both the *Often* and the *Not* column, you do this frequently but you probably put more stress on yourself because you may feel bad that you yelled at an innocent person.
- Look for a combination of a check in the *Rarely* column and a check in the *Very* column. This combination indicates a method that is successful for you, but one that you're not using for some reason. For example, if you checked "Exercise, walk or jog" under *Rarely* and *Very*, exercise reduces your stress but you're not doing it enough. Try to schedule exercise into your routine.

Discussion of Personal Coping Methods

Have participants pair up again, this time with different partners, and compare lists on coping. After 2 minutes, ask them to choose one coping strategy they have in common and one that's unique to each partner.

Initiate a group discussion on the variety of coping strategies available. Ask participants if they know of other coping techniques not already listed on the handout. Some people will inevitably mention "negative" coping techniques. This is a perfect opportunity to talk about the costs and benefits of different coping strategies. For example, choosing to sleep late instead of getting up and going to a dreaded 8:00 a.m. class may provide short-term relief from stress, but it may also create more stress in the long run because of missing class. Ask each participant to identify a positive and negative coping method from the list and share it with the group. Sum up by reminding participants to weigh the costs and benefits of the coping methods they use and to substitute effective coping techniques for the ineffective techniques they may be using.

Symptoms of Stress and Coping Techniques (10 minutes)

Distribute the "Stress Exhaustion Symptoms" handout and instruct participants to place a check next to stress symptoms they *usually* experience. After participants have completed the checklist, ask them if they have several symptoms in a particular area. For example, one individual may experience mostly physical symptoms while another experiences predominantly emotional symptoms. Explain that being aware of our personal stress symptoms helps alert us to slow down and practice a stress management technique. Ask participants how they should choose a coping technique. The technique that works best for their personal stress symptoms is the one to choose.

Provide each participant with a copy of the Symptom Effectiveness Chart. Instruct participants to look down the left column for the symptom(s) they may have. Next, have them look horizontally across the page until they come to a column with an X. This indicates a match between the stress symptom and an effective technique for dealing with it. Describe some of the more popular techniques, such as progressive relaxation and deep breathing. The amount of time required to master each technique varies. Encourage participants to experiment with a variety of techniques to find one that works best for them. Allow time for questions. Go over the "Staircase Effect" handout (see handouts and visual aids).

"Active Remembering" (10 minutes)

Inform participants that we will conclude the presentation with a stress management technique called "guided imagery." Ask them once again to assume a comfortable position, either sitting or lying down. Tell them to uncross their legs and ankles and allow themselves to relax.

Take a deep breath . . . Relax . . . Close your eyes . . . Go back to the beginning of your day . . . What was getting up like for you? . . . How did you feel? . . . Be aware of any thoughts or feelings . . . (pause) . . . Let go of those thoughts and feelings . . . Let go of that part of your day . . . It is the past and you can't change it now.

Think of the hours betwen 9:00 and 11:00 . . . What

was that part of your day like? . . . Be aware of your thoughts and feelings during that part of your day . . . (pause) . . . Let go of that part of your day . . . It is in the past and you can't change it now.

Now think about lunch time . . . Be aware of your thoughts and feelings . . . What were the hours between 11:00 and 2:00 like for you? . . . Let go of your thoughts and feelings during this part of your day . . . They are in the past . . . You can't change them now.

Now be aware of the hours 2:00 and 5:00 . . . What was that part of your day like? . . . Be aware of your thoughts and feelings during this part of your day . . . Let go of those thoughts and feelings . . . Tell yourself that they are in the past . . . You can't change them now.

Be aware of your early evening—the hours between 5:00 and 7:00 . . . What was that part of your day like? . . . Be aware of any thoughts and feelings during that part of your day . . . Let go of the thoughts and feelings you were experiencing during this part of your day . . . They are in the past and you can't change them now.

It is now 8:00 p.m. . . . Quickly go back over your day and be sure you have let go of all thoughts and feelings . . . Experience yourself totally in the present . . . Start to experience yourself relaxing...Experience yourself relaxed . . . Experience yourself totally relaxed.

Conclusion and Evaluation (5 minutes)

Summarize the main points of the workshop:

- It is often our perception of a person, place, or event that determines whether or not it will be stressful.
- What is stressful to one person may not be stressful to another person.
- Identify a successful stress management technique to use on a regular basis.

Ask for questions from participants. Offer resources and referrals for further information. Distribute Lifestyle Workshop evaluation forms and pencils. Allow time for completion and then collect. Briefly list and describe the other Lifestyle Workshops in Stress Management.

Reaction to Frustration

What Your Reaction to a Stuck Window Shade Reveals

Do you ever take those personality tests in the back of magazines? Here's a quiz called, "What Your Reaction to a Stuck Window Shade Reveals About Your Personality." See if you can imagine yourself in one of these descriptions:

Type 1. People who yank the entire assemblage off the window, throw it on the floor, and stomp on it tend to be dynamic and honest in their emotions, although at times they can be severely overreactive.

Type 2. People who cut the stuck shade off at the desired level with a pair of sewing shears are most likely practical and quick-witted, with a sense of humor and a zest for life. They live "for the moment."

Type 3. People who stand by the window for 15 minutes, pulling the shade down longer and longer, waiting for it to snap back up, are usually very patient, calm, and trusting. What they may

lack in intelligence they make up for in warmth and understanding.

Type 4. Those who take the shade down, attempt to repair it, and buy a new one if necessary are the rare, well-adjusted citizens of society. These people are qualified to be surgeons, pilots, and Supreme Court judges. Unfortunately, they seldom run for president.

Type 5. People who fold the shade half-way up and tape it in place are people who can accept imperfection, both in themselves and in others. They are not necessarily neat.

Type 6. People who struggle for a few minutes and say, "I didn't really want the shade up anyway" and then go lie down for awhile, are doing the best they can—probably they're a little shy, and we should not criticize them.

Adapted from "Finding the Real You" by H. Melyan, 1976, October 17, *The Oregonian.*

MOST FREQUENTLY ASKED QUESTIONS

1. *I know I'm stressed! What's the point of identifying the symptoms of stress?*

Often we don't realize we are experiencing stress until we are well into the fight-or-flight reaction. The goal is to recognize the earliest signs of stress and to practice a relaxation technique that minimizes our distress.

2. *What are eustress and distress?*

Eustress refers to the good things to which we must adapt (like winning an award), while distress refers to bad things (like having an automobile accident).

3. *Tell me more about visualization. What is it used for?*

Positive visualization techniques can be used to relieve muscular tension and to reduce or eliminate pain. Visualization exercises may also facilitate recovery from an illness or injury.

4. *How long does it take to learn visualization?*

If you practice visualization exercises two or three times a day for 10 to 20 minutes at a time, you'll benefit most. How quickly you will see results will depend on your goals, your powers of imagination, and your willingness to take the time to practice.

Your Coping Methods: Are They Working?

Coping method	Frequency			Effectiveness		
	Use often	Use some-times	Use rarely	Very effective	Some-what effective	Not effective
Try to act as if nothing happened.						
Get it off your chest; blow off steam.						
Keep it to yourself.						
Drink alcohol; use drugs.						
Exercise, walk, or jog.						
Drink coffee, soda, or tea.						
Smoke cigarettes.						
Use humor to change your perception.						
Use tranquilizers or other medications.						
Take aspirin.						
Take time out for deep breathing.						
Take it out on others; blame someone else.						
Take a bath or shower.						
Watch TV.						
Play or listen to music.						
Apologize even though you were right.						
Engage in hobbies such as reading, cooking, writing, or crafts.						
Talk to a friend or relative.						
Take time to get away from it all.						
Meditate.						
Sleep more.						
Eat more often.						
Take action to prevent the same situation from happening again.						
Other methods you use:						

Note. Adapted from *Stress and Wellness* by J. Robinson, 1985, Champaign, IL: Well Way.

Symptom Effectiveness Chart

Techniques

Symptoms	Progressive relaxation	Breathing	Meditation	Imagination	Self-hypnosis	Autogenics	Thought stopping	Refuting irrational ideas	Coping skills training	Assertiveness training	Time management	Biofeedback	Nutrition	Exercise
Anxiety in specific situations (tests, deadlines, interviews, etc.)	X	X	X	X	X		X	X	X		X			
Anxiety in your personal relationships (spouse, parents, children, etc.)	X	X			X					X				
Anxiety, general (regardless of the situation or the people involved)	X	X	X	X		X	X	X	X			X		X
Depression, hopelessness, powerlessness, poor self-esteem	X	X	X				X	X	X	X			X	X
Hostility, anger, irritability, resentment		X	X			X		X				X	X	X
Phobias, fears	X						X		X			X		
Obsessions, unwanted thoughts		X	X				X							
Muscular tension	X	X		X	X	X						X		X
High blood pressure	X		X			X						X	X	X
Headaches, neckaches, backaches	X	X		X	X	X						X	X	X
Indigestion, irritable bowel, ulcers, chronic constipation	X				X	X						X	X	X

Muscle spasms, tics, tremors	X		x		X	x
Fatigue, tired all the time	X		x	x		x
Insomnia, sleeping difficulties	X		x	x	x	x
Obesity					X	X
Physical weakness						X

Note. From *The Relaxation and Stress Reduction Workshop* (2nd ed.) (pp. 14-15) by M. Davis, M. McKay, and E. Eshelman, 1982, Berkeley: New Harbinger. Copyright 1982. Reprinted by permission.

The most effective techniques for a particular symptom are marked with a large "X," while other helpful techniques for that same symptom are indicated by a small "x."

Stress Exhaustion Symptoms

Check the symptoms of stress exhaustion you've noticed lately in yourself.

Physical

☐ Appetite change
☐ Headaches
☐ Tension
☐ Fatigue
☐ Insomnia
☐ Weight change
☐ Colds
☐ Muscle aches
☐ Digestive upsets
☐ Pounding heart
☐ Accident prone
☐ Teeth grinding
☐ Rash
☐ Restlessness
☐ Foot-tapping
☐ Finger-drumming
☐ Increased alcohol, drug, or tobacco use

Emotional

☐ Anxiety
☐ Frustration
☐ The "blues"
☐ Mood swings
☐ Bad temper
☐ Nightmares
☐ Crying spells
☐ Irritability
☐ "No one cares"
☐ Depression
☐ Nervous laugh
☐ Worrying
☐ Easily discouraged
☐ Little joy

Spiritual

☐ Emptiness
☐ Loss of meaning
☐ Doubt
☐ Unforgiving
☐ Martyrdom
☐ Looking for magic
☐ Loss of direction
☐ Needing to "prove" oneself
☐ Cynicism
☐ Apathy

Mental

☐ Forgetfulness
☐ Dull senses
☐ Poor concentration
☐ Low productivity
☐ Negative attitude
☐ Confusion
☐ Lethargy
☐ Whirling mind
☐ No new ideas
☐ Boredom
☐ Spacing out
☐ Negative self-talk

Relational

☐ Isolation
☐ Intolerance
☐ Resentment
☐ Loneliness
☐ Lashing out
☐ Hiding
☐ Clamming up
☐ Lowered sex drive
☐ Nagging
☐ Distrust
☐ Fewer contacts with friends
☐ Lack of intimacy
☐ Using people

Note. From *Structured Exercises in Stress Management* (Vol. 1) by N. Tubesing and D. Tubesing, 1983, Duluth, MN: Whole Person Associates. Copyright 1983. Reprinted by permission.

The Staircase Effect

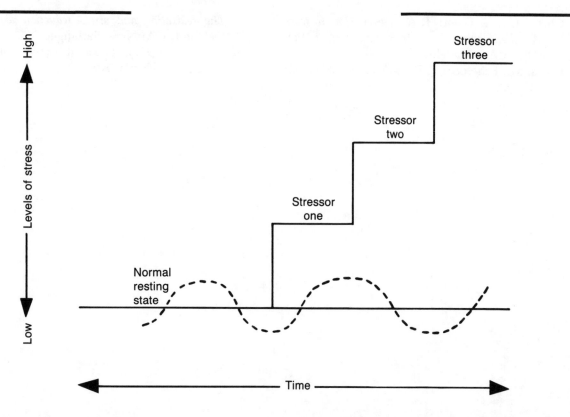

The body is designed to work most effectively when we fluctuate around the normal resting state which is illustrated with the dotted line. However, when we have in-adequate time to return to our normal resting state after exposure to a stressor (stressor one), the physiological response of the next stressor (stressor two) will add to the remaining effects of the previous stress. This buildup or accumulation of stress is most often caused by setting off the stress response for inappropriate and non-life-threatening reasons.

Note. From *Learn to Relax: A 14-Day Program* (p. 15) by J.D. Curtis and R.A. Detert, 1985, LaCrosse, WI: Coulee Press. Reprinted by permission.

REFERENCES

Curtis, J.D., & Detert, R.A. (1981). *How to relax: A holistic approach to stress management.* Palo Alto, CA: Mayfield.

Davis, M., Eshelman, E.R., & McKay, M. (1982). *The relaxation and stress reduction workbook.* Oakland, CA: New Harbinger.

Mason, L.J. (1985). *Guide to stress reduction.* Berkeley: Celestial Arts.

Relaxation Techniques Lifestyle Workshop

PARAPROFESSIONAL PREPARATION MATERIALS

Training Sessions

Competency Exam

Texts and Suggested Readings

WORKSHOP AT A GLANCE

Presenter Information

Most Frequently Asked Questions

Handouts and Visual Aids

References

TRAINING SESSIONS

Relaxation Techniques

Session 1: Workshop Presentation

Time:	60 minutes
Methods:	Presentation, demonstration
Description:	Trainer presents workshop to Lifestyle Educators.
Readings:	The workshop

Session 2: General Adaptation Syndrome

Time:	60 minutes
Methods:	Lecture, discussion
Description:	Information presented on General Adaptation Syndrome and the sources and syptoms of stress. Definition and discussion of stress, the psychophysiology of stress, and the relationship between stress and illness.
Activity:	Complete "Stress Inventory" and "Symptoms Checklist.' Discuss similarities and differences among participants.
Readings:	Introductory material on stress. Psychophysiology and GAS stages.
Competency exam questions:	1, 2, 3, 4, 5, 6, 7, 21, 22, 23, 32

Session 3: The Mind: Friend or Foe?

Time:	60 minutes
Methods:	Lecture, discussion
Description:	Discuss relationship between mind, body, and health. Discuss positive and negative self-talk.
Activity:	Demonstrate mind-body relationship using Chevreul's Pendulum. Practice refuting irrational ideas. Complete and score a beliefs inventory. Practice guided imagery relxation technique.
Readings:	Materials covering the mind-body relationship and self-talk, the workshop
Competency exam questions:	8, 9, 10, 11, 21, 24, 30, 31, 34

Session 4: Relaxation Techniques

Time:	60 minutes
Methods:	Discussion, lecture
Description:	Discuss the "Symptom Effectiveness Chart."
Activity:	Massage demonstration and student practice; progresive relaxation practice
Readings:	This workshop and the *"Positively Stressed!"* workshop. Study various techniques for managing stress, such as meditation, autogenic training, progressive relaxation, and sensory awareness
Competency exam questions:	12, 13, 14, 15, 16, 17, 18, 19, 20, 24, 25, 27, 35

Session 5: "Most Frequently Asked Questions" Review and Hot Seat

Time: 60 minutes

Methods: Discussion, lecture, practice

Description: Review workshop components.

Activity: Hot Seat: Each Lifestyle Educator is quizzed by the other students about the workshop topic for 10 minutes.

Readings: The workshop

Session 6: Practice Workshop Presentation

Time: 60 minutes

Method: Presentation

Description: Each Lifestyle Educator presents 20 minutes of the workshop.

Readings: The workshop

COMPETENCY EXAM

The following questions require brief responses.

1. Give an example of a stressor.

2. Explain Selye's definition of stress.

3. Briefly describe the three stages of the General Adaptation Syndrome.

4. Briefly define eustress and distress and give an example of each.

5. The fight-or-flight response is also known as "stress reactivity." Describe five physiological characteristics of this reaction.

6. According to your texts and lecture, mental stress has caused or aggravated symptoms in what percentage of all hospital inpatients in the U.S.?

7. Imagine yourself presenting a stress management program and describing common symptoms of stress. Identify five physical and five emotional symptoms of stress.

8. Explain what self-talk is and give an example of irrational self-talk.

9. Define *Rational Emotional Therapy* and explain why irrational ideas should be refuted.

10. Why is self-concept an important part of the mind-body relationship?

11. Give an example of a positive affirmation statement.

12. One stress management technique is massage. Briefly explain how massage helps a person to relax.

13. The massage instruction handout gives 10 general tips regarding massage. List five of them.

14. How would you respond to a participant asking "How can I learn more about massage?"

15. Identify four guidelines for practicing progressive relaxation.

16. Based on your readings, describe four advantages of using the progressive relaxation technique to elicit the relaxation response.

17. During your presentation, a student complains, "I tried progressive relaxation once and hated it!" What would your response be?

18. What is meditation?

19. What is autogenic training?

20. What is progressive relaxation?

21. Give an example of a physical cue identifying tension.

22. Explain the "Staircase effect" as it relates to the stress response.

23. Describe three of the physiological changes that occur when a person achieves the relaxation reponse.

24. Identify five reasons why relaxation on a regular basis can be beneficial to one's health.

25. How much time should an individual spend relaxing to achieve benefits?

The following are True/False questions. Check the appropriate blanks.

True   False

_____ _____ 26. Frequent and minor irritants can produce as much stress-associated damage as occasional major life crises.

_____ _____ 27. We have a physiological defense mechanism that protects us against the effects of long-term stress.

_____ _____ 28. Some important components for achieving relaxation are quiet, time, and a desire to listen to the body.

_____ _____ 29. Thinking about an unpleasant event is never as stressful as actually experiencing the event.

_____ _____ 30. Thinking of one's self as useless and powerless can increase one's stress level.

_____ _____ 31. Stress may decrease the body's ability to defend itself against disease.

_____ _____ 32. Overload occurs when people are able to meet the demands placed on them.

_____ _____ 33. The stress produced by a situation depends more on the situation itself than on how the person perceives it.

_____ _____ 34. To be effective, relaxation exercises must always be used at the same time and place.

_____ _____ 35. Our natural, biological fight-or-flight response is very effective against the psychosocial stressors common in an industrialized society.

36. Suggest possible techniques to use in your workshop if an audience participant is one of the following:
    • Recognition Seeker (frequently calls attention to self)
    • Conversationalist (brings up off-the-subject anecdotes and is a noisy distraction)
    • Moralizer (advocates judgmental points of view based on personal convictions)
    • Conservative (convinced that the status quo does not need changing)

TEXTS AND SUGGESTED READINGS

Benson, H. (1975). *The relaxation response.* New York: Avon.

Curtis, J.D., & Detert, R.A. (1981). *How to relax: A holistic approach to stress management.* Palo Alto: Mayfield.

Davis, M., Eshelman, E.R., & McKay, M. (1982). *The relaxation and stress teduction workbook.* Oakland: New Harbinger.

Downing, G. (1972). *The massage book.* New York: Random House.

Greenberg, J.S. (1987). *Comprehensive stress management.* Dubuque, IA: Brown.

WORKSHOP AT A GLANCE

The goal of this workshop is to provide participants with the opportunity to practice several relaxation techniques that they may incorporate into their regular stress management routine. This workshop takes approximately 60 minutes to present. Suggested attendance is 5 to 25 persons.

Objectives

Within the content of this workshop, the following objectives will be met.

- Through "Relaxation Bingo," participants will identify and share their effective relaxation activities.
- Participants will practice two individual relaxation techniques: deep breathing and progressive relaxation.
- Participants will practice massage, an interactive stress management technique.

Workshop Materials

- Workshop sign-in sheet
- Handouts and visual aids: *Relaxation Bingo, Massage Instructions*, and *Posterior Muscle Diagram*
- Lifestyle Workshop evaluation forms and pencils

Note. The physical setting should be conducive to massage and progressive relaxation, preferably a room big enough for participants to lie on the floor. Ideally, have a carpeted room, soft lighting, and minimal noise and distraction.

PRESENTER INFORMATION

Briefly introduce yourself, your background, and any other personal information you choose to share. Describe your health promotion program and the topics available, such as fitness and nutrition. Stress that the workshops are unique because you bring them to their living areas. Lifestyle Workshop paraprofessionals are trained at (your institution or program) to present these workshops. If anyone is interested in the training program, ask him or her to speak with you after the workshop.

The purpose of this workshop is to stimulate ideas about relaxation activities and to practice three specific stress management techniques: deep breathing, massage, and progressive relaxation.

To prepare participants for these activities, briefly describe the sequence of tonight's workshop: Relaxation Bingo, Deep Breathing, Massage, and Progressive Relaxation. Explain that the purpose of these activities is to introduce participants to a variety of techniques they can use to manage their stress.

"Relaxation Bingo" (10 minutes)

Distribute "Relaxation Bingo" handouts and instruct participants to ask each other about the tension-relieving activities they enjoy. Emphasize that making contact with each other and sharing ideas is more important than completing all the items on the sheet. After they have had a chance to meet each other (approximately 8 minutes), ask participants to discuss what they've learned and whether they have any new ideas for relaxation. Suggest other examples that may not have been mentioned, like writing letters, playing an instrument, taking a warm bath, or watching TV.

Deep Breathing Exercise (5 minutes)

At this point, before the massage demonstration and progressive relaxation exercise, explain that there are many techniques available for coping with stress. Suggest that participants experiment with a variety of techniques to find out what works best for them. Tell them to keep in mind that each method varies in the amount of time necessary to master the technique. For example, to master progressive relaxation, one needs to practice twice daily for one to two weeks.

Begin with a deep breathing routine. Instruct participants to get into a comfortable position, either sitting or lying down, loosen restrictive clothing, and uncross legs and ankles.

Begin breathing in deeply through your nose; then exhale through your mouth. Continue breathing in deeply through your nose and exhaling through your mouth. Breathe slowly, deeply, and evenly. Inhale through your nose to a count of four. Now hold your breath for a count of 4. Exhale through the mouth slowly to a count of 8. Repeat this sequence for a total of four times. Notice how you feel. Enjoy the experience.

Massage Demonstration (20 minutes)

Massage is a popular technique used to relieve tension and reduce stress. A common location for muscular tension is in the area of the neck, shoulders, and back. Massage can help relax those muscles and reduce the pain and discomfort you may have when experiencing stress. Massaging these tissues will increase blood flow in the area and help keep tissues elastic and pain-free. Muscle tension causes a build-up of waste products that causes pain. Massage increases circulation, which carries off the waste products, reducing the pain.

Massage is a way to communicate caring without words. Consequently, touch can have a healing effect for both the person giving the massage and the person receiving it. Touching is important to our well-being, however, in our society it is sometimes difficult to find acceptable ways of touching another person. Massage is a good opportunity to touch your roommate, your friend, your parents, and your brothers and sisters. These are tips you can use to give excellent massages:

1. Atmosphere is important! Massage in a comfortably warm room, and avoid drafts. Massage on a firm, comfortable surface, like a carpeted floor or a massage table—not on

a bed or couch, because they do not provide enough support. Massage in a quiet area, or play soft music if you choose. Keep the lighting soft also, avoiding harsh, bright lights.

2. Remove all jewelry that may interfere. (For the massager: rings, wristwatch, bracelets; for the massagee: necklaces and earrings.) Have massagee loosen any restrictive clothing. It is also important that the person giving the massage have short fingernails.
3. Shake your hands to relax them and also to warm them before you begin the massage.
4. Once you begin the massage, *always* maintain contact/touch with the person. If you must move around, at least keep one hand touching the person.
5. Communicate; ask if the person likes what you're doing. Feedback allows you to improve your massage technique.
6. Do not place pressure directly on the spine.
7. Do not tickle—remember that you want your massage to be relaxing.
8. Use circular motions on the back. Long strokes are done in the direction of the heart.
9. Maintain an evenness of speed and pressure.
10. Apply reasonable pressure when you massage—use your weight rather than your muscles to apply pressure. Massage with your entire body, not just your hands.
11. Mold your hands to fit the contours they pass over.
12. Keep your movements steady and smooth.
13. Explore the subcutaneous tissues and muscles of the body as you massage.
14. Don't be offended if the person falls asleep. You've successfully relaxed him or her!

Often the most effective instruction is achieved by demonstration. Begin by demonstrating a back/neck/shoulder massage for participants, allowing them time to practice. Have partners switch positions so that each receives a turn. You may want to present the massage instructions in the following manner.

In the atmosphere you have created for the massage, have the massagee (person receiving the massage) lie on his or her stomach. If the massagee doesn't mind, sit on his or her lower buttocks, otherwise sit beside.

Begin with long, slow, whole-hand stroking movements, starting at the lower back and moving straight up the back toward the neck. Fingertips should be facing each other alongside the spine, but not directly over it. As you stroke up the back, turn hands at the top so that fingertips face outward as you come back down. Take your time doing this. This stroking movement allows both persons to become familiar with each other and to communicate caring. Continue this stroke while you take a deep breath and allow yourself to relax. Focus on your partner even if he or she remains silent.

Next work with your thumbs on the lower back. Using the balls of your thumbs, make short, rapid strokes away from you, toward your partner's head. Work alongside the spine, massaging the muscles from the lower back up to the neck.

Glide your hands up to the top of the shoulders. Using both hands, firmly grasp and knead the entire back and shoulder areas. Observe your partner's response and vary your pressure accordingly. If one particular stroke seems especially enjoyable, continue doing it a little longer.

Next, massage the back of the neck and head. Use your fingertips and the balls of your thumbs to gently knead this area. Using a small circular motion, work from the base of the neck up toward the head. You should be able to feel the muscles beneath. Use smooth, firm strokes down to the base of the neck. Repeat the sequence a couple of times.

With hands located at about the middle of the back, spread your fingers and stroke upward and outward toward the shoulder. Imagine your hands smoothing out the muscle so it lies flat. Repeat.

With hands at the top of the shoulder, gently squeeze and release the upper arm and shoulder muscle (deltoid). Do this several times on each side.

To end the massage, use your fingertips to make feather-light strokes from the neck to the lower back. Finally, very gently remove both hands at the same time.

After completing the massage demonstration, ask if there are any questions. Allow time for participants to talk and relax a moment before continuing to the progressive relaxation exercise.

Progressive Relaxation (20 minutes)

In these exercises, preparation is important because it enables the exercises to be done effectively, for maximal benefit. The first four "rules" below are to be followed for any type of relaxation exercise—deep breathing exercises, meditation, stretching exercises, biofeedback, autogenic training, and visualization. Briefly explain each "rule"; then go on to the Progressive Relaxation Guide.

1. Find a quiet environment. You want to "turn off" both internal and external distractions. Minimize all forms of stimulation—noise, light, odor, movement, etc.

2. Use a mental device of some type to dispel distractions. A word or phrase may be repeated over and over again to "forget" distractions, or you may concentrate on a visual device such as an object or a symbol. You might even concentrate on a particular feeling, as in the progressive relaxation exercises.

3. Adopt a passive (observing) attitude. Empty your mind of any thoughts or distractions. Allow your body to work on itself. Do not force any thoughts or attempt to control the process. Do not worry about how well you are doing. You can best "control" the exercises by NOT controlling them! *This is the most important rule of all.*

4. Assume a comfortable position. You will be remaining in this position for 20 to 30 minutes. If you are in a position that uses your muscles, you are creating a state of tension that will work against relaxation. It is probably best to sit in a chair that supports the body well, or at the least a chair with arms. Some people prefer to do the exercises lying down. If you are using the exercises as a way to induce sleep, this is fine; but if you're doing these exercises in the morning as a way to get "psyched-up" for the day, lying down may not be the best choice.

These are several more pointers to ensure relaxation.

- Loosen constricting garments and remove jewelry. Muscle tension may be triggered by afferent stimulation—that is, information from the sense receptors for touch that pass through nerve pathways to the brain. Thus, minimize tactile input.

- Practice at leat once a day for at least 20 to 30 minutes. Allow enough time. This is very important. Schedule a relaxation period regularly and treat it as you would any other skill—work at it routinely.

- Follow a general order of the muscle groups to be relaxed: face, throat/neck, shoulders/upper back, arms, chest/stomach/lower back, buttocks/thighs, calves/ankles, and feet.

Progressive Relaxation Guide

This is one of many relaxation guides. Remember that gentle, calm presentation is as important as the content of the guide.

Let all your muscles go loose and heavy . . . Just settle back quietly and comfortably . . .

Wrinkle up your forehead now; wrinkle it tighter . . . tighter . . . Now stop wrinkling up your forehead. Relax and smooth it out . . . Picture your entire forehead and scalp becoming smoother, as you relax further . . . Now frown; frown hard, and crease your brows, and study the tension. Let go of the tension again . . . Smooth out the forehead once more. Again, wrinkle your forehead tightly and frown HARD! *Hold it . . . tighter . . . tighter . . . TIGHTER! Let go . . . let go of the tension again, feel it slide away . . . Notice the relaxation . . .*

Now clench your jaws, and grit your teeth. Harder, harder . . . Feel the tension throughout the jaws, hold it! Now relax your jaws . . . Let your lips part slightly . . . appreciate the relaxation . . . Again, clench your jaw, grit your teeth, and press your tongue hard against the roof of your mouth! Feel the tension!!

Now, relax. Breathe deeply and relax . . . Notice the contrast between tension and relaxation . . . Feel the relaxation all over your face, your forehead, jaws . . . The relaxation progresses further and further . . .

Now focus on your neck muscles. Press your head against the floor and feel the tension. Press harder . . . now release. Press your chin against your chest. Hold it there—pressed hard against your chest . . . Let your head return to a comfortable position and study the relaxation . . . Let the relaxation develop . . . feel it spread . . .

Shrug your shoulders up to your ears. Pull them up hard! Hold the tension . . . Drop your shoulders and feel the relaxation . . . Your neck and shoulders are relaxed . . . Shrug your shoulders again, and feel the tension . . . Bring your shoulders forward and HOLD THEM THERE . . . Relax. Drop your shoulders once more and relax . . . Press your shoulders hard against the floor—Press hard! Take a deep breath. Breathe slowly, deeply, and evenly . . . Let the relaxation spread deep into the shoulders and right into your back muscles. Relax your neck, your throat, your jaw, and your forehead, as the pure relaxation takes over and grows deeper . . . deeper . . . deeper . . .

Remember to keep these parts relaxed as you work on the rest of the body.

Now let's relax the arms. Clench your right fist. Clench it tighter and tighter, and focus on the tension. Keep it clenched, and feel the tension in your right fist, hand, and forearm . . . Hold it! Now relax . . . Let the fingers of your right hand become loose . . . Notice the contrast in the feelings . . . Once more, clench your right fist really tightly. Hold it, tighter, tighter, FEEL THE TENSION . . . Now, let go, relax, and let your fingers straighten out . . . Again, notice the difference.

Now repeat this with your left fist. Clench your left fist while the rest of your body relaxes. Clench that fist tighter, tighter, FEEL THE TENSION . . . And now relax . . . Again, enjoy the contrast. Repeat this once more. Clench the left fist, tight and tense . . . Now relax and feel the difference . . . Continue relaxing, and notice your breathing.

Now bend your elbows and tense your biceps. Tense them harder, and study the feeling of tension. Okay, straighten out your arms . . . Let them relax, and feel the difference . . . Let the relaxation develop . . . Once more, tense your biceps, tight! Hold the tension. Observe it carefully. Now straighten your arms and relax . . . Each time, pay close attention to your feelings, both when you tense up and when you relax . . . Continue relaxing your arms even further . . .

Now relax your entire body to the best of your ability . . . Feel that comfortable heaviness that comes with relaxation . . . Breathe easily and freely in and out . . . Notice how your relaxation increases as you exhale . . . Now breathe in and fill your lungs . . . Hold your breath . . . Study the tension . . . Now exhale, feel your chest get loose, and push the air out automatically . . . Continue relaxing and breathe freely and gently . . . Feel the relaxation, and enjoy it.

With the rest of your body as relaxed as possible, fill your lungs again . . . Breathe in deeply and hold it. Now breathe out and appreciate the relief; just breathe normally. Continue relaxing . . .

Now focus your attention on your abdominal muscles —your stomach area . . . Tighten your stomach muscles, tighter . . . Notice the tension . . . And relax, let the muscles loosen, and notice the contrast. Once more, tighten your stomach muscles . . . Hold it . . . tighter . . . TIGHTER! And relax . . . notice the general well-being that comes with relaxing your stomach muscles . . . Now draw your stomach in . . . Pull the muscles in and feel the tension . . . Now relax again . . . let your stomach out . . . Continue breathing normally and easily and feel the relaxation throughout your stomach, chest, back, shoulders, neck, and arms . . . Feel the relax-

ation grow deeper . . . Each time you breathe out, notice the relaxation both in your lungs and in your stomach . . . Notice how your chest and your stomach relax more and more . . .

Let go of all tensions and relax . . . Now flex your buttocks and thighs. Tense these muscles hard! HARDER! Relax and notice the difference. Feel the relaxation spreading . . . Again, straighten your knees and flex your thigh muscles. Hold the tension . . . Hold it tighter . . . tighter . . . Now relax your hips and thighs . . . Allow the relaxation to proceed on its own.

Now press your feet and toes downward, away from your face, so that your calf muscles become tense. Study the tension . . . Relax your feet and calves . . . This time, bend your feet toward your face so that you feel tension along your shins . . . Bring your toes up . . . Hold it! Relax again . . . Keep relaxing for awhile . . . Rotate your right ankle clockwise. Now reverse the direction. Now do the same with your left ankle, beginning clockwise. Then rotate in the other direction.

Tense your feet by squeezing tight with your toes. Hold the tension there . . . Squeeze hard! Now release . . . Wiggle your toes . . . Feel the difference the relaxation makes. One more time, Squeeze your toes tight. Hold it there . . . tighter . . . tighter! Okay, let it go.

Now let yourself relax further all over . . . Relax your feet, ankles, calves, shins, knees, thighs, buttocks, and hips . . . Feel the heaviness in your lower body as you relax still further . . . Now spread the relaxation to your stomach, waist, and lower back. Let go more and more deeply . . . Make sure no tension has crept into your body . . . Relax your neck, your jaws, and all your facial muscles. Keep relaxing your whole body like this for awhile . . . Let yourself relax . . .

Breathe in slowly and deeply and feel yourself becoming heavier . . . Take in a long, deep breath and exhale very slowly . . . Feel how heavy and relaxed you have become . . . Continue breathing deeply, and relaxing . . .

When you wish to get up, count backwards from four to one. You should now feel fine and refreshed, wide awake and calm.

Source: Jacobson, E. (1980). *Progressive relaxation*. Chicago: University of Chicago.

Conclusion and Evaluation (5 Minutes)

Summarize the main points of the workshop:

- There are techniques you can learn to combat stress.
- Progressive relaxation is a helpful individual relaxation technique. It allows you time to clear your mind and focus on yourself.

- Massage is an effective relaxation technique to practice with another person. It is a muscle relaxer, and also allows time for you to focus on yourself.

Ask for questions from participants. Offer resources and referrals for further information. Distribute Lifestyle Workshop evaluation forms and pencils. Allow time for completion and then collect. Briefly list and describe the other Lifestyle Workshops in Stress Management.

MOST FREQUENTLY ASKED QUESTIONS

1. *Why use oil during a massage? What about lotion?*

Using oil during a massage can help cut down on some of the friction created while rubbing the body. Oil is better than lotion because it doesn't soak into the skin as quickly as lotion. Remember to warm the oil to room temperature before applying it to the skin.

2. *Should you always begin a massage at the lower back?*

You can begin a massage wherever you prefer. Regardless of where you begin, be sure to use long, slow strokes, which enable both persons to become familiar with the touching. Once you've made contact with the massagee, always keep at least one hand touching the person throughout the massage.

3. *Can you use these strokes on other parts of the body besides the back?*

Yes. The same basic strokes that are used on the back can also be used on other areas of the body. Remember to massage only on muscle tissue and never directly on the spine or bone. Ask the massagee for feedback on what feels good.

4. *What is a "knot"?*

A "knot" feels like a lump and it is found in particularly tight muscles. These little lumps are either toxic by-products (lactic acid) of muscular exertion or knottings of the connective tissue.

5. *Once you come across a knot, what can you do about it?*

First you will want to massage a much wider area surrounding the tension. This is because the knot is actually an indication of a larger pattern of tension. Next, you will want to massage directly on the tense area slowly and thoroughly, using either the tips of your fingers or the balls of your thumbs. Ask for feedback and adjust the amount of pressure accordingly.

6. *Can massage get rid of headaches?*

A majority of headaches are stress-related and the result of muscle tension. Many people get relief from headaches by eliminating the muscle tension. To do this, massage the shoulder, neck, and scalp area.

7. *How can I learn more about massage?*

An excellent book on the subject is *The Massage Book* by George Downing. It is available at most bookstores. Your public library may also have additional information on massage. If you are interested in a massage class, call your local YMCA or Park District and ask if they offer any.

Relaxation Bingo

Find people here who participate in these activities regularly as a means of relaxation. Ask them to sign their names in the appropriate boxes. Try to find a different person for each activity. Fill in the center square with *your* favorite relaxation activity.

Keeps a journal, diary, or dream notebook	Rides a bike or motorcycle for pleasure	Uses a hot tub, hot springs, steamroom, or sauna	Spends time in the woods, mountains, desert, or beach	Plays a musical instrument or sings
Plays with young children or animals	Runs, jogs, or takes long walks	Works in the yard or garden	Takes naps or sunbaths	Practices a martial art
Spends leisure time in the park	Eats only natural, healthy food	Your favorite	Meditates regularly	Does deep breathing exercises
Listens to quiet music	Enjoys an aerobic sport	Enjoys a craft or manual hobby	Goes hiking or camping	Enjoys a snow or water sport
Practices yoga	Gets and/or gives massages	Reads a lot for pleasure	Attends theatre, concerts, or shows	Practices dancing or gymnastics

Note. From *Structured Exercises in Stress Management* (Vol. 1) by N. Tubesing and D. Tubesing, 1983, Duluth, MN: Whole Person Associates. Copyright 1983. Reprinted by permission.

Massage Instructions

Massage can help you relieve tension and reduce stress. It can help you relax by increasing blood flow to your tension areas (i.e., shoulder, neck, and back) (Figure 1). Increased blood flow relaxes muscles and removes the build-up of waste products caused by tension. (These waste products are what can make your neck hurt.)

A massage is also a way to communicate caring without words. Touch alone can have a healing effect. Massage can be a nice way of saying "I care about you" to a friend, roommate, or family member.

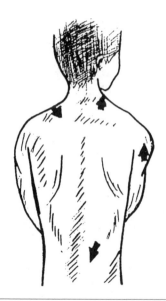

Figure 1. Tension areas.

- Ask what the other person likes.
- Do not use pressure directly on the spine.
- Use circular motions on the back. Long strokes should be done in the direction of the heart (Figure 2).
- Maintain an even, firm pressure by using your body weight rather than muscles to apply pressure.
- Mold your hands to fit the contours they are passing over.
- Don't be offended if your friend falls asleep—you've done well!

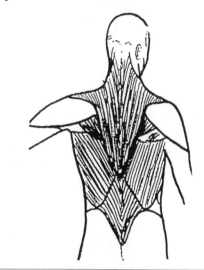

Figure 2. Massage strokes should be done in the direction of the muscle . . . *toward* the heart.

General Tips

- Atmosphere is important! Massage should be done in a comfortably warm room on a firm, comfortable surface. A carpeted floor is perfect. Play soft music and keep the lighting soft.
- Remove all jewelry that may interfere with giving or receiving a massage. This may mean rings, necklaces, bracelets, and watches. Loosen all restrictive clothing.
- Shake your hands to relax and warm them before you start the massage.
- Once you begin the massage, continue to touch the other person.

Massage Instructions

- Have the person lie on his or her stomach. If you feel comfortable (and the person doesn't mind) sit on his or her lower buttocks. Otherwise, you can sit beside the person.
- Begin with long, slow, whole-hand stroking movements; starting at the lower back and moving straight up toward the neck. Take your time; RELAX and breathe deeply; focus on your partner. (See Figure 3.)
- Now, separate your hands and bring them over the shoulder blades toward the floor. Pull your hands back along your partner's sides. Repeat this movement several times.

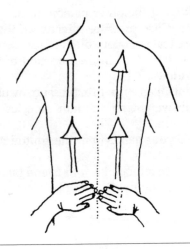

Figure 3.

- Next, work with your thumbs on the lower back. Using the balls of your thumbs, make short rapid strokes away from you toward your partner's head. Work close to the spine just below the waistline; first on the left, then on the right side. (See Figure 4.)

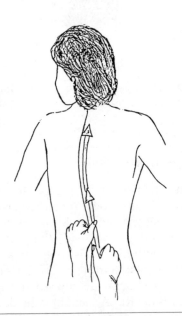

Figure 4.

- Glide your hands to the top of the shoulders. Firmly grasp and knead the entire upper back and shoulder area. Observe your partner's response. Do what he or she likes.
- Next, massage the back of the neck and head. Use your fingers and the balls of your thumbs to gently knead this area. Use a small, circular motion and work from the base of the neck up toward the head. Use a smooth, firm stroke down to the base of the neck. Repeat this several times. (See Figure 5.)

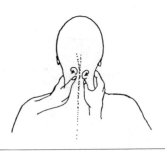

Figure 5.

- With hands placed in the middle of the back, spread your fingers and stroke upward and outward toward the shoulders. Repeat. (See Figure 6.)

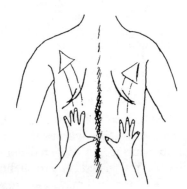

Figure 6.

- With your hands at the top of the shoulders, gently squeeze and release the upper arm and shoulder muscle. Repeat several times on each side. (See Figure 7.)

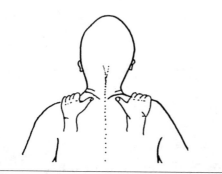

Figure 7.

• To end the massage, use your fingertips to make feather-light strokes from the neck to the lower back. Finally, gently remove both hands.

Contributors: Anne Brinkmann, Mina Coy
Illustrations: Diane Smogor

Note. From *The Massage Book* by G. Downing, 1972, New York: Random House. Adapted by permission.

Posterior Muscle Diagram

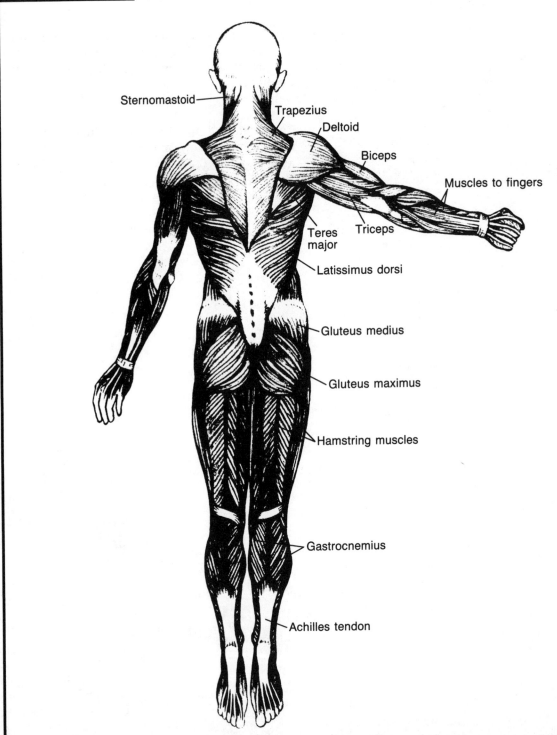

Note. From *The Human Body: Your Body and How it Works* (p. 39) by Ruth Dowling Bruun, M.D., and Bertel Bruun, M.D., Illustrated by Patricia J. Wynn, 1982, New York: Random House. Copyright 1982 by Random House. Reprinted by permission of Random House, Inc.

REFERENCES

Curtis, J.D., & Detert, R.A. (1981). *How to relax: A holistic approach to stress management.* Palo Alto, CA: Mayfield.

Davis, M., Eshelman, E.R., & McKay, M. (1982). *The relaxation and stress reduction workbook.* Oakland, CA: New Harbinger.

Downing, G. (1972). *The massage book.* New York: Random House.

Greenberg, J.S. (1987). *Comprehensive stress management.* Dubuque, IA: Brown.

Jacobson, E. (1938). *Progressive relaxation.* Chicago: University of Chicago.

Mason, L.J. (1985). *Guide to stress reduction.* Berkeley: Celestial Arts.

One-Stop
Time Management
Lifestyle Workshop

PARAPROFESSIONAL PREPARATION MATERIALS

Training Sessions

Competency Exam

Texts and Suggested Readings

WORKSHOP AT A GLANCE

Presenter Information

Most Frequently Asked Questions

Handouts and Visual Aids

References

TRAINING SESSIONS

One-Stop Time Management

Session 1: Workshop Presentation

Time: 60 minutes

Methods: Presentation, demonstration

Description: Trainer presents workshop to Lifestyle Educators.

Readings: The workshop

Session 2: Time Management and Stress

Time: 60 minutes

Methods: Discussion, activities

Description: Explore relationship between time management and stress.

Activity: Complete a time management assessment. Complete a Type-A behavior pattern inventory.

Readings: Materials covering managing personal stress

Competency exam questions: 1, 2, 3, 4, 9, 10

Session 3: The Lakein Method of Time Management

Time: 60 minutes

Methods: Discussion and activities

Description: Discuss the method described in Alan Lakein's book, *How to Get Control of Your Time and Your Life.*

Activity: Present the Lifetime Goals Exercise. Create a list of personal time-wasters. Assign students to calculate how they spend 168 hours a week.

Readings: The workshop, the "Lakein Method"

Competency exam questions: 5, 6

Session 4: Procrastination and Decision Making

Time: 60 minutes

Methods: Discussion, activities

Description: Discuss causes of procrastination and strategies for overcoming it. Discuss and practice decision-making skills related to time management.

Activity: Students complete "Taking Stock of Procrastination" handout.

Readings: Materials on procrastination

Competency exam questions: 7, 8

Session 5: "Most Frequently Asked Questions" Review and Hot Seat

Time: 60 minutes

Methods: Discussion, practice

Description: Review workshop components

Activity: Hot Seat: Each Lifestyle Educator is quizzed by the other students about the workshop topic for 10 minutes.

Readings: The workshop

Session 6: Practice Workshop Presentation

Time: 60 minutes

Method: Presentation

Description: Each Lifestyle Educator presents 20 mintues of workshop.

Readings: The workshop

COMPETENCY EXAM

The following questions require brief responses.

1. How does ineffective use of time lead to stress?

2. According to your text, what are three major areas where time is a potential stressor?

3. Your text describes four kinds of stress caused by poor time management. Identify and briefly explain these.

4. Define goals and explain how goals are relevant to time management and stress reduction.

5. What is the purpose of the ABC method?

6. Explain the significance of an A, B, and C item, respectively.

7. What are five obstacles to effective time management as identified in your text?

8. What are intervention strategies for dealing with these obstacles?

9. Identify five common time-wasters for college students.

10. What are five strategies or techniques for improving time management?

11. Suggest possible techniques to use in your workshop if participant is one of the following:
    • Recognition Seeker (frequently calls attention to self)
    • Conversationalist (brings up off-the-subject anecdotes and is a noisy distraction)
    • Moralizer (advocates judgmental points of view based on personal convictions)
    • Conservative (convinced that the status quo does not need changing)

TEXTS AND SUGGESTED READINGS

Bliss, E.C. (1976). *Getting things done: The ABC's of time management*. New York: Scribner's.

Burka, J.B., & Yuen, L.M. (1983). *Procrastination: Why You Do It, What to Do About It*. Reading, MA: Addison-Wesley.

Lakein, A. (1973). *How to get control of your time and your life*. New York: Signet.

LeBoeuf, M. (1979). *Working smart: How to accomplish more in half the time*. New York: Warner.

Scharf, D., & Hait, P. (1985). *Studying smart: Time management for college students*. New York: Barnes and Noble.

Webber, R.A. (1980). *A guide to getting things done*. New York: Macmillan.

WORKSHOP AT A GLANCE

The goal of this workshop is both to stimulate ideas about poor time management as a source of distress and to educate participants about the role time management plays in organizing and achieving goals. This workshop takes approximately 60 minutes to present. Suggested attendance is 5 to 30 persons.

Objectives

Within the content of this workshop, the following objectives will be met.

- Participants will identify problem areas related to time management, study skills, test anxiety, and procrastination.
- During a time management activity, participants will analyze their weekly committed and free time.
- Following a demonstration of the Lakein time management method, participants will practice organizing and prioritizing their activities.
- Participants will identify tasks that they often procrastinate.
- Using the "Goal-Setting Worksheet," participants will identify their long- and short-term goals.

Workshop Materials

- Workshop sign-in sheet
- Handouts and visual aids: *Goal-Setting Worksheet, Blockades to Success, Weekly Time Schedule, Taking Stock of Procrastination,* and *Time Management Approach: The Lakein Method.*
- Large pad of paper
- Markers
- Lifestyle Workshop evaluation forms and pencils

PRESENTER INFORMATION

Briefly introduce yourself, your background, and any other personal information you choose to share. Describe your health promotion program and the topics available, for example, nutrition and fitness. Stress that the workshops are unique because you bring them to their living areas. Lifestyle Workshop paraprofessionals are trained at (your institution or program) to present these workshops. If anyone is interested in the training program, ask him or her to speak with you after the workshop.

The purpose of this workshop is to stimulate ideas about time management and the role it plays in organizing and achieving goals. Participants will be taught ways to get organized and set goals.

Time Management and Stress (5 minutes)

Pass out the handout "Blockades to Success." After participants complete the survey, explain the four possible impediments to success at school: time management, study skills, test anxiety, and procrastination. Participants may be interested to know how others scored.

Discuss how time stressors are one of the most common sources of anxiety for college students. Offer a personal example of a time stressor. Other examples may be

- finding time to study,
- finding time to clean your room or apartment,
- finding time to do laundry,
- trying to hold a job,
- cooking meals,
- developing relationships, or
- procrastinating.

Explain that when you don't accomplish what you should, you may feel confused, compromised, frustrated, and *stressed*!

Recognizing Common Time-Wasters (15 minutes)

Divide the group into smaller working groups for these two activities. To begin the first activity, pose the question: "How do you spend your week?" There are 168 hours in a week. Have participants take a few minutes to calculate the amount of time spent doing routine activities. Pass out the "Weekly Time Schedule." Give each participant two—one to use now and one for future use. Start by computing *committed time*. For example:

- Sitting in class
- Eating
- Sleeping
- Dressing
- Traveling to and from class or work
- Working
- Participating in meetings

Next, compute flexible or free time. For example: studying (mention that the average student with one lab course spends about 22-26 hours per week studying), and recreational activities. Now review this schedule. Ask participants, "Is your life balanced? Which activities cause you the most stress?"

Suggest that after the workshop participants record in a diary how their time is spent for a week. Tell them to write down their activities in units of 30 minutes at the end of each day. At the end of the week they may want to review the diary and develop a regular schedule that includes time for relaxation.

Brainstorm with participants about common time-wasters for students. Ask, "What do you do when you should be studying or working?" Examples might include these:

- Watch TV.
- Listen to music.
- Talk on telephone.

- Have "bull sessions."
- Get unexpected (and maybe unwanted) visitors.
- Procrastinate.
- Raid the refrigerator.
- Read novels instead of texts.
- Write letters instead of papers.
- Read the newspaper.
- Sleep.
- Shop.

After generating a list of time-wasters, brainstorm about strategies to overcome these. Overcome procrastination by daily making a "To Do" list and following it! Use the "swiss cheese method" of breaking work down into manageable steps. (See Most Frequently Asked Questions.)

Taking Stock of Procrastination (10 minutes)

You may want to present this material by asking participants these questions: Can anyone tell us about a recent incident of procrastination? What happened? Who was involved in the incident? How did you feel? What was the outcome? Was anyone inconvenienced or hurt? What were the consequences? Ask participants to fill out the survey "Taking Stock of Procrastination" to help distinguish between areas in which they procrastinate and those in which they don't. Most people are selective procrastinators.

In each area, have participants consider how much their delaying bothers them. Some things may cause internal or external problems, while others cause none. What distinguishes procrastination from just putting things off is the level of discomfort it creates. Tell participants to be sure to distinguish between procrastination and the things they enjoy (like reading the newspaper) or that need to be done (like housecleaning). If it's really procrastination, there will probably be a nagging feeling of "I've got to get started sooner or later!"

Goal-Setting Activity (5 minutes)

Explain to participants the important role that goals play in managing our time and preventing distress. Setting goals helps people determine how to spend their time. Distribute the "Goal-Setting Worksheet," and direct participants to identify their long- and short-term goals. For example, what they want to accomplish this semester would be a long-term goal, but how they will accomplish it would be a short-term goal.

The Lakein Approach to Time Management (10 minutes)

Explain to participants that the aim of the Lakein approach is to help them

- become **decisive** about time, and thus have greater control over it,
- become more **organized** in the way they think about time: to help them focus on their priorities,
- become **intuitive** about time requirements that will guide them day in and day out, and
- become more **analytical** about time use.

Have participants refer to the Lakein Method handouts and explain the method.

1. Have participants suggest activities for a "To Do" list. Write these on a large sheet of paper so that everyone can see what you're doing.
2. Use the handout "Time Management Approach: The Lakein Method." Have students make a personal "To Do" list on their own papers. Tell them to write for 2 to 3 minutes, intuitively and quickly without censoring.
3. Establish priorities for activities on the class "To Do" list. As = high-value activities, Bs = medium-value activities, Cs = low-value activities. Have participants do the same on their own lists.

4. On the class list, prioritize only the As. Decide which to label A1, A2, A3, and so on. There can be only one A1. Have participants do the same on their lists.

5. Have participants get a new sheet of paper. Tell them: Write your A1 at the top in big letters. Write down all of the activities you can think of that you have to do to achieve A1. Write quickly; don't censor. Be creative! Think of as many alternatives as possible.

6. Now go through all of the activities on the class list and prioritize them with As, Bs, and Cs. Participants should do the same.

7. Next, prioritize these further with A1s, A2s, and so forth. Have participants do this too. Explain that what is left are priorities translated into everyday action terms, that is, a path to accomplishing something.

Discuss this method briefly with the group. Ask for reactions and questions. Tell participants that the "To Do" list may have to be reprioritized as the As are accomplished. This may have to be done on a daily basis.

Conclusion and Evaluation (5 minutes)

Summarize the main points of the workshop:

- Mismanagement of your time can be a source of stress.
- It's important to be aware of where your time goes; keep a diary to record your activities.
- There are strategies you can develop and use to overcome common time-wasters.

Ask for questions from participants. Offer resources and referrals for further information. Distribute Lifestyle Workshop evaluation forms and pencils. Allow time for completion and then collect. Briefly list and describe the other Lifestyle Workshops in Stress Management.

MOST FREQUENTLY ASKED QUESTIONS

1. *Why is time management considered a stress management technique?*

   Practicing time management enables an individual to have some control over potential stressors and thus to minimize distress.

2. *My "To Do" list seems impossible to accomplish. What should I do?*

   Review your list to see if the items listed are too general. The "To Do" list can seem overwhelming unless you list tasks that are specific and limited. To simplify a large task, break it down into manageable parts. For example, instead of "prepare for history final," list the activities involved: study lecture notes, review textbook, re-read quizzes and midterm, and so on.

3. *What is the 80/20 rule?*

   The 80/20 rule basically means that you can be 80% effective by accomplishing the top 20% of your goals. The key is to identify your priorities and concentrate your time and effort on achieving those.

4. *I find the hardest part of any job is just getting started. What can I do?*

   Getting started is hard for a lot of people. It doesn't seem to matter if the task is large or small. It may be especially hard to get started if you aren't sure which task is most important. The ABC method allows you to see what's important compared to what can be eliminated, or at least postponed. You may find it helpful if you look at making a "To Do" list as the starting point of any job. Then, once you've identified your priorities, you've already begun the project!

5. *What do you mean by the "Swiss Cheese Method"?*

   Think of your project as a piece of cheese—to make it resemble swiss cheese, do small amounts of work at a time until your project is finished. For example, if you have to read five chapters of psychology by next week, read one chapter each night rather than five chapters in one night.

Goal-Setting Worksheet

> *"Time is Life. To waste your time is to waste your life; to manage your time is to manage your life."*
> Alan Lakein, 1973, author of *How to Get Control of Your Time and Your Life*

> *"Time is what each person doesn't have enough of, yet each person has all that is necessary."*
> Curtis & Detert, 1981, authors of *How to Relax: A Holistic Approach to Stress Management*

Goal-setting plays a major role in managing your time and preventing distress. Goals are statements related to what you want to do with your time. Goals provide direction and enable you to observe your progress.

Identifying your goals on paper tends to make them more concrete and specific. Spend 2 to 3 minutes answering each of the following questions. Write whatever comes to mind—don't censor your thoughts!

What are my lifetime goals?

How would I like to spend the next 3 years?

If I knew now that I would be struck dead by lightning 6 months from today, how would I live until then?

Now you have a list of goals. You may have even thought of more to do than there is time for. This time constraint creates goal conflicts, which are resolved by setting priorities. This helps you decide which goals are most important to you right now.

Note. Adapted from *How to Get Control of Your Time and Your Life* by A. Lakein, 1973, New York: Signet.

Blockades to Success

Do these statements pertain to you? Put a check next to each one that does.

1. _____ I do my best work under pressure.
2. _____ I often feel hurried by school and/or personal pressures.
3. _____ I have trouble saying "no" to people who ask me to do things for them.
4. _____ I often get behind in my readings and papers.
5. _____ I don't have enough time to spend on personal interests, such as hobbies and sports.
6. _____ I feel that I have to get straight As.
7. _____ I worry that if I fail a test, someone will be disappointed in me.
8. _____ When I take a test, I start blanking out and worry that I won't finish.
9. _____ I panic during a test, worrying that if I don't do well I'll never get into grad school/find a good job/graduate on time, etc.
10. _____ During a test, I worry that I will fail and that everybody is doing better than I am.
11. _____ I find that I get distracted by minor disturbances when I'm studying.
12. _____ I can finish the small tasks, but I rarely have time to finish the larger ones.
13. _____ I read material over and over, but I can't seem to learn it.
14. _____ When I have something on my mind, I can't concentrate on studying.
15. _____ I would rather go out than study, and I often give in to these urges.
16. _____ When I finish a big project, I think "next time I'll start sooner."
17. _____ I usually study by cramming the night before the test.
18. _____ I wish I would get my work done earlier than I do.
19. _____ When I get an assignment, I usually don't start right away.
20. _____ If I leave studying for an exam until the last minute, I panic and have a hard time getting anything done.

If most of your checks are in	You may have a problem with
1-5	Time management
6-10	Test anxiety
11-15	Study skills
16-20	Procrastination

Weekly Time Schedule

Hours	Monday	Tuesday	Wednesday	Thursday	Friday	Saturday	Sunday
7:00- 8:00							
8:00- 9:00							
9:00-10:00							
10:00-11:00							
11:00-12:00							
12:00- 1:00							
1:00- 2:00							
2:00- 3:00							
3:00- 4:00							
4:00- 5:00							
5:00- 6:00							
6:00- 7:00							
7:00- 8:00							
8:00- 9:00							
9:00-10:00							
10:00-11:00							
11:00-12:00							
12:00- 1:00							
1:00- 2:00							
2:00- 3:00							
3:00- 4:00							
4:00- 5:00							
5:00- 6:00							
6:00- 7:00							

Taking Stock of Procrastination

Listed below are common activities, divided into general categories. Check off the activities in which you procrastinate. Are there general areas where you procrastinate more than others?

Your Residence

- ☐ Day-to-day chores (e.g., dishes)
- ☐ Minor home projects or repairs
- ☐ Making your bed
- ☐ Clothes washing/dry-cleaning
- ☐ Grocery shopping
- ☐ Running errands

- ☐ Large home projects
- ☐ Car maintenance and repairs
- ☐ Cleaning
- ☐ Paying bills
- ☐ Returning defective or unwanted merchandise

School

- ☐ Attending classes
- ☐ Completing degree requirements
- ☐ Studying for tests
- ☐ Researching for papers
- ☐ Being on time for meetings
- ☐ Talking with a teacher or advisor

- ☐ Doing bureaucratic tasks
- ☐ Doing homework assignments
- ☐ Returning library books
- ☐ Getting to class on time
- ☐ Writing papers
- ☐ Keeping up with reading for classes

Personal Care

- ☐ Getting physical exercise
- ☐ Reading for personal interest
- ☐ Stopping smoking or use of alcohol or drugs
- ☐ Taking courses/classes for personal interest
- ☐ Shopping for new clothes
- ☐ Taking vacations

- ☐ Getting a haircut
- ☐ Losing weight
- ☐ Pursuing hobbies or personal projects
- ☐ Making medical or dental appointments
- ☐ Making long-term life decisions

Social Relationships

- ☐ Giving gifts or sending cards
- ☐ Asking someone for a date
- ☐ Writing letters
- ☐ Inviting people to your house
- ☐ Being on time for social events
- ☐ Planning recreational activities with other people
- ☐ Telling someone you are upset or angry

- ☐ Calling friends
- ☐ Asking for help or support
- ☐ Giving parties
- ☐ Expressing appreciation
- ☐ Visiting relatives
- ☐ Confronting someone about a problem
- ☐ Ending an unsatisfying relationship

Finances

☐ Paying tuition and fees
☐ Filling out income tax forms
☐ Paying back loans (institutional)
☐ Collecting debts owed to you
☐ Organizing receipts and tax records
☐ Paying or getting insurance
☐ Making financial investments

☐ Balancing your checkbook
☐ Paying parking tickets
☐ Paying back loans (personal)
☐ Budgeting your money
☐ Calling the bank about a problem
☐ Paying credit card bills

Note. Adapted from J. Burka/L. Yuen, *Procrastination*, © 1983, Addison-Wesley Publishing Co., Inc., Reading, Massachusetts. Reprinted with permission.

Time Management Approach: The Lakein Method

TO DO LIST

B   Read 5 history chapters
A_1 Write paper for American lit.
B   Study for geography test
A_2 Write home for money
C   Buy Susan's birthday gift

Step 1: Prioritize list using A, B, C

Step 2: Prioritize As using 1, 2, 3

Step 3: Write activities necessary to accomplish A_1

Step 4: Prioritize again

A_1 Write paper for American lit.
B   Research Mark Twain's life
A   Read Tom Sawyer
C   Outline paper

REFERENCES

Burka, J.B., & Yuen, L.M. (1983). *Procrastination: Why You Do It, What to Do About It*. Reading, MA: Addison-Wesley.

Girdano, D.A., & Everly, G.S. (1986). *Controlling stress and tension: A holistic approach*. Englewood Cliffs, NJ: Prentice-Hall.

Greenberg, J.S. (1987). *Comprehensive stress management*. Dubuque, IA: Brown.

Lakein, A. (1973). *How to get control of your time and your life*. New York: Signet.

McKay, M., Davis, M., & Fanning, F. (1981). *Thoughts and feelings: The art of cognitive stress intervention*. Richmond, CA: New Harbinger.

Whetton, D.A., & Cameron, K.S. (1984). *Developing management skills*. Glenview, IL: Scott, Foresman.

There's More to Eating Than Food Lifestyle Workshop

PARAPROFESSIONAL PREPARATION MATERIALS

Training Sessions

Competency Exam

Texts and Suggested Readings

WORKSHOP AT A GLANCE

Presenter Information

Most Frequently Asked Questions

Handouts and Visual Aids*

References

*Healthy Eating Habits, Healthy You! was written by Michele Easterling, MPH, RD.

TRAINING SESSIONS

There's More to Eating Than Food

Session 1: Workshop Presentation

Time: 60 minutes

Methods: Presentation, demonstration

Description: Trainer presents the workshop to Lifestyle Educators.

Readings: The workshop

Session 2: Body Image

Time: 60 minutes

Methods: Lecture, discussion, activity

Description: Fill out body image survey (see handouts and visual aids), go over workshop, and review materials needed to present workshop.

Activity: University of Pennsylvania's study on Body Image is introduced, along with the questionnaire to be filled in by students. Results from the University of Pennsylvania will be compared to results from class.

Readings: The handout *University of Pennsylvania Body Image Survey*, material on anorexia, bulimia, and cultural expectations of thinness in women; the workshop

Competency exam questions: 1, 2, 3, 4, 5, 20

Session 3: Food Diary and Behavior Modification

Time: 60 minutes

Methods: Lecture, discussion

Description: Pass out seven copies of a food diary to each student. Discuss the proper procedure for filling in a food diary and assign one week's worth of baseline data collection. Introduce and define antecedents, behaviors, and consequences.

Readings: Behavior modification, baseline data collection, contingency contracting, the workshop

Competency exam questions: 7, 14, 16, 19

Session 4: Self-Modification Projects

Time: 60 minutes

Methods: Lecture, discussion

Description: Discuss designing a self-modification project. Discuss the part of the workshop on Managing Eating Behaviors, and assign steps A, B, and C using information collected last week from food diaries. Present an example of a self-modification project. (This includes contract, baseline data, and evaluations 1 and 2.)

Activity: As a group, students design a self-modification project using a sample weekly food diary.

Readings: Behavior modification steps for self-control, the workshop

Competency exam questions: 6, 8, 12, 13, 15

Session 5: Eating Disorders 1

Time: 60 minutes

Methods: Lecture, discussion

Description: Discuss negative eating behaviors. Discuss characteristics of anorexia nervosa and bulimia. Outline the differences and similarities in both the physical and psychological symptoms of these two disorders.

Readings: Eating disorders, diaries of anorexics and bulimics, the workshop

Competency exam questions: 17, 23, 24

Session 6: Eating Disorders 2

Time: 60 minutes

Methods: Lecture, discussion

Description: Discuss the two most common purging methods. Provide students with a list of local resources where help is available. Define bulimarexia, and discuss the cultural norms we have about eating.

Activity: Provide a list of characteristics and symptoms; ask students to indicate whether the characteristic is most commonly associated with anorexia, bulimia, or both.

Readings: Eating disorders, diaries of anorexics and bulimics, cultural norms (socially accepted and expected eating practices), and the workshop

Competency exam questions: 11, 17, 18, 21, 23, 24

Session 7: Positive Eating Behaviors

Time: 60 minutes

Methods: Lecture, discussion

Description: Discuss characteristics that are considered positive eating behaviors, and define the coping and communication skills necessary for those characteristics. For example, choose an article about a dieter from a current women's fashion magazine, and analyze how she fits the characteristics associated with positive eating behaviors.

Readings: Materials on healthy eating habits and the workshop

Competency exam question: 10

Session 8: "Most Frequently Asked Questions" Review and Hot Seat

Time: 60 minutes

Methods: Discussion, practice

Description: Review "Most Frequently Asked Questions" and other workshop components.

Activity: "Hot Seat": Each Lifestyle Educator is quizzed by the other students on the workshop topic for 10 minutes.

Competency exam questions: 9, 22

Session 9: Practice Workshop Presentation

Time: 60 minutes

Method: Presentation

Description: Each Lifestyle Educator presents 20 minutes of the workshop.

COMPETENCY EXAM

The following questions require brief responses.

1. What were the main differences between the males' and the females' results in the University of Pennsylvania Body Image Study?

2. Define these terms from the same study: Ideal, Current, Attractive, and Other Attractive.

3. Explain the difference between "fashion body" and "healthy body."

4. How have female bodies changed from decade to decade starting in the 1950s up to the 1980s?

5. What areas of a woman's body are most significant when she is forming her body image?

6. To resist a tempting situation one needs _____, but if one makes a deliberate effort to change or remove the tempting situation it is called _____.

7. Situations can be divided into two elements, the events that come before a behavior and those that come after it. Name these two elements.

8. Name three common reasons why a self-modification project could fail.

9. In the article, "162 Pounds and Counting Down," explain why Jackie is an example of losing weight properly.

10. Where should one look for professional help with an eating problem?

11. Pick a common negative eating habit and describe the typical behavior(s) that are associated with it.

12. After using a food diary for 2 weeks, a participant discovers that on Sunday afternoons she always ends up having a "food fiesta." Name three behavior modification techniques that could be used to avoid this situation.

13. How does the action that follows a behavior determine whether or not the behavior will happen again?

14. In any self-modification project, why should one expect mistakes to occur?

15. Explain why a food diary is valuable.

16. Name three characteristics of a compulsive eater.

17. Describe one purging method and explain two complications associated with it.

18. In the external cue theory, external factors could be _____, or _____, or _____; internal factors are _____ or _____.

19. Draw and briefly explain the "dieting cycle."

20. Name three cultural norms for eating.

21. Name three criteria to look for when diagnosing anorexia.

22. Name three physical symptoms of anorexia.

23. Name two psychological symptoms of anorexia.

24. Name three criteria to look for when diagnosing bulimia.

25. Name three physical symptoms of bulimia (identify which purging method).

26. Name two psychological symptoms of bulimia.

27. Suggest possible techniques to use in the workshop if a participant is one of the following:
    • Recognition Seeker (frequently calls attention to self)
    • Conversationalist (brings up off-the-subject anecdotes and is a noisy distraction)
    • Moralizer (advocates judgmental points of view based on personal convictions)
    • Conservative (convinced that the status quo does not need changing)

TEXTS AND SUGGESTED READINGS

Barbera-Hogan, M. (1986, October). The nightmare of disturbed eating. *Teen*, p. 27.

Garner, D.M., Garfinkel, P.E., Schwartz, D., & Thompson, M. (1980). Cultural expectations of thinness in women. *Psychological Reports*, **47**, 483-491.

Kirkley, B.G. (1986). Bulimia: Clinical characteristics, development, and etiology. *Journal of American Dietetic Association*, **86**, 468-475.

McCarthy, L.F. (1986, September). The secret lives of dieters. *Mademoiselle*, pp. 264-318.

Nash, J.D. (1986, March). Interruptions: How to avoid backsliding. *Shape*, pp. 56-58.

162 pounds and counting down. (1985, December). *Glamour*, pp. 158-159.

Orbach, S. (1982). *Fat is a feminist issue II*. New York: Berkeley.

Robertson, D.S. (1986, March). Sticking to it: Techniques, tricks, and foolproof planning. *Shape*, pp. 52-54.

Watson, D.L., & Tharp, R.G. (1985). *Self-directed behavior: Self-modification for personal adjustment* (4th ed.). Monterey, CA: Brooks/Cole.

Whitney, E.N., & Hamilton, E.M. (1987). *Understanding nutrition* (4th ed.). St. Paul, MN: West.

Wooley, S., & Wooley, O.W. (1986, October). Thinness mania. *American Health*, pp. 68-74.

WORKSHOP AT A GLANCE

The goal of this workshop is to explore some of the factors that determine one's eating habits, and to introduce self-modification steps for changing negative eating habits into positive ones. The workshop will challenge the participant's views on the role that food plays in their lives and their perceptions of the ideal body types. This workshop takes approximately 60 minutes to present. Suggested attendance is 6 to 30 persons.

Objectives

Within the content of this workshop, the following objectives will be met.

- Participants will choose various ideal and attractive body images and discuss both the concept of body image and how these ideals may differ between the sexes.
- Participants will be introduced to possible causes of negative eating behaviors, such as bulimia and anorexia.
- Self-control steps for managing eating behaviors will be presented.
- Positive eating behaviors will be suggested.
- Local resources will be recommended for participants who prefer more individualized help in overcoming negative eating behaviors.

Workshop Materials

- Workshop sign-up sheet
- Handouts and visual aids: *University of Pennsylvania Body Image Study Survey, Healthy Eating Habits, Healthy You!,* and *Food Diary*
- Blank paper
- Lifestyle Workshop evaluation forms and pencils

PRESENTER INFORMATION

Briefly introduce yourself, your background, and any other personal information you choose to share. Describe your health promotion program and the topics available, such as fitness and nutrition. Stress that the workshops are unique because you bring them to their living areas. Tell them that Lifestyle Workshop paraprofessionals are trained at (your institution or program) to present these workshops. If anyone is interested in the training program, ask him or her to speak with you after the workshop.

This workshop points out some of the less obvious roles that food can play in our lives, along with a brief exploration into the meanings of fat and thin for both men and women. An individual's eating preferences may be pretty well established by this point in their lives, but that doesn't mean they're unchangeable. Self-control techniques will be introduced that will help participants improve their eating habits. Personal and group views on body image and the ideal body type will be challenged and discussed with the use of a survey and questionnaire.

Ideal Body Image (10 minutes)

Introduce the handout of the University of Pennsylvania Body Image study and define the terms *ideal, current, attractive,* and *other attractive.* Direct participants to complete the survey, indicating their choice for ideal, current, attractive and other attractive for the *opposite* sex. Then have them complete the remaining questions. Collect the surveys and give them to a predesignated statistician who will tally the results. Explain results of University of Pennsylvania Study (Fallon & Rozin, 1985).

Involve participants by asking about characteristics of an ideal body type. There may be several definitions of a desirable body type, for example, a high-fashion body or an athletic body. The point is that it's much more important to have the correct percentage of body fat and be in good cardiovascular condition than to try and match a fashion ideal. When health and beauty ideals are not compatible, people diet unnecessarily, as is the case in today's society. Gather photos and magazine ads and compile them on a poster board to show examples of ideal body types from various de-

cades. This would make an excellent visual aid. For example, in the 1950s Marilyn Monroe exemplified the curvaceous figure that men admired and women desired. In the 1960s and 1970s thin was in, and Twiggy best represented the body of the time. Some large-chested women even bound their chests with tape to appear "flatter." The look of the 1980s appears to be lean, yet athletic. It isn't enough to just be thin anymore; the ideal body now has well-defined muscles. Women bodybuilders are saying that muscles and strength represent sexiness. Ask participants to discuss how they feel about these changing standards.

Ask participants to name the parts of a woman's body that are considered the most common problem areas. Usually this list will include hips, abdomen, buttocks, thighs, and breasts. Next, ask about the areas on a man's body that are considered to be the most common concerns. This list will usually include the size of the chest, arms, thighs, and stomach. Next, distribute a blank sheet of paper to each participant. Instruct them to write down five of their own best attributes, for example, their height, eye or hair color, personality, and so on. Have them turn the paper over, and ask them to go through this mental exercise: "Imagine yourself with 20 more pounds of fat on your body frame . . . Think of the changes that would occur because of this extra weight . . . What things would stay the same? Would you feel different about yourself? Would your relationships with others change?"

After participants have had time to think this over, ask them to go back to their original list of attributes and put a star by the ones that would change because of this added weight. Ask participants to share their results and their feelings during the mental exercise.

Negative Eating Behaviors (10 minutes)

Introduce and discuss the origins of negative eating behaviors. Briefly define the major negative eating behaviors. It may be helpful to list the definitions on a poster.

- Bingeing—What is considered a binge to one individual may not be considered a binge to the next. Bingeing is the rapid uncontrolled ingestion of a great deal of food in a relatively short period of time. Some bulimics consume up to 20,000 calories in one sitting.

- Purging—This is a method used to get rid of food rapidly consumed at one sitting. Two of the most common methods are self-induced vomiting and the use of laxatives. An individual may develop a tolerance level after an extended use of laxatives, and what one or two tablets would achieve in the beginning may soon require a whole box of tablets to achieve.
- Anorexia nervosa—Anorexia usually starts out in a teenager as a normal attempt at dieting, but slowly turns into an all-consuming fear of becoming fat. As weight loss continues (often around 25% of original body weight), the individual's attention focuses more and more on food and body size as normal activities are pushed to the side. People who are anorexic will deny that they have a problem and will not perceive themselves as being thin, even at the brink of starving themselves to death. They may still be able to work or study and maintain a social life, but their achievement level will be below their potential. Some individuals will maintain a steady underweight condition, while others who cannot control their food intake struggle with bingeing, purging, and fasting. Because the body is in a state of starvation, there are a number of physical symptoms that usually result in lowered metabolic rate, sensations of coldness in the extremities, malnutrition, decreased heart rate, and low blood pressure.
- Bulimia—This is a cycle of uncontrolled binge-eating followed by purging (such as self-induced vomiting or the use of laxatives). Like anorexia, bulimia may start out as an easy way to get rid of a feeling of fullness from overeating at a meal or as a way to control one's weight. The binge-purge cycle is a response to stress that may range from a very infrequent action to a very severe form where the bulimic is binge-eating and purging 10 or more times a day. A bulimic often feels depressed or guilty after a binge, and both this feeling and the behavior are kept private. The physical effects of frequent vomiting can be permanent tooth damage (or loss) from the corrosive effects of stomach acids on the tooth enamel, as well as damage to the inside of the throat. There also may be serious cardiac problems and a risk of

heart stoppage due to electrolyte imbalances caused by the purging methods.
- Bulimarexia—This disorder is a combination of bulimia and anorexia. The bulimarexic exhibits both the symptoms of self-starvation and those of the bingeing and purging cycle.

There are several reasons negative eating behaviors may develop.

- Negative eating behaviors may develop from a concern about losing weight.
- If disappointments, perceived failures, or rejections are blamed on aspects of personal appearance such as one's weight, an eating disorder may develop.
- Current theories on eating disorders take into consideration both one's heredity (such as a genetic predisposition toward depression) and one's social environment.

Managing Eating Behaviors (15 minutes)

When individuals would like to improve their eating habits, there are some successful behavior modification steps that may be used. The same basic rules of behavior modification can be applied to any habit one wants to change, such as smoking, procrastination, or even swearing.

The ABCs of Control

Discuss the three basic steps that lead toward self-control in the area of eating eating. Define the terms *antecedent, behavior,* and *consequence* (the ABCs of control). You may want to introduce this material by putting these definitions on a poster or handout.

Antecedent is the event or behavior that takes place immediately before the negative eating behavior. For some people it's a stressful event, such as getting into an argument with a boyfriend or girlfriend (the antecedent), that makes them devour a quart of ice cream (the negative eating habit). It is important to understand what triggers a negative eating behavior. Antecedents are also called "cues," and may be physical events, thoughts, emotions, or inner speech.

Behavior is the activity that constitutes the negative habit. The behavior could be anything, ranging from an occasional binge to an actual loss of normal control over food intake.

Consequence is the event or behavior that takes place immediately *after* the negative eating behavior. Consequences affect whether certain acts will be repeated or not. An example of a consequence may be a feeling of depression, anger, or even guilt over a binge; however, the food may have tasted good and provided a calming effect, which are positive qualities.

The effects of these ABCs are influenced by a person's previous experiences in situations that were similar. In other words, once a specific ABC has happened, it has a greater chance of occurring again.

Personal strengths and weaknesses can usually be divided up into areas such as social, emotional, physiological, and psychological. Negative eating behaviors tend to be situational, not "all or nothing." Feeling uncomfortable in a social event may cue an eating binge, but that doesn't mean the person can't control their eating behaviors in other situations.

External cues may prompt some individuals to overeat. Some external cues are social situations, time of day, and the availability of food. Stimulation of the sight, smell, or taste senses may also influence some people more than internal factors like hunger, or physical symptoms of low blood sugar such as dizziness or weakness.

The Food Diary

Hand out and explain the "Food Diary." The purpose of this diary is to monitor participants' eating habits and bring their actions to a conscious level so that the antecedents, behaviors, and consequences become clear. Suggest that they may want to make several copies of this form and keep track of their food intake for several days. Tell them to watch for patterns and analyze the ABCs of their eating styles.

Find solutions to identified problems. In order to change, you need to develop the ability to change the antecedents and consequences that affect your behavior. Be as creative as possible with designing solutions that address the root of the problem. If the problem seems to be situational, such as a tendency to overeat at parties, social gatherings, or when eating out, then you need to think of ways to avoid the cues to eat, and respond

in a more positive manner to those cues you cannot avoid.

Solutions involve anticipating when these situations could occur and planning ahead on how to better handle them. A more specific solution would be to plan for a party where there will be many unusual and delicious appetizers and to eat a small healthy meal before you leave home. When you are at the party, first look at all the appetizers and then decide which ones you like the best. By not starting out hungry, you may avoid stuffing yourself before you have a chance to feel full. Because there are many situations that trigger a negative behavior, list a few examples for participants and ask them to come up with some creative answers.

Try each solution and then evaluate its success. Don't be afraid to try another solution if the first one doesn't work, but remember to give each solution enough time. Don't expect results overnight. Once established, human behavior is hard to change, but with conscious effort and a little time, you can see positive results. Timing is very important in implementing a possible solution. If there are other major changes or events taking place in your life now, then it may be better to wait until things are less eventful when you can give more attention and effort to the solution.

Positive Eating Behaviors (10 minutes)

Introduce and discuss the positive eating behaviors listed here.

- Try not to think of food as either good or bad. Eating a "bad" food that has been eliminated from the diet may lead to guilt feelings.
- Eating sweets or snacks in moderation can fit into a healthy diet plan.
- Don't be a lifelong member of the "Clean Plate Club." Leaving a little food on your plate indicates that you are the one who decides when you're full and it's not the size of the portion that determines how much you must eat.
- Beware of the "dieting cycle." (This would make an excellent visual aid.) This cycle may occur when people diet improperly, for example: At the start of a new diet, the dieter resolves to follow a new eating plan and lose

weight. After a period of time, the individual starts to either crave some favorite food that's been eliminated from this new diet, or the monotony of the new diet strains their willpower. A lapse occurs, and they break the diet and eat a food that's not allowed. After this lapse, they may feel guilty, angry, or depressed, and decide that since they went off the diet, this indicates a "green light" to go ahead and eat many of their favorite foods not included on the diet. This only leads to more feelings of either guilt, anger, or depression, which leads to the start of another cycle that involves another diet. Breaking the dieting cycle involves establishing a regular eating pattern. This doesn't have to be three meals a day, but it is important to decide on a schedule that works and stick with it.

Introduce the analogy of calories consumed per day to the hours of sleep needed per night. A healthy pattern is to sleep a similar amount of hours every night. Eight hours' sleep on both Monday and Tuesday night equals 16 hours in 2 days, but the body doesn't use 16 hours' worth of sleep as efficiently if 0 hours were slept Monday night and all 16 hours Tuesday night. The same is true for calories. The body doesn't use fuel (calories) efficiently if 2,500 calories are eaten Monday and 800 are eaten Tuesday. It's better to eat a balanced amount each day.

There is less likelihood of overeating during a meal if the calories are spread out during the day. This also reduces the chance of bingeing later in the day. Instead of eating all the food served at one meal, save an item or two that could be eaten later as a snack, like yogurt or a piece of fruit. Well-chosen snacks can contribute nutrients to the diet.

Introduce the concept of the four basic food groups. Discuss appropriate portion sizes within each of the food groups. Tell participants that it's important to eat a variety of foods because no one food supplies all the nutrients a body needs. Choosing different foods within the four basic food groups increases the quality of a diet. Talk about the handout "Healthy Eating Habits, Healthy You!"

No one should consume a diet that contains less than 1,200 calories. This causes a slowdown in the body's furnace (basal metabolic rate). For more help with healthy diet planning, there is another Lifestyle Workshop in nutrition, "Designer Diets," which involves actually putting together health diets that can be used during one's lifetime. Tell participants to allow time for the changes in their eating behaviors to become new habits. Tell them to set small, realistic, attainable goals so that each success will encourage them to reach the next small goal. It's best to plan for slip-ups and decide in advance how to deal with it constructively to avoid the same event from happening again.

Take five minutes to provide a list of local resources where participants could get more information on eating disorders or get help with an eating problem. Stress that no individual should be afraid to ask for help. We all need a helping hand at different times in our lives.

Conclusion and Evaluation (5 minutes)

Summarize the main points of the workshop:

- Analyze your eating and activity patterns; remember your ABCs.
- Find the solution to help solve the identified problem.
- Try each solution for a certain time period and then evaluate its effectiveness.

Ask for questions from the participants and offer resources and referrals for further information. Distribute Lifestyle Workshop evaluation forms and pencils. Allow time for completion and then collect. Briefly list and describe the other Lifestyle Workshops in Nutrition.

MOST FREQUENTLY ASKED QUESTIONS

1. *What do you mean by "body image"?*

Body image refers to an individual's own view of his or her body. An individual's body image may be formed and modified many times during his or her life. Different factors such as age, sex, and the environment he or she grew up in can all play a role in how an individual views his or her body. The Body Image Study is one way to encourage workshop participants to examine both their views of themselves and how others view them.

2. *I think my roommate (or close friend) has an eating problem; what can I do to help her?*

Although every situation may differ in the way it needs to be handled, there are some important considerations to keep in mind. First of all, living with or being good friends with a bulimic, anorexic, or compulsive eater can place a strain on your relationship simply due to the nature of the disorder. Having to hide food, finding food missing, using the same bathroom after a purging incident, or just living with secretive behavior can alter your attitude toward your friend. Make sure that you can work through and solve your own feelings of frustration, anger, or pain before you confront your friend about her problem. Be honest and caring; don't accuse or blame her for her problems. Let her know you value her friendship enough to want to help her if she'll let you. A friendship during the good times in life is easy enough to find; however, it is during the rough times that a good friend becomes very precious. You may even want to provide your friend with a few local resources where she can get help.

3. *Why should I go through the trouble of keeping a food diary?*

This is a step most often omitted in the attempt to change negative eating habits because the individual feels that he or she is self-aware already. However, self-knowledge is the key to self-modification. An eating diary, if kept accurately for 1 to 2 weeks, can help you identify problem situations and clarify the events that came right before or after a behavior. Once a negative behavior is narrowed down to one or more specific situations, it can be dealt with effectively. The object is to change the unhealthy relationship between you and food by altering basic attitudes toward eating. Keeping a diary is tedious and a lot of work. It may also be unsettling to come face to face with your bad habits; often this confrontation is not very pleasant, though it is necessary. Too often an individual gives up on trying to eat better, using as an excuse a lack of willpower, or a belief that some greater force is tempting them to eat. A diary helps to put these generalities into specifics so that each specific problem can be overcome. In other words, keeping a diary changes the mountain into smaller, specific molehills.

4. *Is behavior modification always effective in changing a negative eating behavior?*

No, behavior modification is a skill that must be learned and mastered. Sufficient practice and patience is required to master the skill. You may have other priorities that demand more attention. If this is your current situation it's advisable to wait until you can devote more time to behavior change.

5. *How can I become less focused on fashion and more aware of how to reach my own body's healthy potential?*

The first step is to compare the characteristics of a healthy body with those of a fashion body. A few characteristics of a healthy body include a percent body fat that is appropriate for you, a strong cardiovascular system, and muscle strength and flexibility. The fashion body does not often include these characteristics. The second step is to realize that working to attain the characteristics that describe a healthy body will increase your chances of staying healthy and living longer.

6. *Why are women more susceptible to eating disorders than men?*

One of the theories is that women respond to eating in negative ways because our culture equates slimness in women with happiness and success. In college age women the obsession to be thin is very strong. Distorted body image is one problem women face. Women tend to see themselves as being heavier than they are, even when they are of average or below average weight. As long as our culture continues to equate thinness with happiness and success, we will continue to see women turning to anorexia and bulimia to solve their weight "problems."

University of Pennsylvania
Body Image Study

Date _____

Sex	Year in school	Place of residence
☐ Male	☐ Freshman	☐ Residence hall
☐ Female	☐ Sophomore	☐ Sorority
	☐ Junior	☐ Fraternity
	☐ Senior	☐ Private university housing
	☐ Graduate level	☐ Off-campus housing

1 2 3 4 5 6 7 8 9

FEMALE

1 2 3 4 5 6 7 8 9

MALE

Ideal _____ Current _____ Attractive _____ Other _____

If you indicated a thinner "ideal" than "current," do you feel dissatisfied with your present body shape?

☐ Yes   ☐ No   ☐ Does not apply

The pressure in today's society toward being thin is greater for:

☐ Males   ☐ Females   ☐ Equal pressure on both sexes   ☐ Do not feel a pressure

Note. From "Sex Differences in Perceptions of Desirable Body Shape" by A.E. Fallon and P. Rozin, 1985, *Journal of Abnormal Psychology*, **94**, pp. 102-105. Copyright 1985 by the American Psychological Association. Reprinted by permission of the publisher and author.

Healthy Eating Habits, Healthy You!

The following suggestions are intended to help you make healthy food choices and establish an eating pattern that you can live with, now and throughout life.

Establish a regular eating pattern (vs. practicing a binge/starvation diet cycle).

- This doesn't necessarily mean "three square meals a day," but determine an eating pattern that's best for you and stick to it.
- The body uses food more efficiently when distributed throughout the day, rather than having one huge meal.
- When you go for long periods of time without food (i.e., skipping meals), you may be likely to over-eat at the next meal.
- Try to sit down for meals as much as possible. Nibbling or eating on the run may lead to overeating.

Eat a variety of foods in moderate amounts.

- Choose foods every day from the Basic 4 Food Groups: milk and milk products, protein foods, fruits and vegetables, and breads and grain products.
- Avoid too much fat, sugar, and salt (sodium).
- Choose foods rich in starch and fiber—foods such as fruits and vegetables; whole-grain breads, cereals, and grain products; and dried beans and peas.
- If you drink alcohol, do so in moderation.

Don't think of foods as good or bad.

- You may begin to crave "bad" foods if you consider them forbidden. You may then feel guilty or depressed, which could lead to a binge.
- Whether a food could be considered good or bad really depends on how much is eaten and how often. There's nothing wrong with eating several cookies (or chocolate or ice cream, etc.)—sweets *can* fit into healthy eating habits. By allowing these types of food on occasion and then limiting the quantity, you should not feel guilty. If the extra calories are limited over a period of time, weight gain should not occur.

Choose healthy snacks (such as fresh fruit, raw vegetables, yogurt, raisins, peanut butter, or bagels) MOST OF THE TIME.

- Allow yourself an occasional treat if you want. If a candy bar is your particular weakness, you might treat yourself to one on a regular basis—maybe once a week.
- Don't keep snack foods around you that you "can't resist." You can't eat it if it's not available.

Find out more about why you eat.

- Keeping a food diary (listing foods eaten, amounts, when, where, with whom, and emotions while eating) may be a good starting point.
- Do you eat when you're bored, lonely, or frustrated, even if you're not hungry? If so, address these *feelings* instead of eating.
- Say NO to food when you're not hungry.

- Find activities to compensate for feelings (boredom, loneliness, etc.) that make you want to eat. Some suggestions include these:

  Go for a walk or bike ride.
  Do some relaxation exercises.
  Visit with a friend.
  Write a letter.
  Develop a hobby.
  Go to a library or begin a novel you've always wanted to read.
  Keep a list of projects you've been meaning to do and tackle one of them.

Establish a regular exercise pattern that you enjoy.

- Exercise increases energy expenditure (calories burned) and is vital in weight control.
- Exercise on a regular basis also

  improves muscle tone, posture, and general appearance,
  develops strength and endurance,
  increases agility, and
  decreases risk of developing heart disease.

- Moderate, regular exercise can provide a relief from stress, tension, and emotional pressures.

You don't need to weigh yourself every day.

- Everyone experiences small fluctuations in weight on a daily basis. Small increases may discourage you, deterring you from healthy eating habits. Establish a regular schedule for weighing; once a week is often enough.
- Pay more attention to how fit you are (i.e., percent body fat), rather than what the scales say.

Don't expect changes overnight.

- Set goals that are reachable, to improve your eating habits. Start small and approach goals one at a time. When you've accomplished one goal, work toward another.
- Reward yourself (try nonfood rewards) when goals are reached.
- Seek support of friends and family to help you stick with your new, healthy eating habits!

Food Diary Form

Goal: _____ Date: _____

_____

Meal	Food item	Note your feelings before and after eating
Breakfast		
Snack		
Lunch		
Snack		
Dinner		
Snack		

REFERENCES

Begley, S., Okeson, S., Evans, S., Dockser, D., & Burkman, J. (1987, March). When food is the enemy. *Newsweek*, pp. 18-19.

Fallon, A.E., & Rozin, P. (1985). Sex differences in perceptions of desirable body shape. *Journal of Abnormal Psychology*, **94**, 102-105.

Garner, D.M., Garfinkel, P.E., Schwartz, D., & Thompson, M. (1980). Cultural expectation of thinness in women. *Psychology Reports*, **47**, 483.

Gordon, L. (1985, March). How to eat like a naturally thin person. *Glamour*, pp. 214-218.

Kaplan, J., & Aneregg, K. (1982, March). Have we become fitness crazed and fatness crazy? *Vogue*, pp. 398-399.

Kirkly, B.G. (1986). Bulimia: Clinical characteristics, development, and etiology. *Journal of American Dietetics Association*, **86**, 468-472.

Nash, J.D. (1986). *Maximize your body potential: 16 weeks to a lifetime of effective weight management*. Palo Alto, CA: Bull.

Orbach, S. (1980). *Fat is a feminist issue*. New York: Berkeley.

Watson, D.L., & Tharp, R.G. (1985). *Self-directed behavior*. Monterey, CA: Brooks/Cole.

Whitney, E., & Hamilton, E. (1987). *Understanding nutrition* (4th ed.). St. Paul, MN: West.

Winning at Weight Control Lifestyle Workshop

PARAPROFESSIONAL PREPARATION MATERIALS

Training Sessions

Competency Exam

Texts and Suggested Readings

WORKSHOP AT A GLANCE

Presenter Information

Most Frequently Asked Questions

Handouts and Visual Aids*

References

---

*The *Body Composition Form* was written by Bruce Elmore, MS. The *Fast Food Calorie Counter* was compiled by Judy Simon, RD; Sara Kelley, MS, RD; and Michele Easterling, MPH, RD.

TRAINING SESSIONS

Winning at Weight Control

Session 1: Workshop Presentation

Time:	60 minutes
Methods:	Presentation, demonstration
Description:	Trainer presents workshop to Lifestyle Educators
Readings:	The workshop

Session 2: Introduction

Time:	60 minutes
Methods:	Lecture, discussion
Description:	Quiz students on questions used to play the Winning at Weight Control board game.
Readings:	The workshop
Competency exam questions:	1, 2, 3, 4, 30

Session 3: Energy Balance and Weight Control

Time:	60 minutes
Methods:	Lecture, discussion, demonstration
Description:	Discuss the energy balance equation and the ways it can be altered. The difference between body weight and body fat is explained. The method of measuring body fat with calipers is demonstrated.
Readings:	Energy balance and weight control, insurance height and weight tables, and the workshop
Competency exam questions:	5, 6, 7, 8, 10, 14, 16, 26, 27

Session 4: Diets: Healthy Versus Unhealthy

Time:	60 minutes
Methods:	Lecture, discussion
Description:	Characteristics of healthy and unhealthy diets are discussed. New evidence supporting the theory that fat calories add to body fat more than do carbohydrate calories is presented and critiqued. Examples of success stories are shared.
Readings:	Materials on dieting, hunger, and appetite regulation, and responses of the body to fasting and low calorie diets; healthy dieting success stories; the workshop
Competency exam questions:	9, 13, 15, 28, 29

Session 5: Exercise

Time: 60 minutes

Methods: Lecture, discussion

Description: Components of a healthy exercise program are discussed. Students list reasons why exercise helps promote weight loss while dieting.

Activity: Students practice measuring each other's percent body fat under guidance of the instructor.

Readings: Materials on metabolism changes during exercise, nutrition and fitness, definitions of aerobic and anaerobic exercise, and measuring body fat with calipers; the workshop

Competency exam questions: 17, 18, 20, 21, 22, 23, 24, 25, 26, 27

Session 6: "Most Frequently Asked Questions" Review and Hot Seat

Time: 60 minutes

Methods: Discussion, practice

Description: Review "Most Frequently Asked Questions" section of the workshop and other workshop components.

Activity: "Hot Seat": Each Lifestyle Educator is quizzed by the other students on the workshop topic for 10 minutes.

Readings: The workshop

Session 7: Practice Workshop Presentation

Time: 60 minutes

Method: Presentation

Description: Each Lifestyle Educator presents 20 minutes of the workshop.

Readings: The workshop

COMPETENCY EXAM

The following questions require brief answers.

1. Explain the objectives of the Winning at Weight Control game in relation to weight range.

2. How does each team determine its starting weight?

3. If a team answers a question incorrectly, what should you do?

4. Explain what "pound cards" are.

5. Identify the components of both the input and output side of the energy balance equation.

6. Discuss the relationship between the input and output sides and explain how energy balance is achieved.

7. Which of the components on the output side of the energy balance equation accounts for the majority of calories burned in one day?

8. How can you estimate your own basal metabolic rate?

9. Outline at least three components of a healthy diet that could be used for a lifetime.

10. Explain the difference between being overweight and overfat and give an example of each.

11. What problems would you expect to see in an individual who is very flexible, yet has poor muscular strength.

12. Lack of what hormone will prevent a woman from acquiring a large muscle mass from exercise?

13. Of the following weight loss plans, indicate whether each is healthy (H) or unhealthy (U):
    • Emphasizes only caloric restriction. ____
    • Claims quick and easy weight loss. ____
    • Allows at least 1,200 to 1,500 calories per day. ____
    • Provides a list of forbidden foods. ____
    • Emphasizes a short-term program. ____

14. List two ways that exercise is more important to weight control than just in burning calories:

15. What is the "starvation response"?

16. Many studies on overweight individuals point to the real factor of _____ when explaining weight gain, rather than finding that too many calories are being consumed.

17. Aerobic exercise does not produce a(n) _____ debt.

18. Name two long-lasting benefits of aerobic exercise that we talked about in class.

19. What type of breathing occurs with anaerobic exercise?

20. Why is oxygen important in the production of energy?

21. Briefly explain what the acronym FIT stands for.

22. Why is your resting heart rate a good indicator of your present aerobic fitness level?

23. What range in maximum heart rate is recommended to achieve aerobic fitness?

24. What is percent fat?

25. How is fat assessed using skinfold calipers? (Include skinfold sites, skinfold thickness, and the necessary equation in your answer.)

26. Briefly describe the most recent research on fat calories and carbohydrate calories.

27. Name five common reasons that successful dieters maintain their weight losses.

28. Twelve questions will be picked randomly from the game, and you must answer each correctly to receive one point for each question. (This will be done orally.)

29. Suggest possible techniques to use in the workshop if a participant is one of the following:
    - Recognition Seeker (frequently calls attention to self)
    - Conversationalist (brings up off-the-subject anecdotes and is a noisy distraction)
    - Moralizer (advocates judgmental points of view based on personal conviction)
    - Conservative (convinced that the status quo does not need changing)

TEXTS AND SUGGESTED READINGS

Brownell, K.D., Greenwood, M.R.C., Stellar, E., & Shrager, E.E. (1986). The effects of repeated cycles of weight loss and regain in rats. *Physiology and Behavior*, **38**, 459-464.

Danforth, E. (1986, March). Calories: A scientific breakthrough. *Shape*, p. 47.

Katch, V., & Katch, F. (1986, March). Success: Those incredible shrinking women. *Shape*, pp. 60-63.

162 pounds and counting down. (1985, December). *Glamour*, pp. 158-159.

Rhodes, M. (1986, May). New body math. *Self*, pp. 108-110.

Simonson, M., & Heilman, J.R. (1983, August). The fat sex, women. *Self*, pp. 90-91.

Stark, R. (1986, March). Ferreting out fat. *Shape*, p. 48.

Toufexis, A. (1986, January). Dieting: The losing game. *Time*, pp. 54-60.

Whitney, E., & Hamilton, E. (1987). *Understanding nutrition* (4th ed.). St. Paul, MN: West.

WORKSHOP AT A GLANCE

The goal of this workshop is to address basic questions about weight control. Participants will learn that the goal of weight control is *not* merely to lose pounds, but rather to be knowledgeable about foods, calories, and one's body, so that maintaining a healthy weight range becomes a lifetime commitment. This workshop takes approximately 75 minutes to present. Suggested attendance is 4 to 20 persons.

Objectives

Within the content of this workshop, the following objectives will be met.

- Participants will be able to apply general knowledge of nutrition to the various factors involved in weight control.
- Participants will learn how percent body fat and total body weight differ when determining personal ideal body weight.
- Participants will be able to identify the inputs and outputs of energy balance.
- Participants will be presented with the characteristics of a healthy diet.

Workshop Materials

- Workshop sign-in sheet
- Handouts and visual aids: *Energy Balance, Body Composition Form, Fast Food Calorie Counter, Calculating Basal Metabolic Rate*, and the *Winning at Weight Control Game Board*
- Question cards
- Pound Cards
- Playing pieces
- 2 Dice
- Lifestyle Workshop evaluation forms and pencils

PRESENTER INFORMATION

Briefly introduce yourself, your background, and any other personal information you choose to share. Describe your health promotion program and the topics available, like fitness and nutrition. Stress that the workshops are unique because you bring them to their living areas. Lifestyle Workshop paraprofessionals are trained at (your institution or program) to present these workshops. If anyone is interested in the training program, ask him or her to speak with you after the workshop.

Tell participants that the goal of this workshop is to supply factual nutritional information that may lead to developing a healthy attitude about eating that will last a lifetime. Emphasize that knowledge in itself does not guarantee success at weight control; success means maintaining a healthy weight range by eating right and exercising.

Winning at Weight Control (45 minutes)

Explain that the object of the game is to maintain a weight range of five pounds under or over the ideal weight. Ideal weight is a personal decision based on how much you value your health, your athletic performance, fertility (in women), and longevity. You should give yourself a range rather than one "magic" number.

Divide participants into two or more teams. (It's best if each team has four to five players.) Emphasize that although Winning at Weight Control is as much a game of luck as it is a test of knowledge, real weight control is determined by how well behavior and information are managed. Familiarize participants with these rules.

Winning at Weight Control Rules

1. Each team begins the game either over or under its ideal weight. The exact number of pounds is determined by the first roll of the dice.
2. The team farthest from its ideal weight begins the game.
3. This team rolls the dice and moves that number of spaces clockwise from any chosen starting point.

4. The presenter then reads a question from the set of cards matching the color of the square on which the team has landed. The cards vary in point value.
5. The team has 30 seconds to answer.
6. If team answers correctly, it may choose one of the following to keep within the proper 5-pound range:
   - Maintain present weight.
   - Add number of pounds listed on card to its weight.
   - Subtract pounds on card from its weight.
7. If team answers incorrectly, the presenter either adds or subtracts the number of pounds on the card, whichever is more detrimental to team's range.
8. Pound Squares and Cards: Pound Squares are chances. A team that lands on a Pound Square picks the top Pound Card and must add or subtract the given pounds. Pound Cards offer an unpredictability to the game, in the same way that life may be unpredictable for individuals trying to maintain their proper weight.
9. Winner: There could be more than one winning team. A winning team is one that is within 5 pounds of its starting weight.
10. The winning team has the option of having its percent body fat measured (see Appendix A), along with receiving a complimentary button that states: "Winning at Weight Control, I'm _____% fat-free" (to be filled in by presenter after measurement). If only a few of the winning team members wish to have their percent body fat measured, the presenter has the option of taking body fat measurements from any of the other participants who are interested. Play "Winning at Weight Control."

Nutrients (Orange Cards)

These questions are worth 3 pounds each.

1. *A type of fiber called pectin that is found in apples can help reduce cholesterol levels in your blood. (T/F)*

   True. Pectin is one type of fiber that helps bind cholesterol in the intestinal tract so that it's excreted rather than absorbed.

2. *A type of fiber called bran, found in whole grain products such as bread and cereal, can help reduce cholesterol levels in your blood. (T/F)*

   False. Bran is a fiber that increases bulk in your digestive tract to speed up elimination, but it does not help reduce cholesterol levels in your blood.

3. *The RDA per day for vitamin C is 60 mg. This can be met by drinking how much orange juice?*

   a. 1/2 cup
   b. 1 cup
   c. 4 cups
   d. 8 cups

   (a.) One half-cup of orange juice supplies a full day's allowance of vitamin C.

4. *Pick three of the following vitamins that are fat-soluble: A, B complex, C, D, E, and K.*

   Vitamins A, D, E, and K are all fat-soluble. (Refer to question number 14 in Most Frequently Asked Questions section.)

5. *One can increase the amount of iron absorbed from a food (such as a blueberry muffin) by consuming a vitamin C-rich food along with it (such as orange juice). (T/F)*

   True. Vitamin C helps the absorption of iron during digestion.

6. *Rank the following half-cup servings of breakfast cereals according to decreasing fiber content (in other words, most fiber to least):*

   a. cooked oatmeal
   b. Corn Flakes
   c. All Bran
   d. Frosted Mini-Wheats

   The order is: c. All Bran (8.4 g), d. Frosted Mini-Wheats (3 g), a. cooked oatmeal (1.6 g), b. Corn Flakes (0.3 g).

7. *Rank the following forms of apple according to decreasing fiber content (most fiber to least):*

   a. 1/2 cup applesauce
   b. 1/2 cup apple juice
   c. 1 whole apple

   The order is: c. apple (3.6 g), a. applesauce (2.4 g), b. apple juice (0.5 g).

8. *How many types of fiber exist?*

   a. 1
   b. 2
   c. 3
   d. 5

   (d.) Five. Cellulose, hemicellulose, lignin, pectin, and gums/mucilage are all considered fibers.

9. *If the label of a breakfast cereal states that there are 20 g of sugar in one serving, how many teaspoons of added sugar does that equal?*

   a. 2
   b. 3
   c. 5
   d. 10

   (c.) One teaspoon of sugar equals 4 g so there are five teaspoons of added sugar. Also, each gram of sugar equals 4 calories, therefore, 80 of the calories in the cereal came from sugar.

10. *The recommended amount of carbohydrates in a healthy diet is around what percent of total calories?*

    a. 25%
    b. 40%
    c. 55%
    d. 85%

    (c.) The recommended amount of carbohydrates in a diet is 55%.

11. *The recommended amount of protein in a healthy diet is around what percentage of total calories?*

    a. 5%
    b. 12%
    c. 25%
    d. 50%

    (b.) A healthy level that provides enough protein for the body, even if only 1,200 calories a day are eaten, would be about 12% of the daily calories.

12. *There is no difference between natural and synthetic vitamins. (T/F)*

    True. The body uses a vitamin (which is a chemical molecule) in the same way whether the vitamin is from food or man-made.

13. *The recommended amount of fat in a healthy diet is around what percentage of total calories?*

    a. 10%
    b. 20%
    c. 30%
    d. 45%

    (c.) The recommended amount of fat in a healthy diet is 30%. Ideally 10% of the fats should be saturated, 10% should be poly-unsaturated, and 10% should be mono-unsaturated. Americans now consume about 42% of their calories from fat.

14. *Meat may actually contain more fat calories than protein calories. (T/F)*

    True. A T-bone steak provides 20% protein calories and 80% fat calories. In comparison, chicken without skin provides 64% protein calories and 31% fat calories.

15. *Sunlight is the major source of Vitamin D. (T/F)*

    True. Vitamin D helps the body absorb calcium better; the best food source of vitamin D is fortified milk.

16. *Canned sardines and salmon are great sources of calcium. (T/F)*

    True. The soft edible bones in canned fish are rich in calcium.

Weight Control (Yellow Cards)

These questions are worth 2 pounds each.

1. *How many pounds of body fat would be gained if in one week a person ate 7,000 more calories than the body could use?*

   Two pounds, because 3,500 calories = 1 pound body fat.

2. *The unit of energy supplied by food to fuel the human body is called what?*

   A kilocalorie, or commonly called a calorie.

3. *Name the three categories of nutrients that supply calories to the body.*

   Carbohydrates, fat, and protein all supply calories as well as nutrients.

4. *Pound for pound, fat provides over twice as many calories as protein or carbohydrates. (T/F)*

   True. Fat supplies 9 calories per gram while protein and carbohydrates supply only 4 calories per gram.

5. *What does BMR stand for?*

   Basal metabolic rate.

6. *Can one's BMR be decreased by eating a low calorie diet? (Yes/No)*

   Yes. During low calorie diets the body tries to conserve its energy to prevent starvation, which means fewer calories are burned.

7. *During an adult's moderately active day, most calories are used by the body for*

   a. activities such as dressing, fixing meals, and going to school
   b. exercise
   c. BMR

   (c.) BMR accounts for the majority of calories used by the body.

8. *What range of percent body fat would be optimal for an active female college student?*

   a. 4-9%
   b. 10-15%
   c. 20-25%
   d. 30-35%

   (c.) The 20-25% body fat range is considered normal and healthy.

9. *What range of percent body fat would be optimal for an active male college student?*

   a. 3-8%
   b. 13-18%
   c. 20-25%
   d. 35-40%

   (b.) The 13-18% body fat range is considered normal and healthy.

10. *Exercising regularly increases your body's ability to metabolize fat. (T/F)*

    True. A trained body is better able to use fat as energy than is an untrained body.

11. *Some foods are labeled "nutrient dense." These provide*

    a. many calories and many nutrients
    b. a high percentage of needed nutrients
    c. many nutrients compared to calories
    d. many calories compared to nutrients

    (c.) The level of nutrients gained from a food compared to its calories is high.

12. *A good example of a sensible weight-reducing diet is one that*

    a. produces rapid weight loss
    b. emphasizes fruits and vegetables and eliminates starches
    c. does not recommend going below 1,200 calories and includes a variety of foods
    d. includes few nutrient-dense foods

    (c.) The most sensible diet is one that includes a variety of foods and does not go below 1,200 calories. It is also important to include regular exercise in a weight-reducing program.

13. *To maintain physical fitness, one should exercise at least*

    a. once a week
    b. twice a week
    c. three times a week
    d. every day

    (c.) Three times a week, for at least 20 minutes at 60-80% maximum heart rate.

14. *Which of the following is NOT true of regular and moderate exercise?*

    a. Increases appetite
    b. Tones up body muscles
    c. Helps maintain weight
    d. Improves cardiovascular conditioning

    (a.) Studies have shown that there is no significant increase in appetite during long-range exercise programs. Exercise improves the body's ability to distinguish signals of hunger and satiety.

15. *If you eat fewer calories than you expend, what occurs?*

    a. Body water is used for energy
    b. Body protein is stored as fat
    c. Body fat becomes muscle
    d. Body fat is used for energy

    (d.) Body fat is used for energy, to make up the difference in calories. However, if you do not eat enough protein to provide the body with the necessary amino acids, muscle may also be used to supply calories.

16. *Which is the preferred energy source for the body?*

    a. protein
    b. fat
    c. carbohydrate
    d. alcohol

    (c.) Carbohydrates are broken down into the simple sugar glucose, which is the body's preferred energy source.

17. *If your diet contains too much of this nutrient, your kidneys have to work overtime to metabolize it.*

    a. protein
    b. fat
    c. carbohydrate

    (a.) Protein is broken down into individual amino acids, which if not used by the body must be further broken down by the kidneys in order to remove and excrete the nitrogen. Water is needed for this excretion process, which means that the kidneys have to work harder and are unnecessarily stressed.

18. *If your diet provides more protein than your body needs, which one of the following statements is not true?*

    a. More calcium is excreted from the body than normal
    b. Blood cholesterol levels rise if the protein is from an animal source
    c. More muscles are developed if the protein is from an animal source
    d. More saturated fat is consumed if the protein is from an animal source

    (c.) Muscles are developed during normal growth spurts in life and when stress is placed on the muscle during an activity. A diet with added protein will not increase one's muscle size.

Fact or Fiction (Blue Cards)

These questions are worth 1 pound each.

1. *Smokers need more vitamin C than nonsmokers.* (T/F)

   True. Smoking causes a stress on the body that increases the requirement for vitamin C. Two extra servings a day will help.

2. *Between 5% and 10% of the individuals who go on weight-reducing diets reach a desired goal weight and maintain it for a year.* (T/F)

   True. The odds against keeping lost weight off are very slim. A large part of the failure rate can be attributed to the fact that no permanent change may have been made in the individual's eating behavior. Without a permanent change in eating habits, the pounds just sneak back on.

3. *The average American woman eats how many tablespoons of fat per day?*

   a. 3
   b. 6
   c. 9
   d. 12

   (b.) Most women eat six tablespoons of fat, which are mainly saturated animal fats. One tablespoon of polyunsaturated fat per day is all that is needed to meet the requirement of essential fatty acids, which, among their other functions, promote healthy skin and hair.

4. *The tendency for excess body fat to accumulate on thighs is more common for males than females.* (T/F)

   False. Females have a greater tendency to accumulate excess fat on their buttocks, abdominal, and thigh areas.

5. *How many calories does the average woman burn up during an ordinary "moderately active" day?*

   a. about 3,000-3,500
   b. 2,000-2,900
   c. 1,200-2,000
   d. 800-1,100

   (c.) In this society of "automatic" and "instant" products and appliances, the daily caloric expenditure of the 20th-century adult has been reduced a considerable amount compared with the same individual living a century earlier.

6. *You won't have cholesterol in your blood if you eliminate such foods as fatty meats, egg yolks, and whole milk products from your diet.* (T/F)

   False. About 3/4 of the cholesterol in your blood is manufactured by your own body and is used by those body tissues undergoing construction. Lowering one's intake of cholesterol-rich foods and including fiber in the diet can help to lower blood cholesterol levels. This is helpful because when blood cholesterol levels are high, cholesterol is deposited along the inside pathways of the arteries, narrowing them.

7. *Sit-ups are the best way to take fat off the waist.* (T/F)

   False. The only way to lose fat is to burn off more calories than you are consuming. Spot exercises will tone and firm up trouble spots.

8. *Overeating is the basic cause of obesity.* (T/F)

   False. The main cause of obesity is inactivity, not overeating.

9. *You can tell how fat you are by weighing yourself.* (T/F)

   False. The best method of determining body fat composition is underwater weighing. Taking skinfold measurements is a good way of *estimating* percent body fat.

10. *When you are overweight you are also obese.* (T/F)

    False. An obese person is one who carries around an excessive amount of body fat. An overweight person simply weighs more than what is recommended on insurance height/weight tables. Many athletes, such as pro-football running backs, are overweight but not obese.

11. *Height/weight charts tell you your ideal weight.* (T/F)

    False. Height/weight charts are generalizations that cannot take into account the percent of fat on the body. Your weight may be ideal according to the charts, but your percent of fat may be too high. It is a cultural norm to rely on these charts and bathroom scales, but our percent body fat should determine ideal weight.

12. *Low-carbohydrate diets are the fastest way to lose fat.* (T/F)

False. The rapid weight loss during the first few days of these diets is a loss of water that will be regained once the diet is stopped. Since the American diet is already too high in fat, the recommended weight-loss diet is one that's high in complex carbohydrates, low in fats, and involves food from the four basic food groups.

13. *Only fat is lost when you diet.* (T/F)

False. When dieting is the sole means of losing weight, some fat may be lost, but lean body tissue is also lost, even if protein intake is adequate. When exercise is also included in a weight-loss program, practically all of the weight lost is fat.

14. *The role of protein in food is not to supply the body proteins directly to the body, but to supply the amino acids or building blocks from which the body can make its own protein.* (T/F)

True. The amino acids that make up protein are rearranged by the body to make muscles, antibodies, enzymes, and other important protein-based products.

15. *Honey is more nutritious than sugar.* (T/F)

False. The trace levels of nutrients found in honey are insignificant and do not make honey any more nutritious than sugar.

16. *Which is highest in calories?*

   a. one tablespoon butter
   b. one tablespoon margarine
   c. one tablespoon oil
   d. all of the above are equal

(d.) One tablespoon of oil contains approximately 120 calories; butter and fat contain 100 calories.

17. *Which contains more calcium?*

   a. 1 cup skim milk
   b. 1 cup 2% milk
   c. 1 cup whole milk
   d. all of the above are equal

(d.) All provide approximately the same amount of calcium, but if you are watching calories, skim milk should be your choice because of its high nutrient density.

18. *You ate lunch at Wendy's and ordered a double cheeseburger, french fries, and a Frosty. How many tablespoons of fat did you consume?*

   a. 1
   b. 3
   c. 6
   d. 10

(c.) Six tablespoons of fat, most of which are saturated. Over 600 of the 1,310 calories from this meal are fat calories.

19. *A woman in her fifties may weigh the same as she did in her twenties, yet her ratio of fat to muscle has increased over the years.* (T/F)

True. As one ages the amount of lean muscle slowly decreases and the amount of fat usually increases.

20. *A women will need almost twice as much iron during her lifetime as a man will need.* (T/F)

True. During a woman's reproductive years, iron is lost during menstruation.

Pound Cards

These are the "chance" cards of the game. Remind participants, however, that most of the circumstances described are not chance occurrences, but chances to make appropriate decisions.

- Uncontrollable urge hits for a chocolate cream pie . . . gain 2 pounds.
- Take up jogging . . . lose 5 pounds.
- New romantic interest sparks your motivation to get in shape . . . lose 4 pounds.
- Give up dessert at dinner . . . lose 1 pound.
- Midterms: Stock up on M & M's and peanuts for energy . . . gain 2 pounds.
- Stick to your vow to eat fewer fried foods . . . lose 3 pounds.
- Avoid between-meal snacking . . . lose 1 pound.
- The cold and flu have got you down. Dehydration causes you to lose 3 pounds.
- Lost 3 pounds on a fat diet, but gained back an extra 5 pounds . . . gain 2 pounds.
- Linger in cafeteria after a meal and keep nibbling . . . gain 1 pound.
- Your roommate bakes chocolate chip cookies . . . gain 1 pound.

- Indulge in too many late night pizzas . . . gain 2 pounds.
- Start exercising before dinner to reduce your appetite . . . lose 1 pound.
- Stress from finals takes its toll . . . lose 2 pounds.
- Heavy social schedule . . . gain 3 pounds.
- You learn to say no to desserts every night . . . lose 2 pounds.
- Choose TV on Wednesday nights instead of racquetball . . . gain 3 pounds.
- Ride the exercise bike you got for Christmas . . . lose 2 pounds.
- Take the stairs instead of the elevator . . . lose 3 pounds.
- Your boyfriend/girlfriend visits for the weekend and you eat every meal out . . . gain 3 pounds.
- No chance to exercise during finals week . . . gain 1 pound.
- Thanksgiving weekend leaves you feeling stuffed . . . gain 3 pounds.
- Mom sends a care package of homemade goodies . . . gain 4 pounds.
- New Year's resolution to work out more often at the gym . . . lose 3 pounds.
- You realize exercising has social advantages so you begin exercise program . . . lose 4 pounds.
- Spring break is 1 month away and you add 2 hours to your weekly workout . . . lose 3 pounds.
- Use food as a crutch for loneliness . . . gain 4 pounds.
- Start exercising 15 minutes in the morning . . . lose 2 pounds.
- Continuous exercise and conscious eating pays off . . . lose 5 pounds.
- It's your birthday and you take advantage of all those complimentary drinks . . . gain 1 pound.

Nutrition Concepts (10 minutes)

As you can see from the questions asked during the game, there is a lot to know about nutrition. In order to develop a healthy attitude concerning dieting and body weight, you need to learn a few important concepts.

The scale doesn't give all the necessary informa-tion. The best way to determine ideal weight is by measuring body fat composition. Ideal body weight should be viewed as a range of pounds centered around a realistic number. This way you don't have to feel bad when the scale doesn't exactly match that one magic number. Fluctuations around a certain weight should be considered a normal occurrence.

Energy Balance

The second basic concept is understanding the factors that contribute toward maintaining your specific weight range. This is called energy balance.

Energy for the body is provided by calories in food. It takes 3,500 calories to equal 1 pound of body fat. To achieve energy balance (or weight control) the calories consumed must equal the calories burned. The carbohydrates, protein, and fat in food all supply both calories and nutrients to the body. Alcohol also supplies calories, but offers nothing in the way of nutrients.

There are two important ways that calories are burned by the body. They are basal metabolic rate and daily activity, and they make up the output side of the energy balance equation. Basal meta-bolic rate or BMR contributes around two-thirds of the energy spent in a day. People don't often realize that so much energy is going to support the maintenance work of their bodies. This mainte-nance work keeps your heart beating, your lungs breathing, and all the other physiological activities that support life going.

One way to estimate BMR is to multiply your ideal body weight by the factor 10.9. The calories burned from standing, walking, sitting, and other activities are then added on to the calories already burned from BMR. Since BMR remains fairly con-stant, the big factor for increasing energy expen-diture is activity.

The amount of energy burned during an activity depends on how many muscles are used, how in-tensely, and for how long. It is not just exercise but also how active an individual is during the day that determines the amount of calories used up.

To summarize, to balance the scales you need to balance carbohydrates, fats, proteins, and alco-hol with basal metabolic rate (BMR) and physical activity. (This would make an excellent visual aid.)

Healthy Diets

There are so many diets and diet books out that it is important to be able to separate the good ones from the bad. It is a good idea to avoid weight-loss plans that

- emphasize only caloric restriction and fail to include exercise,
- provide an intake of less than 1,200 calories per day,
- eliminate one or more food groups, claim that special foods produce greater weight loss, or require that you buy their special foods,
- claim quick and easy weight loss, or
- emphasize a short-term program.

Weight control progams that are healthy and can be used for a lifetime need to be balanced and adequate in nutrients, to control calories, and to include variety and nutrient-dense foods. When evaluating a weight control program look for plans that

- promote your health and not just weight loss,
- include exercise along with an eating program,
- allow at least 1,200 to 1,500 calories per day,
- use food from the four basic food groups,
- do not classify foods as bad or forbidden, and
- emphasize long-term weight control.

For optimal health, weight control involves eating a nutritious diet and exercising regularly. Remember to discriminate between diets that offer quick weight loss and those that can be safely followed for a lifetime. The three concepts of percent body fat, energy balance, and healthy diet help one to focus on the important issues of weight control.

All of these concepts need to be remembered for you to really win at weight control.

Fat Assessment (10 minutes)

Measure the percent body fat on the winning team members. Also measure others in the workshop if time permits. (The procedure is explained in Appendix A of this workshop.) Select one person from the group to record the skinfold values on the body composition forms.

Conclusion and Evaluation (5 minutes)

Summarize the three main points of the workshop:

- Percent body fat is the most accurate way to determine an individual body weight. Your ideal weight should be viewed as a range of five pounds above and below this number.
- Know the factors that contribute toward maintaining your weight. Calories in = calories out.
- Moderation and variety are the keys to a healthy diet.

Ask for questions from the participants. Offer resources and referrals for further information. Distribute Lifestyle Workshop evaluation forms and pencils. Allow time for completion and then collect. Briefly list and describe the other Lifestyle Workshops in Nutrition.

Fat Assessment

Fat Assessment Procedure

The information provided in Appendix A details proper skinfold techniques and the specific measurement sites used in each skinfold equation. The equation-specific tables needed for determining the percent body fat are also included.

The Skinfold Measuring Method

The proper method for measuring skinfolds is as follows:

1. Firmly grasp the skinfold between the thumb and forefinger and lift up. The subject should not experience pain.
2. Place the contact surfaces of the caliper 1 cm (1/2 inch) above or below the fingers (depth equal to thickness of fold).
3. Slowly release the grip on the calipers, enabling tongs to exert their full (natural) tension on the skinfold.
4. Read skinfold to nearest 0.5 mm after needle stops (1 to 2 seconds after releasing grip on caliper). The skinfold measurement is registered on the dial of the caliper.

Note that the caliper is not to be placed at the base of the skinfold. The correct distance for measurement is approximately midway between the crest and the base of the skinfold.

If repeated measurements vary by more than 1-2 mm, a third measurement should be taken.

Skinfold thickness should be measured separately for each individual without comment or display. Each participant has the right to share or withhold the results of the test. In all cases, interpretation of results should be given individually.

Note that on occasion, one can grasp a fold and include muscle as well as fat. By having the participant contract the muscle, one can feel the muscle pull away. In that case, a new skinfold measurement should be taken.

Skinfold Sites

Body composition is an important component in sports performance, physical fitness, and health. Determining lean body mass or fat weight in the laboratory setting is usually accomplished through hydrostatic weighing. Since it is not always practical or feasible to use this technique, skinfold calipers and equations were developed to serve as a field method for estimating percent body fat.

Research in the area of body composition indicates that averaging the Durnin and Womersley equations with the Pollack, Schmidt, and Jackson equations most closely matches the results of underwater weighing. Therefore the Fat Assessment and Weight Management Lifestyle Workshop uses the mean of the equations as the estimate of percent fat for the workshop participant.

The Durnin and Womersley Sites

The skinfold sites for Durnin and Womersley (1974) for both males and females are these:

- Triceps—locate a point halfway between the bony part of the shoulder and the tip of the elbow. Measure the skinfold with the arm relaxed and hanging in extension.
- Biceps—locate a point halfway between the armpit and the elbow joint. Measure the skinfold with the arm relaxed and hanging in extension.

- Iliac crest—measure the skinfold over the iliac crest (hip) at the midaxillary line (middle of armpit). Measure fold vertically.
- Subscapula—skinfold is taken at the tip of the scapula (shoulder blade) on a diagonal.

The Pollack, Schmidt, and Jackson Sites

The skinfold sites for the Pollack, Schmidt, and Jackson (1980) equation for *females* are triceps, suprailium, and thigh:

- Triceps—measure the fold vertically on the posterior midline of upper arm, halfway between shoulder and elbow with elbow extended and relaxed.
- Suprailium—measure the fold diagonally above crest of the ilium at the spot where an imaginary line would come down from the anterior axillary line.
- Thigh—measure the fold vertically on the anterior aspect of the thigh, midway between hip and knee joint.

The skinfold sites for the Pollack, Schmidt, and Jackson equation for *males* are chest, abdomen, and thigh:

- Chest—measure the fold diagonally, one-half the distance between axillary line and the nipple.
- Abdomen—take a vertical fold at a lateral distance of approximately 2 cm from the umbilicus.
- Thigh—measure the fold vertically on the anterior aspect of the thigh, midway between the hip and knee joints.

Proper use of the following table is critical in estimation of percent fat. Each table is author-specific, since a different group of skinfold sites are used. Also, Pollack, Schmidt, and Jackson have separate tables according to gender. To use the tables correctly, identify the appropriate table for author and gender, find the skinfold sum (in millimeters), and cross-reference that with participant's age to find percent body fat.

Body Fat Calculation Tables (Durnin and Womersley)

Skinfolds (mm)	Males (age in years)				Females (age in years)			
	17-29	30-39	40-49	50+	16-29	30-39	40-49	50+
15	4.8	—	—	—	10.5	—	—	—
20	8.1	12.2	12.2	12.6	14.1	17.0	19.8	21.4
25	10.5	14.2	15.0	15.6	16.8	19.4	22.2	24.0
30	12.9	16.2	17.7	18.6	19.5	21.8	24.5	26.6
35	14.7	17.7	19.6	20.8	21.5	23.7	26.4	28.5
40	16.4	19.2	21.4	22.9	23.4	25.5	28.2	30.3
45	17.7	20.4	23.0	24.7	25.0	26.9	29.6	31.9
50	19.0	21.5	24.6	26.5	26.5	28.2	31.0	33.4
55	20.1	22.5	25.9	27.9	27.8	29.4	32.1	34.6
60	21.2	23.5	27.1	29.2	29.1	30.6	33.2	35.7
65	22.2	24.3	28.2	30.4	30.2	31.6	34.1	36.7
70	23.1	25.1	29.3	31.6	31.2	32.5	35.0	37.7
75	24.0	25.9	30.3	32.7	32.2	33.4	35.9	38.7
80	24.8	26.6	31.2	33.8	33.1	34.3	36.7	39.6
85	25.5	27.2	32.1	34.8	34.0	35.1	37.5	40.4
90	26.2	27.8	33.0	35.8	34.8	35.8	38.3	41.2
95	26.9	28.4	33.7	36.6	35.6	36.5	39.0	41.9
100	27.6	29.0	34.4	37.4	36.4	37.2	39.7	42.6
105	28.2	29.6	35.1	38.2	37.1	37.9	40.4	43.3
110	28.8	30.1	35.8	39.0	37.8	38.6	41.0	43.9
115	29.4	30.6	36.4	39.7	38.4	39.1	41.5	44.5
120	30.0	31.1	37.0	40.4	39.0	39.6	42.0	45.1
125	30.5	31.5	37.6	41.1	39.6	40.1	42.5	45.7
130	31.0	31.9	38.2	41.8	40.2	40.6	43.0	46.2
135	31.5	32.3	38.7	42.4	40.8	41.1	43.5	46.7
140	32.0	32.7	39.2	43.0	41.3	41.6	44.0	47.2
145	32.5	33.1	39.7	43.6	41.8	42.1	44.5	47.7
150	32.9	33.5	40.2	44.1	42.3	42.6	45.0	48.2
155	33.3	33.9	40.7	44.6	42.8	43.1	45.4	48.7
160	33.7	34.3	41.2	45.1	43.3	43.6	45.8	49.2
165	34.1	34.6	41.6	45.6	43.7	44.0	46.2	49.6
170	34.5	34.8	42.0	46.1	44.1	44.4	46.6	50.0
175	34.9	—	—	—	—	44.8	47.0	50.4
180	35.3	—	—	—	—	45.2	47.4	50.8
185	35.6	—	—	—	—	45.6	47.8	51.2
190	35.9	—	—	—	—	45.9	48.2	51.6
195	—	—	—	—	—	46.2	48.5	52.0
200	—	—	—	—	—	46.5	48.8	52.4
205	—	—	—	—	—	—	49.1	52.7
210	—	—	—	—	—	—	49.4	53.0

Note. From "Body fat assessed from total body density and its estimation from skinfold thickness: Measurements on 481 men and women aged 16-74 years" by J. Durnin and J. Womersley, 1974, *British Journal of Nutrition,* **32,** 95. Copyright 1974 by Cambridge University Press. Reprinted by permission of Cambridge University Press.

Percent Fat Estimates for Women, Sum of Triceps, Suprailium, and Thigh Skinfolds*
(Pollack, Schmidt, and Jackson)

Sum of Skinfolds (mm)	Age to the last year								
	Under 22	23 to 27	28 to 32	33 to 37	38 to 42	43 to 47	48 to 52	53 to 57	Over 58
23-25	9.7	9.9	10.2	10.4	10.7	10.9	11.2	11.4	11.7
26-28	11.0	11.2	11.5	11.7	12.0	12.3	12.5	12.7	13.0
29-31	12.3	12.5	12.8	13.0	13.3	13.5	13.8	14.0	14.3
32-34	13.6	13.8	14.0	14.3	14.5	14.8	15.0	15.3	15.5
35-37	14.8	15.0	15.3	15.5	15.8	16.0	16.3	16.5	16.8
38-40	16.0	16.3	16.5	16.7	17.0	17.2	17.5	17.7	18.0
41-43	17.2	17.4	17.7	17.9	18.2	18.4	18.7	18.9	19.2
44-46	18.3	18.6	18.8	19.1	19.3	19.6	19.8	20.1	20.3
47-49	19.5	19.7	20.0	20.2	20.5	20.7	21.0	21.2	21.5
50-52	20.6	20.8	21.1	21.3	21.6	21.8	22.1	22.3	22.6
53-55	21.7	21.9	22.1	22.4	22.6	22.9	23.1	23.4	23.6
56-58	22.7	23.0	23.2	23.4	23.7	23.9	24.2	24.4	24.7
59-61	23.7	24.0	24.2	24.5	24.7	25.0	25.2	25.5	25.7
62-64	24.7	25.0	25.2	25.5	25.7	26.0	26.7	26.4	26.7
65-67	25.7	25.9	26.2	26.4	26.7	26.9	27.2	27.4	27.7
68-70	26.6	26.9	27.1	27.4	27.6	27.9	28.1	28.4	28.6
71-73	27.5	27.8	28.0	28.3	28.5	28.8	29.0	29.3	29.5
74-76	28.4	28.7	28.9	29.2	29.4	29.7	29.9	30.2	30.4
77-79	29.3	29.5	29.8	30.0	30.3	30.5	30.8	31.0	31.3
80-82	30.1	30.4	30.6	30.9	31.1	31.4	31.6	31.9	32.1
83-85	30.9	31.2	31.4	31.7	31.9	32.2	32.4	32.7	32.9
86-88	31.7	32.0	32.2	32.5	32.7	32.9	33.2	33.4	33.7
89-91	32.5	32.7	33.0	33.2	33.5	33.7	33.9	34.2	34.4
92-94	33.2	33.4	33.7	33.9	34.2	34.4	34.7	34.9	35.2
95-97	33.9	34.1	34.4	34.6	34.9	35.1	35.4	35.6	35.9
98-100	34.6	34.8	35.1	35.3	35.5	35.8	36.0	36.3	35.5
101-103	35.3	35.4	35.7	35.9	36.2	36.4	36.7	36.9	37.2
104-106	35.8	36.1	36.3	36.6	36.8	37.1	37.3	37.5	37.8
107-109	36.4	36.7	36.9	37.1	37.4	37.6	37.9	38.1	38.4
110-112	37.0	37.2	37.5	37.7	38.0	38.2	38.5	38.7	38.9
113-115	37.5	37.8	38.0	38.2	38.5	38.7	39.0	39.2	39.5
116-118	38.0	38.3	38.5	38.8	39.0	39.3	39.5	39.7	40.0
119-121	38.5	38.7	39.0	39.2	39.5	39.7	40.0	40.2	40.5
122-124	39.0	39.2	39.4	39.7	39.9	40.2	40.4	40.7	40.9
125-127	39.4	39.6	39.9	40.1	40.4	40.6	40.9	41.1	41.4
128-130	39.8	40.0	40.3	40.5	40.8	41.0	41.3	41.5	41.8

Note. From ''Measurement of cardiorespiratory fitness and body composition in the clinical setting'' by M. Pollack, D. Schmidt, and A. Jackson, 1980, *Comprehensive Therapy*, 6(9), 12-27. Copyright 1980 by Laux Co. Reprinted by permission of the Laux Company, Inc.

*Percent fat calculated by the formula of Siri. Percent fat = $[(4.95/BD) - 4.5] \times 100$, where BD = body density.

Percent Fat Estimates for Men, Sum of Chest, Abdominal, and Thigh Skinfolds*
(Pollack, Schmidt, and Jackson)

Sum of Skinfolds (mm)	Under 22	23 to 27	28 to 32	33 to 37	38 to 42	43 to 47	48 to 52	53 to 57	Over 58
8-10	1.3	1.8	2.3	2.9	3.4	3.9	4.5	5.0	5.5
11-13	2.2	2.8	3.3	3.9	4.4	4.9	5.5	6.0	6.5
14-16	3.2	3.8	4.3	4.8	5.4	5.9	6.4	7.0	7.5
17-19	4.2	4.7	5.3	5.8	6.3	6.9	7.4	8.0	8.5
20-22	5.1	5.7	6.2	6.8	7.3	7.9	8.4	8.9	9.5
23-25	6.1	6.6	7.2	7.7	8.3	8.8	9.1	9.9	10.5
26-28	7.0	7.6	8.1	8.7	9.2	9.8	10.3	10.9	11.4
29-31	8.0	8.5	9.1	9.6	10.2	10.7	11.3	11.8	12.4
32-34	8.9	9.4	10.0	10.5	11.1	11.6	12.2	12.8	13.3
35-37	9.8	10.4	10.9	11.5	12.0	12.6	13.1	13.7	14.3
38-40	10.7	11.3	11.8	12.4	12.9	13.5	14.1	14.6	15.2
41-43	11.6	12.2	12.7	13.3	13.8	14.4	15.0	15.5	16.1
44-46	12.5	13.1	13.6	14.2	14.7	15.3	15.9	16.4	17.0
47-49	13.4	13.9	14.5	15.1	15.6	16.2	16.8	17.3	17.9
50-52	14.3	14.8	15.4	15.9	16.5	17.1	17.6	18.2	18.8
53-55	15.1	15.7	16.2	16.8	17.4	17.9	18.5	19.1	19.7
56-58	16.0	16.5	17.1	17.7	18.2	18.8	19.4	20.0	20.5
59-61	16.9	17.4	17.9	18.5	19.1	19.7	20.2	20.8	21.4
62-64	17.6	18.2	18.8	19.4	19.9	20.5	21.1	21.7	22.2
65-67	18.5	19.0	19.6	20.2	20.8	21.3	21.9	22.5	23.1
68-70	19.3	19.9	20.4	21.0	21.6	22.2	22.7	23.3	23.9
71-73	20.1	20.7	21.2	21.8	22.4	23.0	23.6	24.1	24.7
74-76	20.9	21.5	22.0	22.6	23.2	23.8	24.4	25.0	25.5
77-79	21.7	22.2	22.8	23.4	24.0	24.6	25.2	25.8	26.3
80-82	22.4	23.0	23.6	24.2	24.8	25.4	25.9	26.5	27.1
83-85	23.2	23.8	24.4	25.0	25.5	26.1	26.7	27.3	27.9
86-88	24.0	24.5	25.1	25.7	26.3	26.9	27.5	28.1	28.7
89-91	24.7	25.3	25.9	26.5	27.1	27.6	28.2	28.8	29.4
92-94	25.4	26.0	26.6	27.2	27.8	28.4	29.0	29.6	30.2
95-97	26.1	26.7	27.3	27.9	28.5	29.1	29.7	30.3	30.9
98-100	26.9	27.4	28.0	28.6	29.2	29.8	30.4	31.0	31.6
101-103	27.5	28.1	28.7	29.3	29.9	30.5	31.1	31.7	32.3
104-106	28.2	28.8	29.4	30.0	30.6	31.2	31.8	32.4	33.0
107-109	28.9	29.5	30.1	30.7	31.3	31.9	32.5	33.1	33.7
110-112	29.6	30.2	30.8	31.4	32.0	32.6	33.2	33.8	34.4
113-115	30.2	30.8	31.4	32.0	32.6	33.2	33.8	34.5	35.1
116-118	30.9	31.5	32.1	32.7	33.3	33.9	34.5	35.1	35.7
119-121	31.5	32.1	32.7	33.3	33.9	34.5	35.1	35.7	36.4
122-124	32.1	32.7	33.3	33.9	34.5	35.1	35.8	36.4	37.0
125-127	32.7	33.3	33.9	34.5	35.1	35.8	36.4	37.0	37.6

Note. From "Measurement of cardiorespiratory fitness and body composition in the clinical setting" by M. Pollack, D. Schmidt, and A. Jackson, 1980, *Comprehensive Therapy*, 6(9), 12-27. Copyright 1980 by Laux Co. Reprinted by permission of the Laux Company, Inc.

*Percent fat calculated by the formula by Siri. Percent fat = $[(4.95/BD) - 4.5] \times 100$, where BD = body density.

MOST FREQUENTLY ASKED QUESTIONS

1. *Can I gain weight and lose fat at the same time?*

   Yes. It is possible to lose fat and gain muscle weight at the same time when you combine a diet and exercise program. It is important to notice the loss of fat in obvious body areas such as the waist, hips, and thighs.

2. *What effect will exercise have on my appetite?*

   Contrary to common belief, exercise is not automatically followed by an increase in food intake. This increase takes place only if the individual is already fairly active and then increases his or her activity level even higher. If the person is sedentary, activity can normally be increased without an increase in appetite.

3. *I gained 5 pounds after I started a cardiovascular endurance program, but I look and feel great. What happened? Should I try to lose the 5 pounds?*

   Check your percent body fat to determine if you need to lose weight. It may be that you have gained lean body tissue and lost fat. Muscle tissue is more dense than fat so it weighs more than fat tissue.

4. *Do some foods or food combinations have special chemical properties?*

   No. This is another myth that helps to sell fad diets. The grapefruit-and-egg diet was supposed to have a special chemical combination that "burned" fat off. Unless you get so tired of the one or two foods allowed on these diets that you decrease your caloric intake, you won't lose weight. These diets may actually be dangerous to your health.

5. *What is "cellulite" and how can I get rid of it?*

   "Cellulite" is a term for the type of fatty deposit that is lumpy or bumpy and causes the overlying skin to have a puckered appearance similar to orange peel. Medical authorities maintain that there is no such thing as cellulite and the lumpy bulges are ordinary fat that will respond to a diet and exercise program that increases caloric expenditure.

6. *What is the difference between being obese and being overweight?*

   An individual is considered overweight when he or she is over the height/weight standards used by insurance companies to calculate longevity of the general population. Obesity refers to the percentage of fat in the body. In men, a level of over 25% body fat is considered obese; in women, obesity is defined as over 30% body fat.

7. *What happens when I crash-diet?*

   The body is without many essential proteins, vitamins, and minerals that are often not included in a crash diet, and much of the weight loss is not fat, but lean body tissue.

8. *I want to lose weight on my thighs or stomach only. Is this possible?*

   Spot-reducing is not possible. A person following a proper diet and exercise program will lose body fat throughout the entire body, although a greater percentage of fat loss will be from areas where a greater amount of fat is deposited. If a person has a great deal of fat deposited in the thigh area, then a proportional amount will be lost in this area.

9. *Why shouldn't I go on a one-meal-a-day diet or a starvation (low-calorie) diet?*

This type of diet upsets the body's metabolism. Starvation followed by a large consumption of calories in one meal may cause the body to store more of those calories as fat (as a safety mechanism to prevent starvation), and thus you defeat your purpose. Also, long-term low-calorie diets slow down the metabolism and make it easier to gain fat when a higher calorie diet is resumed. Eating only once a day may cause you to feel deprived during the rest of the day, which is a common reason for breaking a diet.

10. *What happens if I diet but don't exercise?*

Part of your weight loss will be lean body mass. On a diet program approximately 3/4 of the weight loss is fat, while the rest is lean body mass and extracellular fluid. Adding exercise to a reducing plan increases the percent of fat loss to over 90% of the total weight loss.

11. *Aren't carbohydrates bad for you, or don't they at least help to make you fat?*

Carbohydrates have received some false bad press. Carbohydrates contain no more calories than the same amount of protein. A potato is very innocent until butter and sour cream are added. The recommended amount of carbohydrates in a healthy diet is close to 60% of the total calories consumed. Make sure, though, that you're eating complex carbohydrates like those found in bread, pasta, rice, and beans, and not the simple carbohydrates found in candy bars, cakes, and cookies. In nations where the diet is made up of 80% (largely complex) carbohydrates there are very low incidences of obesity.

12. *Are diet soft drinks of any help in losing weight?*

No, there has been no positive proof to indicate that diet soft drinks can help an individual to lose weight. Water, fruit juice spritzers, and low-fat milk offer more to the dieter than an artificially sweetened mixture of syrup and carbonated water. However, due to both heavy advertising by soda companies and already-formed eating habits, diet soft drinks continue to help guilty dieters believe they're saving some valuable calories.

13. *What is a starvation response?*

It is the body's way of conserving energy in order to function on very few calories. When an individual eats less than the amount of calories necessary for basal metabolic function, the body switches into low gear in order to survive. This means that the body is becoming as efficient as possible and thus lowers its basal metabolic rate.

14. *What are the differences between water-soluble and fat-soluble vitamins?*

Fat-soluble vitamins can be stored in the body; water-soluble vitamins cannot and are therefore needed on a daily basis. Vitamins A, D, E, and K are all fat-soluble. They are absorbed through the intestinal membrane into the body with the aid of fats in the diet. Since these vitamins are stored in body fat it is not essential to consume them daily, and taking large doses of these vitamins can build up toxic levels. Eight B-vitamins and vitamin C make up the water-soluble vitamins. These are used up and washed out daily through urine and sweat. These vitamins are more fragile than fat-soluble vitamins, and can be destroyed during food storage, preparation, or processing. Although taking a multivitamin supplement may not hurt an individual, living on vitamin supplements is a poor excuse for bad eating habits. With minimal effort to choose nutrient-dense foods, a normal healthy individual can eat a balanced diet without the need to take additional vitamins.

Energy Balance

Energy is required for growth, body processes (e.g., breathing, digestion), maintaining body temperature, and physical activity. Energy is obtained from the nutrients protein, carbohydrate, and fat, which are provided by the food we eat. The amount of energy in food is measured in units called calories.

Body weight is maintained when energy intake = energy output
(food calories)   (calories used for
metabolism and exercise)

Loss of fat will occur only if energy intake < energy output.

Gain of fat will occur only if energy intake > energy output.

One pound of fat = 3,500 calories so a deficit of 500 calories/day for 7 days = 1 pound fat loss. An excess of 500 calories/day = 1 pound fat gain.

How Can I Determine My Energy Output?

Unfortunately, this is not an easy question to answer. Energy needs depend on body size, age, sex, body composition, and so forth. However, one of the greatest determinants, especially for adults, is physical activity. The exact number of calories used will depend not only on the type of activity, but also on the frequency, intensity, and length of time the activity is performed. Although energy needs vary greatly among individuals, rough estimates for 19- to 22-year-old females are 2,100 and 2,900 calories per day, respectively. One method to estimate your caloric needs is to keep track of your caloric intake for one week and estimate an average daily intake. If your weight remains stable, this would indicate your approximate caloric needs per day.

How Many Calories Should I Consume to Safely Lose Weight?

A healthy, moderately active college student would easily lose 1 to 2 pounds per week on a 1,400-1,500 calorie/day diet. In order to meet nutritional needs, a minimum of 1,200 calories should be consumed from the four food groups—and even then food choices must be made wisely. Increasing physical activity will help assure successful weight loss.

Body Weight—What Does It Mean?

A person's body weight indicates total pounds; it cannot differentiate the percent body fat from muscle, bone, water weight, and so forth. Therefore, a person can appear "normal" on a weight chart but actually be overfat and out of shape. Likewise, a person can be "overweight" (e.g., an athlete), but very fit because he or she has a greater percentage of muscle than fat. This is because muscle weighs more than fat.

Fat's Where It's At?

Measuring percent body fat with a skinfold thickness test is a much better guide for assessing fitness. If you are overfat, a sensible exercise and diet program can do the trick.

The Less Fat, the Better?

No, having too little fat is just as unhealthy as having too much. Some people have distorted body images—imagining themselves fatter than they really are. This can lead to a gross preoccupation with dieting, even to the point of self-induced starvation and death. Maintaining a healthy percent body fat, which is approximately 15% for males and 25% for females, and accepting one's body are two key factors in obtaining good physical and mental health.

Note. Adapted from *Recommended Dietary Allowances* (9th ed.) by the National Research Council, 1980, Washington, DC: National Academy of Sciences; *Nutrition and Exercise for Fitness and Weight Control* (Circular 1230) by the Cooperative Extension Service, 1984, Urbana, IL: University of Illinois.

Body Composition Form

Name _____ Age _____ Date _____

1. Current weight _____

2. Skinfolds

Females	Males	Males & Females
Triceps _____	Chest _____	Biceps _____
Suprailium[a] _____	Abdomen _____	Triceps _____
Thigh _____	Thigh _____	Subscapula _____
		Iliac crest[b] _____
Total _____	Total _____	Total _____

3. Percent fat _____

4. Current fat weight (item 1 × item 3) _____
5. Current lean body weight (item 1 − item 4) _____

6. Desired percent body fat
   Males (average for college age 15%) _____

   Females (average for college age 25%) _____

7. Estimated target weight [item 5 ÷ (1.0 − item 6)] _____

8. Estimated pounds of fat to lose (item 1 − item 7) _____

Note. Columns 1 and 2 from ''Measurement of Cardiorespiratory Fitness and Body Composition in the Clinical Setting'' by M. Pollack, D. Schmidt, and A. Jackson, 1980, *Comprehensive Therapy,* **6**(9), pp. 12-25. Column 3 from ''Body Fat Assessed From Total Body Density and Its Estimation From Skinfold Thickness: Measurements on 481 Men and Women Aged 16-74 Years'' by J. Durnin and J. Womersley, 1974, *British Journal of Nutrition,* **32**, p. 95.

[a]Measure diagonal fold.

[b]Measure vertical fold.

Fast Food Calorie Counter

BASKIN-ROBBINS

Food item (regular 4-oz. scoop)	Calories	Fat (gm)	% Calories from fat
Vanilla	235	13.1	50
Chocolate	264	12.6	43
Strawberry	226	9.6	38
French Vanilla	290	18.9	59
Pralines 'n' Cream	283	13.1	42
Rocky Road	291	11.2	35
Chocolate Mousse Royale	293	13.6	42
Orange Sherbet	158	2.4	14
Dacquiri Ice	136	0.0	0
Raspberry Sherbet	134	0.0	0
Wild Strawberry (low-fat frozen dairy dessert)	90	1.6	16
Sugar Cone	57	1.0	16
Cake Cone	19	0.3	14

ARBY'S

Food item	Calories	Fat (gm)	% Calories from fat
Jr. Roast Beef	218	8.0	33
Regular Roast Beef	353	15.0	38
Super Roast Beef	501	22.0	40
King Roast Beef	467	19.0	37
Beef 'n' Cheddar	490	21.0	39
Bacon 'n' Cheddar Deluxe	561	34.0	55
Ham 'n' Cheese	353	13.0	33
Chicken Breast Sandwich	592	27.0	41
Turkey Deluxe	375	17.0	41
Potato Cakes	201	14.0	63

BURGER KING

Food item	Calories	Fat (gm)	% Calories from fat
Whopper	628	36.0	52
Whopper w/ Cheese	711	42.0	53
Double Beef Whopper	850	52.0	55
Double Beef Whopper w/ Cheese	950	60.0	57
Whopper Junior	322	17.0	48
Whopper Junior w/ Cheese	364	20.0	49
Hamburger	275	12.0	39
Cheeseburger	317	15.0	43
Bacon Double Cheeseburger	510	31.0	55
Whaler Fish Sandwich	488	27.0	50
Whaler Fish Sandwich w/ Cheese	530	30.0	51
Ham & Cheese Specialty Sandwich	471	23.0	44
Chicken Specialty Sandwich	688	40.0	52
Plain Salad	28	0.0	0
French Fries	227	13.0	52
Onion Rings	274	16.0	53
Apple Pie	305	12.0	35

DOMINO'S PIZZA

Food item (2 slices of an 8-slice pizza)	Calories	Fat (gm)	% Calories from fat
Plain Cheese	218	5.9	24
Pepperoni	265	10.2	35
Sausage	246	8.4	31
Double Cheese	284	10.8	34

LONG JOHN SILVER'S

Food item	Calories	Fat (gm)	% Calories from fat
Fish & Fries (3 fish, fries, 2 hushpuppies)	998	55.0	50
Tender Chicken Plank Dinner (4 chicken planks, fries, slaw)	1037	59.0	51
Shrimp, Fish & Chicken Dinner (2 battered shrimp, 1 fish, 1 chicken plank, fries, slaw, 2 hushpuppies	1022	60.0	53
Seafood Platter (1 fish, 2 shrimp, clams, fries, slaw, 2 hushpuppies)	1133	68.0	54
Clam Dinner (clams, fries, slaw)	955	58.0	55
Cajun Shrimp Platter (Cajun shrimp, fries, slaw)	859	52.0	54
Pasta & Seafood Salad (7 oz pasta & seafood, 4 oz lettuce, 2 tomato wedges, 2 crackers	474	33.0	63
Seafood Salad (4.5 oz seafood, 4 oz lettuce, 2 tomato wedges, 2 crackers)	317	25.0	71
Ocean Chef Salad (4 oz lettuce, 1.75 oz shrimp, 2 oz seafood blend, .5 oz carrots, tomato wedge, .75 oz cheese, 2 crackers)	193	7.0	33
Breaded Clams (1 order)	526	31.0	53
Breaded Fish Sandwich	406	15.0	33
Clam Chowder	128	5.0	35
Cole Slaw	182	15.0	74
Fries	247	12.0	44
Hushpuppies	145	7.0	43

DAIRY QUEEN

Food item	Calories	Fat (gm)	% Calories from fat
Cone			
Small	140	4.0	26
Regular	240	7.0	26
Large	340	10.0	26
Chocolate Dip Cone			
Small	190	9.0	43
Regular	340	16.0	42
Large	510	24.0	42
Milkshake (chocolate)			
Small	490	13.0	24
Regular	710	19.0	24
Large	990	26.0	24
Float	410	7.0	15
Banana Split	540	11.0	18
Mr. Misty Freeze (regular)	250	0.0	0
Dilly Bar	210	13.0	56
D.Q. Sandwich	140	4.0	26
Mr. Misty Kiss	70	0.0	0
Heath Blizzard	800	24.0	27
Peanut Buster Parfait	740	34.0	41

WENDY'S

Food item	Calories	Fat (gm)	% Calories from fat
Single Hamburger	350	18.0	46
Double Hamburger	560	34.0	55
Triple Hamburger	900	56.0	56
Single Hamburger w/ Cheese	420	24.0	51
Double Hamburger w/ Cheese	630	40.0	57
Triple Hamburger w/ Cheese	1040	68.0	59
Chicken Sandwich	320	10.0	28
Chili	260	8.0	28
French Fries (regular)	280	14.0	45
Taco Salad	390	18.0	42
Frosty	400	14.0	32
Hot Stuffed Potatoes			
Plain	250	2.0	7
Sour Cream & Chives	460	24.0	47
Cheese	590	34.0	52
Chili & Cheese	510	20.0	35
Bacon & Cheese	570	30.0	47
Broccoli & Cheese	500	25.0	45
Pick-Up Side Salad	110	6.0	49

HARDEE'S

Food item	Calories	Fat (gm)	% Calories from fat
Hamburger	276	15.3	50
Cheeseburger	309	12.8	37
Big Deluxe	503	28.9	52
Bacon Cheeseburger	556	32.8	53
Roast Beef Sandwich	312	12.4	36
Big Roast Beef Sandwich	440	21.5	44
Turkey Club	426	22.3	47
Fisherman's Filet	469	20.1	39
Chicken Filet	510	26.2	46
Hot Dog	346	22.0	57
French Fries (regular)	239	12.9	49
French Fries (large)	406	22.0	49
Apple Turnover	282	13.8	44
Big Cookie	278	15.3	50
Biscuit	257	12.4	43
Egg Biscuit	334	18.7	50
Sausage Biscuit	426	28.3	60
Sausage & Egg Biscuit	503	34.6	62
Bacon & Egg Biscuit	405	25.7	57
Cinnamon 'n' Raisin Biscuit	276	16.2	53
Hashrounds	200	13.0	59

McDONALD'S

Food item	Calories	Fat (gm)	% Calories from fat
Egg McMuffin	340	15.8	42
Hot Cakes w/ Butter & Syrup	500	10.3	19
Scrambled Eggs	180	13.0	65
Pork Sausage	210	18.6	80
English Muffin w/ Butter	186	5.3	26
Hash Brown Potatoes	144	8.9	56
Big Mac	570	35.0	55
Hamburger	263	11.3	39
Cheeseburger	318	16.0	45
Quarter Pounder	427	23.5	50
Quarter Pounder w/ Cheese	525	31.6	54
Filet-O-Fish	435	25.7	53
McD.L.T.	680	44.0	58
Chicken McNuggets (6)	323	20.2	56
French Fries (regular)	220	11.5	47
Apple Pie	253	14.0	50
Vanilla Shake	352	8.4	21
Chocolate Shake	383	9.0	21
Strawberry Sundae	320	8.7	24
Hot Fudge Sundae	357	10.8	27
Hot Caramel Sundae	361	10.0	25
McDonaldland Cookies	308	10.8	32
Chocolaty Chip Cookies	342	16.3	43
Chef Salad	226	13.0	52
Shrimp Salad	99	2.6	24
Garden Salad	91	5.5	54
Chicken Oriental Salad	146	3.9	24
Side Salad	48	2.6	49
Croutons	52	2.2	38
Chow Mein Noodles	45	2.2	44

KENTUCKY FRIED CHICKEN

Food item	Calories	Fat (gm)	% Calories from fat
Original Recipe			
Wing	181	12.3	61
Side Breast	276	17.3	56
Center Breast	257	13.7	48
Drumstick	147	8.8	54
Thigh	278	19.2	62
Extra Crispy			
Wing	218	15.6	64
Side Breast	354	23.7	60
Center Breast	353	20.9	53
Drumstick	173	10.9	57
Thigh	371	26.3	64
Mashed Potatoes	59	0.6	9
Gravy	59	3.7	56
Cole Slaw	103	5.7	50
Biscuit	269	13.6	46
Kentucky Fries	268	12.8	43
Corn-on-the-Cob	176	3.1	16

TACO BELL

Food item	Calories	Fat (gm)	% Calories from fat
Bean Burrito	360	10.9	27
Beef Burrito	402	17.3	39
Beefy Tostada	322	19.6	55
Tostada	243	10.9	40
Bell Beefer	312	13.1	38
Burrito Supreme	422	18.8	40
Combination Burrito	381	14.1	33
Enchirito	382	20.1	47
Pintos 'n' Cheese	194	9.5	44
Taco	184	10.9	53
Fajita Steak Taco	235	10.9	42
w/ Sour Cream	281	15.4	49
w/ Guacamole	269	13.2	44
Nachos	356	19.2	49
Nachos Bell Grande	719	40.7	51

SALAD DRESSINGS

1 oz = 2 tbsp.	Calories	Fat (gm)	% Calories from fat
Bleu Cheese	130	13.5	93
Italian	133	13.7	93
Ranch	139	14.6	95
French	123	10.4	76
Thousand Island	131	11.7	80
Low-Calorie Italian	32	2.8	79
Low-Calorie Thousand Island	69	5.6	73

CARBONATED BEVERAGES

12 oz	Calories	Fat (gm)	% Calories from fat
Cola types	150	0.0	0
Cream Soda	155	0.0	0
Fruit Flavor Soda	166	0.0	0
Gingerale	126	0.0	0
Root Beer	163	0.0	0
Beer	151	0.0	0

Note. Data adapted from *Bowes & Church's Food Values of Portions Commonly Used* (14th ed.), 1985, J.B. Lippincott Co.; and individual restaurant chains.

Calculating
Basal Metabolic Rate

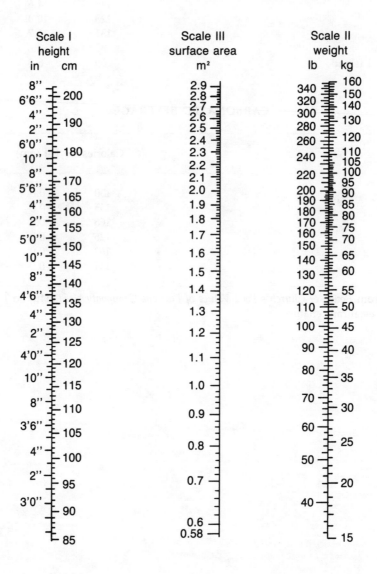

Scale I height		Scale III surface area	Scale II weight	
in	cm	m²	lb	kg
8″		2.9	340	160
6′6″	200	2.8	320	150
4″		2.7	300	140
2″	190	2.6	280	130
6′0″		2.5	260	120
10″	180	2.4		
		2.3	240	110
8″	170	2.2		105
5′6″		2.1	220	100
4″	165	2.0	200	95
	160	1.9	190	90
2″	155	1.8	180	85
5′0″	150		170	80
		1.7	160	75
10″	145	1.6	150	70
8″	140	1.5	140	65
			130	60
4′6″	135	1.4		
4″	130	1.3	120	55
			110	50
2″	125	1.2	100	45
4′0″	120	1.1	90	40
10″	115		80	35
		1.0		
8″	110	0.9	70	30
3′6″	105		60	
		0.8		25
4″	100		50	
2″	95	0.7		20
3′0″	90		40	
	85	0.6 0.58		15

Basal Metabolic Rate According to Age and Sex

Age	BMR (kcal/m²/hr) Men	Women	Age	BMR (kcal/m²/hr) Men	Women
10	47.7	44.9	28	37.8	35.0
11	46.5	43.5	29	37.7	35.0
12	45.3	42.0	30	37.6	35.0
13	44.5	40.5	31	37.4	35.0
14	43.8	39.2	32	37.2	34.9
15	42.9	38.3	33	37.1	34.9
16	42.0	37.2	34	37.0	34.9
17	41.5	36.4	35	36.9	34.8
18	40.8	35.8	36	36.8	34.7
19	40.5	35.4	37	36.7	34.6
20	39.9	35.3	38	36.7	34.5
21	39.5	35.2	39	36.6	34.4
22	39.2	35.2	40-44	36.4	34.1
23	39.0	35.2	45-49	36.2	33.8
24	38.7	35.1	50-54	35.8	33.1
25	38.4	35.1	55-59	35.1	32.8
26	38.2	35.0	60-64	34.5	32.0
27	38.0	35.0	65-79	33.5	31.6
			70-74	32.7	31.1
			75+	31.8	

Worksheet for Calculating Basal Metabolic Rate (BMR)

1. Estimated body surface area = _____
   (see left panel)

2. BMR factor (see above panel) = _____

3. _____ × _____ = _____
   Est. body surface area   BMR factor   BMR

4. _____ × 24 hours = _____
   BMR   Basal metabolic needs for 1 day

Note. From *Fitness for College and Life* by C.A. Bucher and W.E. Prentice, 1985, St. Louis: Times Mirror/ Mosby. Copyright 1985. Reprinted by permission.

Winning at Weight Control
Game Board

| Pound Card | Fact or Fiction | Nutrients | Weight Control | Pound Card |
| | Blue | Orange | Yellow | |

Weight Control — Yellow
Nutrients — Orange
Fact or Fiction — Blue

Winning at Weight Control

Blue — Fact or Fiction
Orange — Nutrients
Yellow — Weight Control

Pound Card

| Pound Card | Yellow | Orange | Blue | Pound Card |
| | Weight Control | Nutrients | Fact or Fiction | |

REFERENCES

Bailey, C. (1978). *Fit or fat?* Boston: Houghton Mifflin.

Brody, J. (1985). *Jane Brody's good food book—Living the high carbohydrate way.* New York: W.W. Norton.

Brody, J. (1981). *Jane Brody's nutrition book.* New York: Bantam.

Hablock, M. (1985, March). Fat savvy, uncover the hidden fat in your food. *Glamour,* pp. 292-293.

Hamilton, E.N., Whitney, E., & Sienkiewicz-Sizer, F. (1982). *Nutrition concepts and controversies* (3rd ed.). St. Paul: West.

Katch, F.I., & McArdle, W.D. (1983). *Nutrition, weight control, & exercise* (2nd ed.). Philadelphia: Lea and Febiger.

162 pounds and counting down. (1985, December). *Glamour,* pp. 158-159.

Osman, J.O. (1981, October). Your weight may be great, but fat's where it's at. *Nutrition News,* **44,** 1.

Stuart, R.B. (1983). *Act thin, stay thin.* New York: W.W. Norton.

Whitney, E., & Hamilton, E. (1987). *Understanding nutrition* (4th ed.). St. Paul, MN: West.

Designer Diets
Lifestyle Workshop

PARAPROFESSIONAL PREPARATION MATERIALS

Training Sessions

Competency Exam

Texts and Suggested Readings

WORKSHOP AT A GLANCE

Presenter Information

Most Frequently Asked Questions

Handouts and Visual Aids*

References

Designer Diets, *Designer Diet Worksheet*, and *Free Foods and Beverages* were written by Sara Kelley, MS, RD, and Clare Sente.

TRAINING SESSIONS

Designer Diets

Session 1: Workshop Presentation

Time: 60 minutes

Methods: Presentation, demonstration

Description: Trainer presents workshop to Lifestyle Educators.

Readings: The workshop

Session 2: Personalizing Exchange Groups

Time: 60 minutes

Methods: Demonstration, discussion, lecture

Description: Instructor demonstrates the proper procedure for dividing up five combination foods using exchange groups.

Activity: Lifestyle Educators present 1-day diets of their own design, using the food models and meal boards from the workshop. Lifestyle Educators pick two combination foods and practice converting them into exchange groups. Results are then discussed. Practice calculating percent carbohydrate, protein, and fat for sample meals.

Readings: Materials on Exchange Groups, the workshop

Competency exam questions: 1, 3, 6, 8, 9, 10, 11

Session 3: Determination of Caloric Needs

Time: 60 minutes

Methods: Lecture, discussion

Description: Define basal metabolic rate (BMR), discuss various methods for determining BMR, and compare differences in their totals. Define activity and criteria for calculating activity calories.

Activity: Students practice working through workshop handout, "Determination of Caloric Needs."

Readings: Materials on energy expenditure and energy balance, the handout "Designer Diets," the workshop

Competency exam question: 4

Session 4: Diet Planning Guides

Time: 60 minutes

Methods: Lecture, discussion

Description: Students will outline the strengths and weaknesses of using Basic 4, Dietary Guidelines, or Exchange Groups for Diet Planning. The nutrient-density concept is discussed and illustrated using exchanges within each of the six food groups.

Activity: Students practice working through workshop handout, *Determination of Caloric Needs.*

Readings: Diet Planning Guides, materials on nutrient density

Competency exam questions: 5, 7

Session 5: High-Carbohydrate Diets

Time: 60 minutes

Methods: Lecture, discussion

Description: Discuss Dietary Guidelines for Americans and how the exchange groups can match these guidelines. Students discuss the main contributors of carbohydrates, protein, and fat from each of the six food groups. More sample meals are presented for calculating total calories and the percentage of carbohydrates, proteins, and fats.

Readings: The workshop, "Exchange Groups" handout

Competency exam questions: 2, 10

Session 6: "Most Frequently Asked Questions" Review and Hot Seat

Time: 60 minutes

Methods: Discussion, practice

Description: Review "Most Frequently Asked Questions" section of the workshop and other workshop components.

Activity: Hot Seat: Each Lifestyle Educator is quizzed by the other students on the workshop topic for 10 minutes.

Readings: The workshop

Session 7: Practice Workshop Presentation

Time: 60 minutes

Method: Presentation

Description: Each Lifestyle Educator presents 20 minutes of the workshop.

Readings: The workshop

COMPETENCY EXAM

1. Explain the goal of the Designer Diets Workshop.

2. Which of the six food groups contribute to a diet high in complex carbohydrates?

3. Which food groups supply both simple and complex carbohydrates?

4. Which food groups contribute fat to the diet?

5. List the six food groups that comprise the exchange groups, the calorie allotment for each, and three examples of exchanges for each group (18 total examples).

6. Fill in the blanks on the "Determination of Caloric Needs" handout. (Pass out the handout with this exam.)

7. Briefly explain nutrient density and give examples of two comparable foods.

8. McDonald's Egg McMuffin can be considered a combination food. Calculate the proper exchanges for its nutritional and caloric value: Calories 331, Carbohydrates (g) 31, Protein (g) 18.5, Fat (g) 14.8.

9. Briefly explain the difference between the Basic 4 and the Exchange Groups as diet planning methods. (Give two pros and two cons of each method.)

10. Provide three examples of polyunsaturated fat exchanges and three examples of saturated fat exchanges.

11. Explain the different fat levels in the meat and milk exchanges, and list the fat levels used for each group in the Designer Diet workshop.

12. Calculate the percent carbohydrate, protein, and fat as well as total calories (approximate and actual) for one of the following meals:

    Breakfast: 1 cup orange juice, 2 soft-boiled eggs, 2 slices wheat bread, 2 strips bacon.

    Lunch: 3 oz broiled chicken breast, 1 cup broccoli and carrots, 1/2 cup wild rice, 1 hard roll, a pat butter, 1/4 small cantaloupe.

    Dinner: Gyros, 2 oz lamb, 1 tomato, 1/2 pita bread, 12 oz Diet Coke.

13. After the 1-day diets have been completed in the workshop, what four points should be covered in the discussion section?

14. Suggest possible techniques to use in the workshop if participant is one of the following:

    - Recognition Seeker (frequently calls attention to self)
    - Conversationalist (brings up off-the-subject anecdotes and is a noisy distraction)
    - Moralizer (advocates judgmental points of view based on personal convictions)
    - Conservative (convinced that the status quo does not need changing)

TEXTS AND SUGGESTED READINGS

Franz, M. D., Barr, P., Holler, J., Powers, M. A., Wheeler, M. L., & Wylie-Rossett, J. (1987). Exchange lists: Revised 1986. *Journal of the American Dietetic Association, 87*, 28-34.

Hamilton, K. (1987, January). Give-up-one-food diet. *Self*, pp. 78-81.

Whitney, E., & Hamilton, E. (1987). *Understanding nutrition* (4th ed.). St. Paul, MN: West.

WORKSHOP AT A GLANCE

The goal of this workshop is to introduce a long-term approach to food selection and calorie control. This system offers a personalized, versatile plan incorporating individual caloric needs and food preferences to eliminate the need for short-term and fad diets. This workshop takes approximately 75 minutes to present. Suggested attendance is 5 to 30 persons.

Objectives

Within the content of this workshop, the following objectives will be met.

- Through the use of the "Determination of Caloric Needs" handout, participants will estimate their daily caloric needs.
- Participants will be introduced to the exchange system of meal planning and diet maintenance.
- In groups, participants will demonstrate their understanding of the exchange system by planning a 1-day diet.

Workshop Materials

- Workshop sign-in sheet
- Handouts and visual aids: *Designer Diets, Designer Diets Worksheet, Free Foods & Beverages, Determination of Caloric Needs, Meal Planning Grid, Exchange Groups* or food model sets from your local Dairy Council ($7.50/set). (Food models are plastic-coated cardboard pictures of food servings with nutrients and caloric information listed on the back.) Or, order *Healthy Food Choices* from The American Diabetes Association, 208 LaSalle St., Suite 1100, Chicago, IL 60604-1003, or phone 312/899-0040.
- Lifestyle Workshop evaluation forms and pencils

PRESENTER INFORMATION

Briefly introduce yourself, your background, and any other personal information you choose to share. Describe your health promotion program and the topics available, like fitness and nutrition. Stress that the workshops are unique because you bring them to their living areas. Tell them that Lifestyle Workshop paraprofessionals are trained at (your institution or program) to present these workshops. If anyone is interested in the training program, ask him or her to speak with you after the workshop.

You may want to introduce this information in the following manner: The purpose of this workshop is to introduce you to a new meal planning system. It emphasizes daily food selection and calorie control, rather than being a predesigned short-term or fad diet. The first half of the workshop involves estimating your individual caloric needs and going over the basics of the system. The second half will be spent in groups actually "designing" a diet.

Energy Balance (10 minutes)

Let's start by looking at the energy balance equation. There are two components of the equation: input and output. These are the most important principles to remember about energy balance.

- To be in energy balance, the amount of food eaten each day has to equal the number of calories burned off each day. If input is greater than output it is called "positive energy balance" and body fat will accumulate. Even as little as 100 calories taken in per day over the amount burned off will add up to 1 pound of extra body fat in 35 days.
- If output is greater than intake it is called "negative energy balance" and weight will be lost. The lost body weight will be more fat than lean body tissue if exercise is also included to induce the negative energy balance.
- Diet-induced negative energy balance results in the loss of less fat and more lean body tissue and is not recommended by nutrition and health experts.
- In other words, to balance the scales, you need to balance carbohydrates, fats, proteins, and

alcohol with basal metabolic rate (BMR) and physical activity.

Calculating Caloric Needs

Next let's look at how to determine caloric needs, keeping these principles in mind. The first step in designing an individualized diet is to get an estimate of the calories each person requires in one day. Distribute the "Determination of Caloric Needs" handout and follow these steps:

1. Estimate desired body weight. Women start at 100 pounds for the first 5 feet of height and add an additional 5 pounds for each inch above 5 feet. For a small body frame, subtract 10% from this total; for a large body frame, add 10%. Men start at 106 pounds for the first 5 feet of height and add an additional 6 pounds for each inch above 5 feet. For a small body frame, subtract 10% from this total; for a large body frame, add 10%.
2. Estimate basal metabolic rate. BMR (basal metabolic rate) is the minimum level of energy required to sustain the body's vital functions and may be viewed as calories expended under total resting conditions. Multiply the desired body weight calculated in step one by a factor of 10. For example, if desired body weight was calculated as 130 pounds, BMR would equal 130 × 10 or 1,300 calories.
3. Estimate calories burned by daily activity. A sedentary individual could be someone who works 40 hours per week—but does not exercise regularly (less than 3 hours per week). Most individuals are considered sedentary because the number of life-simplifying automatic and electrical appliances used throughout the day requires less energy from them. Multiply desired body weight by a factor of 3.

   A moderately active individual is one who exercises regularly between 3 and 5 hours per week at his or her recommended target heart rate. This individual also relies less on automated and electrical appliances and substitutes manual power for those activities. Multiply desired body weight by a factor of 5. A strenuously active individual works

8 hours per day in manual labor or trains 3 to 6 hours per day in an athletic discipline. Multiply desired body weight by the factor 10. (A word of caution for estimating activity calories: It is far better to underestimate activity calories than to discover later that one's daily meal plan includes more calories than the number burned off from activity, causing one to gain fat on a supposed maintenance diet.)

4. Add together BMR calories (step two) with activity calories (step three) to compute the number of calories needed per day.

If an individual wants to lose weight, 2 pounds per week is highly recommended as an upper limit weight loss goal. A reasonable and attainable goal for this system is a loss of 1/2 pound per week. This would promote a greater fat-to-lean-tissue loss ratio, and offer an added flexibility of 250 calories in planning a daily diet. Since the odds are stacked in favor of a dieter gaining back the weight lost within 2 years (97% do), it makes sense to lose weight slowly while learning better eating habits.

If an individual wants to gain weight, it is also recommended that no more than 1 pound per week be set as the weight gain goal. This works out to an additional 500 calories per day added to the original weight-maintaining diet total.

An example could be Amy, who is 5 feet, 6 inches tall and weighs 112 pounds. Her desired weight would be 117 for a small body frame. Her estimated caloric needs equal 1,170 calories for her BMR plus 351 calories for her daily level of activity because she is sedentary. Amy must add 500 calories per day to the 1,521 calories she needs to maintain her weight. This averages to around 2,000 calories per day that Amy's diet should provide in order for her to gain 1 pound per week.

The Exchange System (30 minutes)

The exchange system provides a guide to both the types of food groups to be eaten every day in order to stay healthy, and the quantities needed to stay within an individual's predetermined calorie range; however, the individual decides what specific foods he or she wants to eat and at what times during the day. The exchange system is used instead of the four basic food groups because it involves counting calories and balancing your diet

in terms of the correct percentages of carbohydrates, protein, and fat for optimum health.

Long-Term Benefits

The exchange system can be a long-term eating plan for any healthy individual because of its versatility. All the food portions in each of the six exchange groups have approximately the same number of calories, so a food in the amount listed as an exchange may be substituted for any other food in that same list. In this way, the system can be customized to each person. Short-term diets are often very specific. For example, a typical breakfast might be 1 hard-boiled egg, 2 slices whole wheat bread, 1 teaspoon margarine, 1/2 cup orange juice, and 1 cup 2% milk.

If an individual does not enjoy hard-boiled eggs or wheat bread, a personal substitution might mean upsetting the caloric balance of the diet or changing the total percentages of protein, carbohydrates, and fat. The exchange system allows individuals to break the rules of a preplanned diet. You can customize your meal plan and eat the foods you enjoy. You'll be more likely to follow such a diet because the exchange system meal plan will soon resemble aspects of your old eating habits, including when and what you like to eat. The only changes are the amounts of food eaten and the addition of certain food groups to nutritionally balance your diet.

Foods have been divided into six groups or exchanges. For example, breads and other starches are listed in one group and fats are listed in another. Each exchange group has a certain number of calories, and all the portions listed under one exchange group contain that number of calories. The foods in each exchange group contribute to your daily nutritional needs. Each exchange group has specific vitamin and mineral advantages. No one exchange group can supply all of the nutrients needed in a well-balanced diet. The human body needs all six groups working together to supply all nutritional requirements.

You may have heard the recommendation that Americans need to cut down on fat and increase their intake of complex carbohydrates. Even though you may intend to try to follow this wise recommendation, if you aren't aware of what foods supply complex carbohydrates and what foods are the major contributors of fat, how can the necessary changes be made? This is an extra bonus in using the exchange system. Two of the six exchange groups are loaded with complex carbohydrates: the starch/bread group and the vegetable group. The fat group and many foods in the meat group are the major contributors of fat in your diet.

Meal Planning With Exchange Groups

You have already estimated the number of calories you need for one day, so the next step is to find out how many exchanges you require for your caloric needs. As mentioned earlier, each exchange group contains a particular number of calories. A Meal Plan Table has been worked out (see handouts and visual aids), taking into consideration the U.S. Dietary Goals for consuming a low-fat, high-carbohydrate diet. Most people will be able to incorporate one of these meal plans into their own calorie maintenance diet or as a weight-reducing or weight-gaining diet. Most women can follow the A, B, C, or D meal plan; most men can follow the C, D, or E meal plan.

The bread-starch group has the most exchanges in each of the caloric meal plans because in order to eat a diet high in carbohydrates (55% is recommended), you need to consume a large number of exchanges from this group. (If anyone feels that their individual caloric needs cannot be met by one of these five meal plans, suggest that he or she make an appointment with a registered dietician or obtain a copy of the American Dietetic Association's Exchange Lists.) Pass out "Designer Diets" and the "Designer Diets Worksheet."

Exchange Meal Planning (15 minutes)

The objective of this half of the workshop is to practice using the exchange system by planning a healthy 1-day diet. At this point, distribute the "Meal Planning Grid" and either the "Exchange Groups" handout or food models. (If you are using the food models, poster-size Meal Planning Grids would make an excellent visual aid to display the food models.) Divide the group according to group size.

- If the workshop has the maximum of 20 participants, there should be four groups of 5.
- If the workshop has between 12 and 19 participants, there should be three or four groups.

- If the workshop has between 6 and 11 participants, there should be two groups.
- If five or fewer are involved in the workshop, there should be either one or two groups depending on the level of enthusiasm the participants have about planning a 1-day diet.

Each group may be assigned a particular calorie meal plan (from the Exchange Groups Meal Plan) or given the option of choosing one. Explain that the following is expected from each group when planning their 1-day diets:

- The number of exchanges from each exchange group must equal the number assigned from the Exchange Groups Meal Plan.
- The 1-day diets must be divided into breakfast, lunch, dinner, and one or two snacks.
- At least one combination food is expected per chosen meal plan, and more combination foods are encouraged for the sake of producing a variety of individual 1-day meal plans from the groups.
- Include foods from the Foods for Occasional Use Group to add reality to these typical 1-day diets.

Compliance with these requirements should be checked after a group indicates that it has finished. If there are errors in meeting any or all of these requirements, indicate to the group where the error occurs. Remember, lessons may be learned twice as well after a mistake is revealed and then corrected. (The following would make an excellent visual aid.) If you are using food models, you are encouraged to buy an extra set and arrange each exchange group with food models. Glue the food models on poster boards, one for each exchange group. Place these posters around the room during the explanation of the exchange system.

Group Meal Presentations and Discussion (10 minutes)

Allow the groups to view one another's meal plans. Encourage discussion of various choices used by individual groups and discuss the importance of including a variety from each of the six groups along with using combination foods to fulfill requirements for the daily menu plan.

Briefly explain that some exchanges may be better sources of nutrients than others from the same group. For example, both an orange and an apple are considered fruit exchanges, yet an orange contains 80 mg vitamin C and 0.6 g of fiber, while an apple contains 7 mg vitamin C and 1.1 g fiber. These facts should help individuals get the most nutrition out of the specific exchanges. Depending on time availability, another activity can be used to help participants apply the principles learned during the workshop.

While participants are involved in group menu planning, put together a sample meal that includes a combination food and ask participants to calculate the number of calories in that particular meal. This activity will check their understanding and recall of the calories for each exchange group.

In addition, point out the difference in calories that will occur by doubling the amount of vegetable exchanges versus doubling the amount of fat or meat exchanges for this particular meal.

Conclusion and Evaluation (5 minutes)

Summarize the main points of the workshop:

- Every individual needs a certain number of calories just to maintain weight, and it is important to have an idea of this quantity.
- There are six exchange groups with specific foods, portion sizes, and caloric contents. Combination foods are more difficult to calculate, but it becomes easier to estimate the exchanges as you learn the system. Foods for occasional use should also be included in weight maintenance diets as long as they are not substituted for healthier, more nutrient-dense foods.
- The exchange system is a challenge at first, but gradually you will become more and more familiar with the numbers and types of exchanges.

Ask for questions from the participants. Offer resources and referrals for further information. Distribute Lifestyle Workshop evaluation forms and pencils. Allow time for completion and then collect. Briefly list and describe the other Lifestyle Workshops in Nutrition.

MOST FREQUENTLY ASKED QUESTIONS

1. *Why aren't the "Foods for Occasional Use" translated into exchanges?*

   These foods should not be substituted for foods from which one normally chooses to complete the daily exchanges. Because the goal is to pick a meal plan that has adequate nutrients and calories to maintain ideal weight, it is necessary to use the foods described under each exchange group to complete a daily menu. If sweets or alcohol are included on any particular day, then limit the total calories coming from them to approximately 300 calories and increase your activity level to compensate for these extra calories. Consistently choosing the low-fat meat and milk exchanges will also save you some extra calories to splurge with later.

2. *How can one cup of chicken noodle soup equal one starch exchange?*

   When foods are classified into an exchange group, their composition in terms of carbohydrate, protein, fat, and total calories is the primary consideration. Most of the calories from soup are provided from carbohydrates and a few from protein. This composition most closely resembles the starch exchange group. Some combination foods will make more sense than others, but you can be confident that if you substitute a combination food for its exchange equivalency, your total calories and percentages of carbohydrates, protein, and fat will *not* be significantly different.

3. *Does this mean that a combination food is nutritionally equivalent to its calculated exchanges? Example, 1 cup fruited low-fat yogurt = 1 low-fat milk exchange and 2 fruit exchanges?*

   No, not always. In this particular case the fruit in the fruited yogurt may be equivalent to two fruit exchanges both in calories and in carbohydrates. But the vitamin, mineral, and fiber content is inferior to two fresh fruit exchanges. The protein and calcium content of yogurt is actually slightly higher than the equivalent milk exchange. These differences between foods should be kept in mind when planning how to fulfill your exchange group requirements.

4. *The foods listed under each of the exchange groups don't all have the exact number of calories. Do I still need to count calories when planning my meals?*

   No. The whole idea behind using the exchange groups for meal planning is that you don't have to memorize calories. Each exchange group already has an average number of calories for all the foods and their portion sizes. (Some foods will have a few more calories and others a few less.) If you include a variety of foods from each exchange group, your total daily calories will average out to the total calories of your chosen meal plan. Just pick the calorie meal plan that best suits your weight and learn the number of exchanges in each of its six categories. When you focus your attention away from the calorie content of a food item you can concentrate on your overall diet. Eating a high-carbohydrate, low-fat diet that is within your calorie range is better for your overall health than knowing the calorie content of every food item you put in your mouth.

5. *Why are there three fat levels for the meat and milk exchanges?*

   Fat is the most calorically dense nutrient in food and the varying levels between foods listed in any particular exchange group need to be accounted for. Both the meat and milk exchanges in particular contain varying amounts of fat, so one average caloric value for these two exchange groups would greatly overestimate or underestimate other foods in that group. Each meal plan has been calculated using the medium-fat exchange of 75 calories and the low-fat milk exchange of 120 calories. When planning your diet, try to pick the food items that fall under the low or medium-fat meat and milk exchange groups, and limit the foods under the high-fat categories to twice a week.

6. *There is so much to remember in order to use Designer Diets!*

It may seem overwhelming at first, so don't feel you need to memorize everything. Just try to remember that there are six major exchange groups to choose from every day: starch/bread, meat, vegetables, fruits, fats, and milk. Each of these food groups has a caloric value associated with a given portion size. For example, 1/2 cup cooked vegetables equals 25 calories. Then look at your favorite foods and learn which exchange groups they fall under. As you become more familiar with the foods and portion sizes under each exchange group, the system will start to make more sense. The concept of exchange groups is becoming more popular, so you won't have to feel isolated while using it. Weight Watchers teaches a meal plan based on exchange groups to their participants. Many frozen dinner entrees now list their equivalency in exchanges, as do fast-food restaurants like McDonald's. There are also books that list thousands of combination foods and their exchange group equivalents.

Designer Diets

"Designer Diets" offers a long-term approach to food selection and calorie control, in contrast to most fad diets. It is an easy way to plan meals, monitor calories, and insure that you are meeting your nutritional requirements. First, you need to estimate how many calories you expend in a day's time using the handout "Determination of Your Caloric Needs." Then you are ready to pick the meal plan best suited for you.

The basis of the program is the "exchange." An exchange is simply a serving from a food group. There are six food groups in this program: starch/bread, meat, vegetable, fruit, milk, and fat. Each exchange in a particular food group has approximately the same number of calories and nutrients. For example, each starch/bread exchange has approximately 80 calories. In the 1,500 calorie meal plan, 6 starch/bread exchanges are allowed, which could include 3/4 cup corn flakes (1 exchange), 1 slice of wheat bread (1 exchange), 1/3 cup cooked corn (1 exchange), 1 bagel (2 exchanges), and 3 cups popcorn (1 exchange). The choices are numerous as long as you follow the basic rule: The food must come from the designated food group in the specified quantity. The attached pages list the specific foods and amounts for each of the six food groups.

The exchange system allows you to design a diet which is suited to *your* preferences and is flexible in any eating situation. And the best part—it's an eating plan that won't wear out because it's healthy enough to last a lifetime!

Designer Diets Meal Plan Table

Food groups	Meal plans				
	A	B	C	D	E
Starch/bread	4	6	9	11	13
Meat	4	5	6	7	8
Vegetable	2	3	4	5	7
Fruit	3	4	5	7	8
Milk	2	2	2	2	3
Fat	2	3	5	7	8
Approximate total calories	1,200	1,500	2,000	2,500	3,000
% Carbohydrate	48	50	51	53	53
% Protein	21	20	19	18	18
% Fat	31	30	30	30	29

Designer Diets Worksheet

Breakfast	Lunch

Dinner	Snacks

A			
B		Starch/bread	C
B		Meat	C
B		Vegetable	C
B		Fruit	C
B		Milk	C
B		Fat	C

A. Pick the amount of calories from one of the four suggested meal plans.

B. Fill in the proper number of exchanges needed for this particular meal plan in the column next to the food group.

C. After designing your diet, double-check that the total number of exchanges you've written above matches the number in column B (use check marks).

Free Foods and Beverages

A "free" food or beverage contains less than 20 calories per serving and can be added freely to your meal plan. For those items with a specified serving size, the calories need to be accounted for if more than one serving per day is consumed.

Drinks:
  Bouillon* or broth without fat
  Bouillon, low-sodium
  Carbonated drinks, sugar-free
  Carbonated water
  Club soda
  Cocoa powder, unsweetened (1 tbsp.)
  Coffee/tea
  Drink mixes, sugar-free
  Tonic water, sugar-free

Fruit:
  Cranberries, unsweetened (1/2 C.)
  Rhubarb, unsweetened (1/2 C.)

Vegetables (raw, 1 C.):
  Cabbage
  Celery
  Chinese cabbage**
  Cucumber
  Green onion
  Hot peppers
  Mushrooms
  Radishes
  Zucchini**

Salad greens:
  Romaine
  Spinach

Sweet substitutes:
  Candy, hard, sugar-free
  Gelatin, sugar-free
  Gum, sugar-free
  Jam/jelly, sugar-free (2 tsp.)
  Pancake syrup, sugar-free (1-2 tbsp.)
  Sugar substitutes (saccharin, aspartame)
  Whipped topping (2 tbsp.)

Nonstick pan spray

Condiments:
  Catsup (1 tbsp.)

Horseradish
Mustard
Pickles*, dill, unsweetened
Salad dressing, low-calorie (2 tbsp.)
Taco sauce (1 tbsp.)
Vinegar

Seasonings:
  Basil (fresh)
  Celery seeds
  Cinnamon
  Chili powder
  Chives
  Curry
  Dill
  Flavoring extracts (vanilla, almond, walnut, peppermint, butter, lemon, etc.)
  Garlic
  Garlic powder
  Herbs
  Hot pepper sauce
  Lemon
  Lemon juice
  Lemon pepper
  Lime
  Lime juice
  Mint
  Onion powder
  Oregano
  Paprika
  Pepper
  Pimento
  Spices
  Soy sauce*
  Soy sauce, low-sodium
  Wine, used in cooking (1/4 C.)
  Worcestershire sauce

*400 milligrams or more of sodium per serving
**3 grams or more of fiber per serving

Determination
of Caloric Needs

Estimation of Desired Body Weight

Build	Women	Men
Medium	Allow 100 lb for first 5 ft of height plus 5 lb for each additional inch.	Allow 106 lb for first 5 ft of height plus 6 lb for each additional inch.
Small	Subtract 10%	Subtract 10%
Large	Add 10%	Add 10%

Estimate of Caloric Needs for Adults

Basal Calories

Desirable body weight × 10   = _____

Activity Calories

Sedentary: Desirable body weight × 3   = _____

Moderate: Desirable body weight × 5   = _____

Strenuous: Desirable body weight × 10   = _____

To gain 1/2 lb/week, add 250 calories/day   + _____

To lose 1/2 lb/week, subtract 250 calories/day   − _____

Total daily calories needed to lose or gain weight   = _____

Note. From *Handbook of Clinical Dietetics* by the American Dietetic Association, 1981, New Haven, CT: Yale University. Reprinted by permission.

Meal Planning Grid

This grid can be used in two ways: (a) Enlarge it onto a poster board and give one to each group to plan daily meals. (Choose this method only if you are using the plastic food models.) (b) Reproduce this sheet and give one to each group. Hand out the "Exchange Groups" lists and instruct each group to write the food item and serving size on this sheet.

Breakfast

Lunch

Dinner

Snacks

Exchange Groups

Starch/Bread Exchange Group—80 Calories

Cereals/grains/pasta

1 cup	Cooked cereals (oatmeal)
3/4 cup	Corn flakes
1/2 cup	Grits (cooked)
1/2 cup	Pasta
1/2 cup	Rice (cooked)

Dried beans/peas/lentils

1/2 cup	Blackeye peas (cooked)
1/4 cup	Baked beans

Starchy vegetables

1/2 cup	Corn
1 piece (6 in.)	Corn on cob
1/2 cup	Lima beans
1/2 cup	Peas, green (canned or frozen)
1 small	Potato, baked
1/2 cup	Potato, mashed
2 small	Potatoes, boiled (new)
3/4 cup	Squash, winter (acorn, butternut)
1/3 cup	Yam, sweet potato, plain

Breads

1/2 (1 oz)	Bagel
1/2 (1 oz)	Frankfurter bun
1/2 (1 oz)	Hamburger bun
1 small (1 oz)	Hard roll
1 (6 in.)	Tortilla
1 slice	White bread
1 slice	Whole wheat bread

Crackers/snacks

3 (2-1/2 in. square)	Graham crackers
3 cups	Popcorn (popped, no fat added)
6	Soda crackers

Starch foods prepared with fat

(Count as 1 starch/bread plus 1 fat serving)

1 (2-1/2 in.)	Baking powder biscuit
1 piece (2 in. square)	Corn bread
10 (2 to 3-1/2 in.)	French fries
2 (4 in.)	Pancakes
1 (4-1/2 in.)	Waffle

Meat/Meat-Alternates Exchange Group—75 Calories

Low fat

1 oz	Roast beef*
1 oz	Baked ham*
1/4 cup	Tuna (canned in water)
1/4 cup	Cottage cheese

Medium fat

1 oz	Meat loaf
1 oz	Meat patty
1 oz	Roast beef*
1 oz	Baked ham*
1 oz	Chicken (with skin)
1 oz	Tuna (canned in oil and drained)
1 large	Egg (hard cooked or scrambled with no additional fat)
1 oz	Liver

High fat

1 oz	T-bone steak
1 oz	Pork chop
1 oz	Fried chicken*
1 oz	Fried perch
1 oz	American cheese
1 oz	Cheddar cheese
1 oz	Swiss cheese
1 oz	Bologna
1 (1.6 oz)	Frankfurter (beef, pork, or combination)

*This food may be categorized as either low, medium, or high fat depending on leanness and preparation method.

Vegetable Exchange Group—25 Calories

(All portion sizes, except as noted, are 1/2 cup of any cooked vegetable or vegetable juice and 1 cup of any raw vegetable.)

Vegetables

Asparagus	Coleslaw (1/2 cup)
Beans, green	Greens, cooked
Beets	Okra
Broccoli	Onions
Cabbage, cooked	Summer squash
Carrots	Tomato (1 large)
Cauliflower	Tomato juice

Free vegetables

(See the Free Foods and Beverages handout for a list of other free vegetables.)

Cabbage, raw
Celery
Lettuce
Romaine

Fruit Exchange Group—60 Calories

Fresh fruits

1 medium	Apple
1/2 cup	Applesauce (unsweetened)
1/2 (9 in.)	Banana
1/3 (5 in.)	Cantaloupe
1/2 cup	Fruit salad
1/2 medium	Grapefruit
15	Grapes
1 medium	Orange
1/2 cup or 2 halves	Peaches (canned)
1 small	Pear
1/3 cup or 2 rings	Pineapple (canned)
1-1/4 cup	Strawberries (raw, whole)
1-1/4 cup	Watermelon

Dried fruits and fruit juice

7 halves	Apricots
3 medium	Prunes
2 tablespoons	Raisins
1/2 cup	Orange juice

Milk Exchange Group—120 Calories

Nonfat

1 cup	Skim milk

Whole

1 cup	Whole milk

Lowfat

1 cup	Lowfat milk (2%)
8 oz	Plain lowfat yogurt

Fat Exchange Group—45 Calories

Unsaturated fat

1 tablespoon	French dressing
1 teaspoon	Margarine
20 small or 10 large	Peanuts

Saturated fat

1 teaspoon	Butter
1 strip	Bacon
2 tablespoons	Cream, sour
1 tablespoon	Cream, whipped
2 tablespoons	Half-and-half
1 oz	Sausage links

Foods for Occasional Use—Calories Are Approximate

Alcohol

		Calories
4 oz	Wine	85
12 oz	Beer, regular	150
10 oz	Mixed drink (1.5 oz of 80-proof alcohol)	145

Desserts

		Calories
1/6 of 9-in. pie	Apple pie	405
1/2 cup	Baked custard	150
1	Cake doughnut	125
12 oz	Chocolate milkshake	390
1/2 cup	Chocolate pudding	160
2 tablespoons	Chocolate syrup	95
1	Danish pastry roll	275
1/12 of 9-in. cake	Devil's food cake	235
1 tablespoon	Jelly	50
1 oz	Milk chocolate bar	150
1/2 cup	Orange sherbet	130
10	Potato chips	115
8 oz	Soft drink	95
1/12 of 10-in. cake	Sponge cake	195
1 (3 in.)	Sugar cookie	90
1 teaspoon	Sugar	14
1/2 cup	Vanilla ice cream	140

Combination Foods

1	Beef taco	1 starch/bread 2 meat
1 cup	Beef and vegetable stew	1 starch/bread 1/2 meat 1 vegetable
1/4 of 10-in. pizza	Cheese pizza	2 starch/bread 1 meat 1 fat
1 cup	Chicken noodle soup	1 starch/bread
1 cup	Chili con carne with beans	2 starch/bread 2 meat 2 fat
1 cup	Cream of tomato soup	1 starch/bread 1 fat
1 cup	Macaroni and cheese	2 starch/bread 1 meat 2 fat
1 cup	Spaghetti and meat balls	2 starch/bread 1 meat 1 fat
1 cup	Strawberry yogurt	1 milk 2 fruit

Please note. The food items listed here are a duplication of the Dairy Council's food list. For additional food items, serving sizes, and nutrient information, please refer to the American Dietetic Association and American Diabetes Association *Exchange Lists*.

REFERENCES

American Diabetes Association, American Dietetic Association (1986). *Exchange lists for meal planning.**

Pennington, J.D.T., & Church, H.N. (1985). *Bowes and Church's food values of portions commonly used* (14th ed.). Philadelphia: Lippincott.

Whitney, E., & Hamilton, E. (1987). *Understanding nutrition* (4th ed.). St. Paul, MN: West.

———————————

*Available from American Diabetes Association, 1660 Duke Street, Alexandria, VA 22314, 800-ADA-DISC.

A Winner's Alcohol Facts Game Lifestyle Workshop

PARAPROFESSIONAL PREPARATION MATERIALS

Training Sessions

Competency Exam

Texts and Suggested Readings

WORKSHOP AT A GLANCE

Presenter Information

Most Frequently Asked Questions

Handouts and Visual Aids*

References

---

*"Communicating Your Concerns" was written by Joanne Smogor, MS.

TRAINING SESSIONS

A Winner's Alcohol Facts Game

Session 1: Workshop Presentation

Time: 60 minutes

Methods: Presentation, demonstration

Description: Trainer presents workshop to Lifestyle Educators.

Readings: The workshop

Session 2: Drugs and Drug Education Philosophy

Time: 60 minutes

Methods: Lecture, discussion

Description: Discuss objective methods of drug education and its role in preventing alcohol problems. Cover drug classification and patterns of use.

Readings: Materials on peer approaches to drug prevention, teaching about alcohol objectively, drug categorization and prevalence, levels and patterns of drug-taking

Competency exam question: 15

Session 3: Forms of Alcohol, Use Patterns, and Alcohol's Effects

Time: 60 minutes

Methods: Lecture, discussion

Description: Discuss types of alcohol, various patterns of use, and alcohol's effects.

Readings: Materials on alcohol and its use and the effects of alcoholic beverages on the body, the workshop

Competency exam questions: 1, 2, 8, 9, 10, 11, 12, 13, 14, 15, 16, 27

Session 4: Women and Alcohol

Time: 60 minutes

Methods: Lecture, discussion

Description: Explain how women are affected in unique ways.

Activity: Practice trivia questions from Quarters 1 & 2 (see game directions in workshop).

Readings: Materials on women and alcohol, the workshop

Competency exam questions: 28, 29

Session 5: Social Drinking, Problem Drinking, and Alcoholism

Time: 60 minutes

Methods: Lecture, discussion

Description: Define social drinking, problem drinking, and alcoholism. Explain alcoholism risks, symptoms, and current theories about cause and recovery.

Activity: Generate a list of signals of problem drinking and have students evaluate whether they see any of these signs in themselves or others.

Readings: Social drinking, problem drinking, and alcoholism, the workshop

Competency exam questions: 15, 17, 18, 19, 20, 21, 22, 23, 24, 25

Session 6: Alcohol-Related Problems and Practice Trivia Questions

Time: 60 minutes

Methods: Lecture, discussion

Description: Explain costs of alcohol use to society, how to deal with alcohol emergencies, and how to approach a friend who has a drinking problem.

Activity: Practice trivia questions from Quarters 3 & 4 (see game directions in workshop).

Readings: Materials on costs of alcohol use to society, dealing with alcohol emergencies, and communicating your concerns about another's drinking behavior, the workshop

Competency exam questions: 3, 26, 30

Session 7: "Most Frequently Asked Questions" Review and Hot Seat

Time: 60 minutes

Methods: Discussion, practice

Description: Review "Most Frequently Asked Questions" and other workshop components.

Activity: Each Lifestyle Educator is quizzed by the other students on the workshop topic for 10 minutes.

Readings: The workshop

Session 8: Practice Workshop Presentation

Time: 60 minutes

Methods: Presentation

Description: Each Lifestyle Educator presents 20 minutes of the workshop.

Readings: The workshop

COMPETENCY EXAM

The following are True/False questions. Check the appropriate blanks.

True   False

____ ____ 1. "Proof" on the bottle represents 1/2 the amount of absolute or pure alcohol in the bottle.

____ ____ 2. Alcoholic beverages do not contain calories that cause weight gain.

____ ____ 3. A drunk person is more likely to die from aspirating vomit when lying face down.

____ ____ 4. More men tend to mix drugs with alcohol than women because it is more socially acceptable for them.

____ ____ 5. Most alcoholics are on skid row.

____ ____ 6. Beer drinkers cannot be alcoholics.

____ ____ 7. An individual cannot be an alcoholic if he or she has never been in trouble with the law because of drinking.

The following are multiple choice questions. Circle the letter of the correct answer.

8. About how long does the average person need to completely burn up the alcohol from a standard drink?
   a. 1/2 hour
   b. 1 hour
   c. 1 1/2 hours
   d. 2 hours

9. John went out to the bars on Saturday night and had two beers, a glass of wine, and a whiskey sour in 6 hours. That night he was very sick and vomited. What is the most likely cause of his sickness?
   a. He consumed too much alcohol, so his body's natural defense mechanism made him vomit before his blood alcohol concentration became lethal.
   b. He mixed different kinds of alcohol so the drug effects were magnified.
   c. The congeners in the drinks made him sick.
   d. none of the above.

10. Which of the following cannot minimize the effects of a hangover?
    a. alternating between having a glass of water and an alcoholic drink
    b. taking a nonaspirin pain-reliever while drinking
    c. taking Pepto Bismol before drinking to coat the stomach and slow down absorption

11. Which of the following will help sober you up?
    a. exercise
    b. coffee
    c. a cold shower
    d. time
    e. all of the above

12. Approximately what percentage of adults in the United States drink alcoholic beverages?
    a. 90%
    b. 80%
    c. 70%
    d. 60%

13. Which of the following best describes the effects of alcohol on the central nervous system?
    a. stimulant
    b. depressant
    c. first lowers, then stimulates, inhibitions
    d. first lowers, then depresses, inhibitions

14. A blackout
    a. only lasts for a few minutes.
    b. is directly related to blood alcohol concentration.
    c. occurs when a person passes out.
    d. is a memory loss or alcohol-induced amnesia.
    e. is more than one of the above.

15. The age group with the most problem drinkers is
    a. 18-30.
    b. 30-45.
    c. 40-50.
    d. over 50.

16. Approximately what percentage of alcohol is metabolized in the liver?
    a. 95%
    b. 80%
    c. 70%
    d. 60%

For questions 17 through 22, label each situation with one of the following three choices and briefly explain your answer.

    a. social drinking
    b. problem drinking
    c. alcoholism

17. After studying for her next final exam, Vicki goes out for a few beers with some friends in the middle of finals week; normally she would not drink at all during the week.

18. Rick usually has a beer or two to be comfortable before taking a date to a party where he knows they both will be drinking quite a bit.

19. Everyone from a class goes to happy hour on Fridays. Although Cindy told herself she wouldn't go this week to save money for spring break, she goes and spends some vacation money anyway.

20. Joe occasionally goes out to parties or bars to have a good time with his friends. He usually has several drinks each time he goes out.

21. Mary says to her friend Jill, "I can't wait until the weekend. . . . I'm going to get *so* drunk!" Jill sees Mary do this almost every weekend.

22. Steve forces himself not to drink alcohol during the week, but he spends every weekend in a drunken stupor.

The following questions require brief responses.

23. Define and describe the characteristics of a social drinker.

24. Define and describe the characteristics of a problem drinker.

25. Define and describe the characteristics of an alcoholic.

26. List three direct and three indirect costs of alcohol use to society.

27. Identify the effects of each of the following blood alcohol levels.
    a. .05
    b. .10
    c. .20
    d. .30
    e. .40-.50

28. Explain how the following factors affect absorption of alcohol into the blood stream:
    a. temperature of the drink
    b. dilution of the alcohol
    c. mixing alcohol with carbonated beverages
    d. eating food while drinking
    e. being female

29. List three characteristics of Fetal Alcohol Syndrome.

30. What effects of drinking alcohol impair driving skills?

31. Suggest possible techniques to use in the workshop if a participant is one of the following:
    • Recognition Seeker (frequently calls attention to self)
    • Conversationalist (brings up off-the-subject anecdotes and is a noisy distraction)
    • Moralizer (advocates judgmental points of view based on personal convictions)
    • Conservative (convinced that the status quo does not need changing)

TEXTS AND SUGGESTED READINGS

Duncan, D., & Gold, R. (1982). *Drugs and the whole person*. New York: Wiley.

Finn, P., & O'Gorman, P. (1981). *Teaching about alcohol concepts, methods, and classroom activities*. Boston: Allyn and Bacon.

Hafen, B., & Brog, M.V. (1983). *Alcohol* (2nd ed.). St. Paul, MN: West.

McGuire, P.C. (1975). *The liberated woman*. Center City, MN: Hazelden.

Ray, O. (1983). *Drugs, society and human behavior* (3rd ed.). St. Louis: Mosby.

WORKSHOP AT A GLANCE

The goal of this workshop is to provide general information about alcohol, including the difference between low-risk and high-risk drinking, and social and problem drinking. This workshop takes approximately 60 minutes to present. Suggested attendance is 8 to 20 persons.

Objectives

Within the content of this workshop, the following objectives will be met.

- Through the use of the "Winner's Alcohol Facts Game," participants will discuss and analyze general alcohol information, including acute and long-term physiological effects, patterns of use, and ways of identifying problem drinking.
- Handouts will discuss drinking and driving, approaching someone with a drinking problem, and blood alcohol concentration levels.

Workshop Materials

- Workshop sign-in sheet
- Handouts and visual aids *Blood Alcohol Levels and Driving, Communicating Your Concerns, Blood Alcohol Levels by Gender, Alcohol's Effects Upon The Body*, Football field board, True/false cards and football markers for each team.
- Newsprint and marker or blackboard and chalk
- Bell
- Prizes (suggestion: plastic footballs with institution's logo imprinted)
- Lifestyle Workshop evaluation forms and pencils

PRESENTER INFORMATION

Briefly introduce yourself, your background, and any other personal information you choose to share. Describe your health promotion program and the topics available, like fitness and nutrition. Stress that the workshops are unique because you bring them to their living areas. Tell them that Lifestyle Workshop paraprofessionals are trained at (your institution or program) to present these workshops. If anyone is interested in the training program, ask him or her to speak with you after the workshop.

The purpose of this workshop is to test participants' knowledge of general facts about the effects of alcohol on individuals and society. Through education, individuals are able to evaluate their options, rather than have others (for example, a bar, the media, or peers) make decisions for them. Within the game format, participants are encouraged to share their views and experiences.

A Winner's Alcohol Facts Game (50 minutes)

This game consists of true/false questions arranged in a format to simulate a football game. The questions are in the next section of this outline and are arranged into four quarters: (1) Factors Influencing Alcohol's Effects; (2) Alcohol's Physical and Psychological Effects; (3) Gender Differences and Alcohol; and (4) Risks and Patterns. For each question, a specific yardage can be gained for a correct answer. Each quarter has a maximum possible gain of 100 yards divided among approximately 10 questions. (See game board figure in the handouts and visual aids section.)

Alcohol Facts Game Rules

Divide participants into teams of four to five players, and give each team a set of true/false cards in the team color. Yardage is marked on the game board by two football-shaped playing pieces in the team colors.

Read the question, and then give the teams 5 seconds to make a decision. After 5 seconds, ring the bell and ask each team to hold up the card with what it thinks is the right answer. Those with the right answer will gain yardage. The number of touchdowns scored will determine the winner of the game. Each team starts on the 50-yard line. Each question is worth 5 or more yards each. With each correct response the team's football is moved toward the field goal. After a team scores a touchdown, its football is moved back to the 50-yard line and the process begins again. If a team scores with additional yardage leftover, that amount is subtracted from 50. For example, if a team scores from the 5-yard line on a 15-yard question, it keeps those extra 10 yards and goes back to the 40-yard line instead of the 50.

First Quarter

This quarter's questions concern the factors that influence alcohol's effects.

1. (10 yards) *"Proof" on the bottle represents twice the amount of absolute or pure alcohol in the bottle.*

   True. An 80-proof bottle means that 40% of the total bottle is pure alcohol.

2. (10 yards) *The average person needs about an hour to completely burn up the alcohol in a standard drink. (A standard drink is 5 oz of wine, 12 oz of beer, or 1 1/2 oz of 90-proof liquor.)*

   True. No matter what you drink, it takes your liver about an hour to metabolize a standard drink. An enzyme in the liver called alcohol dehydrogenase is used in the first step of alcohol breakdown. Because you have a finite amount of this enzyme, the maximum rate of alcohol breakdown is set at about one standard drink per hour.

3. (15 yards) *Warm beer intoxicates a person faster than cold beer.*

   True. The body absorbs liquid at body temperature. Because warm beer is closer to body temperature, it is absorbed more rapidly into a person's bloodstream.

4. (10 yards) *A shot of straight liquor will reach the brain and alter behavior faster than one beer or one glass of wine).*

True. The alcohol in a shot of straight liquor is less diluted than in beer or wine so it will be absorbed into the bloodstream and reach the brain faster.

5. (15 yards) *Whiskey mixed with pop will reach the brain and alter your behavior faster than whiskey mixed with water.*

True. Carbonation causes the valve between the stomach and the small intestine to open. About 20% of alcohol is absorbed through the stomach while 80% is absorbed through the small intestine. Because the alcohol reaches the small intestine faster, it is absorbed more quickly into the bloodstream.

6. (10 yards) *Switching standard drinks will make you drunker than staying with one kind of alcoholic beverage. (A standard drink is 5 oz of wine, 12 oz of beer, or 1 1/2 oz of 90-proof liquor.)*

False. Switching drinks won't make a person drunker because alcohol, whether it's beer, wine, or hard liquor, is all the same. The congeners (by-products of fermentation and distillation) and mixtures of nonalcoholic ingredients in alcoholic beverages may make you sick if you're sensitive or allergic to some of them. Congeners are substances other than ethyl alcohol and carbon dioxide that are formed during fermentation and distillation. They may be ketones, acids, aldehydes, or other alcohols.

7. (10 yards) *Drinking milk or Pepto Bismol before drinking alcohol will help prevent you from getting sick because it will protect your stomach lining from becoming irritated.*

False. There is no way to prevent stomach irritation when drinking, in fact, less-diluted liquor may actually cause direct irritation of the throat and stomach. In addition, one or two drinks stimulates the stomach to produce gastric secretions. Vomiting is determined by both stomach irritation and the blood alcohol level, which affects the central nervous system. Neither milk nor Pepto Bismol will prevent both stimuli to triggering vomiting.

8. (15 yards) *There are ways to minimize the effects of a hangover both while you're drinking and after you're drunk.*

True. Headaches, thirst, and nausea can be helped at any time. Drinking nonalcoholic beverages and eating before, during, and after drinking alcohol may help to minimize the effects of a hangover.

9. (5 yards) *Exercise has been shown to facilitate the sobering-up process.*

False. We have already discussed that the liver has a limited amount of enzymes and metabolizes alcohol at a rate of 1/2 ounce of absolute alcohol per hour. There is no way to accelerate the sobering-up process.

Second Quarter

These questions deal with the physical and psychological effects of alcohol.

1. (10 yards) *Alcohol is technically classified as both a food and a drug.*

True. Alcohol is considered a food because it supplies calories that are burned up for energy (although they are "empty" calories because they provide no nutrients), and as a drug because it is a chemical that alters a person's mood.

2. (5 yards) *Alcohol first stimulates and then depresses the central nervous system.*

False. Alcohol depresses the central nervous system by depressing the inhibition center in the brain.

3. (5 yards) *Due to the depressant effects of alcohol on the central nervous system, one can sleep better after drinking.*

False. Research shows that alcohol interferes with the dream or rapid eye movement stage of sleep, which causes frequent awakenings throughout the night.

4. (10 yards) *Alcohol acts as a sexual stimulant upon the body.*

False. Many people think that alcohol is a sexual stimulant because it decreases inhibitions. Although it may increase desire, it actually interferes with sexual arousal and performance because of its depressant effects on the central nervous system.

5. (10 yards) *Alcohol makes you physically warmer.*

False. Many people think that alcohol makes you warmer because of the sensations caused by the irritation of the throat and stomach lining and the feeling of warmth in the limbs. However, you are losing heat because alcohol intake causes the heart to beat faster and the peripheral blood vessels (those near the skin's surface) to dilate (enlarge) and rise closer to the surface. At the same time, the vessels of your internal organs constrict, so more blood goes to the peripheral vessels. All these factors work together to make you feel warmer, but actually increase the heat lost from the body. This is one reason that it's important to watch your alcohol intake when you're participating in winter activities.

6. (10 yards) *A blackout occurs when someone passes out from drinking too much.*

   False. A blackout is a memory loss or alcohol-induced amnesia. It can last from a few seconds to several days. The drinker appears awake and active but is not able to remember what happened during the blackout. Although the cause of blackouts isn't known, research indicates that they are not associated with any specific blood alcohol concentration.

7. (15 yards) *One or two drinks can alter your judgment enough to impair your driving skills.*

   True. As soon as alcohol is introduced into the body, it begins to affect the areas of the brain that control judgment, motor skills, and vision.

   (Note: Use "Blood Alcohol Levels and Driving" handout.)

8. (15 yards) *In a social drinker, some brain damage is likely to occur over a long period of time due to the continual killing of brain cells. (A social drinker is someone who drinks occasionally or regularly at social functions or mealtimes, but whose drinking does not create personal or social problems.)*

   False. No brain damage is caused by social drinking. It is natural for brain cells to die, and social drinking has no proven detrimental physiological effects on the brain.

9. (10 yards) *If you have a friend who has a drinking problem, the best way to help is to drink together so he or she will drink less.*

   False. The best help you can give to a friend is love, support, honesty, and understanding.

   (Note: Use "Communicating Your Concerns" handout.)

10. (10 yards) *A person who "passes out" or falls asleep after drinking should be placed on his or her back to prevent aspiration (inhalation) of any vomitus.*

    False. After drinking, a person should sleep on the side so that any vomit will drain out of the mouth instead of entering the lungs. Lying on the stomach is also dangerous because of the possibility of suffocation.

Third Quarter

The questions in the third quarter pertain to gender differences and alcohol.

1. (5 yards) *More women abstain from drinking alcohol than do men.*

   True. Only 60% of all women drink, compared to 75% of all men.

2. (5 yards) *Among adults who drink, there are more problem drinkers and alcoholics who are female than male.*

   False. A higher percentage of men than women are problem drinkers. Although the exact percentages are difficult to determine for women because they tend to conceal their drinking more than do men, the most current data is that 25% of adult males abstain from alcohol, whereas 75% drink; and, 40% of women abstain, whereas 60% drink. It is estimated that 20% to 40% of males are problem drinkers and that 10% to 30% of women are problem drinkers.

3. (10 yards) *The same amount of alcohol will have the same effect on a woman and a man if both are of the same size and equal weight.*

   False. The reason for this difference is still unknown, but one hypothesis is that the liver metabolizes estrogens with the same system as it does alcohol. The liver prefers to metabolize the estrogen, thus ethanol backs up into a woman's blood.

   (Note: Use "Blood Alcohol Levels by Gender" handout.)

4. (10 yards) *Blood alcohol concentration varies according to a woman's menstrual cycle.*

   True. A woman's blood alcohol level will be higher when she drinks just prior to menstruation than at any other time of the month.

Research indicates that this is because there is a larger amount of estrogen for the liver to metabolize, so the liver is slower and less efficient at metabolizing alcohol than it would be during the rest of the month.

(Note: Use "Alcohol's Effects on the Body" handout.)

5. (5 yards) *No safe level of alcohol use during pregnancy has been established as of today.*

True. Researchers have found that even small amounts of alcohol can lead to miscarriage, or low birth weight and learning disabilities in babies whose mothers drink alcohol during pregnancy. The effects of alcohol may vary according to the level of consumption and stage of pregnancy.

6. (10 yards) *The number of women who drink tends to drop with age.*

True. Generally, women in their mid-thirties drink less than college-age women. However, problem drinking is more common at later ages.

7. (10 yards) *There is a higher rate of problem drinking among women who are employed outside the home than among women who are not.*

True. This has been linked to work environments. Typical "female" jobs are either low-pay, low-status, or unchallenging. In high-level jobs, women often must work harder than men in order to prove themselves. They often face role conflicts, stress, and new social settings.

8. (10 yards) *Women problem drinkers are more likely than men to seek help for their alcohol problems.*

False. Women tend to hide alcohol problems rather than seek help for them. In fact, women tend to quit work due to fears such as losing their children and the greater social stigma of problem drinking in women. Men more readily seek help at alcohol clinics and detoxification programs.

9. (10 yards) *Similar life stresses may initiate problem drinking in both men and women.*

True. Men and women experience similar life stresses that may lead to problem drinking, but they usually occur at different times. Such stresses include job loss or relocation, family death, divorce, and menopause (for women).

10. (10 yards) *Women tend to mix alcohol with prescription drugs more than do men.*

True. Prescription drugs are given more often to women than men, so these drugs are more often mixed with alcohol by women. Men tend to mix illicit drugs with alcohol more frequently than do women.

Fourth Quarter

The questions in the final quarter are about risks and patterns surrounding alcohol.

1. (10 yards) *The percentage of college students who drink is about the same as the national figures for all adult drinkers.*

False. Ninety percent of the college population drinks, while only 70% of the general population does.

2. (10 yards) *It is estimated that one of every five college students who drinks is a problem drinker.*

True. It is estimated that 20% of all college student drinkers are problem drinkers. Ten percent of college students abstain, whereas 90% drink alcohol. Of adult nonstudents, 30% abstain, 70% drink, and 10% are considered problem drinkers or alcoholics.

3. (15 yards) *Most signs of problem drinking and alcoholism are easily identified, but they are usually ignored and thought to be unimportant.*

True. Even the earliest signs of problem drinking can be pointed out by most people, but they are not usually taken seriously. Some examples include driving while intoxicated; hangovers that interfere with activities, classes, or work; and irritability with family or friends.

4. (10 yards) *Someone who can "hold" his or her liquor is at little risk of having a drinking problem.*

False. Tolerance means that the drinker is in a preproblem drinking phase and is already damaging the body.

5. (5 yards) *Most alcoholics tend to be uneducated and/or poor.*

False. Only 5% of all alcoholics are what we consider "skid row" bums. Ninety-five percent of our nation's alcoholics are employed. Forty percent have a college education. Alcoholism is not socioeconomically selective; people from all walks of life are equally susceptible to alcoholism.

6. (10 yards) *Most problem drinkers are middle-aged or older.*

   False. Most problem drinkers used to be in their forties, but recent studies show that the age of most problem drinkers is now between 18 and 30. This transition has occurred within the last 10 years.

7. (10 yards) *Children of alcoholics are at greater risk for becoming alcoholic, even if they are not raised by their own parents.*

   True. Research indicates genetic predisposition to alcoholism. Alcoholism tends to run in the family, but it is not completely understood how that actually happens genetically. Fifty percent of all alcoholics have at least one alcoholic parent.

8. (10 yards) *Anyone can control drinking frequency by exerting willpower.*

   False. Due to genetics and metabolic changes and psychological adaptations, one can easily lose all control over drinking, and the body may start to require alcohol to function normally. Thus, changes in the brain and tissues can cause a loss of control.

9. (5 yards) *Eighty percent of all drownings in the United States each year are alcohol-related.*

   True. Of deaths from various causes, the following percentages were alcohol-related: motor vehicle, 50%; falls, 50%; fires, 25%; drownings, 80%; and all others, 15%.

10. (10 yards) *Of all alcohol-related crimes, assault crimes represent the highest percentage.*

    True. Alcohol was involved for 85% of assault offenders and 90% of assault victims. For other crimes, the following percentages were alcohol-related: homicides (perpetrators & victims), 60%; suicides, 30%; robberies, 80%; sex offenses, 60%; rape victims, 30%; and assault victims, 90%; assault offenders, 85%; child abuse, 70%.

Announce the winning team and give it the prizes.

Conclusion and Evaluation (5 minutes)

Summarize the three main points of this workshop:

- Many factors affect how alcohol influences you: weight, gender, eating while drinking, drinking environment, and dilution of alcohol.
- Alcohol first affects perception, which then has a major effect on behavior.
- The more knowledge of alcohol you have, the wiser your choices will be.

Ask for questions from the participants. Offer resources and referrals for further information. Distribute Lifestyle Workshop evaluation forms and pencils. Allow time for completion and then collect. Briefly list and describe the other Lifestyle Workshops in Drugs and Alcohol Education.

MOST FREQUENTLY ASKED QUESTIONS

1. *Why does carbonation make people get drunk quicker?*

   The carbon dioxide causes the pyloric valve between the stomach and the small intestine to open. This opening makes it easier for alcohol to enter the small intestine, which then increases the rate of alcohol absorption.

2. *What causes a blackout, and why do some people black out more than others?*

   Blackouts occur when someone drinks to excess and experiences an interval of temporary memory loss. This memory loss occurs when alcohol affects the memory banks of the brain and causes alcohol-induced amnesia. A person may be experiencing a blackout even though appearing to be coherent and alert. Variations in body weight, alcohol tolerance, and food in the stomach are some of the reasons people may black out.

3. *What effect does caffeine or a cold shower have on a person who is drunk?*

   Stimulants such as caffeine may reduce the effects of alcohol, but the reduction is so small that they are not recommended as antidotes. Taking a cold shower passes time, but it only results in a cold, wet drunk. Only *time* helps one sober up!

4. *What is the difference between problem and social drinking?*

   Social drinking is simply that—drinking while socializing, having one or two drinks to celebrate. When alcohol adversely affects a person's life, that is evidence of problem drinking.

5. *Is a person who gets drunk at every party he or she goes to a problem drinker?*

   The following should be considered: How often is this person getting drunk and what are the effects on his or her life? If getting drunk is a frequent occurrence and it is affecting this person's life negatively in any way, then he or she might want to consider talking to a counselor or alcohol education professional.

6. *What physiological damage is caused by alcohol abuse?*

   - *Liver.* Milder forms of alcohol abuse lead to excess fat in the liver. After prolonged heavy drinking, the liver becomes swollen and tender, which is symptomatic of acute hepatitis. Hepatitis develops in 1/3 of all chronic drinkers, and severe cases may cause cirrhosis of the liver, which can result in death.
   - *Heart.* Moderate amounts of alcohol relax and dilate blood vessels, causing a slight fall in blood pressure. Studies show that heavy, chronic alcohol use predisposes an individual to coronary artery disease and can cause angina pectoris. Alcohol stresses the main heart muscle, and current thinking is that the same changes (fatty change and fibrosis) that occur in liver cells occur in heart cells.
   - *Brain.* Alcohol depresses the inhibition center of the brain, which is why people often feel more relaxed after drinking alcohol. This depression of the inhibition center may cause a drunk person to do or say things that are out of character. Long-term heavy drinking can result in damage to the centers of memory, coordination, and emotion in the brain. With chronic alcohol abuse, nerves die and are not replaced.

7. *What are the dangers of mixing alcohol and drugs?*

   Mixing alcohol and other drugs may result in increased depression of the central nervous system and respiratory functions, gastrointestinal blood loss, possible seizures, impairment of motor skills, and possibly death. It depends on which drugs are mixed and the quantities taken.

8. *Physiologically, which is the best choice to drink—a 12-oz beer, a 5-oz glass of wine, or a 1-oz mixed drink with hard liquor?*

Each contain equal amounts of alcohol. In terms of nutrition the only benefits would be what was added in the mixed drink. For example, if the mixer is orange juice the drink is high in vitamin C; club soda, on the other hand, has no nutritional value. Overall, there is no significant difference among the three types of alcohol.

9. *Do drinking patterns of college students change when they graduate?*

Drinking habits after college vary among individuals. The only relevant data is that of people now in college, one in five is a problem drinker, whereas this number decreases to one in eight or one in 10 after college. Overall, there is a decrease in alcohol consumption after students leave college.

10. *What does* **tolerance** *mean?*

Tolerance is a term that describes the need for increasing amounts of alcohol to achieve the same reactions formerly produced by smaller amounts of alcohol. Simply stated, it means you need to drink more to get the same results.

11. *What is cirrhosis? How does a person get it? What are its effects?*

Cirrhosis is a severe, irreversible disease that impairs the liver in approximately one of five chronic alcohol users. Cirrhosis is the replacement of functional liver tissue with a type of scar tissue. Eventually, the scar tissue alters the liver's shape and hampers its normal functions, like detoxifying waste products and maintaining blood clotting ability. Abnormal blood flow due to scarring can cause hypertension and gastrointestinal bleeding. These complications can eventually lead to infections, malnutrition, liver cancer, heart failure, "hepatic coma," and death.

12. *If I get drunk regularly, does that mean I'm an alcoholic?*

Not necessarily. What is important to examine is how the alcohol affects your life. Do you miss class because you are hung over? Have you encountered problems with your friends or with the police? If drinking is adversely affecting your life then you may have a drinking problem. Check the phone book for a substance resource center that can give you help or advice.

13. *What are the chances of alcoholism developing in a child of an alcoholic?*

It is estimated that 30% to 50% of children of alcoholics are likely to develop alcoholism.

14. *What are the physiological effects of a one-night drinking binge?*

A one-night binge can have a variety of ill effects. The effects of falling and hurting yourself while drunk or of irritating your stomach lining to the point that you throw up last longer than a hangover. There is also always the possibility of drinking to the point of coma or even death. However, a one-night drinking binge will not do the damage to the body that alcoholism does over time.

15. *How does the body process alcohol?*

The body, through many processes, turns the potentially harmful alcohol into the harmless substances of carbon dioxide and water. The steps to the process are these:

1. Twenty percent of the alcohol is absorbed into the blood stream from the stomach, which is why eating food will slow down the intoxication process. In a person with an empty stomach, alcohol reaches the brain in 20 seconds. In the brain, alcohol suppresses inhibitions, judgment, reasoning, and coordination (in that order).

2. The remaining 80% of the alcohol is absorbed into the blood through the small intestine. If there is too much alcohol to be absorbed, the pyloric valve (the valve from the stomach to the small intestine) will close in order to keep the food and liquid from going into the small intestine. The increased stomach irritation by way of continued exposure of the stomach lining to ethanol may induce vomiting.

3. A small amount (2.5%) of the alcohol leaves the body through perspiration and urination.

4. The blood carries the alcohol from the digestive tract to the liver, where 95% of the alcohol is metabolized (broken down). This is why only time, rather than exercise, coffee, or a cold shower, will sober a person.

5. From the liver, the blood follows its normal course. Because blood is continually circulating, everything you drink will continue through this cycle.

16. *What can I do if I'm with a friend who drinks too much and then tries to drive?*

This is one time in life when it clearly makes sense to interfere in a friend's life. First, before going out to drink, assign one friend as a designated nondrinker and driver. You can rotate so that everyone can drink sometimes. If you haven't planned ahead, offer to drive yourself or, if you have been drinking, offer to call a friend or a cab. If you have to, take away your friend's keys. If your friend is determined to drive, *don't* get in the car.

17. *What are some of the harmful effects of drinking during pregnancy?*

A child born to a mother who drinks during pregnancy tends to be small for its gestational age, may have some degree of mental retardation, and may fail to grow properly. The congenital defects, mental retardation, and behavioral abnormalities that occur from heavy drinking during pregnancy are called Fetal Alcohol Syndrome (FAS). Many problems of FAS are often attributed to drinking, especially drinking during the first trimester of fetal growth when major organs (brain, lungs, heart, etc.) are developing. However, one problem is that a woman generally isn't aware she is pregnant until she's already two months along. As a rule of thumb, there is no safe time during pregnancy to drink.

18. *Why do college-age women drink more than women in other age groups?*

"Atmosphere" is one of the many factors related to women's increased drinking in college. Many social functions for college women center around alcohol and getting drunk, such as fund-raising events sponsored by beer distributors and happy hour with the gang every Friday afternoon. Drinking is also a way to gain acceptance among peers and is often associated with new experiences.

19. *Is there any particular socioeconomic group of women that have a drinking problem?*

No, women and men from all walks of life are equally susceptible to drinking problems.

20. *What causes heavier drinking to occur more often in older women than it does in older men?*

Because women are more often confronted with increasing pressures later in life than are most men, alcoholism becomes a greater threat. Many women experience life and role changes or stresses that put them at higher risk for developing alcohol-related problems later in life. A typical example is a woman who tries to be a good wife and mother along with maintaining a successful career. Another common crisis for older women is the "empty-nest stage" when her children have left home, which may cause her to feel unsettled about her purpose in life.

21. *Do men have higher alcohol tolerance levels than women?*

There is no definitive data that has found differences in gender significant to alcohol tolerance.

22. *Why is alcohol metabolism affected by the menstrual cycle?*

The menstrual cycle affects alcohol absorption because of the changing balances of sex hormones. During the premenstrual period, a woman absorbs alcohol most rapidly and therefore will get drunk more quickly. The liver is called upon to perform the function of metabolizing both estrogen, which controls the menstrual cycle, and the alcohol, slowing down the rate at which the alcohol can be metabolized.

23. *Why do women seem to drink less than men?*

Historically it has been socially unacceptable for women to drink. This dates back to ancient Greece and Rome, where women were required to kiss their male relatives to prove they hadn't been drinking. In colonial America, women were allowed to drink but only in privacy, not in public places or after dinner with men. This helped establish the ambiguous image of women as either righteous and moral or drunken and loose. Although this view is not as prevalent today, there is still a strong social stigma regarding women and alcohol consumption, which results in women hiding drinking problems and feeling reluctant to seek help and treatment.

24. *Men often become more violent when they get drunk. Why do women become very emotional (crying, depressed)?*

Since alcohol depresses the central nervous system, it changes behavior patterns, and the emotions expressed depend on the individual. It is possible that the distinct pattern of men commonly becoming violent and women commonly becoming emotional is based on socialization. An individual's mood and initial purpose for drinking may also be significant. These emotions or feelings will probably surface once his/her inhibitions are reduced.

25. *Do women recover faster from alcoholism than men?*

There are so many factors in alcoholism recovery that it is hard to determine whether one sex recovers faster than the other. Alcoholism recovery is an individual problem that cannot be generalized by gender.

Blood Alcohol Levels and Driving

Blood Alcohol Levels (percentage)

Body wt (lb)	1	2	3	4	5	Drinks per hour* 6	7	8	9	10	11	12
100	.038	.075	.113	.150	.188	.225	.263	.300	.338	.375	.413	.450
120	.031	.063	.094	.125	.156	.188	.219	.250	.281	.313	.344	.375
140	.027	.054	.080	.107	.134	.161	.188	.214	.241	.268	.295	.321
160	.023	.047	.070	.094	.117	.141	.164	.188	.211	.234	.258	.281
180	.021	.042	.063	.083	.104	.125	.146	.167	.188	.208	.229	.250
200	.019	.038	.056	.075	.094	.113	.131	.150	.169	.188	.206	.225
220	.017	.034	.051	.068	.085	.102	.119	.136	.153	.170	.188	.205
240	.016	.031	.047	.063	.078	.094	.109	.125	.141	.156	.172	.188

Under .05 Driving is not seriously impaired (although some research indicates fine motor skills may be impaired at .02 or .03 level).	.05 to 0.10 Driving becomes increasingly dangerous.	.10 to .15 Driving is dangerous. Legal drunkenness in most states.	Over .15 Driving is very dangerous. Legal drunkenness in every state.

*One drink equals 1 oz of 80-100 proof liquor, 12 oz of beer, or 5 oz of wine.

Communicating Your Concerns

It is not so much the *amount* one drinks, *what* one drinks, or *when* one drinks that determines problem drinking, but rather *what happens* when one drinks alcohol. What happens when you drink alcohol may affect you in these different life areas: social, academic, financial, legal, personal, and health. For example, you may:

- End up in an acute injury clinic.
- Go to class or work after drinking.
- Get arrested for driving under the influence (DUI).
- Offend or hurt a date/friend while drunk.
- Do something that you later regret.

There may be times when you see someone's drinking get out of line. You may be affected *directly* (something is said by that person that embarrasses you) or *indirectly* (you see the person act in ways he or she would not normally act, which would be embarrassing to him or her). When you see these kinds of things, it may be helpful to talk to that person about your concerns.

Guidelines for Discussing Alcohol Abuse

1. Choose a time and place that is comfortable when the person is sober.
2. Decide whether the person will respect your feelings or if there is a more appropriate person (e.g., best friend, roommate) whom he or she will listen to.
3. Find out if anyone else was affected the same way you were by that person's drinking behaviors.
4. Describe the specific actions or remarks that bothered you. Do not be vague about the consequences of the behaviors you described.
5. Do not criticize, diagnose, or judge your friend's actions (e.g., ''You have a drinking problem''). Explain that you want to share your concerns because you care for him or her.
6. After sharing your list of behaviors, let your friend accept or reject what you have said. Do not get into excuses; stay on the offensive.

Be aware that your friend may react in several ways (e.g., thankful, angry, upset, or indifferent). If he or she reacts defensively, do not take it personally, but rather feel good about doing your friend a service that may not be recognized as such at that time. For further information and resources about alcohol, problem drinking, and learning how to talk to someone about their drinking, call Alcoholics Anonymous/Alanon, your local mental health department, or look for substance abuse counselors and clinics in the phone book.

Blood Alcohol Levels by Gender

Comparisons of Blood Alcohol Levels by Sex, Weight, and Consumption

Absolute alcohol (oz)	Beverage intake in 1 hr	Blood alcohol levels (mg/100 ml)					
		Female (100 lb)	Male (100 lb)	Female (150 lb)	Male (150 lb)	Female (200 lb)	Male (200 lb)
1/2	1 oz spirits* 1 glass wine 1 can beer	0.045	0.037	0.03	0.025	0.022	0.019
1	2 oz spirits 2 glasses wine 2 cans beer	0.090	0.075	0.06	0.050	0.045	0.037
2	4 oz spirits 4 glasses wine 4 cans beer	0.180	0.150	0.12	0.100	0.090	0.070
3	6 oz spirits 6 glasses wine 6 cans beer	0.270	0.220	0.18	0.150	0.130	0.110
4	8 oz spirits 8 glasses wine 8 cans beer	0.360	0.300	0.24	0.200	0.180	0.150
5	10 oz spirits 10 glasses wine 10 cans beer	0.450	0.370	0.30	0.250	0.220	0.180

Note. From *Drugs, Society & Human Behavior* (4th ed.) by O. Ray and C. Ksir, 1987, St. Louis: Times Mirror/Mosby. Copyright 1987. Reprinted by permission.

*100-proof spirits.

Alcohol's Effects on the Body

A number of factors will determine how individuals react differently, given the same amount of alcohol, or on different occasions:

Speed of drinking—The more rapidly the beverage is ingested, the higher the peak blood alcohol concentration (BAC). The liver metabolizes about 1/2 ounce of alcohol per hour.

Presence of food in the stomach—Eating while drinking slows down the absorption rate. When alcoholic beverages are taken with a substantial meal, peak BAC may be reduced by as much as 50%.

Other chemicals in the beverage—The greater the amount of nonalcoholic chemicals in the beverage, the more slowly the alcohol is absorbed (e.g., vodka is absorbed more rapidly than beer or wine).

Body weight—A larger person has more blood and requires greater amounts of alcohol to reach a given BAC.

Drinking history/tolerance—Increasing amounts of alcohol are needed to result in the physical and behavioral reactions formerly produced at lesser concentrations, if there is a long history of drinking.

Environment—There may be differences in alcohol's effects depending upon where one drinks (e.g., local bar, with family, hostile environment, etc.).

The drinker's expectations—Many people become intoxicated on less alcohol merely because they have that expectation before they begin drinking.

General state of emotional and physical health—Many people seem more susceptible to the effects of alcohol when they are extremely fatigued, have recently been ill, or are under emotional stress and strain. The usual amount of alcohol may result in uncomfortable effects.

Sex differences—Given the same amount of alcohol, and proportional to body weight, females will generally have a higher BAC than their male counterparts, due to less body fluids to dilute the alcohol and also due to more body fat. Females are generally more affected by alcohol just prior to menstruation. Females taking birth control pills or medications containing estrogen may remain intoxicated longer than those who do not, due to the liver's function of metabolizing both.

Other drugs—Prescription, over-the-counter, illicit, and unrecognized drugs all have potential reactions with alcohol. One should be aware of the additive and synergistic effects when these drugs are mixed with alcohol.

When you drink alcohol, 20% is absorbed immediately into the bloodstream, with the rest quickly processed through the gastrointestinal tract. Alcohol, classified as a depressant drug, affects the functions of the brain.

BAC	*This much alcohol causes . . .*
.05	Lowered alertness; released inhibitions; mental relaxation, disrupted judgment; less concern about environment.
.10	Impaired movements and coordination; slowed reaction time; exaggerated emotions; impaired vision.
.20	Marked abnormality of bodily and sensory functions; feeling of need to lie down; inability to stand or walk without help; confusion/tears/rage occur easily.
·.30	Stupor and near unconsciousness; lack of comprehension of what is seen or heard.
.40-.50	Loss of feeling; unconsciousness; shock; breathing and heartbeat possibly stop.

Game Board

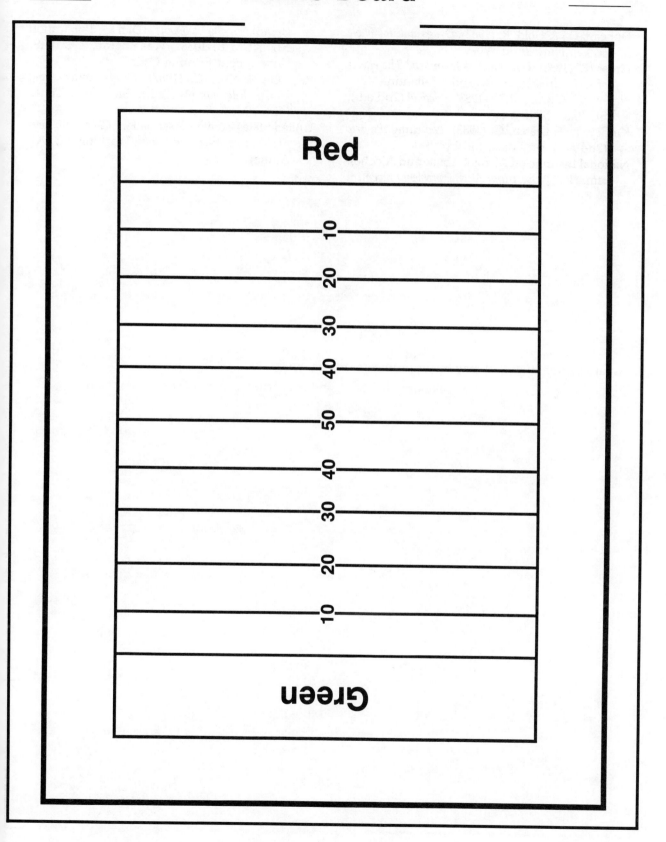

REFERENCES

Duncan, D., & Gold, R. (1982). *Drugs and the whole person*. New York: Wiley.

Gross, L. (1983). *How much is too much? The effects of social drinking*. New York: Ballantine.

Hafen, B., & Brog, M.V. (1983). *Alcohol* (2nd ed.). St. Paul, MN: West.

Kinney, J., & Leaten, G. (1983). *Loosening the grip* (2nd ed.). St. Louis: Mosby.

National Institute on Alcohol Abuse and Alcoholism. (1981). *Spectrum: Alcohol problem prevention for women by women*. (DHHS Publication No. ADM 81-1036). Washington, DC: U.S. Government Printing Office.

Ray, O., & Ksir, C. (1987). *Drugs, society, and human behavior* (4th ed.). St. Louis: Times Mirror/Mosby.

United States Brewers Association. *Cheers! Six keys to operating responsible pubs*. Washington, DC: Author.

Marijuana and Cocaine Education Game Lifestyle Workshop

PARAPROFESSIONAL PREPARATION MATERIALS

Training Sessions

Competency Exam

Texts and Suggested Readings

WORKSHOP AT A GLANCE

Presenter Information

Most Frequently Asked Questions

Handouts and Visual Aids

References

TRAINING SESSIONS

Marijuana and Cocaine Education Game

Session 1: Workshop Presentation

Time: 60 to 90 minutes

Methods: Presentation, demonstration

Description: Trainer presents workshop to Lifestyle Educators

Readings: The workshop

Session 2: Drug and Drug Education Philosophy

Time: 60 minutes

Methods: Lecture, discussion

Description: Discuss objective methods of drug education and its role in preventing drug problems. Cover drug classification, patterns of use, and methods of administration.

Readings: Materials on peer approaches to prevention, teaching about drugs objectively, categorization and prevalence, levels and patterns of drug-taking

Competency exam questions: 1, 2, 3, 4

Session 3: Drug Classification, Levels of Use, and Effects on Performance Tasks

Time: 60 minutes

Methods: Lecture, discussion, practice

Description: Define different classifications of cocaine and marijuana; discuss various methods and types of use and their effects on performance tasks.

Activity: Practice the game questions for Classification, Methods and Types of Use, and Effects on Performance Tasks.

Readings: Materials on classification, use, and effects of cocaine and marijuana; the workshop

Competency exam questions: 1, 2, 3, 4, 5, 11, 12

Session 4: Psychological and Physiological Effects, Addictions, and Patterns of Use

Time: 60 minutes

Methods: Lecture, discussion, practice

Description: Psychological and physiological effects, addictions, and patterns of use are explained.

Readings: Materials on physiological and psychological effects of cocaine and marijuana and patterns of drug use, the workshop

Competency exam questions: 3, 6, 8, 9, 10, 13

Session 5: History, Legalities, and Drug Testing

Time: 60 minutes

Methods: Lecture, discussion, practice

Description: Explain history of cocaine and marijuana use, legal issues in drug use, types of drug tests, and related issues.

Activity: Practice game questions for History, Legalities, and Drug Testing.

Readings: Materials on history of cocaine and marijuana use, legal issues, and drug testing; the workshop

Competency exam questions: 7, 13, 14

Session 6: "Most Frequently Asked Questions" Review and Hot Seat

Time: 60 minutes

Methods: Discussion, practice

Description: Review "Most Frequently Asked Questions" and other workshop components.

Activity: Each Lifestyle Educator is quizzed by the other students on the workshop topic for 10 minutes.

Readings: The workshop

Session 7: Practice Workshop Presentation

Time: 60 minutes

Method: Presentation

Description: Each Lifestyle Educator presents 20 minutes of the workshop.

Readings: The workshop

COMPETENCY EXAM

1. Explain the three major factors that influence how a drug affects a person.

2. Distinguish among drug use, misuse, and abuse.

3. Distinguish among experimental use, occasional use, and compulsive use.

4. Explain how oral versus nasal ingestion affect the user's ability to titrate a drug.

5. Fill in the information requested below for marijuana and cocaine.

   Route of administration:

   Average mg of dose:

   Percentage of dose absorbed:

   Peak effects (minimum):

   Length of high (minimum):

6. List three ways a marijuana high affects learning ability.

7. Briefly outline the history of marijuana use from 2700 B.C. to the present.

8. What are the psychological effects of low and high doses of marijuana?

9. What are the physical effects of marijuana use?

10. Describe the physical and psychological effects of cocaine use.

11. What are the medical uses of marijuana?

12. What are the medical uses of cocaine?

13. Describe the use of marijuana in the college population from 1960 to present, including a change of trends in those who have ever used, occasional users, and daily users.

14. Briefly outline the highlights of the history of cocaine use.

15. Suggest possible techniques to use in the workshop if a participant is one of the following:
    • Recognition Seeker (frequently calls attention to self)
    • Conversationalist (brings up off-the-subject anecdotes and is a noisy distraction)
    • Moralizer (advocates judgmental points of view based on personal convictions)
    • Conservative (convinced that the status quo does not need changing)

TEXTS AND SUGGESTED READINGS

Duncan, D., & Gold, R. (1982). *Drugs and the whole person*. New York: Wiley.

Kozel, M.J., & Adams, E.J. (1985). *Cocaine use in America: Epidemiologic and clinical perspectives.* (NIDA Research Monograph Series No. 1). Washington, DC: U.S. Government Printing Office.

National Institute on Drug Abuse. (1981). *Marijuana and health*. (DHHS Publication No. ADM 81-945). Washington, DC: U.S. Government Printing Office.

National Institute on Drug Abuse. (1986, April). *Prevention networks: Cocaine use in America.* Washington, DC: Government Printing Office.

Ray, O., & Ksir, C. (1987). *Drugs, society, and human behavior* (4th ed.). St. Louis: Times Mirror/Mosby.

WORKSHOP AT A GLANCE

The goal of this workshop is to increase participants' knowledge about cocaine and marijuana, enabling them to sensibly evaluate these two drugs. This workshop takes approximately 60 minutes to present. Suggested attendance is 6 to 20 persons.

Objectives

Within the content of this workshop, the following objectives will be met.

- Through the use of the game "Marijuana and Cocaine: A Double Trouble Game," participants will discuss and analyze cocaine and marijuana information.
- Participants will examine and discuss the following issues surrounding cocaine and marijuana: classification, methods and types of use, patterns of use, addictions, history of use, physiological and psychological effects, and legalities related to possession and use.

Workshop Materials

- Workshop sign-in sheet
- Handouts and Visual Aids: *Cocaine Addiction*, game board and four dry-erase boards, erasers, and markers; or small chalkboards, chalk, and erasers; bell; paper for keeping score; and prizes.
- Lifestyle Workshop evaluation forms and pencils

PRESENTER INFORMATION

Briefly introduce yourself, your background, and any other personal information you choose to share. Describe your health promotion program and the topics available, like fitness and nutrition. Stress that the workshops are unique because you bring them to their living areas. Lifestyle Workshop paraprofessionals are trained at (your institution or program) to present these workshops. If anyone is interested in the training program, ask him or her to speak with you after the workshop.

The purpose of this workshop is to test participants' knowledge of general facts about cocaine and marijuana. Through education, individuals are better able to evaluate their options, rather than allowing other influences to make their decisions. Within the game format, participants are encouraged to share their views and experiences.

Marijuana and Cocaine Education Game (50 minutes)

Contestants choose from various categories and are given answers to which they must respond with the correct question. Questions start, "Who is . . . ," "What is . . . ," "Where is . . . ," or "When was . . ." When choosing a category the participant also asks for a specific point amount, for example, "Classifications, for 200 points." The answers are divided into seven categories: Classification, Methods and Types of Use, Patterns of Use and Addictions, History, Physiological and Psychological Effects, Legalities, and Performance Tasks and Drug Testing. The answers range in value from 100 to 500 points: questions of greater difficulty are worth more points.

Marijuana and Cocaine Game Rules

Divide participants into teams of two or more, and give each team a marker, an eraser, and a dry-erase board. Have the first team choose the category and point level. Each team should write on the board its response-question to the given answer. The correct question will never be "What is cocaine?" or "What is marijuana?" Call time after 15 seconds, and have each team show its question. Points are awarded to each team with the correct question.

There is no penalty for an incorrect question. Have the next team to the right choose the next category and question. Proceed playing for 45 minutes.

After 45 minutes, announce the final category. Instruct each team to write a wagered number of points on its board and then give the answer. A correct question means the number of wagered points is added to the team's previous total. An incorrect question means the number of points wagered is subtracted from the team's previous total. The team with the highest point total wins. A sample Game Board with four representative categories is shown in the handouts and visual aids section.

Classification

This category tests participants' knowledge of drug classification.

100 points—*Plant from which marijuana is made.*
  What is cannabis or hemp?

200 points—*Plant from which cocaine is derived.*
  What is the coca plant?

300 points—*Physiological classification or effects of cocaine.*
  What is a stimulant?

400 points—*Low, medium, or high? The dosage of marijuana that classifies its effects as sedative-hypnotic.*
  What is low?

500 points—*Legal classification of cocaine and marijuana.*
  What is a narcotic?

Methods and Types of Use

This category tests participants' knowledge of drug use methods.

100 points—*Device used to smoke marijuana by inhaling gases.*
  What is a waterpipe or bong?

200 points—*Average cost of 1 gram of cocaine.*
  What is $100?

300 points—*Drug form derived from cocaine hydrochloride using baking soda and water.*

What is crack?

400 points—*A more potent form of marijuana derived from the plant resin.*

What is hashish?

500 points—*Two of the three conditions treated medically with marijuana.*

What are asthma, glaucoma, and chemotherapy nausea? (Cancer is an acceptable response in place of chemotherapy nausea.)

Patterns of Use and Addiction

This category tests participants' knowledge of patterns of use and addiction.

100 points—*Method of cocaine with the greatest risk of addiction.*

What is freebasing?

200 points—*2.0%, 4.0%, 6.0%, or 8.0%. Percentage of college students using marijuana daily (based on latest figures from the National Institute on Drug Abuse).*

What is 6.0%?

300 points—*18 to 25, 26 to 35, or over 35. Age group containing the largest share of "current" users of cocaine (one or more times in the last month).*

What is 18 to 25?

400 points—*Zero deaths per year.*

How many deaths are caused by marijuana overdose?

500 points—*Leads to weight loss, insomnia, and anxiety.*

What is compulsive use of cocaine, or addiction?

History

This category tests participants' knowledge of the historical uses of drugs.

100 points—*Psychoanalyst who used cocaine to treat depression, alcoholism, and morphine addiction.*

Who is Sigmund Freud?

200 points—*South American Indians who chew coca leaves even today.*

Who are the Incas?

300 points—*2700 B.C., 100 B.C., or A.D. 1200? First recorded use of marijuana.*

What is 2700 B.C.?

400 points—*Popular 1876 world-event where marijuana was available in the Turkish Pavilion.*

What is the World's Fair?

500 points—*Alcoholic beverage introduced in 1863 that prompted the Pope to title Angelo Mariani a "benefactor of humanity."*

What is "vin mariani" or wine with cocaine?

Physiological and Psychological Effects

This category tests participants' knowledge of the physiological and psychological effects of drug use.

100 points—*Dilated pupils and talkativeness.*

What are the signs of a cocaine high?

200 points—*Acute panic anxiety reaction.*

What is the primary symptom of a marijuana overdose?

300 points—*Two of the three most common causes of death from cocaine use.*

What are stroke, heart attack, or seizures?

400 points—*Characteristic cycle associated with cocaine use that reinforces continuous use.*

What is the cycle of euphoria and depression?

500 points—*Set, setting, and dose.*

What are the three major factors determining how a drug affects an individual?

Legalities

This category tests participants' knowledge of drug laws.

100 points—*Beverage company prosecuted by the Food and Drug Administration in 1909 for not including in its beverage what its name implied.*

What is Coca-Cola?

200 points—*1937.*

What year did marijuana become illegal?

300 points—*A life sentence in 12 states.*

What is the maximum penalty for selling cocaine?

400 points—*The same penalty as selling the real thing.*

What is the penalty for selling a "look-alike" substance?

500 points—*Twice the normal penalties.*

What is the penalty for an adult selling cocaine to a minor?

Performance Tasks and Drug Testing

This category tests participants' knowledge of various drugs' effects on performance capabilities.

100 points—*Cocaine effect that prompted its use in the Bavarian Army in the 1880s.*

What is reduction in fatigue or prolonged worker performance?

200 points—*Methods of drug testing that must be voluntary unless the person is under arrest with probable cause for drug use.*

What are a blood test or urine test?

300 points—*Interferes with ability to maintain following-distance and lane position.*

How does marijuana affect driving?

400 points—*Half-life of about one week. (Half-life means half of the drug remains in the body while half is gone.)*

What is the half-life of THC (delta-9-tetrahydrocannibinol)?

500 points—*Two ways a marijuana high affects learning ability.*

What are memory, concept formation, reading comprehension, or problem solving? (Name any two of the four for a correct response.)

Final Jeopardy Question

The team with the most points chooses one of the two categories: marijuana or cocaine. After the choice is made, each team writes on its board the number of points it is willing to wager from its total. Read the answer and allow 20 seconds for a written response. Each team displays its answer and the amount wagered.

Marijuana

A San Francisco community with one of the country's largest marijuana-using populations in the 1960s and 1970s.

What is Haight-Ashbury?

Cocaine

Specialized medical branch that uses cocaine as a local anesthetic.

What is ear, nose, and throat? (Accept nasal surgery as correct response.)

Calculate final team points. Announce winning team and give prizes.

Conclusion and Evaluation (5 minutes)

Summarize the two main points of the workshop:

- Our attitudes about the use of certain drugs are embedded in a cultural and societal context. Views handed down through history affect our attitudes whether they are based on fact or folklore.
- Remember, it's how you use a drug, not the drug itself, that classifies as use, misuse, or abuse. Abuse is using the drug in circumstances or at doses that significantly increase its hazard. The handout "Cocaine Addiction" on page 326 points out characteristics of addiction.

Ask for questions from participants. Offer resources and referrals for further information. Distribute Lifestyle Workshop evaluation forms and pencils. Allow time for completion and then collect. Briefly list and describe the other Drugs and Alcohol Lifestyle Workshops.

MOST FREQUENTLY ASKED QUESTIONS

1. *How much is an average hit or "line" of cocaine?*

   A line of cocaine to snort averages 25 mg. A typical hit to freebase is 120 mg.

2. *What percentage of college students use cocaine, marijuana, and other drugs at least once a year?*

   Alcohol 90%, marijuana 42%, cocaine 17%, stimulants 12%

3. *Does one develop a tolerance to cocaine?*

   Yes, tolerance to the euphoric effects develops quickly, but the level at which toxic effects occur remains unchanged.

4. *Is marijuana physically addictive?*

   Yes, mildly. Physical addiction depends upon the appearance of a withdrawal syndrome when the drug is stopped. In some cases chronic users have stopped with no noticeable signs of withdrawal, whereas others have displayed depression, tremor, and agitation as a withdrawal syndrome.

5. *How does marijuana affect sexual performance?*

   In high doses it may act as a sedative and decrease performance.

6. *How many people actually use cocaine?*

   According to the National Institute on Drug Abuse (1986) an estimated 4.6 million people are current users and 200,000 to 1 million are compulsive users.

7. *When did cocaine use begin?*

   Coca was rarely seen outside of South America until the mid-1800s. About that time the cocaine alkaloid was isolated by German physicians and its medicinal properties were explored.

8. *What are cocaine's physiological effects?*

   Cocaine narrows blood vessels; increases heart rate, blood pressure, and respiration rate; and deadens the appetite. After the initial euphoria has passed, a physiological depression occurs that is characterized by a feeling of dullness and tenseness.

9. *What are the consequences of chronic marijuana use?*

   The limited research that has been completed indicates no major health consequences that occur in high percentages. Further investigation on this issue is needed.

Cocaine Addiction

Only recently has cocaine been considered an addictive substance. For many years researchers were telling us that cocaine was not an addictive drug, with the implication that its use was relatively harmless. We now know that although cocaine does not appear to be physically addictive in the sense of narcotics, barbiturates, or alcohol, it does appear to be one of the most addicting substances known in terms of need and compulsion, loss of control, and continued use despite negative consequences. These terms are defined by thoughts and emotions that are related to them.

Need and Compulsion

- feeling hooked
- preoccupation with thoughts concerning cocaine
- sacrifice of other responsibilities and interests for cocaine
- strong desire for cocaine upon sight, smell, or mention
- distress at the thought of not being able to locate cocaine

Loss of Control

- inability to turn down cocaine if it is offered
- inability to limit the extent of use
- inability to stop cocaine usage despite repeated attempts

Continued Use Despite Negative Consequences

- impaired physical or mental functioning
- negative effects on marital/family relationships
- negative effects on employment
- legal involvements
- financial losses

Game Board

Patterns of use and addiction	Methods and types of use	Legalities	Performance tasks and drug testing
100	100	100	100
200	200	200	200
300	300	300	300
400	400	400	400
Leads to weight loss, insomnia, and anxiety	500	500	500

REFERENCES

Duncan, D., & Gold, R. (1982). *Drugs and the whole person*. New York: Wiley.

Kozel, N.J., & Adams, E.H. (1985). *Cocaine use in America: Epidemiologic and clinical perspectives*. (NIDA Research Monograph Series No. 1). Washington, DC: U.S. Government Printing Office.

National Institute on Drug Abuse. (1981). *Marijuana and health*. (DHHS Publication No. ADM 81-945). Washington, DC: U.S. Government Printing Office.

National Institute on Drug Abuse. (1986, April). *Prevention networks: Cocaine use in America*. Washington, DC: U.S. Government Printing Office.

Ray, O., & Ksir, C. (1987). *Drugs, society, and human behavior* (4th ed.). St. Louis: Times Mirror/Mosby.

Who's Calling the Shots? Lifestyle Workshop

PARAPROFESSIONAL PREPARATION MATERIALS

Training Sessions

Competency Exam

Texts and Suggested Readings

WORKSHOP AT A GLANCE

Presenter Information

Most Frequently Asked Questions

Handouts and Visual Aids

References

TRAINING SESSIONS

Who's Calling the Shots?

Session 1: Workshop Presentation

Time: 60 minutes

Methods: Presentation, demonstration

Description: Trainer presents workshop to Lifestyle Educators.

Readings: The workshop; "A Winner's Alcohol Facts Game" is also an excellent reference for this workshop.

Session 2: Drug and Drug Education Philosophy

Time: 60 minutes

Methods: Lecture, discussion

Description: Discuss objective methods of drug education and its role in preventing alcohol problems. Cover drug classification and patterns of use.

Readings: Material on peer approaches to drug prevention, teaching about alcohol objectively, drug categorization and prevalence, levels and patterns of drug-taking

Competency exam question: 20

Session 3: Forms of Alcohol, Use Patterns, and Alcohol's Effects

Time: 60 minutes

Methods: Lecture, discussion

Description: Alcohol types, use patterns, and effects

Activity: Have each Lifestyle Educator complete the "Find Out Why *You* Drink" handout for discussion.

Readings: Materials on alcohol and its use, effects of alcoholic beverages on the body, the workshop

Competency exam questions: 1, 2, 3, 11, 12, 13, 14, 15, 16, 17, 19, 22, 24, 25, 26, 27, 28, 29, 30, 41, 43, 46, 47, 50

Session 4: Social Drinking, Problem Drinking, and Alcoholism

Time: 60 minutes

Methods: Lecture, discussion

Description: Define social drinking, problem drinking, and alcoholism. Explain alcoholism risks, symptoms, and theories about cause and recovery.

Activity: Generate a list of signals of problem drinking and have students evaluate whether they see any of these signs in themselves or others.

Readings: Materials on social drinking, problem drinking, and alcoholism; the workshop

Competency exam questions: 6, 7, 8, 9, 10, 19, 20, 21, 31, 32, 33, 34, 35, 36, 37, 38, 39, 44, 45, 50, 51

Session 5: Alcohol-Related Problems and Legal Regulations

Time: 60 minutes

Methods: Lecture, discussion

Description: Costs of alcohol use to society, how to deal with alcohol emergencies, and how to approach a friend who has a drinking problem. Discuss how laws attempt to regulate alcohol use.

Readings: Materials on costs of alcohol use to society, dealing with alcohol emergencies, and communicating your concerns about another's drinking behavior; the workshop

Competency exam questions: 4, 23, 42, 49, 52, 53

Session 6: Factors Influencing Drinking Behavior

Time: 60 minutes

Methods: Lecture, discussion

Description: Discuss the factors influencing drinking behavior.

Readings: Materials on the influences of family, peers, and the media on drinking behavior; the workshop

Competency exam questions: 5, 18, 37, 38, 39, 45, 48

Session 7: Show "Calling the Shots"

Time: 60 minutes

Methods: Presentation, discussion

Description: Show film and review discussion questions in manual.

Activity: Practice threading and operating the film projector.

Readings: The workshop

Session 8: "Most Frequently Asked Questions" Review and Hot Seat

Time: 60 minutes

Methods: Discussion, practice

Description: Review "Most Frequently Asked Questions" and other workshop components.

Activity: Each Lifestyle Educator is quizzed by the other students on the workshop topic for 10 minutes.

Readings: The workshop

Competency exam questions: 54, 55

Session 9: Practice Workshop Presentation

Time: 60 minutes

Methods: Presentation

Description: Each Lifestyle Educator presents 20 minutes of the workshop.

Readings: The workshop

COMPETENCY EXAM

The following are multiple choice questions. Circle the letter of the correct answer.

1. About how long does the average person need to completely burn up the alcohol in a "standard" drink?
    a. 1/2 hour
    b. 1 hour
    c. 1 1/2 hours
    d. 2 hours

2. Which of the following will help sober you up?
    a. exercise
    b. coffee
    c. a cold shower
    d. time
    e. all of the above

3. Approximately what percentage of adults in the United States drink alcoholic beverages?
    a. 90%
    b. 80%
    c. 70%
    d. 60%

4. Which of the following best describes the effects of alcohol on the central nervous system?
    a. stimulant
    b. depressant
    c. first lowers, then stimulates, inhibitions
    d. first lowers, then depresses, inhibitions

5. Which of the following was not found to be a public perception of alcohol?
    a. Hard liquor is more damaging than other forms.
    b. Moderate consumption should be encouraged.
    c. Drunk driving penalties need to be tightened.
    d. Wine is like a food and considered in the same class as Coke or Pepsi.

6. The age group with the most problem drinkers is
    a. 18-30.
    b. 30-40.
    c. 40-50.
    d. over 50.

7. Approximately what percentage of alcohol is metabolized in the liver?
    a. 95%
    b. 80%
    c. 70%
    d. 60%

8. In comparing alcohol revenues of the liquor industry to the cost of alcohol use to society,
    a. revenues are far greater than the costs.
    b. costs are far greater than the revenues.
    c. revenues and costs are about equal.

9. Which of the following best describes alcohol absorption into the bloodstream?
   a. 80% is absorbed through the liver.
   b. 80% is absorbed through the stomach.
   c. 80% is absorbed through the intestines.
   d. 80% is absorbed through the brain.

For questions 10 through 12, choose one of the following three phrases to complete the sentence:
   a. . . . a higher percentage of college students . . .
   b. . . . a higher percentage of adults . . .
   c. . . . similar percentages of college students and adults . . .

10. In comparing college students and adults, _____ abstain from alcohol.

11. In comparing college students and adults, _____ are problem drinkers and alcoholics.

12. In comparing college students and adults, _____ are social drinkers.

For questions 13 through 18, label each of the following situations:
   a. social drinking
   b. problem drinking
   c. alcoholism

_____ 13. After studying for her next final exam, Vicki goes out for a few beers with some friends in the middle of finals week; normally, she would not drink at all during the week.

_____ 14. Rick usually has a beer or two to be comfortable before taking a date to a party where he knows they both will be drinking quite a bit.

_____ 15. Everyone from a class goes to happy hour on Fridays. Although Cindy told herself she wouldn't go this week to save money for spring break, she goes and spends some vacation money anyway.

_____ 16. Joe occasionally goes out to parties or bars to have a good time with his friends. He usually has several drinks each time he goes out.

_____ 17. Mary says to her friend Jill, "I can't wait until the weekend . . . I'm going to get *so* drunk!" Jill sees this happen almost every weekend.

_____ 18. Steve forces himself not to drink alcohol during the week, but he spends every weekend in a drunken stupor.

The following are short essay questions.

19. Discuss techniques used by alcohol advertisers to appeal to the following target audiences: men, women, college students.

20. Discuss some of the issues involved in removing alcohol ads from television, radio, and print media.

21. Explain how the environment and expectations of the drinker can interact to produce different effects from the same dosage of alcohol.

22. List three direct and three indirect costs of alcohol use to society.

23. Identify the effects of each of the following blood alcohol levels: .10, .20, .30, .40-.50.

24. What are the three purposes of advertising? Why does the liquor industry believe that alcohol advertising does not have the same purposes?

25. What attitudes about alcohol's role does advertising promote?

26. What four kinds of information are most likely to be learned from an alcohol advertisement?

27. Suggest possible techniques to use in your workshop if participant is one of the following:
    • Recognition Seeker (frequently calls attention to self)
    • Conversationalist (brings up off-the-subject anecdotes and is a noisy distraction)
    • Moralizer (advocates judgmental points of view based on personal convictions)
    • Conservative (convinced that the status quo does not need changing)

TEXTS AND SUGGESTED READINGS

Alcohol advertising changing. (1986). *The Bottom Line on Alcohol in Society, 7*(3), 36-40.

Duncan, D., & Gold, R. (1982). *Drugs and the whole person.* New York: Wiley.

Hafen, B., & Brog, M.V. (1983). *Alcohol* (2nd ed.). St. Paul, MN: West.

The impact of alcoholic beverage advertising. (1981). *The Bottom Line on Alcohol in Society, 4*(4), 2-17.

Liquor industry tackles its biggest problem. (1986). *The Bottom Line on Alcohol in Society, 7*(1), 14-15.

Ray, O., & Ksir, C. (1987). *Drugs, society, and human behavior* (4th ed.). St. Louis: Times Mirror/Mosby.

Under the influence. (1984). *The Bottom Line on Alcohol in Society, 6*(1), 5-9.

WORKSHOP AT A GLANCE

The goal of this workshop is to educate participants on how the alcohol advertising industry, campus bars, and personal experiences influence people's drinking behaviors. This workshop takes approximately 75 minutes to present. Suggested attendance is 5 to 15 persons.

Objectives

Within the content of this workshop, the following objectives will be met.

- By using the film "Calling the Shots," information about general alcohol use and abuse is presented along with techniques advertisers use to encourage people to drink.
- Participants will examine what factors influence the effects of alcohol.
- Participants will evaluate differences among low-risk and high-risk drinking and social and problem drinking and will discuss how to approach someone they feel needs help.
- Participants will examine their own motivations for drinking behaviors.

Workshop Materials

- Workshop sign-in sheet
- Handouts and visual aids: *Alcohol's Effects on the Body, Blood Alcohol Levels by Gender, Communicating Your Concerns, Find Out Why You Drink,* and the film *Calling the Shots,** which can be ordered from: Cambridge Documentary Films, Inc./Box 385/Cambridge, MA 02139, or phone: (617) 354-3677.
- Film projector
- Screen
- Lifestyle Workshop evaluation forms and pencils

---

*If for any reason, you are not able to obtain the film, you will find the structure of this workshop is designed to stimulate questions and provide answers that are covered in the film.

PRESENTER INFORMATION

Briefly introduce yourself, your background, and any other personal information you choose to share. Describe your health promotion program and the topics available, like fitness and nutrition. Stress that the workshops are unique because you bring them to their living areas. Tell them that Lifestyle Workshop paraprofessionals are trained at (your institution or program) to present these workshops. If anyone is interested in the training program, ask him or her to speak with you after the workshop.

In this workshop we will examine the prevalence and impact of alcohol advertising and other influences on drinking behaviors. By developing a better understanding of these influences, we will be better able to choose whether or not to be affected by them.

Film: Calling the Shots *(35 minutes)*

This film will take approximately 25 minutes to show. The discussion following the film should last about 10 minutes. You may want to present this material in the following manner.

Lots of things in our everyday lives influence the choices we make about alcohol. One example is the people we live with. Your roommates or floor residents may influence your drinking behavior by encouraging or discouraging you to adopt behaviors similar to theirs. (Ask participants for other examples of things that may influence drinking behaviors.) However, we may not always pay conscious attention to these influences. In fact, it's doubtful that many of us have stopped to think about how our families or friends influence our alcohol drinking.

An even more subtle influence is the role advertising plays in our drinking behavior. The film gives many examples of techniques that the alcohol beverage industry uses to influence consumer behavior. The film's narrator, Jean Kilbourne, is a media analyst and educator who gives us tremendous insight into the field of advertising and its effects.

Here are a few possible discussion questions you might use to elicit responses from workshop participants:

- How many of you have seen some of the advertisements in the film?
- Which ads did you find most powerful or manipulative?
- Did you find any advertising techniques that particularly appealed to what you want out of life?
- Do you think we consciously think of the appeals in the ads?
- The unconscious nature of the appeals may give some insight into the startling statistics presented. Did any of the statistics surprise you?

Point out that the film explained four different target groups for alcohol advertising: men, women, problem drinkers and alcoholics, and college students. What different techniques were used to appeal to these different groups?

Men. Advertisements that appeal to a macho image and to sport involvement.

Women. Drinking alcohol is the way to get to a man. And, "light" beers and wines are marketed to fit women's needs and for women's concern over weight control.

Problem Drinkers and Alcoholics. Twenty-three percent of the drinkers in this country consume 93% of the alcohol. Advertisers play upon this group's vulnerability. Advertisers try to establish that abusive drinking levels are really accepted norms of behavior.

College Students. About 2/3 of all advertising in campus newspapers is for alcohol, mostly beer. Techniques used by alcohol advertisers ridicule many of the basic elements of the college experience, such as learning, student organizations, science, and graduation. Beer distributors know that many students choose a brand of beer during college that they will drink for many years, so they want very much to convince college students to buy their brand.

"Calling the Shots" illustrates the multitude of different advertising techniques. Overall we become more aware of subtle messages and techniques to affect our consumer behavior with alcoholic beverages.

Creating a Campus Bar (15 minutes)

Now we'll bring the focus to your campus to look at ways campus bars encourage students to drink. Campus bars use lots of advertising in the local newspapers and on the radio to attract students to their establishments. In addition to advertising, campus bars use a variety of techniques to encourage their patrons to drink more.

Setting Up the Bar

We're going to look at these techniques by dividing into groups to create a campus bar. In setting up the bar, we need to know a little about alcohol's effects on our patrons and the role their blood alcohol level plays in their actions. Hand out "Alcohol's Effect on The Body" and "Blood Alcohol Levels by Gender"; discuss how this information can be used in a bar.

Divide participants into groups of four to five to "create a bar." The object of the bar is to sell the most alcohol and make the most money. Suggest that participants think about the following factors in creating their bars:

- the name of the bar
- whether it will serve food
- whether it will have a dance floor
- what clientele will be targeted
- the atmosphere or theme
- types of drinks to be offered
- location
- waiters/waitresses
- seating arrangements
- whether it will serve drink specials or happy hours
- hours of operation
- whether there will be games or entertainment

Give the groups 10 minutes to design their bar, then have them share their results. Ask participants to explain why they made the choices they did. Discuss how each of the characteristics affects alcohol consumption and blood alcohol level.

Discussion of "Cheers!" Guidelines

The U.S. Brewers Association distributes a set of guidelines called "Cheers! Six Keys to Operating Responsible Pubs." Here are some excerpts. Discuss whether or not the bars near your campus follow them.

- Make diversions available. Offer sections of the bar for pinball, darts, pool, and television. Provide sufficient lighting; a darker atmosphere is more conducive to drinking.
- Feature appealing foods. Protein-rich foods such as cheese and crackers or pizza can slow the absorption of alcohol. Providing good food can draw in more people and add to profits.
- Give nonalcoholic beverages equal billing. Provide an atmosphere in which students feel comfortable ordering nonalcoholic beverages.
- Use on-site aids for alcohol education. For example, posters, coasters, and napkins can carry messages on drinking and driving.
- Maintain high personnel standards. Bartenders and managers must have a responsible attitude toward acceptable drinking behavior. If the bar and personnel are potentially liable for contributing to alcohol-related accidents, extensive training may be needed.
- Follow constructive promotional practices. Maintain a philosophy of selling a moderate amount to many, in contrast to 2-for-1 drinks and low-cost happy hours. Offer entertainment to divert attention from preoccupation with just drinking.

Ask the group whether it is reasonable to expect campus bars to regulate themselves to promote low-risk drinking instead of maximizing profit.

On a Personal Level . . .

Now bring the discussion to a more personal level. We came up with a lot of things that influence drinking behaviors: family, friends, class load, general health-promoting habits, and advertising, just to name a few. Now look at some of the personal motivators for alcohol use.

Hand out "Find out Why *You* Drink . . ." This handout is for participants' information so that they can see some of the factors that influence their behavior. Have participants share any information or insights they feel comfortable discussing.

Conclusion and Evaluation (5 minutes)

Summarize the three main points of the workshop:

- Advertisers use a variety of techniques to encourage people to drink.

- Your family and friends influence your attitudes about drinking.
- Your knowledge of factors that influence drinking will help you make choices that are most beneficial for you, not for the alcohol industry.

Ask for questions from the participants. Offer resources and referrals for further information. Distribute Lifestyle Workshop evaluation forms and pencils. Allow time for completion and then collect. Briefly list and describe the other Lifestyle Workshops in Drugs and Alcohol Education.

MOST FREQUENTLY ASKED QUESTIONS

1. *What tactics do bars use to get people to drink more?*

Bars offer drink specials to attract customers. Small, crowded dance floors cause people to feel warmer and to drink more to cool down. When customers have to talk over loud music, they get thirsty because their throats get dry. Salty munchies also make people thirsty and likely to drink more.

2. *Why does the TV industry allow beer and wine commercials but not hard liquor commercials?*

Recently Seagrams attempted a $10 million TV ad campaign stating that a 12-oz can of beer, a 5-oz glass of wine, and a 1 1/4-oz shot of hard liquor all contained the same amount of alcohol. The networks refused to run the Seagrams' ads because of their long-standing prohibition against liquor ads (the TV industry is afraid of negative public reaction because the general public perceives hard liquor as harmful). Seagrams then ran the ads in newspapers and magazines instead. In August of 1985, the Federal Bureau of Alcohol, Tobacco, and Firearms ruled that not only was Seagrams' data accurate, but that the ads might help to shatter the consumer's view that wine and beer are "safe" beverages (*Newsweek*, Sept. 2, 1985, pg. 46).

3. *How much money do college newspapers make from alcohol ads?*

The following example details the alcohol ads in the University of Illinois campus newspaper, the *Daily Illini*. In 1985, there were 168,039 inches of local advertisements, 14,000 of which were alcohol-related (8.3% of the total). In 1985, there were 14,468 inches of national advertisements—1,295 were alcohol-related (8.9% of the total). Alcohol-related ads took up 15,295 inches of the *Daily Illini*'s advertising space in 1985. Alcohol ads ranked fourth in ads displayed (behind food, clothes, and stereos and records). Interestingly, first-quarter alcohol ads for 1986 went down 34% from the same period the previous year. The editor felt this drop was due to both local pressure and the fact that they stopped issuing a Saturday paper. Alcohol was highly advertised on Saturdays.

4. *Have drunk-driving accidents gone down since DUI (driving under the influence) laws went into effect in 1982?*

Since passage of the DUI laws, nationwide traffic fatalities have dropped: 28,000 in 1980; 28,100 in 1981; 25,600 in 1982; and 22,500 in 1983. That's an 18% decrease in fatalities since 1981.

5. *Are there different laws for advertising beer and wine?*

Many laws are the same, but a few are different. Both wine and beer advertisements

- should encourage proper use of alcohol,
- cannot correlate alcohol and success,
- must appeal only to those over 21,
- may not show alcohol and a car,
- may not degrade any ethnic or minority group,
- may not make false medicinal claims, and
- may not be sexually exploitative.

In addition, wine must be depicted with food and may not be advertised during a TV show that glamorizes alcohol. The Brewers Industry of America has developed additional rules for beer advertisements that work to their advantage in marketing.

- Beer ads should not associate beer drinking with situations requiring a high degree of alertness.
- Ads should not refer to the "strength" of the alcohol.
- Ads should not associate beer with crime or illegal activities.
- Taverns displayed in ads must be well-kept.

- Any comparisons between competitors must be fair.
- Alcohol should never be shown to enhance education.
- Beer ads on TV should not represent on-camera drinking, including any sound effects of drinking.
- Ads should never show littering.

6. *What effect do drinking habits of parents have on their children?*

Parental drinking habits play an important role in the formation of childrens' drinking habits. It has been shown that the children at highest risk are those at the ends of the spectrum. This means both children of parents who drink heavily and children of parents who abstain are the most prone to have drinking problems. Alcoholism has also been shown to be hereditary, though little is known about what causes this genetic link.

7. *How much does college affect a person's drinking habits, or are they established before that person comes to college?*

This is a question of patterns. If you have established patterns they may change slightly, but if you never drank before, this is when you will establish a pattern of consumption. The increased availability on campus does increase consumption for some people, however, it is a very individualistic change.

8. *Is subliminal seduction still used in advertising?*

Subliminal seduction is still used with a fair amount of regularity, as evidenced in many magazines and newspapers. For example, when an ad contains a drawing of a large beer can, this is a subliminal message implying quantity. It has been proven that when quantity and availability are implied, consumption increases.

Alcohol's Effects on the Body

A number of factors will determine how individuals react differently, given the same amount of alcohol, or on different occasions:

Speed of drinking—The more rapidly the beverage is ingested, the higher the peak blood alcohol concentration (BAC). The liver metabolizes about 1/2 ounce of alcohol per hour.

Presence of food in the stomach—Eating while drinking slows down the absorption rate. When alcoholic beverages are taken with a substantial meal, peak BAC may be reduced by as much as 50%.

Other chemicals in the beverage—The greater the amount of nonalcoholic chemicals in the beverage, the more slowly the alcohol is absorbed (e.g., vodka is absorbed more rapidly than beer or wine).

Body weight—A larger person has more blood and requires greater amounts of alcohol to reach a given BAC.

Drinking history/tolerance—Increasing amounts of alcohol are needed to result in the physical and behavioral reactions formerly produced at lesser concentrations, if there is a long history of drinking.

Environment—There may be differences in alcohol's effects depending upon where one drinks (e.g., local bar, with family, hostile environment, etc.).

The drinker's expectations—Many people become intoxicated on less alcohol merely because they have that expectation before they begin drinking.

General state of emotional and physical health—Many people seem more susceptible to the effects of alcohol when they are extremely fatigued, have recently been ill, or are under emotional stress and strain. The usual amount of alcohol may result in uncomfortable effects.

Sex differences—Given the same amount of alcohol, and proportional to body weight, females will generally have a higher BAC than their male counterparts, due to less body fluids to dilute the alcohol and also due to more body fat. Females are generally more affected by alcohol just prior to menstruation. Females taking birth control pills or medications containing estrogen may remain intoxicated longer than those who do not, due to the liver's function of metabolizing both.

Other drugs—Prescription, over-the-counter, illicit, and unrecognized drugs all have potential reactions with alcohol. One should be aware of the additive and synergistic effects when these drugs are mixed with alcohol.

When you drink alcohol, 20% is absorbed immediately into the bloodstream, with the rest quickly processed through the gastrointestinal tract. Alcohol, classified as a depressant drug, affects the functions of the brain.

BAL	*This much alcohol causes . . .*
.05	Lowered alertness; released inhibitions; mental relaxation, disrupted judgment; less concern about environment.
.10	Impaired movements and coordination; slowed reaction time; exaggerated emotions; impaired vision.
.20	Marked abnormality of bodily and sensory functions; feeling of need to lie down; inability to stand or walk without help; confusion/tears/rage occur easily.
.30	Stupor and near unconsciousness; lack of comprehension of what is seen or heard.
.40-.50	Loss of feeling; unconsciousness; shock; breathing and heartbeat possibly stop.

Note. Reprinted by permission from ALCOHOL by Brent Hafen and Molly Brog. Copyright © 1983 2/E by West Publishing Company. All rights reserved.

Blood Alcohol Levels by Gender

Comparisons of Blood Alcohol Levels by Sex, Weight, and Consumption

Absolute alcohol (oz)	Beverage intake in 1 hr	Blood alcohol levels (mg/100 ml)					
		Female (100 lb)	Male (100 lb)	Female (150 lb)	Male (150 lb)	Female (200 lb)	Male (200 lb)
1/2	1 oz spirits* 1 glass wine 1 can beer	0.045	0.037	0.03	0.025	0.022	0.019
1	2 oz spirits 2 glasses wine 2 cans beer	0.090	0.075	0.06	0.050	0.045	0.037
2	4 oz spirits 4 glasses wine 4 cans beer	0.180	0.150	0.12	0.100	0.090	0.070
3	6 oz spirits 6 glasses wine 6 cans beer	0.270	0.220	0.18	0.150	0.130	0.110
4	8 oz spirits 8 glasses wine 8 cans beer	0.360	0.300	0.24	0.200	0.180	0.150
5	10 oz spirits 10 glasses wine 10 cans beer	0.450	0.370	0.30	0.250	0.220	0.180

Note. From *Drugs, Society & Human Behavior* (4th ed.) by O. Ray and C. Ksir, 1987, St. Louis: Times Mirror/Mosby. Copyright 1987. Reprinted by permission.

*100-proof spirits.

Communicating Your Concerns

It is not so much the *amount* one drinks, *what* one drinks, or *when* one drinks that determines problem drinking, but rather *what happens* when one drinks alcohol. What happens when you drink alcohol may affect you in these different life areas: social, academic, financial, legal, personal, and health. For example, you may:

- End up in an acute injury clinic.
- Go to class or work after drinking.
- Get arrested for driving under the influence (DUI).
- Offend or hurt a date/friend while drunk.
- Do something that you later regret.

There may be times when you see someone's drinking get out of line. You may be affected *directly* (something is said by that person that embarrasses you) or *indirectly* (you see the person act in ways he or she would not normally act, which would be embarrassing to him or her). When you see these kinds of things, it may be helpful to talk to that person about your concerns.

Guidelines for Discussing Alcohol Abuse

1. Choose a time and place that is comfortable when the person is sober.
2. Decide whether the person will respect your feelings or if there is a more appropriate person (e.g., best friend, roommate) whom he or she will listen to.
3. Find out if anyone else was affected the same way you were by that person's drinking behaviors.
4. Describe the specific actions or remarks that bothered you. Do not be vague about the consequences of the behaviors you described.
5. Do not criticize, diagnose, or judge your friend's actions (e.g., ''You have a drinking problem''). Explain that you want to share your concerns because you care for him or her.
6. After sharing your list of behaviors, let your friend accept or reject what you have said. Do not get into excuses; stay on the offensive.

Be aware that your friend may react in several ways (e.g., thankful, angry, upset, or indifferent). If he or she reacts defensively, do not take it personally, but rather feel good about doing your friend a service that may not be recognized as such at that time. For further information and resources about alcohol, problem drinking, and learning how to talk to someone about their drinking, call Alcoholics Anonymous/Alanon, your local mental health department, or look for substance abuse counselors and clinics in the phone book.

Find Out Why You Drink . . .

Some of the reasons people give for drinking alcohol are listed below. Read the lists and put a mark beside the reasons for drinking that most closely resemble your own. After you have read each list and marked your responses, tally how many marks you made in each of the three groups, then look at the bottom of the page to find out why *you* drink.

Group 1

I drink because it helps me . . .
  feel more like my real self.
  feel less depressed, frustrated, or angry.
  feel like I'm just as good as or better than other people.
  have something to do; it keeps me from being bored.

Group 2

When I drink I . . .
  drink very quickly, gulping my beverage.
  sometimes black out or forget things.
  become aggressive and sometimes fight or argue.
  often drink alone.

Group 3

I drink so that . . .
  I will feel more comfortable in a party environment.
  I will feel more socially accepted.
  I will feel more popular and more relaxed.
  my friends will stop pressuring me.

If you have more marks beside the items in the first group of statements, you probably drink to change your moods or attitudes. If the majority of your marks is in the second group, you probably drink for physical reasons. If most of your marks are in the third group of statements, you probably drink for social reasons.

REFERENCES

Duncan, D., & Gold, R. (1982). *Drugs and the whole person*. New York: Wiley.

Gross, L. (1983). *How much is too much? The effects of social drinking*. New York: Ballantine.

Hafen, B., & Brog, M.V. (1983). *Alcohol* (2nd ed.). St. Paul, MN: West.

Kinney, J., & Leaten, G. (1983). *Loosening the grip* (2nd ed.). St. Louis: Mosby.

National Institute on Alcohol Abuse and Alcoholism. (1981). *Spectrum: Alcohol problem prevention for women by women*. (DHHS Publication No. ADM 81-1036). Washington, DC: U.S. Government Printing Office.

National Technical Information Service. (1983). *Alcohol involvement in U.S. traffic accidents: Where it is changing*. (NHTSA Technical Report No. DOT HS 806 733). Springfield, VA: National Highway Traffic Safety Administration.

Ray, O., & Ksir, C. (1987). *Drugs, society, and human behavior* (4th ed.). St. Louis: Times Mirror/Mosby.

United States Brewers Association. *Cheers! Six keys to operating responsible pubs*. Washington, DC: Author.

Speaking of Sex . . . Lifestyle Workshop

PARAPROFESSIONAL PREPARATION MATERIALS

Training Sessions

Competency Exam

Texts and Suggested Readings

WORKSHOP AT A GLANCE

Presenter Information

Most Frequently Asked Questions

Handouts and Visual Aids*

References

---

*Intimate Communication: Where Did They Go Wrong? and Sexual Choices: Spontaneous or Safe? were written by Beth Chamberlain.

TRAINING SESSION

Speaking of Sex . . .

Session 1: Workshop Presentation

Time:	60 minutes
Methods:	Presentation, demonstration
Description:	Trainer presents workshop to Lifestyle Educators.
Readings:	The workshop

Session 2: Coming to Terms With Your Sexuality

Time:	60 minutes
Methods:	Lecture, discussion, brainstorming, scenario discussion
Description:	Definition and components of sexuality. Explore and clarify the meanings and origins of values.
Activities:	Brainstorm to generate discussion of prevalent sex myths in our society and a general discussion of why they are myths. Lifestyle Educators list advantages and disadvantages of being male and female. Discuss sex role stereotypes and gender identity. Read and discuss values clarification exercise.
Readings:	Materials on sexuality and values clarification
Competency exam questions:	1, 2, 3, 4

Session 3: Barriers to and Enablers for Communication of Intimate Needs

Time:	60 minutes
Methods:	Discussion, role-playing, practice
Description:	Discussion of ways to effectively communicate intimate needs and resolve values conflicts that may arise in an intimate relationship.
Activities:	Role-play situations of communicating about contraception and sexually transmitted disease. Discuss and practice facilitating workshop handout "Sexual Choices: Spontaneous or Safe?" Discuss and practice facilitating workshop handout "Intimate Communication: Where Did They Go Wrong?"
Readings:	The workshop
Competency exam questions:	5, 6, 7, 8, 9, 10, 11, 12, 13, 14, 15, 16, 17, 18, 19

Session 4: "Most Frequently Asked Questions" Review and Hot Seat

Time:	60 minutes
Methods:	Discussion, practice
Description:	Review "Most Frequently Asked Questions" and other workshop components.
Activity:	Hot Seat: Each Lifestyle Educator is quizzed by other students on workshop topic for 10 minutes.
Readings:	The workshop

Session 5: Practice Workshop Presentation

Time: 60 minutes

Method: Presentation

Activity: Each Lifestyle Educator presents
20 minutes of the workshop.

Readings: The workshop

COMPETENCY EXAM

This test will depend on the abilities of paraprofessionals to write short-answer and short-essay responses.

1. Define the term *sexuality*, including the necessary components for a complete definition.

2. Give an example of a sexual value, and name the three steps one must go through to make a value one's own.

3. Why is values clarification an important part of intimate communication?

4. What are four influences that may shape our values?

5. What are the four types of intimacy exhibited in relationships? Give an example of each.

6. What are three benefits of discussing sexual needs with your partner?

7. How is discussing sexual intimacy different from discussing other types of intimacy? Why?

8. What are three reasons someone might give for entering into a sexually intimate relationship?

9. Based on the article "Are You Ready for Sex?" give at least five criteria of a person who is ready for sexual intimacy.

10. What effect do alcohol and other drugs have on sexual decision-making?

11. Give and explain two examples of conflicts between sexual needs.

12. Define and describe the process of "active listening."

13. Give an example of a conflict between verbal and nonverbal communication.

14. What is the difference between open-ended and closed questions? Give an example of each.

15. At a workshop someone claims that it's only fair for a woman to have sexual intercourse after a date if the man has spent a great deal of money on her. How would you respond?

16. You are leading the "Sexually Speaking" workshop and a participant asks you, "What is the best reason for wanting to have sex?" What is your reply?

17. A participant claims that it's a person's right to expect sexual intimacy if the partner does not say "no" or does not physically try to stop him or her. Indicate how you would address this statement.

18. Julie is a sexually active woman. Although she doesn't feel she must be "in love" with a sexual partner, she feels physically attractive and desirable when someone wants to become sexually intimate with her. Her parents are very strict, and she feels that sex is one way for her to express her independence. She also believes that sex is the only way to hold on to someone. Besides, she doesn't want her friends to think that she is a prude, and she wants to fit in when her friends talk about sexual experiences. Knowing Julie's motives or reasons for intercourse, how do you think these reasons may affect her relationships?

19. You are having a conversation with a student who is unsure about whether she's ready to become sexually intimate with her boyfriend. Based on your knowledge of sexual needs and communication, indicate concrete guidelines she may use to resolve her conflict. Be specific regarding ways to foster communication between herself and her partner.

20. Suggest possible techniques to use in the workshop if participant is one of the following:
    • Recognition Seeker (frequently calls attention to self)
    • Conversationalist (brings up off-the-subject anecdotes and is a noisy distraction)
    • Moralizer (advocates judgmental points of view based on personal convictions)
    • Conservative (convinced that the status quo does not need changing)

TEXTS AND SUGGESTED READINGS

Allgur, E. (1985). Are you ready for sex? Informed consent for sexual intimacy. *SIECUS Report*, **13**(6), 8-9.

Carrera, M., & Calderone, M. (1980). The SIECUS/UPPSALA principles basic to education for sexuality. *SIECUS Report*, **8**(3), 8-9.

Ferguson, T., & Strayhorn, J. (1982). Better communication: Use facilitative messages. *Medical Self-Care*, **16**, 34-37.

Ferm, D. (1971). *Responsible sexuality now*. New York: Seabury.

Franceour, R. (1984). *Becoming a sexual person*. New York: Wiley.

Gordon, S. (1979). Coming to terms with your own sexuality first. *Journal of School Health*, **49**(5), 247-250.

Strayhorn, J. (1977). *Talking it out: A guide to effective communication and problem solving*. Champaign, IL: Research Press.

WORKSHOP AT A GLANCE

The goal of this workshop is to provide participants with necessary skills to identify and effectively communicate intimate needs. This workshop takes approximately 60 minutes to present. Suggested attendance is 10 to 20 persons.

Objectives

Within the content of this workshop, the following objectives will be met.

- Different types and reasons for intimacy in a relationship will be explored.
- Participants will practice expressing their needs and considering their partners' needs through the "Sexual Bill of Rights" exercise.
- Participants will demonstrate concrete examples of communication guidelines in order to resolve two hypothetical conflicts.

Workshop Materials

- Workshop sign-in sheet
- Newsprint, easel, and markers
- Handouts and Visual Aids: *Intimate Communication: Where Did They Go Wrong?*, and *Sexual Choices: Spontaneous or Safe?*
- Blank paper
- Lifestyle Workshop evaluation forms and pencils

PRESENTER INFORMATION

Briefly introduce yourself, your background, and any other personal information you choose to share. Describe your health promotion program and the topics available, such as fitness and nutrition. Stress that the workshops are unique because you bring them to their living areas. Lifestyle Workshop paraprofessionals are trained at (your institution or program) to present these workshops. If anyone is interested in the training program, ask him or her to speak with you after the workshop.

You may want to present this information in the following manner: For many people, college is a time when the meaning of the word "independence" is fully understood. No longer is anyone there to tell you when you should be home or whom you may go out with. By the same token, *you* are now the only person who can ultimately make the decisions for yourself and live with the benefits or consequences of your actions. One of the decisions that must be made is how to conduct yourself in a sexually responsible manner, both to yourself and to others. This workshop will enable you to explore your feelings about whether you want to be sexually active, and if so, with whom, and will help you learn how to communicate these decisions to a prospective partner.

Types of Intimacy (5 minutes)

There are at least four different types of intimacy that may be desired in a given relationship.

- Intellectual intimacy: Your relationship is based to some extent on intellectual exchange with another person.
- Emotional intimacy: Emotional attachment is a major aspect of the relationship, as with close friends and family members.
- Spiritual intimacy: Some higher level of spiritual commonality is shared. This might occur in awareness groups or religious groups.
- Physical intimacy: Some level of physical involvement is important to the relationship.

Discuss how some relationships include all of these types of intimacy, while others include a few or only one.

Reasons for Physical Intimacy (5 minutes)

Physical intimacy means that you have made the decision to include some form of sexual activity in the relationship. People have different reasons for choosing to be sexually active in a relationship. Ask the participants to list some reasons for sharing sex in a relationship and list their answers on newsprint. Here are some important reasons the group may discuss.

- Expression of love and caring
- Playful activity
- Duty or responsibility to partner
- Cure for loneliness
- Proving independence from parents or former lovers
- Peer pressure
- Physical pleasure
- Means of personal gain
- Pleasing your partner
- Reproduction
- Experimenting or curiosity

Do not attempt to evaluate these reasons. Discuss that different people have different values and that when or why one wants to become sexually active is an individual decision.

Needs Clarification and Communication (20 minutes)

Sometimes two people in a relationship have different needs for sexual intimacy. Discuss how to handle such a conflict: The first step is to determine your personal needs, motivations, and values. In doing this, you must understand why you hold these values, and why you feel these motivations and needs. It is important here to separate your needs and values from those of your parents and friends. In addition to determining your feelings about intimacy, you should consider other issues such as sexual responsibility, contraception, and sexually transmitted disease prevention.

Sexual Bill of Rights

Hand out blank paper and ask participants to title it "My Bill of Rights." Ask participants to list the rights they expect in an intimate relationship. To stimulate thinking, offer examples, such as the following:

- I have the right to know if my partner has a sexually transmitted disease.
- I have the right to say "no" to any sexual advances.
- I have the right to discuss contraception *before* becoming intimately involved.

Ask participants to share examples from their Bill of Rights with the group, and list these on a sheet of newsprint taped to the wall. Ask the group how they feel these rights could be communicated in a relationship. Now ask each participant to list his or her *responsibilities* as a partner. Start another list on a clean sheet of newsprint. Some examples might be these:

- I am responsible for telling my partner about any sexually transmitted diseases I carry.
- I am responsible for clearly communicating my sexual needs and limits to my partner.
- I must take responsibility to use or ask my partner to use a condom and be prepared to use a safe method of birth control.

The second step is to communicate your needs to your partner. This may be difficult because social messages are still against talking about sexual intimacy—that it's not a subject "nice" people discuss. Another reason sex isn't discussed is that many people lack the vocabulary to carry on a meaningful discussion.

The Language of Intimacy

Divide participants into three groups. Direct one group to think of all the terms possible for female sexual anatomy, another to think of all the possible terms for male sexual anatomy, and the third group to think of all possible terms for sexual intercourse. When the groups have finished, discuss these questions:

- Why do we have so many different slang terms for sexual words?

- Would you use different terms when talking to your parents than talking with your friends? Your partner? Why?
- What kinds of feelings did you experience while brainstorming about these terms?

Once it has been explained that being comfortable with sexual terminology will make discussions of sexual needs, motivations, and values easier, share these guidelines for fostering intimate communication.

- You are responsible for your own sexual fulfillment. You must tell your partner what level of intimacy you feel comfortable with. It is important to communicate what feels good and what doesn't. Remember that no one can read your mind!
- Acknowledge your fears. It is okay to realize that you are afraid to bring up issues related to sexual intimacy. Once you realize what your fears are and why they exist, you can take steps to conquer them.
- Decide when and where you want to discuss sex. Too often people wait until they are sexually aroused to discuss sexual issues. It's best to discuss sexual intimacy, contraception, and sexually transmitted diseases when you have a clear head and can rationally discuss your needs.
- Listen actively. Communicating means more than just talking. Many problems with communication surface because the listener does not really hear or understand the message. This can be prevented by clarifying or rephrasing the message before you respond to it.
- Use "I" messages rather than "You" messages. "I" messages include I feel, I want, I hear, I need, I don't understand. "I" messages open channels of communication and promote a blameless atmosphere. Only use "you" messages in a positive manner: "You really make me feel good."
- Stay focused. Don't use blanket statements like "we always" or "we never." If something bothers you, cite a specific example such as "On our last date, I felt angry when our conversation about contraception was interrupted by the basketball game on TV" rather than "We are always interrupted by things when we talk" (McKay, Davis, & Fanning, 1983).

Dilemmas in Sexual Decision-Making (20 minutes)

Now that you have discussed some guidelines for communicating, introduce situations where needs may conflict and discuss how these situations could be resolved. Hand out "Intimate Communication." Read the questions to the group and lead a discussion. Follow the same process for the handout "Sexual Choices." After reading the scenario from the handout, discuss what would be a good time and place to discuss sexual intimacy, contraception, and sexually transmitted diseases? Also discuss using "I" statements, such as "I feel like I'm ready to become physically intimate with you and I'd like to hear your needs," or "I have a friend who has experienced an unplanned pregnancy in his relationship. I want to make sure that we can prevent that from happening to us."

Again, stay focused. Practice using statements like, "There may be other areas of our relationship we need to discuss, but right now I'm really interested in hearing what you feel your needs are regarding physical intimacy."

Conclusion and Evaluation (5 minutes)

Summarize the main points of the workshop:

- There are different types of intimacy and many reasons for intimacy.
- Be honest—clarify and express your own intimate needs as well as considering your partner's needs.
- Stay focused on your needs and encourage open communication with your partner.

Ask for questions from the participants. Offer resources and referrals for further information. Distribute Lifestyle Workshop evaluation forms and pencils. Allow time for completion and then collect. Briefly list and describe the other Lifestyle Workshops in Sexuality.

MOST FREQUENTLY ASKED QUESTIONS

1. *Are the issues discussed here specific to heterosexual relationships?*

   No. Some of the issues in heterosexual relationships also come up in some homosexual relationships. There may be additional issues in both kinds of relationships that are specific to the individuals involved. However, since relationships take place between two individuals, many of the dilemmas may be similar.

2. *Is there any ultimately correct decision to make?*

   Only you can know what is best for you; sometimes this is very hard, for in every relationship something different may be right. There are no steadfast rules. What is important is that you understand your values and are comfortable with them when entering into a relationship.

3. *What is the best reason to have sex?*

   There are many reasons people decide to have sex, ranging from the expression of love to having a playful physical activity. Your sexual values will dictate *your* best reasons for having or not having intercourse.

4. *What effects does alcohol have on sexuality?*

   Alcohol lessens inhibitions and so increases desire, but because it is a depressant, it decreases sexual capability. People under the influence of alcohol may not use good judgment in making decisions. It is important to practice safe drinking in social situations.

5. *How do you know what values are really yours and not ones imposed by friends and parents?*

   You need to think about what you *personally* value—not what your friends or parents value. Think, for example, what you would do if you were alone with someone on a deserted island. You knew you would be rescued in a few days. No one would know what went on but you and this person, who will not pressure you in any way. What would you do? If you feel good about your behavior, your values will be consistent with your actions.

6. *How do you objectively tell someone your feelings about sexual activities and not come off looking "easy" or like a "prude"?*

   Sometimes you may be misinterpreted, but if you are honest, you can hope that others will respond honestly and not make assumptions. Maybe you could teach others the merits of speaking honestly without anyone feeling you are "easy." If someone feels your honesty is "prudish," perhaps you need to reevaluate your relationship with that person. That person may need some lessons in communication and relationships.

7. *How can I remain spontaneous and still prevent conflicts in intimate communication?*

   With the independence of making choices about sexual behavior comes the responsibility to you and your partner to discuss issues surrounding sexual needs, contraception, and STDs. You have to decide whether you want to base your relationship on spontaneity or open communication and then live with those consequences.

8. *How do you resolve a situation where experiences you've had (or want to have) conflict with your value system?*

You need to look at the specific experience and understand the reason you made or want to make that decision. Figure out whether it conflicts with your values because of fear or whether it actually goes against your values. You might try talking with friends or a counselor just to get a clear perspective, not to have them tell you what to do.

9. *What does having sex "for procreation only" mean?*

Having sexual intercourse for procreation means for the sole purpose of reproducing. A person with this belief would feel that sex is only acceptable when a couple is trying to have children.

10. *Does this workshop assume that everyone has had sexual intercourse?*

No. Please don't feel that we expect everyone who attends this workshop to be sexually active. We are talking about past and present as well as potential future situations. We emphasize that "sex" means different things to different people, so please interpret the word to fit your values and lifestyle.

11. *Isn't it always the female who sets limits on how far to go sexually?*

Definitely not. If a male isn't comfortable with what a couple is doing or thinks things are going too far, he has just as much right to say "stop." In fact, part of this workshop is meant to encourage both males and females to decide what types of activities are acceptable in a relationship and when. Too often men are caught in a stereotypical role and feel pressure to have intercourse. Men should know themselves and be able to set some limits if they choose, just like women.

12. *How can I tell my partner what hurts without sounding like I'm blaming or without making him or her feel defensive?*

The key to facilitating communication is remaining positive. Try to focus on emphasizing what feels good. Use "I" language to remove the blame from the other person. There is a big difference between, "I really like it when you . . ." as opposed to "You always stroke me too hard." Everyone has different ideas about what feels good, and the only way to find out from your partner is to ask!

Intimate Communication:
Where Did They Go Wrong?

Kevin and Terri met in college and had been dating for several months. They felt close to one another and really enjoyed spending time together. Kevin was Terri's first serious boyfriend. However, Kevin had dated quite a few people before meeting Terri. The only problem with their relationship was that they had different views about where sex fits into a relationship. Terri liked the physical and romantic intimacy they shared but strongly valued her virginity. Kevin was more sexually experienced and wanted more physical intimacy. He was becoming frustrated and decided to voice his feelings to Terri one night when things were becoming more and more physically intimate:

Terri, you don't seem to be interested in having sex with me and I really feel that it's important to include this in our relationship to become closer. If you really love me, you will understand my needs.

Terri, upset and hurt, replied, "You always ask me to do things I don't want to do. You obviously don't care about me enough to understand why I can't sleep with you. Maybe you should go find someone who will!" With that she stormed out of the room leaving a confused and frustrated Kevin behind.

Questions for Discussion

1. *What are Terri's needs in this relationship?*
2. *What are Kevin's needs in this relationship?*
3. *What guidelines for open communication were violated by Kevin and Terri?*
4. *Based on your understanding of Kevin's and Terri's individual needs, how would you rewrite the communication between them?*

Sexual Choices:
Spontaneous or Safe?

You and your close friend, John, are discussing his relationship with Judy, a steady girlfriend. John thinks that they are both ready to think about making sex a part of their relationship. Unfortunately, they have not yet discussed it, and John has some confusion about the best way to bring up contraception and sexually transmitted diseases without offending Judy. On one hand, he wants to be spontaneous and romantic by just letting it happen; but on the other hand, he has a friend who recently fathered a child due to poor planning.

He asks you for advice about whether he should bring up these issues. Based on your knowledge of intimate communication, what concrete suggestions would you give him to resolve his dilemma?

REFERENCES

Crooks, R., & Baur, K. (1987). *Our sexuality* (3rd ed.). Menlo Park, CA: Benjamin/Cummings.

Franceour, R. (1984). *Becoming a sexual person.* New York: Wiley.

Hyde, J. (1986). *Understanding human sexuality* (3rd ed.). New York: McGraw-Hill.

McKay, M., Davis, M., & Fanning, P. (1983). *Messages: The communication book.* Oakland, CA: New Harbinger.

Choosing Contraceptives Lifestyle Workshop

PARAPROFESSIONAL PREPARATION MATERIALS

Training Sessions

Competency Exam

Texts and Suggested Readings

WORKSHOP AT A GLANCE

Presenter Information

Most Frequently Asked Questions

Handouts and Visual Aids

References

TRAINING SESSIONS

Choosing Contraceptives

Session 1: Workshop Presentation

Time: 60 minutes

Methods: Presentation, demonstration

Description: Trainer presents workshop to Lifestyle Educators.

Readings: The workshop

Session 2: Overview of Contraception

Time: 60 minutes

Methods: Lecture, discussion, brainstorming activity

Description: Overview of male and female sexual anatomy and physiology. Overview of contraception and birth control methods, including theoretical and actual effective rates, oral contraceptives, diaphragm, cervical cap, sponge, condom, IUD, permanent methods, natural family planning, withdrawal, and chance.

Activity: Brainstorm about terms for sexual anatomy and activity. Discuss slang vocabulary used in sexual communication, including why terms may reflect different values.

Readings: Materials on anatomy, physiology, and contraception, the workshop

Competency exam questions: 15, 17, 18

Session 3: Issues in New Contraceptive Technology

Time: 60 minutes

Methods: Lecture, discussion, presentation, brainstorming activity

Description: Analysis of new contraceptive technologies and factors affecting contraceptive decision-making.

Activity: Participants brainstorm about reasons that someone may not use a particular contraceptive method and potential ways to enhance contraceptive use.

Readings: Materials on factors that affect contraceptive methods and use in the college population, the workshop

Competency exam questions: 2, 3, 4, 5, 6, 7, 8, 9, 10, 11, 12, 13, 14, 15, 16, 17, 18

Session 4: "Most Frequently Asked Questions" Review and Hot Seat

Time: 60 minutes

Methods: Discussion, practice

Description: Review "Most Frequently Asked Questions" section of the workshop and other workshop components.

Activity: Hot Seat: Each Lifestyle Educator is quizzed by the other students on the workshop topic for 10 minutes.

Readings: The workshop

Session 5: Practice Workshop Presentation

Time: 60 minutes

Method: Presentation

Description: Each Lifestyle Educator presents
20 minutes of the workshop.

Readings: The workshop

COMPETENCY EXAM

The following questions require brief responses.

1. Explain the function of each sexual anatomy structure listed below:
   - Ovary:

   - Fallopian tube:

   - Uterus:

   - Cervix:

   - Vagina:

   - Clitoris:

   - Penis:

   - Seminiferous tubules:

   - Epididymis:

- Vas deferens:

- Prostate:

- Cowper's gland:

- Urethra (male):

2. Name two slang terms used to describe sexual intercourse and discuss the values that may be reflected by each.

3. Name the two hormones (synthetic or natural) that make up the combined Pill, and explain their mechanism of action. How is this mechanism different from that of the mini-Pill?

4. The Pill's danger signals fit the mnemonic device "ACHES." What do each of these letters stand for?

5. What are the three *female* barrier contraceptive methods? How would you suggest a student obtain each?

6. What are three ways a male can participate in the use of a diaphragm?

7. Two side effects of condom use are allergy to rubber and insufficient lubrication. Discuss two ways these might be corrected.

8. List two benefits and disadvantages of the combined Pill and the condom.

9. Define reflexive ovulation and list three possible causes.

10. Explain the step-by-step process for the use of spermicidal jelly, foam, and suppositories.

11. Indicate whether a back-up method is suggested for each of the following methods: Pill, IUD, Diaphragm, Condom, and Sponge.

12. What are two *temporary* conditions that may cause the birth control pill to be less effective?

13. Describe the difference between theoretical and actual effectiveness rates. Give two reasons that the effectiveness rates differ.

14. List the three methods of determining fertile times using natural family planning. Briefly describe how each method is used.

15. How do tubal ligation and vasectomy work to prevent pregnancy? Be specific when naming structures involved.

16. Name three reasons people might not use contraception even when they have all of the factual information necessary for decision making.

17. What is the effectiveness rate of the chance method?

18. You are an educator in a family planning clinic. Based on your knowledge of lifestyle issues regarding contraceptive choices, indicate which method(s) would be appropriate to each situation and which method(s) you would not advise. Present your rationale for each decision.
    - A woman who is sexually active with many partners.

    - Someone who is deeply concerned with future fertility and feels comfortable with her sexual partner.

    - A 38-year-old woman who is a smoker and would like maximal male involvement in birth control.

    - A woman who is not yet sexually active but intends to be soon. She is very concerned with spontaneity due to her inexperience with sexual intercourse.

    - A woman who is adamantly against abortion and is therefore concerned with both the effectiveness and mechanics of various methods. She prefers the fewest potential side effects.

    - Someone who has difficulty remembering things but has a steady partner very involved in contraception.

19. Suggest possible techniques to use in the workshop if a participant is one of the following:
    - Recognition Seeker (frequently calls attention to self)
    - Conversationalist (brings up off-the-subject anecdotes and is a noisy distraction)
    - Moralizer (advocates judgmental points of view based on personal convictions)
    - Conservative (convinced that the status quo does not need changing)

TEXTS AND SUGGESTED READINGS

Cherniak, D. (1979). *A book about birth control.* Montreal: Montreal Health Press.

Cooke, C., & Dworkin, S. (1979). *The Ms. guide to a woman's health.* Garden City, NY: Anchor Press/Doubleday.

Franceour, R. (1984). *Becoming a sexual person.* New York: Wiley.

Hatcher, R., Guest, F., Stewart, F., Stewart, G., Trussel, J., Bowen, S., & Cates, W. (1988). *Contraceptive technology 1988-1989* (14th ed.). New York: Irvington.

Hister, N., & Macrina, D. (1985). The health belief model and the contraceptive behavior of college women: Implications for education. *Journal of American College Health, 33,* 245-251.

Planned Parenthood Federation of America. (1982). *Basics of birth control.*

U.S. Department of Health and Human Services (PHS). (1987, Winter). *Facts about AIDS.*

U.S. Department of Health and Human Services (PHS). (1986). *Surgeon General's report on acquired immune deficiency syndrome.*

WORKSHOP AT A GLANCE

The goal of this workshop is to provide current, accurate information on contraception and birth control, thereby promoting participants' informed contraceptive choices. This workshop takes approximately 60 minutes to present. Suggested attendance is 10 to 20 persons.

Objectives

Within the content of the workshop, the following objectives will be met:

- Through a demonstration and the use of the handout "Birth Control Guide At a Glance," participants will be able to compare and contrast various contraceptive methods for appropriateness, effectiveness, methodology, and risks.
- Participants will assess their lifestyles and attitudes relative to various contraceptive choices.
- Using the film "Condom Sense," the use of condoms as a method of choice is encouraged.

Workshop Materials

- Workshop sign-in sheet
- Handouts and visual aids: *Birth Control Guide at a Glance, Effectiveness Rates,* and the film: *Condom Sense** which can be ordered from: Perennial Education, Inc., 930 Pitner Avenue, Evanston, IL 60202.
- Birth control bag containing an example of each method and a plastic pelvic model
- 24 condoms
- Lifestyle Workshop evaluation forms and pencils

---

*If for any reason you are not able to obtain the film, you will find the structure of this workshop is designed to present the information covered in the film.

PRESENTER INFORMATION

Briefly introduce yourself, your background, and any other personal information you choose to share. Describe your health promotion program and the topics available, such as nutrition and fitness. Stress that the workshops are unique because you bring them to their living areas. Lifestyle Workshop paraprofessionals are trained at (your institution or program) to present these workshops. If anyone is interested in the training program, ask him or her to speak with you after the workshop.

You may want to present this in the following manner: It is by no means a secret that college students are a very sexually active segment of the population. It is also no secret that many students do not have intercourse for the purpose of reproduction. Many people are not aware of the different contraceptive choices available, or they are not accurately informed about how to properly use these methods. In this workshop, we discuss all the different methods of contraception and birth control, specifically the effectiveness rates, methodology, risks and side effects, and some lifestyle benefits and disadvantages. As a result of this program, participants may be better able to make informed decisions about which method to use and to use the method correctly every time. If you're not sexually active right now, this information may be useful in the future.

Film Presentation and Contraception Instruction (55 minutes)

Show the film "Condom Sense" (15 minutes) and lead a birth control and contraceptives discussion (40 minutes). Explain that Quiz Questions (**QQ**) will be asked of the group during the workshop. A condom will be given to the person who answers correctly. The Quiz Answers (**QA**) to the **QQ**s will have been given in the film.

QQ: *What's the difference between contraception and birth control?*

QA: Birth control prevents live births, but fertilization can occur. Contraceptives prevent the egg and sperm from meeting.

Generate a list of questions people might ask themselves when looking for a method of contraception or birth control. You may want to list these on a poster board and leave it up during the workshop. This would make an excellent visual aid.

- How effective is it?
- Are there side effects?
- Will it affect my future fertility?
- How comfortable do I feel about touching myself?
- How comfortable is my relationship with my partner?
- Will this have an impact on my religious beliefs?
- Do I have a good memory?

Show the poster "Effectiveness Rates" (see handouts and visual aids section) and leave it up during the workshop. Explain the two effectiveness rates that will be given with each method: (a) *Theoretical*—this rate is for the perfect person who uses the method correctly every time. The theoretical rate shows how effective the method is when the only chance for failure is if the *method* fails. (b) *Actual*—this rate takes into consideration that people make mistakes. The actual rate shows how effective the method is when failure is due to incorrect usage. Hand out "Birth Control Guide at a Glance." This handout will be referred to throughout the workshop. Discuss each method of contraception or birth control using the same format:

- Show the device or explain the method.
- Explain mechanism of action or how it works.
- Explain methodology or how it's used.
- Discuss the effectiveness rates, both theoretical and actual.
- Discuss side effects and possible long-term complications.
- Discuss benefits and advantages.
- Discuss medical contraindications or inadvisability.
- Discuss lifestyle considerations, including male participation.
- Answer questions.

Some methods, such as the Pill, may take longer to explain than others.

Oral Contraceptives

This is a discussion of the combined and mini-Pill methods. Pass the pill pack around so everyone in the group can examine it.

Explain the mechanism of action for the combination pill. A synthetic estrogen that prevents ovulation is combined with synthetic progesterone (progestin) that prevents the thickening of the uterine lining and thickens cervical mucous. In this way, sperm have a harder time reaching the egg, and if the sperm and egg do meet, implantation cannot occur. The Pill mimics pregnancy; it tricks your body into thinking it's pregnant.

Explain the mechanism of action for the mini-Pill. The mini-Pill contains progestin only. A woman can ovulate, but the uterine lining will not allow implantation. The mini-Pill is used by women who cannot take estrogen for physical or personal reasons.

Methodology

1. Start taking pills the Sunday after your period begins.
2. Take one pill every day for 21 days. Take the pill at the *same time* each day. Some women try to associate pill-taking with an activity such as breakfast to help them remember to take them.
3. Contraceptive pills put you on a 28-day cycle. You do not take pills for the last 7 days of the cycle, although you are still protected. You should menstruate during this week. Begin the next pack the next Sunday, whether or not bleeding is still occurring.
4. Use a back-up method for your first 3 weeks on the Pill, because it takes the body a while to adjust to the hormones.
5. There may be spotting or lack of menstruation during the first cycle. This is normal, but if it persists past the first month, call your health-care provider.
6. Nearly everyone forgets a pill occasionally. Don't get too upset, but try to remember your pill every day. If you miss one pill, take it when you remember and take the next one at the correct time. Try to space pills 12 hours apart. If you miss two pills, take them in one day spaced 12 hours apart, and take the next

two pills the following day spaced 12 hours apart. Use a back-up method for the rest of the cycle and call your health-care provider if your next period is delayed. If you miss three pills, throw the pack away and use a back-up method. You should begin your period soon. Start a new pack of pills the Sunday following your period, and use a back-up method for the first 3 weeks of the new cycle.

Effectiveness Rates

Combined Pill: theoretical, 99.5%; actual, 98%
Mini-Pill: theoretical, 99%; actual, 97.5%

Side Effects and Treatments

Side effects of the Pill are similar to the symptoms of the first few months of pregnancy. Suggested treatments are given for some side effects.

- Nausea/vomiting. Take the pills either with a meal or at bedtime.
- Spotting and/or irregular bleeding. Take the pill at the same time every day to prevent uneven levels of estrogen in your body.
- Depression and/or moodiness. Take Vitamin B-complex.
- Weight gain or loss. Weight gain is due to water retention, so try to reduce salt intake and exercise a lot. Statistically, as many women lose weight on the Pill as gain weight.
- Breast tenderness.

Complications of Prolonged Use

The Pill does not cause complications, but it does increase your risk of getting them:

- Blood clotting disorders—heart attack, stroke, hypertension (primarily in women over 35 who smoke)
- Liver problems
- Hormone suppression for some months after going off the Pill
- Be aware of the Pill's danger signals. If you exhibit any of these, call your health-care provider immediately.
  a. Abdominal pain (severe)

b. Chest pain, shortness of breath (severe)
c. Headaches
d. Eye problems (blurred vision or loss of vision)
e. Severe leg pain (in calf or thigh)
f. Dizziness, weakness, fainting, or numbness in arms or legs are also signals that you should watch for.

Benefits and Advantages

- Menstrual changes. Periods become shorter, lighter, and less painful with less blood loss. The risk of anemia, or iron deficiency, is decreased. Periods are also regulated.
- Decreases symptoms of PMS (Pre-Menstrual Syndrome).
- Acne may subside.

Medical Contraindications

Your clinician should screen for these before prescribing the Pill for you:

- high blood pressure
- diabetes
- immobilized limb (the Pill may increase the chance of reducing blood circulation to the limb)
- cancer of any reproductive organ
- bulimia (women who induce vomiting and/or diarrhea may expel a pill if they vomit within 2 hours after taking it; laxatives also decrease pill absorption
- blood-clotting disorders such as heart pain, heart attack, or stroke, especially if there is a history of these in your family
- interactions with other drugs (the Pill may conflict with other prescribed drugs; always tell a clinician you are taking the Pill and use a back-up method while taking any other medication, especially antibiotics)

Lifestyle Considerations

Discuss some of the issues involved. For example, with the Pill there is no interruption of lovemaking, the body is affected all the time, a good routine is necessary, you have to see a doctor and get pelvic exams, and, most important, you must remember to take it every day.

A man can participate in this method of contraception by

- helping the women remember to take a pill every day;
- using a back-up method, such as a condom, when needed;
- going along to the clinic; and
- sharing the cost of the pills.

The Diaphragm

When all the questions about oral contraceptives are answered, pass diaphragms around the room. Explain the mechanism of action. (A diagram would be an excellent visual aid.) A latex rubber dome covers the cervix (the entrance of the uterus) and provides a barrier between sperm and the cervix. When a diaphragm is used with spermicide, sperm are immobilized.

Methodology

The diaphragm must be fitted by a physician or clinician, because women have different-sized vaginas and require different-sized diaphragms. Be certain everyone can see a demonstration of insertion using a plastic pelvic model:

1. Check for holes, especially around and near the rim.
2. Place 1 to 2 teaspoons of spermicidal jelly in the dome (demonstrate). Spread it around the dome and, if desired, on the rim and the back.
3. Insert the diaphragm (the woman should be in a comfortable position).
4. Make sure the cervix is covered by inserting a finger and checking (the cervix feels like the tip of the nose).

QQ: *How long is a vagina?*

QA: On the average, 4 to 5 inches.

5. When the diaphragm is in place, neither the woman nor her partner should be able to feel it.
6. If the woman feels the diaphragm, she should go back to the clinic to have it refitted.
7. Diaphragm with jelly can be inserted 2 hours

before intercourse. If longer than 2 hours, add more jelly before intercourse.

8. Diaphragm should be left in place 8 hours after intercourse.

QQ: *How long do sperm live?*

QA: 72 hours. You need to leave diaphragm in for at least 8 hours to allow the spermicide to work effectively, although it should kill sperm on contact.

9. If you have intercourse more than once within an 8-hour period, add more jelly with an applicator (demonstrate).

Demonstrate diaphragm removal. Remember to make certain again that everyone can see what is being demonstrated. To remove diaphragm, hook your finger under the rim and pull it out. Clean it with mild soap and water, dry it, and return it to its case. Never leave the diaphragm in for longer than 24 hours.

Effectiveness Rates

Theoretical, 98%; actual, 81%

Side Effects and Treatments

- Allergy to the rubber or the jelly. If this occurs, try a different brand of jelly.
- If you have a 10-pound weight gain or loss, your diaphragm needs to be refitted.
- The fit of your diaphragm should be rechecked 2 to 3 weeks after your initial fitting and/or your becoming sexually active.
- The lifetime of a diaphragm is 1 to 2 years, depending on frequency of usage. If it puckers or becomes discolored, have it replaced.
- Some women do not use the diaphragm during menstruation because it traps blood and bacteria, resulting in odor.
- If the diaphragm is left in for more than 8 to 10 hours during menstruation, the risk of TSS (Toxic Shock Syndrome) is increased. Be aware of the symptoms—high fever, diarrhea, vomiting, muscle aches, and rash.

Benefits and Advantages

You only need to use it when you're going to have intercourse, so it's not acting on your body all the time. Spermicidal jelly can help prevent STD transmission. There are no medical contraindications.

Lifestyle Considerations

Discuss some of the issues. For example, how do you feel about touching yourself? Will this method embarrass you or your partner? You'll need privacy, it's messy, and it interrupts lovemaking. It only works if inserted, and it's not a good method if you're forgetful. You'll need to go to a health-care professional for fitting. A partner can insert and withdraw the diaphragm, clean it, and check it for holes—basically, he can do everything except wear it.

The Sponge

Pass around a Today® sponge. Explain the mechanism of action. The sponge acts as a barrier placed over the cervix. It blocks the sperm from entering the uterus and traps sperm within the sponge. The sponge releases spermicide to kill sperm.

Methodology

Demonstrate, using a plastic pelvic model. Again, make certain everyone can see this demonstration.

1. Wet the sponge with 2 tablespoons of water. *Do not* drench it in water and squeeze it out because the spermicide will rinse out.
2. Fold it and place it in the vagina over the cervix.
3. With a finger, check to make sure it's in place. Because it is so thick, you won't feel the cervix; you are checking to make sure that is the case.
4. One reason for sponge failure is a lack of education about insertion. If you're concerned, make an appointment for help with insertion. Another problem is that one size does not fit all.
5. Although the instructions say you can have intercourse repeatedly for 24 hours, we suggest a condom be used with the sponge *every time* to increase its effectiveness.
6. You should not be able to feel the sponge.
7. Leave the sponge in for 8 hours after the last act of intercourse. To remove the sponge,

grab the string and pull it out. Throw it away—sponges can only be used once.

Effectiveness Rates

Theoretical, no rate is established yet; actual, 80-90%

Side Effects and Treatments

- Dislodging of sponge. Check it periodically to make sure it's in place.
- If the sponge is left in for longer than 24 hours the risk of Toxic Shock Syndrome is increased. Be alert for any symptoms.
- Do not use the sponge during menstruation, because that also increases the risk of TSS.

Benefits and Advantages

May help prevent STD transmission because of the non-oxynol-9 spermicide content.

Medical Contraindications

History of TSS

Lifestyle Considerations

Discuss some of the issues. For example, will I have trouble using this method correctly? Like the diaphragm, you only use it during intercourse. The sponge can be purchased over-the-counter. The lack of proper fit lowers its effectiveness rate; are you willing to use a condom? Will you remember to use it? A male can participate in this contraceptive method by inserting the sponge, withdrawing it, and checking to make sure it's in place.

Cover all the questions about the sponge and then present the following information:

The Cervical Cap

Explain what it looks like or show a picture, if available. (This would make an excellent visual aid.) Explain the mechanism of action: The mechanism of action is the same as the diaphragm. You must be part of a national study, because the cervical cap has not been approved by the FDA, so it's considered experimental in the U.S. See your health-care provider if you are interested in the cervical cap.

Methodology

The cervical cap can be inserted like a diaphragm, and left in place for days.

Effectiveness Rates

Theoretical, 98%; actual, 87%

Because the cervical cap is still in the testing stage, little information is available about its side effects. Discuss all questions about the cervical cap before continuing.

Condoms

Unroll and put a condom over your hand to demonstrate. Explain the mechanism of action: The latex rubber sheath provides a barrier between the penis and vagina. Ejaculated sperm is trapped in the condom.

Methodology

Demonstrate these steps on fingers or fist of presenter.
1. Roll the condom over the erect penis to the base of the penis. Leave 1/2 inch at the top if there is no reservoir tip.
2. Condom must be placed on the penis before penetration because pre-ejaculatory fluid contains sperm.
3. After intercourse, withdraw the penis while still erect. Hold the tip of the condom so semen doesn't drip into the vagina.
4. Throw the condom away. Condoms are *not* reusable.
5. If the condom breaks during intercourse, add another application of spermicide immediately.

Don't use a condom that is more than 2 years old. Don't store condoms in wallets or glove compartments of cars because heat will damage them. Condoms need to be used every time intercourse occurs.

Effectiveness Rates

Theoretical, 98%; actual, 90%

The effectiveness rate of condoms and spermicides used together is between 96% and 98%.

Side Effects and Treatments

- Allergy to rubber. Use natural-skin condoms made from sheep intestines.
- Loss of sensation. Some men do complain of this, but an offsetting benefit is being able to keep an erection longer.
- Not enough lubrication or too much friction during penetration. Try using spermicidal cream or jelly on the condom or use water-soluble lubricant (i.e., KY jelly). Do not use petroleum jelly because it is not water-soluble, won't wash out of the vagina, and can erode the condom.

Benefits and Advantages

Condoms are helpful in preventing the transmission of STDs if used every time (for anal as well as vaginal intercourse). Condom use is essential for protection from the AIDS virus. There are no medical contraindications.

Lifestyle Considerations

Discuss issues. For example, are you concerned about sexually transmitted diseases? In light of the AIDS epidemic, sexually active people can no longer afford not to be concerned. Condoms are easy to use, inexpensive, and easy to carry around. There is some interruption of lovemaking, though. A female can participate by rolling the condom on and taking it off. This can be incorporated into lovemaking. A woman also can help her partner to remember to use a condom.

Vaginal Spermicides (Jellies, Foams, Creams, Suppositories)

Pass foam and suppositories among participants. Explain the mechanism of action: Kills sperm on contact with the non-oxynol-9 spermicide content. The spermicide provides a barrier by covering the cervix.

Methodology

1. Insert jelly, with an applicator. The applicator is filled with cream, jelly, or foam, then inserted into the vagina all the way back to cover the cervix.
2. Jelly, foam, or cream can be inserted up to 15 minutes before intercourse.
3. A suppository must be inserted 15 minutes before intercourse so vaginal lubrication can melt the waxlike substance.
4. A suppository is inserted with fingers into the vagina directly next to the cervix. It must cover the cervix.

Spermicide must be reapplied each time intercourse occurs.

Effectiveness Rates

Theoretical, 95-98%; actual, 82%

Side Effects and Possible Long-Term Complications

Allergy to spermicide. Change brands or type of spermicide.

Benefits and Advantages

Spermicide may provide *some* protection against transmission of some STDs. There are no medical contraindications.

Lifestyle Considerations

Discuss some of the issues. For example, will this method interrupt spontaneity of lovemaking so you or your partner will enjoy lovemaking less? Spermicides can be messy, but they're inexpensive and a good back-up method. Men can purchase and insert the spermicide, and they can help remind their partners to use it every time. A spermicide's effectiveness is greatly increased when used with a condom.

The Intrauterine Device

Hold up the IUD in its case. Explain the mechanism of action: The IUD is a foreign object in the woman's uterus; it produces an inflammatory response that prevents implantation. The IUD immobilizes sperm. The progestin that is emitted is absorbed into the uterine walls; its effects are similar to those of the mini-Pill. The IUD is a method of birth control—that is, it is considered to induce abortion.

Methodology

Explain the following steps and procedures to the group.

1. The IUD is inserted by a clinician during menstrual bleeding. The cervix is dilated with a speculum, and an instrument, the IUD inserter, is used to place the plastic IUD in the uterus.
2. A string attached to the IUD hangs through the cervix into the vagina. The string needs to be checked frequently, especially after menstruation, to make sure the uterus did not expel the IUD. A sexual partner should not feel the string during intercourse.
3. After insertion, a woman may experience heavy bleeding and cramping.
4. The woman should not have intercourse for 48 hours after insertion.
5. It is necessary to use a back-up method for the first 3 months after insertion and at fertile times.

An IUD should be removed by a clinician. One should never try to remove it herself. The IUD needs to be replaced yearly.

Effectiveness Rates

Theoretical, 98.5%; actual, 95%

Side Effects and Treatments

- Heavier bleeding, cramping, and longer menstrual periods. Take iron supplements and a nonaspirin pain-reliever.
- Spotting, bleeding, and cramps after insertion. Take nonaspirin pain reliever.
- Spontaneous expulsion of IUD
- Perforation of the uterus
- Increased risk of iron deficiency or anemia
- Increased risk of pelvic inflammatory disease (PID), an infection of the uterus and fallopian tubes. The risk for PID increases with multiple partners because the more partners, the more bacteria one is exposed to. PID can lead to sterility and even death.
- Increased risk of ectopic pregnancy. Of women who get pregnant while using an IUD, 50% have miscarriages, so if you become pregnant while using the IUD, have it removed immediately.

QQ: *What is ectopic pregnancy?*

QA: When the ovum implants outside of the uterus, usually in the fallopian tube (show this on a pelvic model).

IUD Danger Signals

If you have any of these, call your health-care provider immediately:

Period late or absent
Abdominal pain
Increased body temperature
Noticeable, foul discharge
Spotting, bleeding, clots, heavy periods

Medical Contraindications

- Pelvic infections, including gonorrhea
- Known or suspected pregnancy
- Abnormal uterine bleeding
- History of ectopic pregnancy
- Endometriosis

- Anemia
- Severe dysmenorrhea (painful menstruation)
- Abnormal pap smear
- Multiple sexual partners

Women who want to have children should not use the IUD because of the risk of sterility.

Lifestyle Considerations

Discuss some of the issues. For example, have you carefully reviewed the pros and cons of using an IUD? Will you seek medical attention if a problem arises? There is no interruption of lovemaking. You will need to see a doctor and have pelvic exams regularly. It's a good method if you are forgetful and desire spontaneity. You will risk getting a PID and this method may not be a good choice for young, childless women. The man can participate in this birth control method by going with the woman when the IUD is inserted, checking the IUD string, and reminding her to get the IUD replaced when needed.

QQ: *What is the history of the IUD?*

QA: In desert cultures, stones were put in the vagina and uterus of female camels to control their population.

Sterilization (Tubal and Vasectomy)

Obviously, demonstration is not possible, but you may want to show a diagram of the fallopian tubes (female) and of the vas deferens (male), where the incisions are made. Explain the mechanism of action: Both vasectomy and tubal sterilization involve removing part of the reproductive system, to make it impossible for sperm and ovum to meet.

Methodology: Vasectomy

(Refer to diagram of male anatomy if you have one.)

1. The vas deferens is cut and cauterized. The procedure can be performed on an outpatient basis.

2. The male can still ejaculate but he ejaculates semen without sperm. Sperm are still produced but not ejaculated; instead sperm disintegrates.

QQ: *What percentage of semen fluid is sperm?*

QA: Only 2%.

Methodology: Tubal Sterilization

(Refer to diagram of female anatomy if you have one. This is a more complicated procedure.)

1. The fallopian tubes are blocked by ligation, coagulation, or mechanical occlusion with clips, bands, or rings.
2. Ovulation still occurs but the egg, which cannot pass through the tube, quickly disintegrates.

Effectiveness Rates

Close to 100%.

Side Effects and Treatments

Once the person has recovered from surgery there should be no physical side effects. There is a slightly increased risk of ectopic pregnancy after tubal sterilization. Some men and women suffer from psychological problems dealing with their voluntary or involuntary decision. Individuals should be prepared to deal with their feelings about themselves, their partner, and their decision.

Benefits and Advantages

Sterilization offers the highest degree of contraceptive protection. The procedures are safe, effective, and permanent. There are no medical contraindications.

Lifestyle Considerations

Discuss some of the issues. For example, have you thoroughly explored your reasons for sterilization? How will you feel if you change your mind or change partners? Are you certain you will not change your mind about wanting children?

Natural Family Planning (NFP)

Demonstrate by showing a graph of the days of the menstrual cycle with indications of menstruation, safe days, and ovulation. Explain the mechanism of action: It is necessary to know a woman's fertile times and to abstain from intercourse then.

Methodology

Methods are used simultaneously to chart fertile times when abstinence must be practiced.

- Calendar or rhythm method
- Basal body temperature method (BBT)
- Billings cervical mucous technique

Couples must go for NFP counseling to learn how to practice charting these methods. It takes at least 6 months before this method is effective. It is advisable to find out whether your health-care provider offers NFP counseling. This method is used by couples who, for personal or religious reasons, choose not to use contraception. It is also used by couples trying to become pregnant.

Effectiveness Rates

Theoretical, 80-98%; actual, 76%

Side Effects

None.

Benefits and Advantages

- Safe
- Inexpensive or free
- Acceptable to many religious groups
- Helpful for planning or preventing pregnancy
- Women learn more about their menstrual cycle

Medical Contraindications

- Irregular intervals between menses
- History of anovulatory cycles
- Irregular temperature charts

Lifestyle Considerations

Discuss some of the issues. For example, are you prepared to keep careful and accurate daily records? Are you willing to abstain from intercourse during certain days of each month? The male can participate by helping with charting, keeping commitment, and accepting the long periods of abstinence during fertile periods. He can help the couple explore lovemaking alternatives.

Answer questions from the group and bring up these questions participants may want to ask their health-care providers:

- Which contraceptives are available from the health-care provider?
- Are any free?
- What are the average costs?
- Are appointment times or walk-in hours available?

Conclusion and Evaluation (5 minutes)

Summarize the main points of the workshop:

- Know as much as you can about your choice of contraception.
- Think about your own lifestyle and contraceptive choices accordingly.
- Get your partner involved in your contraceptive method—it's a shared responsibility.

Ask for questions from the participants. Offer resources and referrals for further information. Distribute Lifestyle Workshop evaluation forms and pencils. Allow time for completion and then collect. Briefly list and describe the other Lifestyle Workshops in Sexuality.

MOST FREQUENTLY ASKED QUESTIONS

1. *Isn't an IUD like an abortion?*

   The IUD is considered an abortifacient and, therefore, some people are opposed to using it. It depends on your definition of when life begins. The IUD is a method of birth control, not contraception.

2. *Does the pill affect future fertility?*

   You should be off the Pill for 6 to 18 months before trying to conceive. About 25% of Pill patients take at least 24 months to conceive, especially those with history of irregular periods. It takes a while for the regular ovulatory cycle to reinstate itself. Pills probably do not compromise fertility in any permanent way. However, post-Pill fertility cannot be guaranteed. Ten to fifteen percent of all American couples are infertile for reasons unrelated to Pill use (Hatcher et al., 1988).

3. *Isn't the sponge a good method because you can have repeated intercourse for 24 hours without adding anything, and then you can just throw it away?*

   Some women use this method incorrectly because they drench the sponge in water and then squeeze it out, washing away all the spermicide. Or there is insufficient suction, due to incorrect placement or a fault in the sponge itself, and the sponge has been found in the vagina turned upside-down or torn. If a woman is concerned about not placing it in correctly, she should make an appointment for a fitting. The actual effectiveness rate of the sponge alone is 80-90%, but it's best to always use a condom as well.

4. *How much do the risks of heart disease and cardiovascular side effects increase for women using the Pill who smoke or are older?*

   Heart attacks and strokes have been found to occur more in women who use the Pill than in nonusers. For women under 35 years of age who smoke, the annual excess death rate (for Pill users) is 1 per 10,000, while for nonsmokers under 35 years of age the excess death rate is 1 per 77,000. These risks are higher for Pill users who smoke, although these side effects occur in a small segment of the Pill-user population. Death rates due to cardiovascular complications are lower than death rates due to pregnancy (Hatcher et al., 1988).

5. *What about the morning-after Pill?*

   The morning-after Pill (MAP) is a massive dose of estrogen and progestin. It is legal and FDA-approved as a birth control pill but its effects on a developing embryo are not yet known. Four pills are taken within 48 hours, and the first pill must begin within 72 hours after unprotected intercourse. The MAP does not prevent ovulation; it changes the uterine lining to prevent implantation of an ovum. The patient's needs, medical history, and history of unprotected intercourse must be taken into account. The MAP is unlikely to be given twice. The risks are the same as the combined Pill and nausea may result.

6. *What is the best method of birth control for college-age women?*

   There is no "best" method. The choice depends on the physical, moral, and emotional needs of each individual or couple. However, certain methods, such as the IUD, are associated with more risks for young, childless women. A birth control method is only as effective as the user, for example, a diaphragm must be used every time.

7. *Why do so many of my friends have sex and not use birth control?*

For many, this is a moral question. Society and some religions tell us it's bad to have sex, so not using birth control is a sort of punishment. Others are forgetful or are risk-takers. After the first time they have unprotected intercourse and do not become pregnant, they may feel safe not using birth control. Actually, the chance of getting pregnant (or impregnating) without using birth control is 90% for the first year of nonuse of contraception or birth control.

8. *I've heard of people getting pregnant through pantyhose or underwear. Can this happen?*

It is highly unlikely, but possible—especially if the woman's clothes are moist enough from her lubrication to provide a medium for sperm to live and travel in.

9. *Is there really a difference among condoms, for example, ribbed, pleasure dots, and so on?*

Some may notice a difference, while others do not. Some features that are significant are reservoir tips and lubrication. The reservoir tip catches the ejaculate, and the lubrication decreases friction during intercourse and therefore helps prevent breakage.

10. *Can a woman get pregnant during her period?*

Yes! A woman can ovulate any time during her menstrual cycle. Reflexive ovulation can be caused by

- diet change,
- weight change,
- physical trauma,
- emotional stress, or
- sexual excitement.

11. *Is there a difference between birth control and contraception?*

Yes. Contraception prevents the egg and sperm from meeting. Birth control refers to preventing a fertilized ovum from implanting within the uterus in order to develop. For example, the IUD is a birth control method because the egg and sperm can meet, but the ovum cannot implant within the uterus because it will be dislodged by the IUD. Birth control can also refer to planning births. Many religious persons do not believe in using contraceptive methods, so they opt for natural family planning methods, which prevent births by advocating periodic abstinence.

12. *Does the Pill cause cancer?*

Evidence suggests that the Pill protects against ovarian and endometrial cancer. The Pill also helps protect against pelvic inflammatory disease, benign breast disease, ectopic pregnancy, and ovarian cysts. Many studies have reached contradictory results, so not all evidence is completely reliable.

13. *What do you do if a condom breaks during intercourse?*

If it breaks before ejaculation put on a new one and insert an extra application of contraceptive jelly, cream, or foam into the vagina. Do not douche. Douching can push the sperm further into the uterus. If the condom breaks during ejaculation, insert more jelly, cream, or foam immediately. Condom breakage can be prevented by adequate lubrication, leaving a reservoir tip, and decreasing friction during intercourse.

14. *I heard that IUDs should only be used after a woman has all the children she wants. Why?*

An IUD increases risks of infections and diseases such as pelvic inflammatory disease, which can cause infertility. Approximately 1/3 of IUD-related pregnancies result from undetected partial or complete expulsion of the IUD. But pregnancies can also occur with an IUD in place, and there is then approximately a 50% chance that a spontaneous abortion will occur if the IUD is left in place (Hatcher et al., 1988).

15. *As a man, how can I be responsible for birth control, unless I use a condom?*

The first rule in male responsibility for birth control is, Never assume your partner is using some form of birth control. If you aren't certain, ask her. The best relationships are built on communication. Males can help their partners remember to take pills or can check to make sure diaphragms, sponges, and IUDs are in place. They can insert vaginal spermicides, diaphragms, and sponges as well as withdraw diaphragms and sponges. Men can also help pay for contraceptives and accompany the woman to her medical appointments.

16. *Can a man feel a diaphragm?*

If he does, it is usually only the cup and not the rim. The cup feels pretty much like the vaginal wall (warm, soft, and wet) so it is not uncomfortable. If he feels the rim of the diaphragm it probably isn't correctly placed.

17. *I've heard of women losing weight from the Pill. How typical is this?*

Some women lose weight, have oiler or drier hair or skin, or have increased or decreased sex drives. These and other minor side effects occur because of the hormone interactions with each woman's individual chemistry. If such side effects become a problem, a woman can get a different prescription, or choose another method of contraception.

18. *Why are diaphragms different sizes?*

Diaphragms are fitted to each woman. Some women have fattier vaginal linings than others, so they require smaller diaphragms. A diaphragm is sized (by a clinician) by inserting different-sized rings in the vagina around the cervix. The largest size a woman can wear is the one prescribed.

19. *Why have most IUDs been taken off the market?*

At this time, the only IUD available is the Progestasert. Some IUDs have been proven to cause sterility in some women so companies that produced IUDs were forced to take them off the market.

20. *How are contraceptive effectiveness rates calculated?*

Effectiveness rates are calculated according to how many women per 100 women per year get pregnant using the method (not necessarily for the first time). This does not include women trying to get pregnant. This is according to *Contraceptive Technology 1988-1989* (Hatcher et al., 1988).

21. *How does the pill prevent PID?*

Several mechanisms are at work. The Pill decreases uterine contractions, thickens cervical mucous, decreases the dilation of the cervix during the menstrual flow, and reduces the amount of menstrual fluid each month. These mechanisms act to prevent bacteria from traveling up the reproductive system and to provide a less favorable environment for bacterial growth (Hatcher et al., 1988).

22. *What are some noncontraceptive benefits of oral contraceptives?*

There is a decreased incidence of PID, ovarian and endometrial cancer, benign breast disease, ovarian cysts, rheumatoid arthritis, and anemia in women using the Pill (Hatcher et al., 1988).

Birth Control Guide
at a Glance

Method	Effectiveness	Advantages	Disadvantages	Good for those who	Bad for those who
Pill	96-99%	Most effective method when used properly Possible decreased cramps and flow during menstrual period Periods very regular No interruption during sex play Possible weight gain or loss	Requires trip to doctor Possible annoying side effects Long-term effects still being researched Possible spotting between cycles	Have a routine Have a good memory Have heavy, crampy periods Have sexual intercourse frequently	Hate taking drugs or pills Hate doctors and pelvic exams Are forgetful Do not have on-going sexual relationship or activity
IUD	95-98%	Nothing to remember No interruption during sex play "Mess-free!"	Requires trip to doctor Possible heavy, long, crampy periods Possible spotting and cramping between periods Can be expelled from body Possible infections, hemorrhage, or perforation of the uterus	Want a method with no "bother" Are forgetful Are risk-takers	Have painful or long periods Have pelvic abnormalities or infections Dislike touching their genitals Have more than one sexual partner (increases risk of infection)

Method	Effectiveness	Advantages	Disadvantages	Good for those who	Bad for those who
Foam, cream/jelly, suppositories	78-97%	No side effects except possible allergic reactions Always available without a doctor's prescription Acts as a lubricant	Can be "messy" For greater protection partner should use condom **Can interrupt sex play** Temptation to "skip it, just this once" Suppositories tend to "burn" or create warm sensation	Need birth control right away Hate doctors and pelvic exams **Have a cooperative partner** Have patience and sense of humor	Hate the "mess" Are risk-takers Don't fit anywhere in the **"good"** category
Condom	90-97%	Always available without a doctor's prescription Helps stop spread of venereal disease No side effects Helps prevent premature ejaculation Gives the male a part in contraception	Interrupts sex play Decreases sensation for some men Temptation to "skip it, just this once"	Need birth control right away Are comfortable with their sexuality Are concerned about venereal disease Want to prevent early ejaculation	Lose an erection if interrupted Are concerned about any loss of sensation Are risk-takers
Diaphragm with jelly or cream	83-97%	No side effects Condom not necessary Jelly acts as lubricant	Can be "messy" Some positions during intercourse not advisable Can interrupt sex play Temptation to "skip it, just this once" Requires trip to doctor	Have sexual intercourse infrequently Have privacy Have patience and sense of humor Are nursing mothers	Dislike touching their genitals Dislike mess or interruption Are risk-takers Are dieting

Method	Effectiveness	Advantages	Disadvantages	Good for those who	Bad for those who
Sponge	80-90%	No harmful side effects Soft and comfortable when in place Spermicide acts as lubricant, but is not drippy Can wear it throughout 24 hours and have repeated intercourse without applying additional spermicide Available without a prescription Mess-free	Temptation to "skip it, just this once" Should not be used when menstruating Possible irritation to spermicide Might get expensive depending on frequency of intercourse Takes "know-how" and practice to remove it easily Effectiveness still under research	Dislike going to doctors Need birth control immediately Are nursing mothers Dislike messiness of other spermicides	Are risk-takers Dislike touching their genitals Have ever had toxic shock syndrome

Male Participation in Birth Control

Birth control method	Two heads are better than one (male participation in birth control)	The most common causes of birth control failure
Pill	If uncertain as to whether a woman is "protected," ask her: "Are you on the Pill?" Offer to accompany her to the family planning clinic and help pay for exams and pills. Help her remember to take a pill every day and to renew prescription. If she missed pills, use condoms or abstain *without complaining* for the designated time period. 1 pill — 1 week 2 pills — rest of package 3 pills — until she's back on pill for 2 weeks	Missing a pill or pills and either not knowing what to do *or* knowing but not using the back-up method for the proper time period. Going off the Pill due to annoying side effects and not using another method immediately. Some women think that the Pill "stays in their system" after they've quit taking it. (The day after you quit the Pill could be the day you get pregnant!) Going off the Pill and using rhythm as the next method. After quitting the Pill, a woman has no way of knowing when she will ovulate next. It could be the next day; it could be in six months! Going off the Pill "for a rest" as directed by the doctor and not using another method of birth control. This happens *especially* if the doctor hasn't suggested another method to use in the meantime.
IUD	Check the string during lovemaking. Offer to accompany her to family planning clinic and help pay for exams and IUD. Use condoms as a back-up method for two months after initial insertion of IUD.	The woman had not faithfully checked the string which tells her the device is still in place . . . and the device had been expelled from the uterus, leaving her unprotected. The woman had the IUD removed due to side effects and didn't use another method after its removal.
Foam, cream/jelly, suppositories	Put the foam in for her during lovemaking. Don't tempt her to "skip it, just this once." Be patient, uncomplaining. Help keep an eye on the supplies to avoid running out. Help pay for supplies.	The woman "skipped it, just this once." The woman put the foam in more than a half hour ahead of time, and it turned to liquid. It dripped outside the vagina, leaving little or nothing to block the cervix. The woman douched too soon after the foam had been applied. It takes 6 to 8 hours for the foam's spermicide to kill the sperm, so it must be left inside the body for at least 6 to 8 hours.

Birth control method	Two heads are better than one (male participation in birth control)	The most common causes of birth control failure
Condom	Use condom without complaining. Try different brands if one is unsuitable for either of you. Use it *every* time and *as directed*. Help keep an eye on the supplies to avoid running out.	The man "skipped it, just this once." The man touched his penis to the vaginal area or penetrated the vagina *before* putting on the condom. There are droplets that seep from the penis before ejaculation that contain sperm; thus a pregnancy could result. The man forgot to hold the condom on while pulling out after intercourse, and the condom slipped off . . . usually remaining in the vagina with its contents spilled. The condom was poor quality *or* the condom did not have a reservoir tip, and there was no slack allowing room for the semen. The condom broke.
Diaphragm and jelly/cream	Learn how to put in the diaphragm during lovemaking. Be patient. Don't complain. Help her remember to reinsert more jelly if intercourse is repeated. Offer to accompany her to family planning clinic and help pay for the exam and supplies.	The woman "skipped it, just this once." The woman didn't apply the jelly or cream or applied very little. The jelly or cream was applied once and intercourse was repeated later without another application. The diaphragm "bounced" or moved during female orgasm, which allowed sperm to get behind the device and swim into the cervix. The woman lost or gained more than 10 pounds and did not get the diaphragm refitted. The woman didn't insert it properly.
Sponge	Learn how to insert sponge during lovemaking and how to remove it. Help pay for it. Help keep an eye on supplies.	The woman "skipped it, just this once." It "fell out" during a bowel movement sooner than 6 hours after intercourse. It was inserted wrong. It was removed or fell out sooner than 6 hours after intercourse.

Note. From *Birth Control Guide at a Glance* by the Hope Clinic for Women, 1979. Copyright 1979 by the Hope Clinic for Women, Ltd. Reprinted by permission.

Effectiveness Rates

Method	Theoretical (%)	Actual (%)
Combined Pill	99.5	98
Mini Pill	99	97.5
Diaphragm (with spermicide)	98	81
Sponge	89-91	80-90
Cervical cap	98	87
Condoms	98	90
Foams, jellies, creams, suppositories	95-97	82
IUD	98.5	95
Tubal ligation	99.6	99.6
Vasectomy	99.6	99.6

REFERENCES

Crooks, R., and Baur, K. (1987). *Our sexuality* (3rd ed.). Menlo Park, CA: Benjamin/Cummings.

Franceour, R. (1984). *Becoming a sexual person*. New York: Wiley.

Hatcher, R., Guest, F., Stewart, F., Stewart, G.,

Trussell, J., Bowen, S., and Cates, W. (1988). *Contraceptive technology 1988-1989* (14th ed.). New York: Irvington.

Hyde, J. (1986). *Understanding human sexuality* (3rd ed.). New York: McGraw-Hill.

Loving Smart:
An STD Prevention Game
Lifestyle Workshop

PARAPROFESSIONAL PREPARATION MATERIALS

Training Sessions

Competency Exam

Texts and Suggested Readings

WORKSHOP AT A GLANCE

Presenter Information

Most Frequently Asked Questions

Handouts and Visual Aids*

References

Facts About AIDS was compiled and written by Mary Ellen O'Shaughnessey, MA.

TRAINING SESSIONS

Loving Smart: An STD Prevention Game

Session 1: Workshop Presentation

Time: 60 minutes

Methods: Presentation, demonstration (It is important to keep current with rapidly changing information concerning STDs.)

Description: Trainer presents workshop to Lifestyle Educators.

Readings: The workshop

Session 2: Overview of Sexually Transmitted Diseases—Part 1

Time: 60 minutes

Methods: Lecture, discussion

Description: Discussion of major sexually transmitted diseases: gonorrhea, syphilis, chlamydia, and herpes. Discussion of primary and secondary prevention strategies.

Readings: Materials on sexually transmitted diseases, the workshop

Competency exam questions: 1, 2, 3, 6, 7, 8, 9, 10, 11, 13, 15, 16, 17, 18, 20, 22, 24, 25, 27, 28, 30

Session 3: Overview of Sexually Transmitted Diseases—Part 2

Time: 60 minutes

Methods: Lecture, discussion, quiz

Description: Continued discussion of sexually transmitted diseases: vaginitis, monilia, genital warts, pubic lice, NGU (nongonococcal urethritis), PID (Pelvic Inflammatory Disease)

Activity: Quiz on information presented in Session 2

Readings: Materials on sexually transmitted diseases, the workshop

Competency exam questions: 1, 2, 5, 6, 7, 9, 10, 11, 13, 15, 16, 17, 20, 21, 22, 29, 30

Session 4: Acquired Immune Deficiency Syndrome (AIDS)

Time: 60 minutes

Methods: Lecture, discussion, quiz

Description: AIDS—its transmission, effects, and specific high- and low-risk behaviors

Activity: Quiz on material presented in Sessions 2 and 3

Readings: Up-to-date AIDS facts and information, the workshop

Competency exam questions: 4, 11, 12, 14, 19, 23, 26, 32

Session 5: "Most Frequently Asked Questions" Review and Hot Seat

Time: 60 minutes

Methods: Discussion, practice

Description: Review "Most Frequently Asked Questions" section of the workshop and other workshop components

Activity: Hot Seat: Each Lifestyle Educator is quizzed by the other students on the workshop topic for 10 minutes.

Readings: The workshop

Session 6: Practice Workshop Presentation

Time: 60 minutes

Methods: Presentation

Description: Lifestyle Educator presents 20 minutes of the workshop.

Readings: The workshop

COMPETENCY EXAM

The following questions require brief responses.

1. What do the following abbreviations stand for?

   STD

   SRD

   PID

   NGU

   AIDS

2. Explain the difference between primary and secondary prevention of STDs. Give one example of each.

3. What percentage of women with gonorrhea are asymptomatic?

4. How is the HIV transmitted sexually?

5. What organism is the most common cause of NGU?

6. Name three ways a clinician can screen for an STD.

7. Name two sexual activities that could lead to transmission of an STD.

8. What are the two different kinds of herpes simplex and where would you find the lesions caused by each?

9. What three STDs are considered curable or treatable with antibiotics?

10. Vaginal discharge is a normal part of the menstrual cycle. What changes indicate a possible STD? (Name three.)

11. Discuss three aspects of a sexual lifestyle that could put one at high risk for contracting an STD.

12. What are the two main opportunistic diseases people with AIDS die from?

13. Why is it important for partners to discuss STDs? Give examples of when and how the topic could be brought up.

14. What are two high-risk sexual activities associated with AIDS transmission?

15. List two public resources for STD information.

The following are True/False questions. Check the appropriate blanks.

True   False

_____   _____   16. If you check for symptoms on a sexual partner, anonymous sex poses little or no risk.

_____   _____   17. Douching after intercourse won't prevent STDs.

_____   _____   18. Once herpes sores go away, you shouldn't return to unprotected intercourse in case they come back.

_____ _____ 19. In terms of AIDS, it isn't dangerous to give blood and it's now safer to receive it.

_____ _____ 20. STDs are a result of poor personal hygiene.

_____ _____ 21. Vaginitis cannot be sexually transmitted to a male.

_____ _____ 22. For women, an annual pap smear and regular pelvic exam are sufficient checks for STDs.

_____ _____ 23. College students who are heterosexual and not IV drug users should be safe from contracting AIDS.

The following questions require short essay responses.

24. Discuss five strategies for primary prevention of STDs. Give the rationale behind each.

25. While you are giving the workshop, a participant adamantly claims that AIDS is "a gay disease." Based on your knowledge of AIDS incidence and transmission, describe your response to this statement.

26. Suggest possible techniques to use in the workshop if a participant is one of the following:
    • Recognition Seeker (frequently calls attention to self)
    • Conversationalist (brings up off-the-subject anecdotes and is a noisy distraction)
    • Moralizer (advocates judgmental points of view based on personal convictions)
    • Conservative (convinced that the status quo does not need changing)

TEXTS AND SUGGESTED READINGS

American Red Cross/U.S. Public Health Service. (1986). *AIDS and your job. Are there risks?*

American Red Cross/U.S. Public Health Service. (1986). *AIDS, sex and you.*

American Red Cross/U.S. Public Health Service. (1986). *Facts about AIDS and drug abuse.*

Corsaro, M., and Korzeniowsky, C. (1981). *STD: A common sense guide.* New York: St. Martins.

Donahue, D. (1985, Summer). Chlamydia: New diagnostic technology. *Hotliner: VD National Hotline Newsletter* (American Social Health Association), pp. 1-6.

Franceour, R. (1984). *Becoming a sexual person.* New York: Wiley.

Illinois Department of Public Health. (1985). *AIDS information for the general public.*

U.S. Department of Health and Human Services (PHS). (1986). *Surgeon General's report on acquired immune deficiency syndrome.*

U.S. Public Health Service/Center for Disease Control. (1987, Spring). *Facts about AIDS.*

WORKSHOP AT A GLANCE

The goal of this workshop is to educate students about the causes and modes of transmission for various sexually transmitted diseases, and to discuss which sexual activities are high-risk for infection. This workshop takes approximately 75 minutes to present. Suggested attendance is 6 to 20 persons.

Objectives

Through the content of this workshop, the following objectives will be met.

- By playing the game "Loving Smart," sexuality issues and myths will be discussed.
- By playing the game "Loving Smart," causes, modes, and transmission of common sexually transmitted diseases will be discussed.
- Both primary prevention techniques of sexually transmitted diseases and low-risk practices will be discussed.

Workshop Materials

- Workshop sign-in sheet
- Handouts and visual aids: *Common Sexually Transmitted Diseases (STDs), Can You Pass the Safe Sex Test?, Facts About A.I.D.S., Loving Smart game board, game cards, game questions* typed on pink, blue, green, and yellow index cards, *4 sets of game pieces, clear acrylic boxes,* and *colored gumballs* in pink, blue, green, and yellow.
- Two condoms for each participant
- Lifestyle Workshop evaluation forms and pencils

PRESENTER INFORMATION

Briefly introduce yourself, your background, and any other personal information you choose to share. Describe your health promotion program and the topics available, like fitness and nutrition. Stress that the workshops are unique because you bring them to their living areas. Tell them that Lifestyle Workshop paraprofessionals are trained at (your institution or program) to present these workshops. If anyone is interested in the training program, ask him or her to speak with you after the workshop.

This workshop will focus on the *prevention* of STDs (sexually transmitted diseases). STDs are a group of infectious diseases, spread from person to person by sexual relations or by other close physical contact. They have different causes, symptoms, treatment, and consequences. Prevention entails some sexual lifestyle modifications, but the purpose of STD prevention is to permit people to continue to enjoy their sex lives. Prevention doesn't mean you have to discontinue intimacy, just that you may have to change certain practices. Prevention techniques can be embarrassing or seem silly, but isn't it better to take precautions than to find symptoms after it's too late? Having a sense of humor and open communication with a sexual partner can help to make prevention less of a chore.

correctly answering the questions at designated spaces (see Game Board in handouts and visual aids).

Note. Scientific advances occur at a rapid rate. Please check information for current accuracy.

Loving Smart Game Rules

1. Every cup begins in the middle.
2. Start from the presenter's right side and move counterclockwise. The first team rolls the dice and moves in any direction they choose. There are four different colored squares.
3. Pink = true/false questions
   Yellow = definitions or listing
   Green = short answer and advanced true/false questions
   Blue = more difficult short answers
4. Presenter asks the question and gives the team 15 seconds to answer. Presenter explains the correct answer after team gives its answer.
5. If team answers any question correctly, it rolls again.
6. If team gives three correct answers in a row, the next team gets to roll, so that everyone gets a chance to play the game.

Loving Smart Game (45 minutes)

It's important to understand that sexual practices don't cause diseases. Germs cause diseases, and it's obvious that germs have no morals. They are oblivious to the context of sexual behavior; they don't care if people know each other or love each other, if partners are of the same or opposite sex, or if anyone is enjoying sex. Germs are only interested in a warm, moist home. If one person is infected, transmission can occur in a sexual act. Some of the most common STDs are gonorrhea, syphilis, NGU or nongonococcal urethritis (caused mostly by the chlamydia bacteria), herpes, and Acquired Immune Deficiency Syndrome or AIDS.

To play this game, split participants into groups of no more than five, and try not to have more than four groups. The objective of the game is to fill each team's cup with all four colors of pieces by

Sex and STDs (Pink Cards)

The pink cards are true/false questions.

1. *If you check for symptoms on a sexual partner, anonymous sex poses little or no risk.*

   False. Many symptoms cannot be seen. For instance, semen may be invisibly infected. Anonymous sex is risky because it's likely that either partner has had other anonymous sexual encounters, and the more sexual partners one has, the more bodily secretions are exchanged, increasing chances of infection.

2. *After you've finished medication for a treatable STD, you can resume your regular sexual lifestyle.*

   False. After treatment you are at risk of reinfection, which may or may not be as serious as the first. It is a good idea to use a condom for 3 to 6 months after treatment to prevent reinfection.

3. *Decreasing the number of times you have sex is the only way to decrease the chance of getting an STD.*

   False. Being sexually active doesn't mean you'll get an STD, just that you're at risk. More important than decreasing your sex life is limiting the exchange of bodily secretions. This can mean changing sexual practices or limiting your partners.

4. *If you're taking medication for an STD and your symptoms disappear and you feel better, it's okay to stop taking the medication.*

   False. Never stop taking medication before the medication is finished according to your clinician's instructions. The germ can still be active in your body even though your symptoms are gone. If your partner is being treated she or he should also continue to take the medication for its duration.

5. *Douching after intercourse won't prevent STDs.*

   True. Vaginal or anal douching doesn't protect either partner from transmission. It can even push infective materials farther into the body, enhancing the transmission of disease. Douching also can upset the normal pH of the vagina, which can cause irritation and possible infection, and can wash away the bacteria normally present in the vagina.

6. *Once herpes sores go away, you should not return to unprotected sexual activity in case they come back.*

   True. Even if sores go away, the virus frequently remains dormant in the body's nerve tissues for awhile. It is possible to shed the virus without having lesions but the virus can later multiply and cause sores again. Sores last from 2 to 6 weeks. Recurrences last from 1 to 10 days, are less severe, and recur in 65% to 75% of all herpes victims. Recurrences can be triggered by sunlight, menstruation, fever, physical trauma, friction during intercourse, or emotional stress. Condoms should *always* be used with intercourse for lowest risk of transmission.

7. *Getting an STD is a direct result of a promiscuous sexual lifestyle.*

   False. An STD can be transmitted in a single sexual encounter. Germs cannot discriminate among their hosts; they are only interested in finding a warm, moist home.

8. *If a sexual partner has an STD and is treated, you have nothing to worry about if you have no symptoms.*

   False. If a partner is infected, chances are you've been infected also, so you should be screened, and treated if necessary. It is most effective to treat partners simultaneously. Remember that for some STDs symptoms may not be obvious without screening.

9. *There is a cure for herpes.*

   False. As of now there is a treatment that relieves symptoms (the sores), but it is not a cure.

10. *One of the greatest risks for getting AIDS is from anal intercourse.*

    True. Anal sex may tear the rectal lining, allowing any virus that may be in the ejaculate to easily enter the bloodstream.

11. *Use of condoms may help prevent AIDS and other STDs.*

    True. If there is no contact with infected semen, there is little risk of transmission during sex. The consistent use of condoms may reduce transmission, but it's unproven whether condoms prevent infection with HIV (Human Immunodeficiency Virus) antibodies. Natural ''skins'' may not be as effective in preventing transmission of some STDs (primarily viruses) as latex condoms.

12. *AIDS is a gay disease.*

    False. Disease knows no lifestyle. The disease was introduced into the American population through homosexual men and intravenous drug users, but in Africa, where it originated, the ratio of men to women carrying the disease is 1:1 in a mainly heterosexual population.

13. *AIDS can't be transmitted by ''dry kissing'' or sharing a glass.*

    True. Although the virus has been found in saliva and tears, there have been no documented cases of these methods of transmission. Also, the concentration of the virus in saliva is low and is found in only a small percentage of AIDS victims. Kissing is relatively safe, although it is not known whether future cases won't be found to be transmitted in this way. Dry kissing poses no risk.

14. *If your roommate has AIDS, chances are you won't get it.*

True. Unless you are sexually involved with an infected roommate or sharing needles with him or her, there appears to be no risk.

15. *In terms of AIDS transmission, it isn't dangerous to give blood, and it is only slightly risky to receive it.*

True. AIDS can be transmitted by sharing needles, but needles used to take blood are disposable, so as a donor you are never exposed to someone else's blood. All blood is now screened for HIV antibodies, so no blood containing the antibodies is transfused; therefore, receiving blood is also safer now. *Note:* If you need a transfusion, your risk of death by not having it is higher than the risk of receiving contaminated blood.

16. *One can contract herpes by touching dirty doorknobs or contaminated eating utensils.*

False. The organism responsible for herpes does not survive readily outside the body; direct transmission is required.

17. *Homosexuality is a pathology, a mental sickness.*

False. Homosexuality is not a disease; it is a sexual orientation and a way of life for many people. It is a prejudice to believe that homosexuals are mentally ill.

18. *STDs are the result of poor personal hygiene.*

False. STDs require transmission from an infected person. These organisms do not exist in normal body flora.

19. *STDs have reached epidemic proportions.*

True. There are an estimated 3 million cases of chlamydia and 20 million sufferers of genital herpes.

20. *Some people have a natural immunity to STDs.*

False. If you are a member of the human race you are susceptible to contracting an STD.

Definitions (Yellow Cards)

Yellow cards require definitions or listing.

1. *List two sexual activities that could lead to an STD.* (Name any two of the following.)

   • Oral, anal, or vaginal intercourse *with an infected person.*

   • Anal or vaginal intercourse *without a condom.*
   • Fisting, rimming, or water sports with an infected person. (Fisting is inserting the fist into the anus. Rimming is anal-oral sex. Water sports is urinating on or being urinated on by partner.)

2. *List two sites on males where venereal warts occur.* (Name any two of the following.)

   • Glans
   • Foreskin
   • Urethral opening
   • Shaft of penis
   • Scrotum
   • Anus
   • Rectum

3. *List two sites on female sexual organs where genital warts occur.* (Name any two of the following.)

   • Vulva
   • Perineum (area between vaginal opening and anus)
   • Vagina
   • Cervix
   • Anus
   • Rectum

4. *Define the difference between* primary *and* secondary *prevention and which is better?*

   Primary prevention is what you do to keep from getting or giving an STD (such as using condoms or spermicidal jelly). *Secondary* prevention is minimizing the consequences once you have a disease. Primary prevention is always better, because you never get the disease.

5. *List two STDs that produce symptoms of pain, itching, or burning with urination.*

   • Chlamydia
   • Gonorrhea
   • Nongonoccocal urethritis (NGU)
   • NSU, or nonspecific urethritis cervicitis

6. *Define two factors that indicate that you're at high risk for getting an STD.*

   • If you have symptoms such as painful urination (gonorrhea or NGU), a chancre (syphilis), dysmenorrhea (gonorrhea), discharge or itching (vaginitis, monilia, lice, herpes, or gonorrhea) or painless growths (warts). There may also be no symptoms—80% of women with gonorrhea are asymptomatic.

- If your partner tells you she or he has symptoms.
- If your sexual lifestyle puts you at risk, such as having multiple partners, using unsafe or risky sexual practices, and having anonymous sex.

7. *Define the two types of herpes simplex and list where you might find the lesions caused by each?*

   Herpes simplex I is an oral infection on the lip, mouth, or facial area, commonly called a cold sore. Herpes simplex II is genital lesions. Either strain can cause the disease on either the mouth or genitals. It is spread by either intimate physical contact with an infected person or by direct contact with an infected area, which can then transmit the virus to another site on the body.

8. *List two modes by which AIDS can be transmitted.* (Name any two of the following.)

   - direct blood contact or transfusions
   - sexually through bodily secretions
   - sharing needles

9. *Define chlamydia.*

   A bacterial infection that is now the most common STD diagnosed, chlamydia trachomatis affects both males and females. It can be passed to a newborn as it passes through the birth canal, although its most common route of transmission is through sexual intercourse. It is the most common cause of nongonococcal urethritis and pelvic inflammatory disease, and in both sexes it can lead to infertility.

10. *Define PID.*

    Pelvic inflammatory disease is an infection of any of the pelvic organs. It has a high correlation to sterility in women.

11. *Define NGU and the organism that is typically responsible for NGU.*

    Nongonococcal urethritis is an infection of the urethra in males and is very common. NGU is usually caused by the chlamydia organism.

12. *List two of the four STDs that must be reported to the State Department of Public Health.* (Check your state's requirements.)

    - Gonorrhea
    - Syphilis
    - AIDS
    - Chlamydia

13. *List three STDs that are considered curable or treatable with antibiotics.*

    - Gonorrhea
    - NGU
    - Syphilis

14. *List two STDs that may cause lesions in the genital region.*

    - Herpes, which is usually painful and recurring.
    - Syphilis, which is usually not painful and does not recur but rather progresses to more serious stages.

15. *List five STDs.*

    - Gonorrhea
    - Syphilis
    - Chlamydia
    - Herpes
    - Venereal warts
    - AIDS
    - NGU
    - Pubic lice

More About Symptoms and Treatments (Green Cards)

Questions on green cards require participants to supply one word answers or more advanced true/false answers.

1. *Certain sexual acts can produce bacteria, germs, and viruses.*

   False. There is nothing inherently disease-causing about any sexual act; one person must already be infected for transmission to occur.

2. *Once the chancre from syphilis disappears, the disease is gone.*

   False. The chancre is the first stage of syphilis. If left untreated, secondary syphilis sets in after about 6 weeks as the bacteria spreads. Some of the symptoms include mild fever, headache, lack of appetite, bone pain, and a rash. The rash can be spots appearing almost anywhere on the body and may vary in color on different colored skins.

3. *If you currently have an STD and are under treatment, you should tell your partner and limit your activity.*

   True. Tell your partner what you would want to be told. Be specific; give the name of the disease and the treatment you have received. Encourage your partner to be examined. Also, *use a condom* and your imagination (that is, forego intercourse if possible, but some other sexual activities are okay). Always exchange names and phone numbers with your partners.

4. *Tetracycline, which is used to treat many STDs, should not be taken with milk products or antacids.*

True. These reduce the absorption of the drugs. Also, a woman taking oral contraceptives should inform her physician of this before she is prescribed any medication. Some drugs, including tetracycline, may reduce the effectiveness of the Pill.

5. *Vaginitis cannot be sexually transmitted to a male.*

False. Vaginitis is transferred by intimate physical contact, so the bacteria, fungus, or yeast can be transferred to the penis and can cause irritation. Also, some men have no symptoms but carry the microbe in the urethra or prostate.

6. *Women taking oral contraceptives are at a higher risk for developing some STDs.*

True. Recent research documents that women taking oral contraceptives are more likely to contract STDs. The two reasons for this are that women on the Pill tend to have more sexual partners, creating a greater risk for exposure to a variety of STDs, and that the Pill changes the pH of the vagina, making a more hospitable environment in which bacteria can flourish.

7. *An annual pap smear and regular pelvic exam for women are sufficient screening for STDs.*

False. Special testing needs to be done on your pap smear and special checks need to be made for STDs. Specifically request an STD check, and inform your clinician of your sexual habits so he or she can assess whether you need screening.

8. *If your male partner has an STD, you can contract it orally (in the throat or mouth).*

True. Many, though not all, infections can be transmitted this way. Bacteria and germs like moist, warm places; if the infection is on the penis or in the semen, it can be transmitted into a partner's mouth or throat through oral sex.

9. *The herpes virus can be transmitted only when you or your partner have sores.*

False. Some people are infectious yet remain asymptomatic.

10. *A woman who wears tight jeans or sits cross-legged for a long time increases her chances of getting vaginitis or a urinary tract infection.*

True. These practices can force bacteria into the vagina and urethra and should be avoided. Also, sitting cross-legged can decrease blood flow to the groin area, so there is less chance for the blood cells to fight off infection. Tight jeans trap moisture and heat, making infection more likely.

11. *Sores on or around the genitalia are the only symptoms to be aware of for the transmission of herpes.*

False. There may also be flulike symptoms, including headaches, fatigue, and lymph swelling. Usually these occur just before lesion outbreak. Be aware that sores around the mouth can spread to genitals through oral or genital contact.

12. *You can't get the HIV from a person who has no symptoms.*

False. Anyone carrying the virus is contagious, and 70% to 80% of those carrying the virus may never develop symptoms.

13. *Of all the people who test positive with HIV antibodies, 20% to 30% will develop AIDS.*

True. Based on present knowledge, scientists predict that within 5 years, 20% to 30% of those infected with the HIV will develop an illness that fits an accepted definition of AIDS.

14. *College students who are heterosexual and not intravenous drug users should be safe from contracting AIDS.*

False. Most of the college population is at risk. Many students are sexually active and one may not know whether a potential partner is bisexual or an IV drug user. College students may experiment with drugs as well as alternative sexual practices and lifestyles. An increased number of partners increases the risk of infection.

15. *Homosexuals caused AIDS because of their sexual practices.*

False. Homosexuals didn't cause AIDS. They were just the first unfortunate Americans to get it. The acts some homosexuals practice, such as anal intercourse with many partners over time, are high-risk activities for transmitting the HIV. There are no sexual acts homosexuals practice that heterosexuals don't also practice in some form.

16. *Closing gay bars and bathhouses will probably stop the spread of AIDS.*

    False. Bathhouses and bars don't cause AIDS—the practices that occur there do. If these places are closed, people can still have anonymous sex elsewhere. As long as bars are open, education can occur there. Closing gay bars might be followed by closing singles' bars, because they too lead to pickups and anonymous sex.

17. *It is not possible to have more than one STD at a time.*

    False. Organisms can coexist in the body.

18. *Herpes can be spread through kissing.*

    True. Oral and genital lesions can transmit the virus to oral and genital regions.

19. *Lesbians get fewer STDs than any other segment of the population.*

    True. They do not get STDs carried by sperm through penile penetration, thus lowering their risk substantially.

Filling in the Details (Blue Cards)

Questions on blue cards require participants to provide more detailed short answers.

1. *What is the primary sign of syphilis and where does it appear?*

    A chancre, a painless sore that develops on mucous membranes, appears on the site where the bacteria first entered the body. It begins as a lump that erodes as the bacteria multiply and healthy cells are destroyed. Its surface becomes smooth and dull red. The chancre feels rubbery and has clear edges. If the chancre becomes infected with other bacteria, it may be painful. Common sites are near the genital area, on internal genitalia on women, and on the anus, rectum, mouth (mucous membranes), and throat.

2. *What are two of the most common symptoms of STDs in men?* (Name any two of the following.)

    - burning or itching during urination
    - lesions, warts, or chancres on genitals
    - unusual discharge from penis

3. *Name two ways STDs are transmitted.* (Two of the following.)

    - direct skin contact with infected area
    - direct contact of mucous membranes, including mouth, throat, eye, vagina, and anus
    - direct contact of bodily secretions from an infected person (such as semen in vagina, mouth, and anus)

4. *Vaginal discharge is common in some women. Name two changes that indicate a possible STD.* (Name any two of the following.)

    - increased discharge
    - foul smell
    - change in color of discharge
    - burning or itching with discharge
    - different consistency (for example, thick, cottage-cheesy)

5. *Name two common vaginal infections.* (Two of the following.)

    - trichomonas vaginalis (trich)
    - monilial vaginitis (yeast)
    - gardnerella
    - NSU (nonspecific urethritis)

    Note: These are not necessarily transmitted sexually. Bacteria can enter the vagina in many ways, such as from wearing noncotton underpants, sitting cross-legged, or wearing tight jeans.

6. *Name two aspects of a sexual lifestyle that can put you at high risk for getting an STD.*

    - multiple partners
    - unsafe sexual practices
    - anonymous sex

7. *AIDS is 100% fatal.*

    True. AIDS is a syndrome that breaks down the immune system, which then allows a multitude of infections and diseases to occur. These are called opportunistic diseases, and it is these that AIDS victims die of. Currently, there are no antiviral drugs available that have been proven to cure AIDS.

8. *Name two of the first symptoms of AIDS (the opportunistic infections).* (Any two of these are correct.)

    Fever, weight loss, fatigue, persistent diarrhea, swollen lymph nodes, purplish-red lesions, shortness of breath, night sweats, and cough.

9. *Name the two highest risk groups for AIDS.*

Sexually active homosexual and bisexual men and past or present users of illegal intravenous drugs.

10. *What are the two main illnesses people with AIDS develop?*

- Pneumocystic carinii pneumonia, a parasitic infection of the lungs (the most common cause of death in AIDS patients)
- Kaposi's Sarcoma, a rare type of cancer

11. *Women cannot transmit AIDS to men.*

False. If a woman has an open cut in her vagina, anus, or mouth and a man has an open cut on an organ that comes into contact with one of the woman's sores through oral, anal, or vaginal intercourse, a woman can transmit AIDS to a man. Also, low levels of HIV have been detected in vaginal secretions, but research has not yet proven that transmission occurs in this mode. Female-to-male transmission is much less common than male-to-female transmission.

12. *What key function has to occur to transmit AIDS?*

AIDS can be transmitted sexually by the exchange of bodily secretions including semen, blood, and urine of an infected person. The key is that AIDS has to get into the blood system, where the virus lives, and this occurs when any bodily secretion enters the bloodstream, such as when friction from anal or vaginal intercourse produces tears, allowing secretions to easily enter the bloodstream.

13. *How are STDs diagnosed?*

STDs are diagnosed by screenings, which include a visual exam, a lab culture of discharge or urine and a blood test.

14. *Name one way to minimize your risk of infection or further complications if a sexual partner tells you she or he has or may have an STD.*

- See a doctor for screening.
- Check yourself; do a self-exam. (This should be followed by a screening in case you are asymptomatic).

- Abstain from intercourse.
- Use a condom for intercourse.

Primary Prevention and Symptoms (10 minutes)

Primary prevention is actions or behaviors that will help prevent STDs. Here are some primary prevention steps you can take to help keep yourself safe and healthy. (You may want to put these on a handout or poster. This would make an excellent visual aid.)

Abstinence. The only absolute guarantee against STDs is abstinence from intimate physical contact. This doesn't mean you can't hold hands, embrace, or kiss. It does mean you must refrain from activities that include the exchange of bodily fluids. (Point to the appropriate picture.)

Limit Your Partners. Don't have intimate relations with several partners or with a person who has several partners. The more partners, the greater the risk. This does not mean you must decrease your sex life, just limit the circle of partners with whom your sexual activity includes the exchange of bodily secretions. This may require a lifestyle change for some people.

Get to Know Your Partner. The more you know about a potential partner the better you can evaluate the potential risks the person presents. It is a good idea to talk before you engage in intimacy. This can cause embarrassment, but may also prevent it and worse later. Perhaps the best way to get information is to give it. Tell your partner if you've had an STD. This is difficult, but keeping a sense of humor helps. After all, wouldn't you rather know these things about a person before an encounter rather than after?

Selectivity. This is the goal of getting to know your partner better. You have a better basis for being selective about partners when you know a lot about them. Avoid high-risk sex, for example:

- If a partner has many other partners
- If an encounter is so casual that you learn nothing about your partner's lifestyle (this

person probably has other casual or anonymous encounters and would therefore be high-risk)

- If a person has been diagnosed with an STD, has symptoms, or has tested positive on the AIDS/HIV antibody test
- If a person injects drugs and shares needles

Limit Your Practices. The only way to prevent STDs is by not engaging in activities that include the exchange of bodily fluids or secretions including semen, blood, urine, and stool and by not having direct contact with the mucous membranes or skin of an infected person.

- Avoid *sexual* contact with an infected person. This doesn't mean you can't hug, massage, talk on the phone, look at magazines, or mutually masturbate.
- Avoid penetration—anal, oral, or vaginal. These acts include the exchange of bodily secretions.
- Avoid acts that cause slight damage to body tissue (such as anal or vaginal intercourse without proper lubrication). This increases the chance for bodily fluids to enter the bloodstream.
- Avoid acts that include direct or indirect oral or anal contact with high-risk partners.
- Avoid group sex—the more partners, the higher the risk.

Observation. This means looking *before* you begin sexual contact. Some people try to take a shower with their partner to get a better look in good light. Another way to get a look is to undress each other (with the lights on) as part of foreplay. If you see any suspicious sores, rashes, or discharges, ask about them. Have the courage to say no or at least to delay sex if you are concerned with potential risks.

Urinating. Urinating after sex can help prevent infection. For men it may prevent urethritis (an infection in the urethra) and for women it may help prevent vaginitis and urinary tract infections, because you may flush out the bacteria that entered during penetration.

Hygiene. As a part of hygiene and urinating, women should always wipe from front to back so germs from the anus do not enter the vagina. Both sexes should wash genitals with soap and water thoroughly and dry them thoroughly. For uncircumcised men it is important to wash under the foreskin because bacteria can get trapped there.

Also, the penis should be washed after anal intercourse and before engaging in any other sexual activity. Always wash your hands after any anal contact.

Lubrication. Adequate lubrication is important for all penetration, but particularly anal. The friction caused by inadequate lubrication can cause tears in the anus or vagina, which can then be sites for the transmission of infections such as AIDS because these tears open into the bloodstream. Use a water-soluble lubricant that is unlikely to cause allergies. Don't use petroleum-based lubricants, because they do not wash out. Also, do not touch the tube of lubricant with fingers that have recently had anal contact—wash your hands first.

Use Vaginal Contraceptive Creams, Jellies, and Foam. These can kill bacteria as well as sperm. They are probably useful against gonorrhea, chlamydia, and some forms of vaginitis.

Use Condoms. Condoms are one of the best preventive measures for most STDs when put on before contact and removed properly. But they only protect the parts of the body they separate (i.e., cervix, penis, vagina, and anal linings). Many infections can be prevented by using condoms. But remember, condoms can break or slip!

Stay Informed. New research is being conducted all the time. It is a good idea to read about STDs—especially about an infection you have or one for which your sexual lifestyle puts you at risk. If you understand all your symptoms, you can be an informed patient and can ask the clinician intelligent questions. You can take control over your health, and staying informed is a big part of that.

Secondary Prevention (5 minutes)

Have any unusual symptoms checked out by a physician. Discharge from the penis can mean chlamydia NGU—anywhere from minimal mucous to profuse puslike discharge, or gonorrhea—clear or creamy and ranging in color from white to yellow to yellow-green.

Vaginal discharge in women can mean:

- chlamydia;
- herpes—thin, white vaginal discharge;
- vaginitis, trich, gardnerella, nonspecific urethritis (NSU), yeast infection; or

- gonorrhea—foul-smelling, excessive, or different-colored vaginal discharge.

Other symptoms include problems when urinating, such as burning, itching, blood, or other discomfort; herpes sores on penis. Sores may last 6 weeks, then disappear, but the infection *isn't* cleared up. Herpes is incurable. Go to your health-care provider for STD screenings. Ask your physician how often you should be screened. This depends on your sexual lifestyle (sexual practices, number of partners, etc.). Remember, a pap test is *not* an STD check for women. Ask specifically for an STD screening. Find out if your health-care provider will do the HIV antibody test upon request, and ask whether the results will remain confidential.

Handouts and Discussion (10 minutes)

Discuss the following handouts and ask for questions from the participants.

- Common Sexually Transmitted Diseases (STDs)

- Can You Pass the Safe Sex Test?
- Facts About AIDS
- Hand out condoms for everyone.

Conclusions and Evaluation (5 minutes)

Summarize the main points of the workshop:

- The more you know about sexually transmitted diseases, the better your chances of practicing low-risk behavior.
- Take an active role in your own sexual health and practice primary prevention.
- If you suspect an STD symptom, have it checked by a physician immediately.

Ask for questions from the participants. Offer resources and referrals for further information. Distribute Lifestyle Workshop evaluation forms and pencils. Allow time for completion, then collect. Briefly list and describe the other Lifestyle Workshops in Sexuality.

MOST FREQUENTLY ASKED QUESTIONS

1. *Are heterosexual men at risk of getting AIDS?*

   Under certain circumstances, yes. Heterosexual drug injectors are at high risk, as are heterosexual partners of female drug injectors. Also, a significant percentage of heterosexual AIDS victims report a history of multiple and frequent female partners, including prostitutes. The more partners a person has, the higher the risk. Bisexuals and their partners are also at risk for AIDS, particularly female partners of bisexual men.

2. *How do I know whether I should be screened for the HIV antibody?*

   You should be screened if you practice any high-risk activity (such as anal intercourse, intravenous drugs, or anything where there is potential for exchange of bodily fluids) or your partner is in a high-risk group or you have been monogamous with that partner for less than 5 years.

3. *Can herpes I be transformed into herpes II?*

   No. Herpes simplex I is confined to the face and mouth. It can be transmitted to the genital area by oral/genital contact, but it does not become herpes simplex II. HSV II is genital herpes, which can similarly be transmitted to the mouth/genital area by oral/genital contact, but does not become HSV I.

4. *If I call my health-care provider for an STD examination, what should I expect the doctor or nurse will do?*

   For men who are asymptomatic, they do a urine culture, and for men with symptoms, a urethral culture. A culture of urethral cells will be extracted from the penis, then tested. For women, a culture of discharge will be taken during a pap smear and a variety of tests may be performed appropriate to the suspected disease. For both sexes, a full visual exam of the genital area will be made.

5. *Can a condom guarantee prevention of STDs?*

   No. A condom reduces the chances of acquiring an STD by preventing the transmission of infected semen. But condoms only protect certain areas of the body. For example, oral sex without a condom will not prevent transmission. Natural skins provide less protection than latex.

6. *What is NGU?*

   NGU stands for nongonococcal urethritis. It is any inflammation of the urethra not caused by gonorrhea. NGU is most often caused by a bacterium called chlamydia trachomatis. The major symptom is painful urination.

7. *What is PID?*

   PID stands for pelvic inflammatory disease. A woman with PID has an infection of one or more pelvic organs. The infection may result from delaying treatment of an STD, which may spread through the reproductive tract. The two diseases most often involved are gonorrhea and chlamydia. The organ usually infected is the fallopian tubes, but the uterus and ovaries can also be affected. Symptoms include lower abdominal pain, back pain, fever, chills, nausea, pain during intercourse, and abnormal vaginal bleeding.

8. *What is gonorrhea?*

Gonorrhea is an STD caused by bacteria transmitted during intercourse. It usually causes burning urination and discharge in men. Women often have no symptoms; those that do have some vaginal discharge and irritation of the vulva.

9. *What are genital warts?*

Genital warts are warts found in women on the vulva and perineum and in men on the glans, foreskin, and urethral opening. Warts are caused by a virus similar to the one that causes warts elsewhere on the body.

10. *What is syphilis?*

Syphilis is an STD caused by a bacteria. It is spread by intimate contact with an infected person through mucous membranes. The symptoms of primary syphilis are a chancre sore that's usually painless and does not recur where the bacteria first entered the body. Secondary syphilis is characterized by mild fever, headache, lack of appetite, and bone pain. A rash can develop anywhere, and round gray patches can develop in the mouth. Secondary syphilis is highly contagious.

11. *How and when do I tell a potential partner that I have herpes?*

The important thing to remember is to discuss the issue with your partner *before* you engage in any sexual contact. You may want to choose a private, quiet setting that will facilitate discussion. Don't wait until minutes before intercourse, as rational discussion is most difficult at that time. Contact the STD/VD Hotline at (800)227-8922 for any further suggestions or factual information.

12. *Why should I be concerned about AIDS if I'm not homosexual or an IV drug user?*

Most of the sexually active college population is at risk. You may not know whether a partner is bisexual or uses or has used IV drugs. If you don't have a clear, accurate idea about your partner's sexual history, the best way to decrease your risk, short of abstinence, is using latex condoms.

13. *If so many women are asymptomatic for gonorrhea, how can I protect myself from contracting gonorrhea if I'm planning to have intercourse?*

If you and a female partner are monogamous, your risk for contracting gonorrhea is *very* low. If, however, you are unsure about your partner's sexual history (number of partners, anonymous sex, etc.) you should always wear a condom to be safe. Open communication combined with complete honesty is the key here.

Common Sexually Transmitted Diseases (STDs)

Name	Symptoms	Potential complications	Importance of treatment	Special instructions	Prevention
Syphilis (*Treponema pallidum*)	Primary (3 weeks postexposure): chancre on penis/ vagina/rectum/ anus/cervix	Brain damage, heart disease, condylomata lata, spinal cord damage, blindness	Essential	Use condoms for 1 month. Return to clinician for follow-up at 3, 6, 12, and 24 months.	Avoid multiple partners.
Gonorrhea (clap, or drip, *Neisscria gonorrhea*)	May be asymptomatic; vaginal/ penile discharge Male: Painful urination; tenderness in lymph nodes, testicular/ abdominal pain, fever Female: Dysmenorrhea, painful intercourse, postcoital bleeding, abnormal discharge	Sterility, blindness, eye infections, pelvic inflammatory disease, arthritis	Essential	Refrain from oral/genital sex. Use condoms or avoid intercourse.	Avoid multiple partners. Spermicides offer some protection. Use condoms.

Name	Symptoms	Potential complications	Importance of treatment	Special instructions	Prevention
Chlamydia/NGU (*chlamydia trachomatis*)	Male: Burning on urination, frequent urination, white to yellow-green discharge. Female: Vaginal discharge, symptoms of pelvic inflammatory disease	Urethritis, cervicitis, pelvic inflammatory disease, pneumonia of newborn, infertility	Essential	Use condoms for length of treatment. Refer sexual partner for exam.	Avoid multiple partners.
Herpes genitalis	Many blister-like sores on vulva, cervix, penis; painful intercourse; itching of vulva, penis; painful urination	Recurrence, meningitis, neonatal herpes, encephalitis	No known treatment	Report herpes to OB if pregnant. Wear loose underwear. Avoid intercourse or use condoms if sores are present.	Have an annual Pap smear. Avoid oral/genital and genital/genital intercourse when sores are present. Keep area dry and clean.
Bacterial vaginosis (nonspecific vaginitis, *Hemophilus vaginalis*, *Gardnerella vaginalis*)	Yellow, green discharge (chalky white); pain on urination; vaginal itching; painful intercourse; foul odor of discharge	Recurrent infections are common.	When needed	Use condoms for length of treatment.	Avoid multiple partners.
Monilia (*Candidiasis albicans*, yeast infections*)	Thick, cottage cheese-like discharge; itching; redness of external genitalia	Recurrence	When needed	Wear cotton underwear. Treatment may be needed for 2 cycles.	Use betadine/vinegar douches. Lose weight if obese.

Name	Symptoms	Potential complications	Importance of treatment	Special instructions	Prevention
Pubic lice (crabs, *Phthirus pubis*)	Itching, lice in pubic hair	Inflammation of the lymph nodes, shedding of skin	If infected, must treat	Remove all visible signs of lice, wash with soap and water and Kwell Shampoo. Avoid intercourse.	Maintain good hygiene.
Acquired Immuno-deficiency Syndrome (*HIV, LAV, HTLV III, ARV*) (AIDS)	General symptoms: unexplained weight loss, night sweats, extreme fatigue, lymph node enlargement	Kaposi's sarcoma, pneumocystis carinii pneumonia	None available	Those testing positive with HIV antibodies should try to avoid other infections, inform partners, and avoid risks.	Avoid exchange of body fluids with high-risk individuals.
Genital warts (*Condyloma acuminata*)	Single or multiple painless growths on vulvovaginal area, penis, perineum	May destroy tissue, may obstruct birth canal in pregnant women	Should be examined for warts.	Abstain from sexual activity or use condoms during treatment.	Limit partners. Check for symptoms before sexual contact.

Note. Data are from *Contraceptive Technology 1988-89 14th Revised Edition* (pp. 1-43) by R.A. Hatcher, F. Guest, F. Stewart, G.K. Stewart, J. Trussell, S.C. Bowen, & W. Cates, 1988, New York: Irvington. Copyright 1988 by Irvington. Adapted by permission.

Can You Pass the Safe Sex Test?

Sexual practices (Things I do or could see myself doing sometime)	Check if statement applies	What the experts say*		
		Safe	Possibly safe	Unsafe
Have multiple partners			X	
Vaginal or anal intercourse without condoms (with a person in a high-risk group)				X
Vaginal or anal intercourse (with a person not in a high-risk group)			X	
Hugging		X		
Dry kissing		X		
Wet kissing (frenching)			X	
Sexual activities that involve the exchange of body fluids				X
Anonymous sex			X	
Vaginal or anal intercourse using condoms			X	
Intercourse using lubricants (water-soluble)			X	
Having sexual contact with someone who injects drugs			X	
Having sexual contact with someone positive for HTLV-3 antibodies			X	
Oral sex with ejaculation				X
Oral sex without ejaculation			X	
Massage		X		
Masturbating		X		

Note. Adapted from *Can You Pass the Safe Sex Test?* by the San Francisco AIDS Foundation, 333 Valencia St., Fourth Floor, San Francisco, CA 94103. (415) 863-AIDS.

*Remember, there is nothing inherently disease-causing about any sexual act; one person must already be infected for transmission to occur. Certain sexual acts promote tissue breakage and, therefore, potential for body fluid exchange is increased.

Facts About AIDS

AIDS is a serious condition characterized by the breakdown of an individual's immune system, which fights off disease and infections. People who have AIDS are vulnerable to serious illnesses that would not be a threat to anyone whose immune system was functioning normally. These illnesses are referred to as "opportunistic" infections or diseases.

What Causes AIDS?

Investigators have discovered the virus that causes AIDS. Different groups of investigators have given it different names, but they all appear to be the same virus. The virus is called human T-lymphotropic virus, type 3 (HTLV-3); lymphadenopathy associated virus (LAV); or human immunodeficiency virus (HIV). Infection with this virus does not always lead to AIDS. Preliminary results of studies show that most infected persons remain in good health; others may develop illness varying in severity from mild to extremely serious.

Who Gets AIDS?

Ninety-eight percent of AIDS cases have occurred in the following groups of people:

- Sexually active homosexual and bisexual men with multiple partners (65%)
- Present or past abusers of intravenous drugs (17%)
- Homosexual and bisexual men who are also intravenous drug abusers (8%)
- Persons with hemophilia or other coagulation disorders (1%)
- Heterosexual contacts of someone with AIDS or at risk for AIDS (4%)
- Persons who have had transfusions with blood or blood products (2%)
- Infants born to mothers infected with AIDS (1%)

Some 2% of patients do not fall into any of these groups, but researchers believe that transmission occurred in similar ways.

What Are the Symptoms of AIDS?

Most of the symptoms of AIDS are similar to those associated with colds, bronchitis, and the stomach flu. However, if these symptoms or a combination of symptoms appear, and if there is a possibility of exposure to AIDS, medical attention should be sought. Symptoms include an unexplained, increasing, persistent fatigue; persistent fever, chills, and night sweats not accompanied by a known illness and lasting longer than several weeks; unexpected weight loss of over 10 pounds in less than two months; swollen glands (lymph nodes), unexplained by other illness and lasting longer than two weeks; creamy white patches on the tongue or the mouth; persistent diarrhea; persistent, frequent dry cough (not from smoking or common respiratory infection), shortness of breath, or difficulty breathing; pink or purple flat or raised blotches that don't go away and don't pale when pressed (these lesions are *not* common in women with AIDS).

How Contagious Is AIDS?

Casual contact (i.e., kiss on the cheek, handshake, etc.) does not spread the virus; *no* family member of anyone with AIDS has been known to contract the disease, with the exception of fetal transmission. Although the AIDS virus has been found in saliva and tears, there have been no cases in which exposure to either was shown to result in transmission.

How Is the Virus Transmitted?

Transmission of the virus from one person to another occurs primarily through high-risk sexual activities, use of needles contaminated with the virus (e.g., IV-drug users sharing needles), and direct contact with contaminated blood. Infants may also be infected by their mothers prior to or during birth and through breast feeding.

How Long After Exposure to HIV Does a Person Develop AIDS?

The time between infection with HIV and the onset of symptoms (the incubation period) seems to range from about 6 months to 5 years and possibly longer. Not everyone exposed to the virus develops AIDS.

How Is AIDS Diagnosed?

There are no clear-cut symptoms that indicate the loss of immunity. The diagnosis of AIDS usually depends on the presence of opportunistic diseases. Certain tests that demonstrate damage to various parts of the immune system, such as specific types of white blood cells, support the diagnosis. The presence of opportunistic diseases, plus a positive test for antibodies to HIV, can also make possible a diagnosis of AIDS.

Is There a Laboratory Test for AIDS?

As with most other viral infections, there is no single test for diagnosing AIDS. There is now a test for antibodies (substances produced in the blood to fight disease organisms) to the virus that causes AIDS. Presence of HIV antibodies means that a person has been infected with the virus; it does not tell whether the person is still infected. The antibody test is used to screen donated blood and plasma and to assist in preventing cases of AIDS resulting from blood transfusions or use of blood products.

What Are Some of the Diseases Common in People With AIDS?

About 85% of the AIDS patients studied have had one or both of two rare diseases: pneumocystis carinii pneumonia (PCP), a parasitic infection of the lungs; and a type of cancer known as Kaposi's sarcoma (KS). KS usually occurs anywhere on the surface of the skin or in the mouth. In early stages, it may look like a bruise or blue-violet or brownish spot. The spot or spots persist and may grow larger. KS may spread to, or appear in, other organs of the body. PCP has symptoms similar to any other form of severe pneumonia, especially cough, fever, and difficulty in breathing. Other opportunistic infections include unusually severe infections with yeast, cytomegalovirus, herpes virus, and parasites such as toxoplasma or cryptosporidia. Milder infections with these organisms do not suggest immune deficiency.

Is There a Danger of Contracting AIDS From Donating Blood?

No. Blood banks and other blood collection centers use sterile equipment and disposable needles. The need for blood is always acute, and people who are not at increased risk for getting AIDS are urged to continue to donate blood as they have in the past.

How Is AIDS Treated?

Currently, there are no antiviral drugs available anywhere that have been proven to cure AIDS, although the search for such a drug is being pursued vigorously. Some drugs have been found that inhibit the AIDS virus, but these do not lead to clinical improvement. Though no treatment has yet been successful in restoring the immune system of an AIDS patient, doctors have had some success in using drugs, radiation, and surgery to treat various illnesses of AIDS patients. Therapeutic agents are needed for all stages of AIDS infections, to block action of the virus once infection has occurred, and to build up immunity in patients who have developed AIDS symptoms. Eventually, a combination chemotherapy to combat the virus and restore the immune system may be the most effective therapy.

Can AIDS Be Prevented?

Yes. Cases of AIDS related to medical use of blood or blood products are being prevented by use of HIV antibody screening tests at blood donor sites, and by members of high-risk groups voluntarily not donating blood. There is no vaccine for AIDS itself.

Note. Adapted from *Surgeon General's Report on Acquired Immune Deficiency Syndrome* by the U.S. Department of Health and Human Services, 1986, Washington, DC: U.S. Government Printing Office; *AIDS and Your Job—Are There Risks?* by the American Red Cross, 1986, American Red Cross; *Women and AIDS* by the Women's AIDS Network, 1984, San Francisco: AIDS Foundation.

Game Board

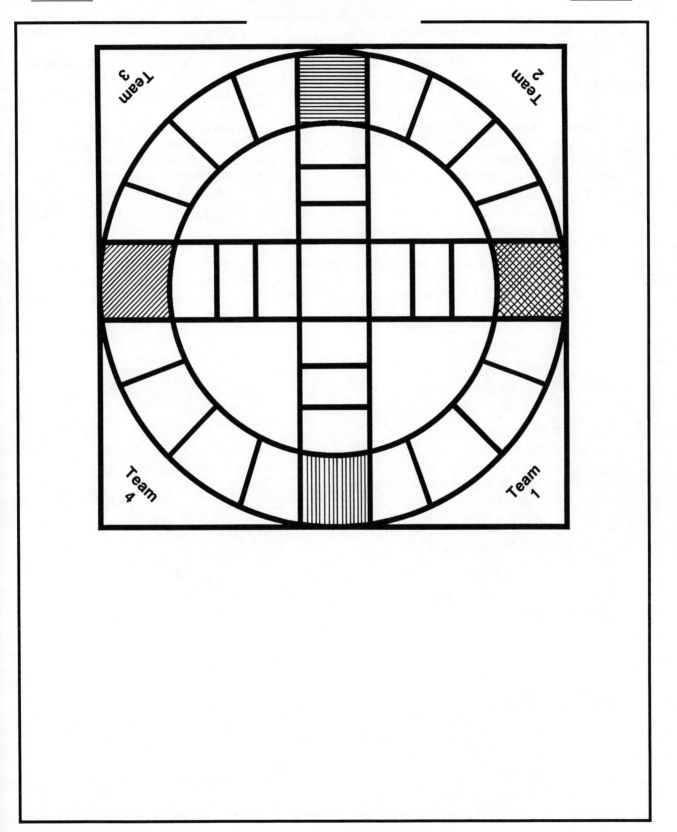

REFERENCES

American Red Cross & U.S. Department of Health and Human Services. (PHS). (1986, October). *AIDS and your job—are there risks?* (AIDS-20).

Franceour, R. (1984). *Becoming a sexual person.* New York: Wiley.

Hatcher, R., Guest, F., Stewart, F., Stewart, G., Trussell, J., Bowen, S. and Cates, W. (1988). *Contraceptive technology 1988-1989* (14th ed.). New York: Irvington.

Holmes, K., Mardh, P., Sparling, P., and Weisner, P. (Eds.) (1984). *Sexually transmitted diseases.* New York: McGraw-Hill.

Hyde, J. (1986). *Understanding human sexuality* (3rd ed.). New York: McGraw-Hill.

San Francisco AIDS Foundation. (1984). *Guidelines for AIDS risk reduction.*

U.S. Department of Health and Human Services (PHS). (1987, Winter). *Facts about AIDS.*

U.S. Department of Health and Human Services (PHS). (1986). *Surgeon General's report on acquired immune deficiency syndrome.*

Acquaintance Rape Prevention Lifestyle Workshop

PARAPROFESSIONAL PREPARATION MATERIALS

Training Sessions

Competency Exam

Texts and Suggested Readings

WORKSHOP AT A GLANCE

Presenter Information

Most Frequently Asked Questions

Handouts and Visual Aids*

References

---

*Acquaintance Rape: How—Why? was written by Lela Jones Olzweski, MS.

TRAINING SESSIONS

Acquaintance Rape Prevention

Session 1: Workshop Presentation

Time: 60 minutes

Methods: Presentation, demonstration

Description: Trainer presents workshop to Lifestyle Educators.

Readings: The workshop

Session 2: Introduction to Acquaintance Rape

Time: 60 minutes

Methods: Film, discussion

Description: Film *Rethinking Rape* is used as an introduction to the topic. *Rethinking Rape* can be ordered from Film Distribution Center, 1028 Industry Drive, Seattle, WA 98188; (206)575-1517

Activity: Assignment—Interview three friends about acquaintance rape. Is it a problem? Why does it happen? Is it anyone's fault?

Readings: The workshop

Competency exam questions: 1, 7, 18, 19, 20, 28

Session 3: Attitudes Toward Rape

Time: 60 minutes

Method: Discussion

Description: Students share feedback from the previously assigned interviews, and trainer leads a discussion on attitudes toward rape and acquaintance rape.

Activity: Complete and discuss the workshop handout "Attitude Assessment Survey."

Readings: Materials on state rape and sexual assault laws, readings on rape and acquaintance rape, the workshop.

Competency exam questions: 1, 5, 10, 19, 20, 21, 30

Session 4: Facilitating Workshop Film or Story, Bill of Rights, and Assertiveness Exercises

Time: 60 minutes

Methods: Demonstration, discussion, practice

Description: Discuss ways to facilitate the film or story as an introduction, including possible reactions. Practice guiding the "Bill of Rights" activity and the assertiveness exercise.

Activities: Lifestyle Educators develop a "Bill of Rights." Role-play the assertiveness exercise.

Readings: Film discussion guide, assertiveness training, the workshop

Competency exam questions: 2, 3, 4, 6, 7, 8, 9, 11, 12, 13, 14, 15, 16, 23, 25, 26, 28

Session 5: "Most Frequently Asked Questions" Review and Hot Seat

Time: 60 minutes

Methods: Discussion, practice

Description: Review "Most Frequently Asked Questions" section and other workshop components.

Activity: Hot Seat: Each Lifestyle Educator is quizzed by the other students about the workshop topic for 10 minutes.

Readings: The workshop

Session 6: Practice Workshop Presentation

Time: 60 minutes

Method: Presentation

Description: Each Lifestyle Educator presents 20 minutes of the workshop.

Readings: The workshop

COMPETENCY EXAM

The following are True/False questions. Check the appropriate blanks.

True   False

_____ _____ 1. Most men rape because of strong sexual urges.

_____ _____ 2. One of the goals of this workshop is to help women learn to withdraw trust when it is not deserved.

_____ _____ 3. The least frequent coercive strategy used in sexual assault of acquaintances is physical violence.

_____ _____ 4. The "Bill of Rights" developed at the workshop will be appropriate for every participant.

_____ _____ 5. Under law in many states, men or women may be charged with the crime of sexual assault against either men or women.

_____ _____ 6. "I think you're disgusting" is an example of an "I" message, rather than a "you" message.

_____ _____ 7. If the preventive and protective measures listed in the workshop are followed, a woman will avoid being raped.

_____ _____ 8. Pleading and quarreling are ineffective rape-avoidance strategies.

_____ _____ 9. Every person who is a sexual assault victim should get tested for possible sexually transmitted diseases.

_____ _____ 10. If a victim was drunk at the time of the assault, the courts will be less likely to prosecute the rapist.

The following are matching questions. Put the letter representing the answer into the space to the left of the question.

a. 5
b. 10
c. 18
d. 84
e. 50

_____ 11. Percent of rape victims who are men.

_____ 12. Average age of acquaintance rape victims in *Ms.* magazine study.

_____ 13. Percent of acquaintance rape victims assaulted on the man's territory.

_____ 14. Percent of victims who make a report to the police.

_____ 15. Percent of victims who know their attacker.

The following questions require brief responses.

16. The four steps in acquaintance rape are

17. List five rights that might be on a "Sexual Bill of Rights."

18. Define stranger rape.

19. Define sexual assault.

20. Define sexual harassment.

21. Define *consent* according to the state Sexual Assault Law's provisions.

22. If a person is raped, what should he or she do and not do afterward? List four possibilities.

23. List six things a woman can do to help protect herself from becoming an acquaintance rape victim.

The following questions require short essay responses.

24. You have just finished showing the film "The Party Game," and one of the participants is crying. What do you do?

25. What does the term *desensitization* mean in the context of acquaintance rape? Give an example with your explanation.

26. What is the *broken record* technique? Why is this taught in the acquaintance rape prevention workshop?

27. Speculate on the reasons that acquaintance rape may happen in cases when the following events occur: The woman asks the man out, the man pays for the date, and they go to his apartment.

28. The effects of acquaintance rape on the victim are different than the effects of stranger rape. What are three of the differences?

29. How are alcohol and acquaintance rape related?

30. Define and explain the differences between acquaintance rape and date rape.

31. Suggest possible techniques to use in the workshop if a participant is one of the following:
    • Recognition Seeker (frequently calls attention to self)
    • Conversationalist (brings up off-the-subject anecdotes and is a noisy distraction)
    • Moralizer (advocates judgmental points of view based on personal convictions)
    • Conservative (convinced that the status quo does not need changing)

TEXTS AND SUGGESTED READINGS

Alberti, R., & Emmons, M. (1986). *Your perfect right: A guide to assertive living*. San Luis Obispo, CA: Impact.

Bart, P., & O'Brien, P. (1984). Stopping rape: Effective avoidance strategies. *Signs: Journal of Women, Culture, and Society*, **10**(11), 83-101.

Bateman, P. (1982). *Acquaintance rape awareness and prevention*. Seattle: Alternatives to Fear.

Cherniak, D. (Ed.). (1984). *A book about STDs*. Montreal: Montreal Health Press.

Garner, A. (1980). *Conversationally speaking*. New York: McGraw-Hill.

Merton, A. (1985, September). Return to brotherhood—An exposé of fraternity life today. *Ms.*, **14**(3), 60.

Morrison, E., & Underhill-Price, M. (1974). *Values in sexuality—A new approach to sex education*. New York: Hart.

Parrot, A. (1985). *Acquaintance rape and sexual assault prevention training manual*. Ithaca, NY: Cornell University.

Pritchard, C. (1985). *Avoiding rape on and off campus*. Wenonah, NJ: State College Publishing.

Schwartz, J. (1986, February). Acquaintance rape comes into open. *Newsweek on Campus*, p. 12.

Sweet, E. (1985, October). Date rape: The story of an epidemic and those who deny it. *Ms.*, **14**(4), 56.

WORKSHOP AT A GLANCE

The goal of this workshop is to discuss values about and societal myths surrounding acquaintance rape. Information will be provided about various protective measures, including assertiveness training. This workshop takes approximately 75 to 90 minutes to present. Suggested attendance is 10 to 25 persons.

Objectives

Within the content of the workshop, the following objectives will be met.

- Participant will be able to define rape and acquaintance rape, and define behaviors that constitute rape.
- Through the "Attitude Assessment Survey on Rape," participants will discuss and analyze attitudes about rape and sexuality.
- By viewing and discussing the film "The Party Game," or use of the story, "Acquaintance Rape: How—Why?", the participants will learn some behaviors that contribute to acquaintance rape; experience and process the emotional impact of the film; and begin to be aware of preventive techniques.
- Participants will begin to consider the components of their own needs in a healthy relationship by designing a "Bill of Rights."
- Through assertiveness training exercises, participants will begin to learn techniques for expressing their rights to others.
- Participants will be introduced to preventive and protective measures, including the role of alcohol, and given sources for further information on prevention and protection.

Workshop Materials

- Workshop sign-in sheet
- Handouts and visual aids: *Attitude Assessment Survey on Rape; Acquaintance Rape: Definitions and Statistics; Acquaintance Rape: Prevention and Protection; Resource and Referral Information Sheet**; the film *The Party Game*, which is distributed by MTI Teleprograms, Northbrook, IL; or *Acquaintance Rape: How—Why?* (Appendix A).

*Construct a resource and referral handout for your campus. Provide the names of local counseling, mental health, and rape crisis facilities and/or counselors, with addresses and phone numbers. If your community has ride services, provide phone numbers, costs, and hours of operation. Hospitals may offer services for people who have had too much to drink. If your university or local community police department has designated sexual assault investigators, provide their names and phone numbers. Also provide the names and phone numbers of available medical care for sexual assault victims. Provide information regarding self-defense and protection classes. Check with your local police department and women's resources centers.

- Newsprint, marker, tape
- State laws on rape and sexual assault
- Lifestyle Workshop evaluation forms and pencils

Note: This workshop has been designed for a *female* audience. We have found that some males have felt offended when attending this workshop. Please consider developing a different workshop for a mixed audience.

PRESENTER INFORMATION

Introduction (5 minutes)

Briefly introduce yourself, your background, and any other personal information you choose to share. Describe your health promotion program and the topics available, like fitness and nutrition. Stress that the workshops are unique because you bring them to their living areas. Lifestyle Workshop paraprofessionals are trained at (your institution or program) to present these workshops. If anyone is interested in the training program, ask him or her to speak with you after the program.

You may want to present this in the following manner: The purpose of this workshop is to educate and inform. As women, we have been raised to try to please other people, especially men. In helping you learn to be more aware of your own needs and limits, and to say "no" when appropriate, we are not trying to turn you against men. Rather our goal is to keep you from being harmed in a way that could significantly affect your relationships with both men and women. The goal of prevention programs is to help women move toward the ideal of being able to trust, but also to be able to withdraw that trust when the situation warrants—to be able to give freely of one's self, but not to lose one's self. We will discuss what acquaintance rape is, and how to make ourselves less vulnerable to it.

If the group is small, have participants introduce themselves to make the discussion more intimate. The subject matter of this workshop is obviously sensitive and needs a facilitator who can guide the discussion gently and effectively. This outline provides many suggestions to help you.

Rape Attitude Assessment Survey (15 minutes)

This survey (see handouts and visual aids) is designed to help participants begin thinking about their attitudes concerning rape. There are no right or wrong answers. Urge participants to answer on the basis of their first impressions. Pass out the survey and pencils. Give participants 5 minutes to complete the survey. Ask for a show of hands indicating how many participants answered *true*

or *false* to each question in order to begin the discussion. Ask participants their reasons for their answers.

Discussion Suggestions

If participants are not willing to discuss the questions, reassure them that their answers reflect what they have been taught and that there are no right or wrong answers—just different viewpoints. You might say, "The workshop tonight will be more meaningful to you if you share your thoughts and opinions with the other people here."

If no one is answering, make sure that you are allowing enough time (count to 30 before responding after a question). Use your judgment about how to lead the discussion. Keep the workshop structured, but not rigid. Ask for a show of hands indicating how many participants strongly agree or agree with questions 6, 7, 8, 11, or 22, and ask for their reasons.

As the discussion ends, tell the participants that many of the items on the survey reflect traditional attitudes about rape in our society. Strong agreement or belief in the truth of many of these attitudes has been identified by feminists as contributing to both rape and the continuation of sexism. We must always remember that no woman "asks" to be raped or dehumanized. Rape is the sexual expression of violence, not the violent expression of sexuality. Acknowledge participants' contributions to the discussion.

The Party Game (20 minutes)

This is a film depicting acquaintance rape. The film takes approximately 10 minutes to show. If this film is not available, use the alternative discussion aid "Acquaintance Rape: How—Why?" (Appendix A) and discussion outline.

Preface the film by explaining that *The Party Game* depicts a possible acquaintance rape situation. Although the film wouldn't win any awards for acting and is dated, the emotions viewers experience may be quite strong. Viewers should be reminded that they are safe in the workshop and that the people in the film were *acting*. Although the film shows a hometown party, similar situations occur in bars and parties on college campuses. After the film, comment on the emotional effects the film may have had on viewers. The situation in the film can be upsetting to some people. If participants are upset by it, remind them that emotions are neither good or bad and that whatever they may be feeling is OK.

Film Discussion

To help focus the discussion about the film, outline some of the typical steps in acquaintance rape situations. Take a few minutes to think about the following points:

- What factors contributed to the problem?
- What role did peer pressure and alcohol have?
- What could the participants have done to prevent the situation?

Allow the group 2 minutes to think about these questions. Discourage discussion during this time; you may also have to ask people not to get up. If the group has trouble focusing quietly, you might suggest that everyone close their eyes while they think. The film also has a discussion guide to which you may want to refer.

Ask the group, "Was Kathy being raped?" Ask if anyone would be willing to share thoughts on why she believes Kathy was raped. Occasionally, someone will say that Kathy was not raped, in which case you might ask, "Did she deserve to be treated in the way she was by Mark? Why not?" This can be a difficult discussion starter, but the other participants may open up if they disagree with someone who says Kathy was not raped. Be sensitive to acknowledging everyone's opinion. Ask each of the following questions, and if you have newsprint, write down some of the ideas as people talk.

- *What factors contributed to the situation?* Kathy felt alone and self-conscious; Mark was on the make; poor communication and misunderstandings, etc.
- *What role did peer pressure and alcohol play?* Both Kathy and Mark felt that they should be with someone; Mark was drinking a lot; Kathy continued to drink even after she didn't want to.

- *What could the participants have done to prevent the situation?* The host/hostess could have made sure Kathy felt comfortable; Kathy could have been more assertive; someone could have come out on the porch with them; Mark could have stopped when Kathy resisted.

There are four steps in acquaintance rape that can serve as warning signals. The movie showed each of these:

Four Steps to Acquaintance Rape

1. Intrusion: Violation of the personal space of the victim; this may be through touch, intimate or explicit conversation, or by entering a place that is considered private (your home or room). This usually occurs in public where the victim feels safe. (Kathy was uncomfortable with the way Mark danced with her.)
2. Desensitization: As the intrusions continue, the victim becomes desensitized, dismissing them as harmless, predictable, and inevitable. She may feel that because she said nothing earlier, it's too late now. A pattern is established in which one's need for space has not been asserted. (Kathy may feel she gave Mark "permission" to take advantage of her because she agreed to go outside with him.)
3. Isolation: When the aggressor and the victim are finally alone together, the pattern of intrusion is repeated, but to further extremes. Because the victim has been desensitized, she does not assert herself now. (Kathy and Mark first went outside, then to the pool where no one would be able to see or hear them.)
4. Assault: The victim is unaware of the danger she faces because her defenses are down. It is not until the assault is well-advanced that she begins to realize that she is in danger. Unfortunately, once she does assert herself, it may be too late.

There are five coercive strategies used by men who assault women. These vary in frequency, but in cases of acquaintance rape, the order is usually as follows: convince verbally, ignore protests, restrain physically, threaten, and initiate physical violence.

"Bill of Rights" (10 minutes)

Put up blank paper or sheet of newsprint; label it "Bill of Rights." As an introduction to this activity, you may want to present these ideas in the following manner: One element in many acquaintance rape situations is that the people involved did not communicate clearly about their intentions, limits, and feelings. This is particularly true for women, who are socialized to put other's needs before their own, and as a result do not express what they intend, feel, want, or do not want. In many situations this may be appropriate, but in a potentially dangerous situation, it is not.

The next activity is designed to enable you to begin the process of thinking about your needs and beliefs. Although you may not have articulated it, each of you already has a set of beliefs about the expression of your own sexuality. We're going to develop a set of beliefs called a "Bill of Rights"— and we'll try to come up with a sample set of rights as a group. Please note that each person has a *different* Bill of Rights, based on her own ethical and religious philosophy. To introduce this, pose these questions: How would you compose a Sexuality Bill of Rights? What do you believe you have the right to expect?

Have the group develop a Bill of Rights. Begin with an example that is very important to sexuality: The right to have access to accurate information about sexuality. Developing a Bill of Rights may be difficult, so be cautious about beginning to talk too soon. Often the most articulate participants are those with the most traditional attitudes about sexuality; you may need to balance traditional views with more nontraditional ones. Try not to be judgmental, but rather encourage the participants. Some rights that might be expressed are these:

- the right to say *no* to sex
- the right to be sexually active
- the right to choose the partner, time, and place for sexual activity
- the right to avoid unwanted pregnancy and STDs
- the right to change one's mind about involvement with someone
- the right to stop sexual activity
- the right to enjoy sexual activity

Mention that if each person were writing her own bill, each might be different, and even people with the same list might act on these rights in different ways. Defining your rights is the first step. Later in the workshop, ways you can express these rights to others will be discussed.

Definitions, Laws, and Statistics (10 minutes)

You may want to present this in the following manner: "Next we're going to take a very brief look at some definitions, our state law, and statistics. It will be brief because we only have a limited amount of time tonight. There will be time for questions after the workshop, and I'll be handing out some pamphlets that cover this material in greater depth."

Hand out "Acquaintance Rape—Definitions and Statistics." Explain that the definitions represent points on a continuum, and often it is difficult to determine the category of a particular assault. The average age of the victim is 18 (in the range of 15 to 21). For many college-age women it is their first time away from home. Peer pressure to drink and be sexually active is intense, and some women are not aware of the danger in which they may place themselves in new situations. Present your state laws on rape and sexual assault. Define *consent*, various categories of sexual assault, *threat*, and *force*. Include appropriate classes of misdemeanors and felonies.

Assertiveness Exercises (10 minutes)

The next and perhaps most important step is to begin to learn prevention and protection techniques. The first of these techniques offers ways of expressing yourself that will help you convey a clearer picture of your rights and limits to others. Often this is called assertiveness training, although we will barely touch on the surface of all the possible assertiveness techniques.

Practice telling other people how *you* feel and think, rather than what you think of *them*. These are commonly called "I" statements, because you start your sentence with the word "I," rather than with "you." For example, if you're dancing with someone who is holding you too close, say "I'm uncomfortable dancing this close," which tells your partner how you feel. Giving the person a "you" message such as, "You're too pushy" will put them on the defensive.

If the person you're with doesn't respond to polite requests (and if the person has been drinking this may be especially true), you may need to be very direct about what you want the person to do. For example, if your dancing partner continues to pull you too close, you may need to give a direct message such as "Let go of my hips while we dance." Beware of adding "please" or "ok?" to direct messages—these will only give the other person permission to ignore your demand.

There is a very simple and effective technique for resisting what someone else wants you to do. All you do is repeat your refusal to each and every reason that the other person gives you. Then you won't get into arguments about reasons because it becomes obvious that you won't be swayed. For example, if your dancing partner wants you to go up to his room to dance with him there, say, "No, I'm not going upstairs with you," or "You probably do have a great stereo, but I'm not going upstairs with you," or "I know that you'd like to show me your computer, but I'm not going upstairs with you."

Mention that this technique works in many situations and can be very powerful. Ask for a volunteer to role-play this with you as practice. If you can get a volunteer, continue the imaginary conversation about the dancing partner. It helps to have thought ahead of some reasons to be going upstairs. The volunteer only has to say *no* every time. You'll find that the volunteer often gets a round of applause from the other participants after the demonstration.

Preventive and Protective Measures (10 minutes)

Some acquaintance rapes can be averted if you learn the various preventive and protective measures we are about to cover. However, it is not always possible to prevent a rapist from attacking. Many rapes are planned ahead of time. *Never blame the victim* if she did not use these strategies. In a crisis, the victim may go into shock and respond automatically—it is very difficult to remember to think through a list like this. Because we often respond automatically in a crisis, prevention is crucial. This is why it is important to avoid alcohol and not to go out alone with someone you don't know well. Before discussing the actual prevention and protection strategies, list some situations in which acquaintance rape is most likely to occur. These situations occur

- after a chance meeting, such as at a party or bar,
- with someone known to the victim from the neighborhood, such as a neighbor or repair person, or
- in a dating situation when the woman asks the man out, the man pays for the date, and they go to his house or apartment.

The victim is vulnerable in these situations both because of mixed communications about what each person wants and because she ends up alone with the potential attacker. Refer to the handout "Acquaintance Rape: Prevention and Protection." Emphasize the following points on the handout:

- Staying in control of your environment can be as simple as carrying enough money for a phone call and cab fare; then you aren't dependent on someone else for a ride.
- Avoid being alone with someone until you know him well enough. Especially avoid being alone at *his* place. A good rule is to go to public places for the first three dates.
- Play music softly, if you are alone. Or, consider turning it off, in case you need to scream.
- Pace your drinking and eat while you're drinking. Alcohol and drugs are implicated in many acquaintance rapes; often both persons have been drinking. Alcohol lowers inhibitions, impairs judgment, and slows reaction time.
- Trust your feelings! Better safe than sorry.
- Pleading and quarrelling are ineffective because it then appears that the victim is admitting the attacker has her in his power. The attacker wants control of the victim, and pleading demonstrates that he has this control.
- Doing something disgusting, such as making yourself vomit, can be very effective. Anything potentially disgusting may discourage the attacker.

Conclusion and Evaluation (5 minutes)

Summarize the main points of the workshop:

- Understand the attitudes and values you hold about rape.
- Being aware of the way acquaintance rapes usually occur will alert you to a dangerous situation.
- Clearly expressing yourself and knowing some assertiveness techniques will help you defend your limits.

Ask for questions from the participants. Hand out "Resources and Referrals for Sexual Assault Prevention Services and Services for Victims." Distribute Lifestyle Workshop evaluation forms and pencils. Allow time for completion, then collect. Briefly list and describe the other Lifestyle Workshops in Sexuality.

APPENDIX A

Acquaintance Rape: How—Why?

by Lela Jones Olzweski

Melanie was perched on the bar stool, straining to look through the dim, smoke-filled room for her roommate, Julie. She knew that if she got up, someone would take her seat. Standing would be far worse: The only place to stand that wasn't full of couples embracing was by the dance floor. Last time she'd stood there, one of the dancers had slammed into her and spilled her drink all over. Where was Julie?! She had begged Melanie to come along, so she wouldn't be alone—and now Julie was dancing with some guy from her psych class!

Melanie felt someone squeeze in between her bar stool and the one behind her and she heard him ask for a pitcher. She wondered why he didn't go down to the end of the bar where there was more room *and* a bartender, but she figured he must have his reasons. As he made his way out, he turned to Melanie and said, ''Your glass is empty—and my pitcher is full. A problem I can rectify!'', which is what he did. Surprised, Melanie started to protest that she didn't want any more to drink, but he didn't seem to be listening. Putting his pitcher down on the bar, he said, ''Drink up, fair lady! A toast to you!'' and clinked his glass to hers. What could she do but drink? It hardly seemed polite to do anything else, when he was toasting her. ''My name's Jeff. What's yours?''

Not waiting to hear her reply, Jeff continues, ''That's a fascinating necklace you have on. Did someone special give that to you?'' As Melanie explained that it was a birthday present from her sister, Jeff reached for the chain and, sliding his hand down her neck, picked up the pendant. Melanie felt self-conscious, since the pendant hung just inside the top of her blouse. After looking at it briefly, Jeff carefully put the necklace back in-

side her blouse. Melanie jumped slightly, shocked that he was being so forward. ''Feels good, huh? Don't worry—I'm harmless—just ask any of the girls here!'' Still feeling awkward, Melanie realized that she was being prudish and that he had only wanted to look at the necklace anyway.

Jeff continued to talk, asking questions, but usually not listening to Melanie's answers. Every time her glass got half empty, he filled it up. He talked about a film he'd seen the night before and described in detail the love scene at the end. Melanie was distressed at the turn in the conversation, so she asked him if he wanted to dance, just to get him to stop talking.

The dance floor was crowded, and Julie was nowhere to be seen. The first song they danced to was a fast one, and it was too loud to talk. When the next one started, Melanie realized it was a slow song and started to go back to the bar. Jeff grabbed her around the waist, saying, ''Where're you going? This is a great song!'' and began to dance. There wasn't much she could do, and dancing was better than listening to his stories, so she figured, Why not?

Jeff put his arms around her, pulling her close. They swayed to the music, and as they danced, Jeff slid his right hand up and down Melanie's back. Gradually, he pulled her closer and closer, until his whole body was rubbing against hers. Melanie kept trying to pull away, but every time she did, Jeff would whisper in her ear, ''Don't fight it, just feel the music! Relax. Trust me.'' Melanie realized that she was probably making too much out of it, so she tried to relax. They were only dancing, after all.

When the song ended, Melanie looked again for Julie, because it was almost closing time. She

433

didn't see her, but she did see Elise, another friend of theirs, so she asked whether Elise had seen Julie. "Oh, she left with that guy from her psych class," Elise replied, "and she told me to tell you to have a good time, but not to wait up for her." "Great," replied Melanie without enthusiasm, "Now I get to walk home in the rain. And it's all the way across campus!"

"That's no problem," interrupted Jeff. "My place is just around the corner, and my roommate's gone for the weekend, so I've got his car. We can dash through the rain, stop in for a nightcap, and you'll stay nice and dry in the car on the way home! Sounds great, right?" A ride did sound better to Melanie than walking alone through the rain and the night. She'd be safer riding than walking, that was for sure. "Well, OK. But no nightcap for me," answered Melanie. "I'd just as soon get home and in bed. Tomorrow's an early day."

Jeff's place *was* just around the corner, but when they got there, Jeff insisted that they go in, saying, "My roommate's keys are in the apartment; no sense in standing in the rain." As they walked in, he turned on the stereo, walked into the kitchen, and opened two beers. "Here's your nightcap!" he said, handing one to Melanie. "Drink up!" Surprised, Melanie said, "I told you that I didn't want a nightcap. I need to get home and to bed." Jeff replied, "Come on, what's your problem? Besides, I enjoyed dancing with you so much, I want one last dance." "Please," Melanie said impatiently, "I need to get home." "First we dance," insisted Jeff, setting his empty beer down and pulling Melanie close.

Melanie began to dance, but as Jeff reached to unbutton her blouse, she grabbed at his hand. "Don't do that. Just take me home! Please." "You're not getting away that easy," answered Jeff, gripping her hands behind her back, "You loved dancing with me at the bar, and you'll love it even more here." And he again reached down, unbuttoning all the buttons on her blouse. Realizing that Jeff was serious, Melanie struggled to get away, but Jeff just gripped her harder. "I don't want to hurt you, but I'll have to if you don't quit struggling."

"I don't want to dance anymore. Please let go of me, OK?" pleaded Melanie. "Sure," shouted Jeff, "I've got just the thing for you! You'll love it!" Twisting her arm behind her back, Jeff shoved Melanie over to the couch, forced her down on it, and straddled her firmly. Before she fully understood what was happening, Jeff had his pants unzipped and her skirt up. "Stop it!" she screamed, "You can't do this to me!" "Don't worry, it won't take long, and you might even enjoy it!"

As she fought his attack in vain, Melanie thought, "How could this happen! Why did it happen?"

MOST FREQUENTLY ASKED QUESTIONS

1. *Why do men rape?*

   Men don't rape for sexual fulfillment. They rape to gain or retain power and control over their victim. Rape is a violent crime in which sex is used against a victim.

2. *If a woman goes to a party where she doesn't know anyone, gets drunk, goes to a guy's room, and begins fooling around with him, isn't she setting herself up? How can we blame the man?*

   Everyone makes mistakes. However, making a mistake does not mean that one deserves to have a criminal act perpetrated against her.

3. *Is there any way to prevent acquaintance rape?*

   There are a lot of protective measures you can take; however, there may be times when you find yourself in a situation where the aggressor cannot be reasoned with. There may be no way to protect yourself against superior strength, threats of harm, or violence.

4. *How can a woman go out with a man for six months and not know he's capable of rape?*

   It is impossible to know everything about a person. Anyone is capable of raping. It is important to be aware that if a person feels threatened by someone else then rape or sexual assault may be used to assert a sense of power or control.

5. *What should I do if I get raped?*

   If you feel ready, call the police. You can either formally report the rape or just talk unofficially with an officer. However, the best thing to do is call the local rape crisis center. They have hotlines and advocates who will accompany you to the hospital or to the police. Also, in any case, whether the rape occurred the night before or 6 months before, going for counseling is an excellent idea. Rape crisis counselors can help victims work through their feelings of shame, guilt, and fear.

6. *If I report and try to prosecute the assailant, what are the chances of him or her going to jail?*

   The answer to this question will depend on your state's sexual assault laws. Research those laws and provide the answer. For example, since the new Illinois Criminal Sexual Assault law went into effect so recently (July 1984), it is difficult to determine how effective the law has been in sending convicted rapists to jail. Convictions are very difficult with acquaintance rape, because alcohol is involved in so many cases. When the victim is intoxicated and judgment is impaired, the court will question how clear the memory is of the incident. When the victim cannot clearly remember what happened, the court will be less likely to prosecute.

7. *What about sexual harassment? Is it also acquaintance rape?*

   If sexual harassment is a serious problem, in some cases it is related to acquaintance rape. One definition is any unwanted sexual gesture, physical contact, or statement that a reasonable person would find offensive, humiliating, or an interference with his or her required tasks or career opportunities.

   When sexual harassment proceeds to the point of physical contact, it enters the realm of sexual assault. Even if sexual harassment does not fit the technical legal definition of sexual assault, it is against the law, and it may be a legal violation of regulations governing your institution or workplace. (All cases of sexual harassment should be reported to appropriate authorities within the university. Reports are confidential.)

8. *Do men ever get raped? Do women ever rape men?*

Men are victims of rape in about 10% of all reported cases. Usually it is men who rape men, but there are documented cases of women raping men. The most common effect of the latter is temporary impotence.

9. *If someone gets raped, is the morning-after Pill available?*

Whether or not a doctor prescribes the morning-after Pill depends on many factors, including your medical history. You will need to ask your health-care provider what his or her policy is on the morning-after Pill.

10. *I've heard that the police won't believe a woman who says she's been raped and that they're very insensitive even when they do believe her. So why should she call the police?*

It's true that in the past, and probably in some places today, the police have been accused of being insensitive. This has been a serious concern of feminists and rape crisis workers in the U.S. and is one reason rape crisis centers began sending advocates with rape victims to make police reports.

However, this lack of sensitivity has changed significantly over the past 10 years, as society's attitudes about rape have begun to change. In many communities, police officers get special training in working with rape victims. Often, a female officer is assigned to rape cases. If you are concerned, call the local rape crisis center, and ask for someone to go to talk to the police with you.

11. *If I try to fight off an attacker, won't I just get hurt worse? Wouldn't I be better off giving in quietly?*

For years, women were told not to resist a rapist, for fear that they would be harmed more if they resisted. Some defense strategies, mentioned in the workshop, suggest that fleeing, shouting, or resisting may work much more effectively than more passive strategies. Sometimes a women has no choice, if she is overcome by her attacker's strength or by a weapon. Fighting back is not advised if your life may be in danger.

Attitude Assessment Survey on Rape

Do not spend too much time thinking about the answers for the following questions. The primary purpose of this survey is to have you examine your attitudes and beliefs about male and female sexuality that you may have grown to take for granted.

True/False

_____ 1. Because a man must physically enter a woman in sexual intercourse, men will always tend to be sexually dominant and women sexually submissive.

_____ 2. Men have stronger sexual drives than women; most men are more easily aroused than women.

_____ 3. Sometimes even the best of men loses control of himself sexually.

_____ 4. Some women deserve to be raped.

_____ 5. Women never really know what they want from a man, so they often send mixed signals.

Circle the number that corresponds to the strength of your feeling.

| 1 = Strongly Agree | 2 = Agree | 3 = No Opinion | 4 = Disagree | 5 = Strongly Disagree |

6. Women invite rape by their actions, appearance, or behavior.	1	2	3	4	5
7. Society condemns rape.	1	2	3	4	5
8. Rape is motivated by sexual needs.	1	2	3	4	5
9. In sex, *no* means maybe or yes.	1	2	3	4	5
10. When having sex with a new person, it is best to state what you want and don't want before you actually do anything sexual.	1	2	3	4	5
11. It is the woman's responsibility to set sexual limits.	1	2	3	4	5
12. In a dating relationship a woman is largely out to take advantage of a man.	1	2	3	4	5
13. Men are only out for one thing: sex.	1	2	3	4	5
14. A woman who initiates a sexual encounter will probably have sex with anybody.	1	2	3	4	5
15. Women only mean *no* when they physically resist.	1	2	3	4	5
16. Any female can get raped.	1	2	3	4	5

1 = Strongly Agree	2 = Agree	3 = No Opinion	4 = Disagree	5 = Strongly Disagree

17. If a woman engages in necking or petting and she lets things get out of hand, it is her own fault if her partner forces sex on her. 1 2 3 4 5

18. One reason that women falsely report a rape is that they frequently have a need to call attention to themselves. 1 2 3 4 5

19. Any healthy woman can successfully resist a rapist if she really wants to. 1 2 3 4 5

20. When women go around braless or wearing short skirts and tight tops, they are just asking for trouble. 1 2 3 4 5

21. Being roughed up is sexually stimulating to many women. 1 2 3 4 5

22. Women have the same need for a sexual outlet as do men. 1 2 3 4 5

23. Many women have an unconscious wish to be raped and may unconsciously set up a situation in which they are likely to be attacked. 1 2 3 4 5

Note. From *Acquaintance Rape and Sexual Assault Prevention Training Manual* by A. Parrot, 1985, Ithaca, NY: Cornell University. Adapted by permission.

Acquaintance Rape
Definitions and Statistics

Acquaintance Rape Definitions and Statistics

Rape—Forced Penis-Vagina Intercourse. By this definition only women can be raped, and only by men; 15% of college women are rape victims.

Sexual Assault—A Forced Sexual Act. May or may not include intercourse; both women and men can be assaulted, and either can commit assault; 52% of college women experience sexual victimization.

Stranger Rape. The victim does not know the person committing the assault; 16% of the women raped do not know their attacker.

Acquaintance Rape. The victim knows the person committing the assault, perhaps only slightly; 84% of the women raped know their attacker.

Date Rape. The victim has an ongoing dating relationship with the attacker; 50-75% of the women do not identify the experience as rape.

Differences Between Stranger Rape and Acquaintance Rape

- The victim feels to blame for consenting to a date.
- Friends may not believe the victim, or she may think they won't believe her.
- The emotional trauma is different because the victim trusted the attacker.
- The victim may lose faith in her own ability to judge people or to trust men.
- Fifty percent of the women raped are assaulted on the man's "turf." Ninety-five percent of the women raped do not make a report to the police.

If You Are Raped, Get Help

1. Don't change your clothes, shower, or douche.
2. Call your clinic or emergency room.
3. Call a rape hotline for assistance.
4. Go to a hospital for an exam, even if you don't plan to press charges. The police will give you a ride there.
5. Request testing for sexually transmitted diseases.
6. Find someone to talk with such as a counselor from a rape hotline or university or college counseling center.

REMEMBER THAT RAPE IS NOT YOUR FAULT—NO ONE ASKS TO BE RAPED!

Acquaintance Rape: Prevention and Protection

Know the Problem

- Understand what rape is.
- Understand the communication process.
- Remember: Rape can happen to anyone, including *you*.

Know Yourself

- Decide what *you* want and don't want.
- Know your rights.
- Know your alcohol tolerance.

Define Your Limits

- State clearly what you do, and do not, want.
- Stay in control of your environment: Be aware of changes, such as the end of the party; double-date, especially in new relationships; stay in public places.
- Drink alcohol moderately: Realize that alcohol and drugs affect your behavior. Remember that beer, wine, and hard liquor contain the same amount of alcohol per drink. Eat before drinking and while drinking. Pace yourself to only 1 drink per hour.
- Develop a buddy system with another woman: Don't leave a bar or party without your "buddy." Remember the designated driver system works here also.

Defend Your Limits

- Be assertive: Assertiveness training helps. Take a self-defense class.
- Say "No!" loudly and clearly.
- Dress to move easily.
- Trust your instincts and feelings.
- Do anything you can think of to get out of danger: Lock yourself in another room, make yourself vomit, climb out a window.
- Use proven rape-avoidance strategies. Flee—use any excuse to get away. Scream—yell "Fire!," not "Rape!" Use physical force. Sometimes reasoning works.
- Don't use ineffective strategies: pleading, quarreling.

REFERENCES

Alberti, R., & Emmons, M. (1986). *Your perfect right: A guide to assertive living*. San Luis Obispo, CA: Impact.

Bart, P., & O'Brien, P. (1984). Stopping rape: Effective avoidance strategies. *Signs: Journal of Women, Culture, and Society, 10*(11), 83-101.

Bateman, P. (1982). *Acquaintance rape awareness and prevention*. Seattle: Alternatives to Fear.

Cherniak, D. (Ed.). (1984). *A book about STDs*. Montreal: Montreal Health Press.

Garner, A. (1980). *Conversationally speaking*. New York: McGraw-Hill.

Merton, A. (1985, September). Return to brotherhood—An exposé of fraternity life today. *Ms.*, p. 60.

Morrison, E., & Underhill-Price, M. (1974). *Values in sexuality—A new approach to sex education*. New York: Hart.

Parrot, A. (1985). *Acquaintance rape and sexual assault prevention training manual*. Ithaca, NY: Cornell University.

Pritchard, C. (1985). *Avoiding rape on and off campus*. Wenonah, NJ: State College Publishing.

Schwartz, J. (1986, February). Acquaintance rape comes into open. *Newsweek on Campus*, 12.

Sweet, E. (1985, October). Date rape: The story of an epidemic and those who deny it. *Ms.*, p. 56.

About the Author

Martha Imrie Carey received a BS in health education at the University of Wisconsin-LaCrosse. In 1984, while completing her master's degree at the University of Oregon, she received a Secretary's Award for Innovations in Health Promotion and Disease Prevention, sponsored by the U.S. Department of Health and Human Services.

Martha taught health education at Portland (OR) State University and is now the Director of Health Education for McKinley Health Center at the University of Illinois at Urbana-Champaign. In this capacity she developed the Lifestyle Workshops training program, one of the largest paraprofessional health education programs in the country.

A member of the American College Health Association and the American Alliance of Health Education, Martha enjoys playing softball and walking in her leisure time.